# Influence of FinTech on Management Transformation

Amira Sghari
*Faculty of Economics and Management, University of Sfax, Tunisia*

Karim Mezghani
*Al Imam Mohammad Ibn Saud Islamic University, Saudi Arabia & University of Sfax, Tunisia*

A volume in the Advances in Finance, Accounting, and Economics (AFAE) Book Series

IGI Global
PUBLISHER of TIMELY KNOWLEDGE

Published in the United States of America by
IGI Global
Business Science Reference (an imprint of IGI Global)
701 E. Chocolate Avenue
Hershey PA, USA 17033
Tel: 717-533-8845
Fax: 717-533-8661
E-mail: cust@igi-global.com
Web site: http://www.igi-global.com



Library of Congress Cataloging-in-Publication Data

Names: Sghari, Amira, 1982- editor. | Mezghani, Karim, 1979- editor.
Title: Influence of fintech on management transformation / Amira Sghari, Karim Mezghani, editors..
Description: Hershey, PA : Business Science Reference, [2021] | Includes bibliographical references and index. | Summary: "This book consolidates knowledge in management in a context of digital transformation offering explanations of how the management transformation in financial institutions and companies is closely related to the emergence of fintech"-- Provided by publisher.
Identifiers: LCCN 2020036920 (print) | LCCN 2020036921 (ebook) | ISBN 9781799871101 (hardcover) | ISBN 9781799871118 (paperback) | ISBN 9781799871125 (ebook)
Subjects: LCSH: Financial institutions--Management. | Finance--Technological innovations. | Organizational change.
Classification: LCC HG173 .I5236 2021 (print) | LCC HG173 (ebook) | DDC 332.1068/4--dc23
LC record available at https://lccn.loc.gov/2020036920
LC ebook record available at https://lccn.loc.gov/2020036921

This book is published in the IGI Global book series Advances in Finance, Accounting, and Economics (AFAE) (ISSN: 2327-5677; eISSN: 2327-5685)

British Cataloguing in Publication Data
A Cataloguing in Publication record for this book is available from the British Library.



For electronic access to this publication, please contact: eresources@igi-global.com.

# Advances in Finance, Accounting, and Economics (AFAE) Book Series

ISSN:2327-5677
EISSN:2327-5685



**MISSION**

In our changing economic and business environment, it is important to consider the financial changes occurring internationally as well as within individual organizations and business environments. Understanding these changes as well as the factors that influence them is crucial in preparing for our financial future and ensuring economic sustainability and growth.

The **Advances in Finance, Accounting, and Economics (AFAE)** book series aims to publish comprehensive and informative titles in all areas of economics and economic theory, finance, and accounting to assist in advancing the available knowledge and providing for further research development in these dynamic fields.

**COVERAGE**

- Field Research
- Risk Analysis and Management
- Economics of Innovation and Knowledge
- Entrepreneurship in Accounting and Finance
- Interest Rates and Annuities
- Finance
- Environmental and Social Accounting
- Microeconomics
- Economic Indices and Quantitative Economic Methods
- E-Accounting

IGI Global is currently accepting manuscripts for publication within this series. To submit a proposal for a volume in this series, please contact our Acquisition Editors at Acquisitions@igi-global.com or visit: http://www.igi-global.com/publish/.

The Advances in Finance, Accounting, and Economics (AFAE) Book Series (ISSN 2327-5677) is published by IGI Global, 701 E. Chocolate Avenue, Hershey, PA 17033-1240, USA, www.igi-global.com. This series is composed of titles available for purchase individually; each title is edited to be contextually exclusive from any other title within the series. For pricing and ordering information please visit http://www.igi-global.com/book-series/advances-finance-accounting-economics/73685. Postmaster: Send all address changes to above address. 

## Titles in this Series

*For a list of additional titles in this series, please visit:*
*https://www.igi-global.com/book-series/advances-finance-accounting-economics/73685*

***Machine Learning Applications for Accounting Disclosure and Fraud Detection***
Stylianos Papadakis (Hellenic Mediterranean University, Greece) Alexandros Garefalakis (Hellenic Mediterranean University, Greece) Christos Lemonakis (Hellenic Mediterranean University, Greece) Christiana Chimonaki (University of Portsmouth, UK) and Constantin Zopounidis (Technical University of Crete, Greece)
Business Science Reference • © 2021 • 330pp • H/C (ISBN: 9781799848059) • US $225.00

***Corporate Governance and Its Implications on Accounting and Finance***
Ahmad Alqatan (University of Portsmouth, UK) Khaled Hussainey (University of Portsmouth, UK) and Hichem Khlif (University of Sfax, Tunisia)
Business Science Reference • © 2021 • 425pp • H/C (ISBN: 9781799848523) • US $195.00

***Recent Applications of Financial Risk Modelling and Portfolio Management***
Tihana Škrinjarić (University of Zagreb, Croatia) Mirjana Čižmešija (University of Zagreb, Croatia) and Bryan Christiansen (Global Training Group, Ltd, UK)
Business Science Reference • © 2021 • 432pp • H/C (ISBN: 9781799850830) • US $195.00

***Fostering Innovation and Competitiveness With FinTech, RegTech, and SupTech***
Iustina Alina Boitan (Bucharest University of Economic Studies, Romania) and Kamilla Marchewka-Bartkowiak (Poznan University of Economics and Business, Poland)
Business Science Reference • © 2021 • 300pp • H/C (ISBN: 9781799843900) • US $215.00

***Bridging the Gender Gap in Digital Financial Inclusion***
Puja Singhal (Sashakt-A Centre of Empowerment, India) and Rosy Kalra (Amity University Uttar Pradesh, India)
Business Science Reference • © 2021 • 300pp • H/C (ISBN: 9781799850120) • US $215.00

*Innovative Strategies for Implementing FinTech in Banking*
Yousif Abdullatif Albastaki (Ahlia University, Bahrain) Anjum Razzaque (Ahlia University, Bahrain) and Adel M. Sarea (Ahlia University, Bahrain)
Business Science Reference • © 2021 • 367pp • H/C (ISBN: 9781799832577) • US $225.00

IGI Global
PUBLISHER of TIMELY KNOWLEDGE

701 East Chocolate Avenue, Hershey, PA 17033, USA
Tel: 717-533-8845 x100 • Fax: 717-533-8661
E-Mail: cust@igi-global.com • www.igi-global.com

# Editorial Advisory Board

# Table of Contents

# Detailed Table of Contents

Directives and regulations legislated to increase the confidence payment transformation and users by instructive the rights and obligations of all mobile payments parties, providing the requirements for transformation such as interoperability, likewise users requisites such as security and customer protection. This chapter provides a brief overview of these directives and raises to some critical matters that have to be taken into consideration for successful management transformation of a pan-European mobile payment service in the Fintech context.

## Section 3
## Empirical Experiences and Applications



FinTech has become an increasingly important phenomenon around the world in recent times. This is substantiated by a growing interest from researchers, academicians, and policymakers. While the adoption of FinTech appears to be widely regarded as a strategic priority for financial institutions worldwide, the empirical evidence on the managerial challenges under FinTech is very scant, especially from the perspective of developing countries. With this in mind, this chapter aims at providing empirical evidence on the managerial challenges emanating from FinTech within the context of Zimbabwean commercial banks. The study establishes seven challenges, namely, customer retention, regulatory compliance, technology risk, increased competition, cyber-attacks, the inadequacy of IT employees, and system downtimes. The recommendations to deal with these challenges are proffered and the suggestions for further study are captured.



The evolution of information and communication technology (ICT) affects all areas of activity including the financial industry. Indeed, it leads to rapid development of innovative and modern financial services, namely financial technology (Fintech). The latter is not well defined in the literature. This descriptive chapter aims to propose a comprehension of the Fintech concept based on three interpretations: Fintech as financial services relying on digital technologies, Fintech as startups and IT companies, and Fintech as an industry. An analysis of the components of the Tunisian Fintech ecosystem is then presented. The latter is mainly composed-of Central Bank of Tunisia, fintech startups (financing, payments, loyalty program, blockchain and cryptocurrencies, exchange services and insurance, and technology, IT, and infrastructure), technology developers, traditional financial institutions, and financial customers.



This chapter will provide an analysis of market moves, and innovation sources, from newcomers and incumbent players, based on core and periphery networks theory; and additional survival analysis and VSR model, based on organizational population ecology. The French market neobanks, which are a subpart of fintech, are dominantly set up by entrepreneurs. On the contrary, online banks usually have universal banks as shareholders. Does this difference matter regarding market strategies? Is innovation coming only from peripheral actors like online banks and moreover neobanks, or do large retail banks at the heart of the banking system try to integrate or promote it? The author will discuss these topics to conclude with mixed evidence. Hence, if neobanks, on one hand, tend to converge towards the core; universal banks, on the other hand, are growingly accepting peripheral actors.



The aim of this chapter is to study the online banking quality and its impact on the satisfaction and loyalty of the consumers. To reveal the quality's importance, the authors studied the Attijari Bank online services, namely Webank. The results of this chapter demonstrate that this bank respects all the quality norms and criteria: reliability, responsiveness, competence, courtesy, credibility, access, communication, understanding the customer, collaboration, continuous enrollment, content, accuracy, ease of use, timeliness, aesthetics, security, and diverse features that led to its success.

# Preface

Digital financial services are starting to become increasingly popular with consumers, thereby fostering a favorable climate for digital entrepreneurship: mobile payment, Blockchain, etc. Research trying to understand and explain this phenomenon focuses on FinTech, an emerging field of research which attracts a lot of attention but remains little explored (Ryu, 2017). Indeed, there is not yet a clear definition of "FinTech" which is the subject of a consensus among researchers (Milian et al., 2019). For some authors, FinTechs are financial innovations that upset the financial market (Anand & Mantrala, 2019). For others, they are startups, based on financial innovations, which have changed the ecosystem (Palmié et al., 2019). What is therefore the FinTech? What are their different types? Are they the source of entrepreneurial opportunities ? What are the components of the FinTech ecosystem? How can we qualify the relationships between them?

Liu et al. (2020) discuss the importance of the variety of FinTech business models and their ability to solve financial market problems. At this level, several questions can be asked: What are the characteristics of FinTech business models? How FinTech can influence the business models of traditional financial players (banking, insurance)?

Wonglimpiyarat (2018) lists current research topics dealing with FinTechs such as mobile payment, and Blockchain. The latter, through its multiple platforms and applications (value transfer, financing, asset recognition, etc.), promotes entrepreneurial opportunities (Chen & Bellavitis, 2020). What are the entrepreneurial opportunities favored by Blockchain ? Is Blockchain entrepreneurship an appropriate solution for financial inclusion?

In the ecosystem, the relationship between its "traditional financial players (banking, insurance)" and "FinTech" components remains ambiguous (Lee & Shin, 2018): is it a collaborative relationship or rather a competitive one?

Noting the lack of research work on these themes, this book attempts to shed light on this area in order to bridge the gap between the discourse of practitioners and the literature.

This book aims to:

- Define the concept of FinTech and its ecosystem;
- Define concepts in relation with management transformations caused by FinTech;
- Present new theoretical and empirical frameworks related to the topics;
- Share useful experiences and best practices to deal with the new technological changes.

Regarding its contributions, this book is divided into three interrelated sections. The first section is titled "Insights From the Blockchain Technology". Three chapters (1-3) are included in this section dedicated to the study of Blockchain technology.

In the first chapter, the authors' objective is to classify different banks according to their Blockchain initiatives examining their strategic scope. In order to achieve this objective, they surveyed Blockchain initiatives of forty-five international banks and analyzed the different business models as management transformation for the banking industry. The authors developed a taxonomy of 5 different business models.

The purpose of the second chapter is to highlight how the implementation of the Blockchain technology has shaped a new way of trading commodities for global companies. The author proposes relevant examples in order to properly understand the influence of the Blockchain technology on the commodities' business. Specifically, it mainly handles the perceived renovation on each step of the physical commodity transaction life cycle, through the negotiation of the contract terms to the delivery to final clients' companies. The author also emphasizes the role of FinTech in transforming the means of trading commodities in the financial markets at different strands: a network of worldwide payment systems, easing and security of payments, a timely search for new financing sources, opportune data for investors, an enhancement of derivatives products' trading, etc.

In the third chapter, the authors emphasize that the major issue of Blockchain technology is the lack of regulatory measure framework to boost its acceptability among many countries of the world. They examine the regulatory standard measures of Blockchain technology as panacea for Blockchain technology acceptability. Evidence shows that absence of regulatory measure standard is fear to non-acceptability and accessibility of Blockchain technology.

Section 2 is dedicated to the presentation of "Managerial and Cultural Transformations in the Era of FinTech". Three chapters (4-6) are integrated in this section.

In the fourth chapter, the author sheds the light on drivers, features and challenges of FinTech, and discusses the elements and attributes of its ecosystem and the diversity of FinTech models operating in the financial industry. The author also emphasizes the role of a FinTech culture as a vibrant digital, agile, customer-centric, creative technology-driven, and entrepreneurial culture in a digitalized and changing world.

The fifth chapter deals with the Big data management in the era of FinTech. The authors emphasize the need of managers for big data tools in order to get meaningful insights from the huge volumes of such data. They investigate the big data management issues in the context of FinTech and propose a framework for big data management tools adoption based on expected benefits and challenges.

Regarding the managerial issues linked to Regulatory Perspective, the sixth chapter provides an overview of these directives and raises to some critical matters that have to be taken into consideration for successful management transformation of a pan-European mobile payment service in the FinTech context.

Section 3 is titled "Empirical Experiences and Applications". This section contains four chapters (7-10) from several proposals that were submitted by researchers from different countries.

In the seventh chapter, the author provides an overview of Managerial Challenges under FinTech. The author attempt providing empirical evidence on the managerial challenges emanating from FinTech within the context of Zimbabwean commercial banks. Seven challenges, namely, customer retention, regulatory compliance, technology risk, increased competition, cyber-attacks, the inadequacy of IT employees, and system downtimes are established and recommendations to deal with these challenges are proffered.

The eighth chapter, titled "FinTech's Interpretations and Tunisian Ecosystem Analysis", describes the Tunisian fintech ecosystem. The latter is mainly composed of Central Bank of Tunisia, Fintech Startups (Financing, Payments, Loyalty program, Blockchain and cryptocurrencies, Exchange services and Insurance, and Technology, IT and Infrastructure), Technology developers, Traditional Financial Institutions and Financial customers.

The ninth chapter highlights the Competition between neobanks and online banks in the French retail banking market and reactions from universal banks. It provides an analysis of market moves, and innovation sources, from newcomers and incumbent players, based on core and periphery networks theory; and additional survival analysis and VSR model, based on organizational population ecology. On the French market neobanks, which are a subpart of fintech, are dominantly set up by entrepreneurs. On the contrary, online banks usually have universal banks as shareholders. According to the author, if neobanks, on one hand, tend to converge towards the core, universal banks, on the other hand, are growingly accepting peripheral actors.

The tenth chapter is dedicated to the understanding the importance of the online banking quality and its impact on the satisfaction and loyalty of the Tunisian consumers. The authors demonstrate that the bank, object of the study, respects all the quality norms and criteria, namely, reliability, responsiveness, competence, courtesy, credibility, access, communication, understanding the customer, collaboration, continuous enrollment, content, accuracy, ease of use, timeliness, aesthetics, security and diverse features which led to its success.

We hope this book can help readers to better understand the Influence of FinTech on Management Transformation and thus can inspire other researchers to explore new related issues.

## REFERENCES

Anand, D., & Mantrala, M. (2019). Responding to disruptive business model innovations: The case of traditional banks facing fintech entrants. *Journal of Banking and Financial Technology*, *3*(1), 19–31. doi:10.100742786-018-00004-4

Chen, Y., & Bellavitis, C. (2020). Blockchain disruption and decentralized finance: The rise of decentralized business models. *Journal of Business Venturing Insights*, *13*, e00151. Advance online publication. doi:10.1016/j.jbvi.2019.e00151

Lee, I., & Shin, Y. J. (2018). Fintech: Ecosystem, business models, investment decisions, and challenges. *Business Horizons*, *61*(1), 35–46. doi:10.1016/j.bushor.2017.09.003

Liu, J., Li, X., & Wang, S. (2020). What have we learnt from 10 years of fintech research? A scientometric analysis. *Technological Forecasting and Social Change*, *155*, 120022. Advance online publication. doi:10.1016/j.techfore.2020.120022

Milian, E. Z., Spinola, M. M., & de Carvalho, M. M. (2019). Fintechs: A literature review and research agenda. *Electronic Commerce Research and Applications*, *34*, 100833. Advance online publication. doi:10.1016/j.elerap.2019.100833

Palmié, M., Wincent, J., Parida, V., & Caglar, U. (2019). The evolution of the financial technology ecosystem: An introduction and agenda for future research on disruptive innovations in ecosystems. *Technological Forecasting and Social Change*, *151*. Advance online publication. doi:10.1016/j.techfore.2019.119779

Ryu, H. S. (2017). What makes users willing or hesitant to use Fintech? The moderating effect of user type. *Industrial Management & Data Systems*, *118*(3), 541–569. doi:10.1108/IMDS-07-2017-0325

Wonglimpiyarat, J. (2018). Challenges and dynamics of FinTech crowd funding: An innovation system approach. *The Journal of High Technology Management Research*, *29*(1), 98–108. doi:10.1016/j.hitech.2018.04.009

# Acknowledgment

The editors would like to acknowledge authors and reviewers for their engagement in the process of developing this challenging book, through collective sense-making efforts aiming to explore the different ways of management transformation in the era of Fintech.

Their sincere gratitude goes also to Mrs. Nicole Hagan (Assistant Development Editor at IGI Global), Mr. Eric Whalen (development editor at IGI Global) and Ms. Jan Travers (Director of Intellectual Property and Contracts at IGI Global) for their ongoing support.

*Amira Sghari*
*Laboratory PRISME (LR18ES24), Faculty of Economics and Management, University of Sfax, Tunisia*

*Karim Mezghani*
*Imam Mohammad Ibn Saud Islamic University, Saudi Arabia & University of Sfax, Tunisia*

# Section 1

# Insights From the Blockchain Technology

# Chapter 1
# Blockchain Technology and New Business Models for Banks in the Financial Services Industry

**Vincent Sabourin**
*ESG University of Quebec at Montreal, Canada*

**Mike Cyrille Aka-Brou**
*ESG University of Quebec at Montreal, Canada*

## ABSTRACT

*In recent years, the financial technology of blockchain has become a disruptive innovation that is transforming the management of banks. If blockchain represents an opportunity for financial services, it also represents a severe threat of financial disintermediation. What are the business models available to banks when deploying a business model to integrate the blockchain technology? In this chapter, the authors surveyed the strategic intent of 45 international banks for blockchain technology and analyzed the different business models that might facilitate a management transformation for the banking industry. They developed a taxonomy of five different business models. They were labeled as the following: the coordinators, the integrators, the solution providers, the disrupters, and the explorers.*

DOI: 10.4018/978-1-7998-7110-1.ch001

## INTRODUCTION

In recent years, FinTech is responsible for major innovations in financial services. FinTech can be categorized as companies that combine financial and technological attributes in their business models. Recently, the rise of FinTech has attracted much interest since they challenge incumbents such as established banks and financial institutions (Eickhoff *et al.*, 2017).

Over the last decade, the financial services industry has developed a strategic interest in information technology (IT). Literature has argued that financial services are experiencing a fundamental management transformation (El Sawy & Pereira 2013; Lucas Jr. *et al.*, 2013). Sia *et al.* (2016) has argued that FinTech represents "a new generation of financial technology startups that are revolutionizing the financial industry". FinTech has been dubbed by Teo & Lee (2015) as "innovative financial services or products delivered via technology" that are radically transforming financial services.

The foundations of the FinTech revolution have been described in the literature by relying on three separate pillars of innovation (Gomber *et al.*, 2018). First, we have massive amounts of capital available for technology innovation for financial services in a highly fertile area of the global economy. According to The Economist (2015), from payments to wealth management, from peer-to-peer lending to crowdfunding; a new generation of FinTech has been able to access a significant stream of revenues. For instance, Goldman Sachs estimates are worth $4.7 trillion in 2015.

Second, FinTech has developed new technologies and designed new services for the finance industry that are different from what the conventional companies offer. They address financial needs for investment, mitigation and precaution with radically new ways. The FinTech revolution is transforming financial services operations and several elements of financial services such as productivity, performance analysis, systems design, forecasting and money management (Hatzaskis *et al.*, 2010).

Third, these financial technologies are transforming business models; and financial intermediation is achieved with a higher level of personalization based on digital applications and big data analytics. They also substituted for traditional banks and their services in new ways. For example, deploying financialized business processes, allowing lending on a crowdfunded, platform-based business or offering hybridized services delivered through attractive non-banking channels (PwC, 2016; Gozmnan, 2018).

Among those financial technologies, blockchain technology has become elemental for FinTech. In recent years, blockchain technology transformed banking to become the most disruptive FinTech in the financial services industry (Gomber *et al.*, 2018)

## THEORETICAL BACKGROUND

Research has argued that FinTech is a substantial factor contributing to the management transformation of business models for the financial services industry. Puschmann (2017), defines them as "incremental or disruptive innovations in the context of the financial services industry induced by IT developments resulting in new intra- or inter-organizational business models, products and services, organizations, processes, and systems."

For their part, Eickhoff *et al.*, (2017) defined FinTech as a combination of the following characteristics: (i) information technology that is often (ii) startups with (iii) their innovative product or services.

Alongside the gamut of financial industry, FinTechs are looking for new pathways to design successful business models that could yield a significant management transformation. Industry and academic observers believe this connate to a revolution for financial services leading to radical improvements in efficiency, customer centricity, and informedness provided by these new financial technologies (Gomber *et al.*, 2018). These financial technologies have attracted much interest since they challenge incumbent financial service businesses and traditional banking intermediation. (Schmitt & Weber, 2017).

## BLOCKCHAIN TECHNOLOGY

Research has indicated that for over twenty years, the diffusion of blockchain technology has been an underlying trigger for a progressive transformation of the financial services industry through technological developments in financing, insurance and payment-related business functions (Gomber *et al.*, 2017). Furthermore, the primary disruptive trigger of blockchain was considerably enhanced with the introduction of new functionalities and with the digitization of securities exchanges in the mid-1990s; and even earlier, by the offering of new financial exchanges at a much lower cost with no human intervention (Gomber *et al*, 2018).

Over the last decade, the technology of blockchain has become a topic of interest in the research. Zhao *et al.* (2016) has presented blockchain and associated business models as a set of three generations of technologies in which; a) Blockchain 1.0 refers to the digital currency, b) Blockchain 2.0 leads to digital finance, and c) Blockchain 3.0 is associated with the digital society (Zhao *et al.*, 2016).

More recently, blockchain technology has reached extraordinarily high interest among academics, businesspeople, and consultants (The Economist, 2015). In the financial market arena, blockchain engineering has emerged as a game-changer, as it allows a management transformation with radically new business models and disruption of existing banking models (Nofer *et al*, 2017). Blockchain engineering is gaining momentum with much more diverse uses, along with the ever-increasing amounts of actors involved in its implementation (Nowinsky & Kozma, 2018)

However, blockchain still faces a myriad of issues. For instance, research has indicated that securities clearing and trading, cost complexity, scalability, IT security, along with a host of nontechnical issues such as legal, regulatory, and taxation treatment are yet to be resolved. In settlement and clearing, for a counterparty, the risks are inherent (Gomber *et al.*, 2018). These authors point to the recreancy of trading where high-throughput and low-latency requirements might hinder the use of existing blockchain implementations for high volume asset classes, for instance, equities and listed derivatives.

## Blockchain Definitions

Blockchain technology has several facets and could be defined in the following ways:

## Blockchain as a Set of Transactions

Blockchain is a chain of transactions, a shared asset, a way to gain efficiency or an innovation. Blockchain technology is composed of a chain of data packages where a block comprises multiple transactions (Nofer *et al.*, 2017b). Blockchain technology can be propitious for FinTech as it can assist a revolution in the financial services industry and especially for banks as they form a critical stratum of this industry.

A blockchain consists of data sets that are composed of a chain of data packages where a block comprises multiple transactions (Nofer *et al.*, 2017). Thus, it is possible to undertake an infinity of transactions in the blockchain. These transactions are very secure and include "the transfer of money, assets, and information via the internet, without the participation of an intermediary such as a bank" (Swan, 2015). Blockchain could potentially minimize the intermediaries, like banks, by lowering the transaction costs between the clients and depositors.

## Blockchain is a Shared Asset and a Decentralization System Without a Third-Party Intermediary

Blockchain could be defined as a distributed database of records or a public ledger. It is a shared asset between the users of the network and could be compared to the system of an exchange network. The users generate the content, whereby the efficiency of the network depends on the number of users. The increase in the number of users is beneficial for the network. It is also a public electronic ledger, similar to a relational database that can be openly shared across a diversiform, and that creates an unchangeable and incorruptible record of their transactions (Mearian, 2017).

Blockchain technology relies on the concept of decentralization. Blockchain furnishes services plugged with coeval technology to each user which makes this system decentralized to the very core. The redundancy of an intermediary can be stated as the hallmark of this decentralized system. This decentralized system has spawned the latest financial products such as smart contracts where the users are the only adherents in this peer-to-peer network and interact directly within their secure sub-network; avoiding the hassle of obtaining approvals from a central body.

## Blockchain as a Secure, Private and Immutable System

The blockchain system has been designed for assuring more security and more privacy to users. With its decentralized system, a central authority for oversight is deemed redundant.. This omission helps users to avoid risks like data breach, stolen data or unauthorized use of personal data. The blockchain system makes good use of an intricate and sophisticated system of cryptography that impedes hacking to virtually impossible.

The blockchain system has the particularity to be immutable. Once any information or data is integrated into the blockchain, it is impossible to remove or modify it. As explained by Mearian, blockchain creates an unchangeable and incorruptible record. Each transaction is time-stamped and linked to the previous one (Mearian, 2017). The data is stored in strings and any attempt to doctor a transaction is immediately thwarted.

## Blockchain Transparency and Traceability

The blockchain system is reputed for offering maximum transparency and traceability. All operations are saved in the database, and accessible to everyone within the network. Each adherent of the network has the same right to the information. This system can serve banking industry as an excellent contrivance against money laundering because of real-time data rendering on all transactions (Yap, 2017). Many countries and institutions are investing heavily in blockchain machinations with their indigenous sovereign-backed digital currency platforms. (Yap, 2017). Trustworthy and accessible information in real-time presents an indispensable ratchet for risk management, and a mean of prevention against a financial crime and crisis (IFLR, 2016).

## Blockchain as an Innovation for Operational Efficiency

The financial services industry has shown an interest in blockchain because of its innovation and improvisation in enhancing operational efficiency. Blockchain will facilitate and streamline processes such as international transfers which, through conventional banking, can be very complicated. Further, it will reduce transactions cost by removing commissions and fees charged by different intermediaries. Blockchain, like the internet, is an open, global infrastructure that allows companies and individuals to make transactions by effacing the middleman and thereby, substantially reducing the cost of transactions and the time-lapse of working through third parties (Underwood 2016).

Blockchain technology is a technical innovation but also an economic innovation (Liebenau & Elaluf-Calderwood, 2016). Blockchain technology offers new opportunities; on both technical and economic agendum. Blockchain is an innovation that, apart from opening new perspectives for financial services, demands a major overhaul of the industry's business model.

In conclusion, blockchain is a disruptive technology that represents a strategic opportunity as well as a threat to the financial service industry.

## BUSINESS MODELS

One of the preoccupations of the literature on FinTech has to do with the nature and creation of business models that integrate financial technology like Blockchain. FinTech can be accounted for challenging established business models as well as service offerings in the financial industry. (Gomber *et al.*, 2017). In order to comprehend the true scale of Blockchain's impact on financial services industry's need for change, it is imperative to review the different definitions of a business model in the literature.

The concept of business models has several and diverse definitions (Zott, Amit & Massa, 2011). One of the earliest definitions was supplied by Osterwalder, Tucci & Pigneur (2005). Business model was defined as a "conceptual tool that contains a set of elements and their relationships and allows expressing the business logic of a specified firm as a description of the value company offers to one or several segments of customers and the architecture of the firm and its network of partners for creating, marketing, and delivering value and sustainable revenue streams".

According to Timmers, for a majority of authors, a business model is, therefore; an architecture of the product, service, and information flow, including a description of the various business actors and their roles; a description of the potential benefits for the various business actors and a description of the sources of revenue (Timmers, 1998). This definition highlights the critical role of a business model in a company's strategy.

This definition is consistent with Wirtz *et al.* (2016) which states that "a business model represents an aggregated representation of the relevant activities of a company. It describes how marketable information, products, and services are generated using a company's value-added component". They argue that "in addition to the architecture of value creation, customer, and market components are taken into consideration to achieve the superordinate goal of generating, or rather, securing the competitive advantage". To fulfill this latter purpose, a current business model should always be critically regarded from a dynamic perspective, thus within the consciousness that there may arise a need for the business model to evolution or improvise, due to internal or external changes over time. (Wirtz *et al.*, 2016).

Another definition is that a business model is an "organizational system built for a specific purpose" (Geissdoerfer *et al.*, 2018). This definition presses the need for delineating the aims and goals of a company, in terms of monetary profits and organizational expansion, before its commencement. Zott *et al.* (2011) indicate that the current literature on business models could be classified based on three generic themes: a) e-business models whereby organizations make use of information technology; b) strategic problems where business models handle topics such as firm performance, value creation, and competitive advantage; and c) the management of technology and innovation. Research has constantly arrived at the illation that understanding components of a business model might facilitate a categorization and taxonomic development for business models in financial services (Alt & Zimmermann, 2001; Osterwalder *et al.*, 2005).

Previous research is replete with discussion on the components of a business model. An overview of the components of a business model is provided by Alt & Zimmermann (2001), who identified six typical components; mission, legal issues, revenues, processes, structure and engineering. Mission is referred to as one of the more crucial elements of a company. It encompasses an understanding which ranges from corporate strategy down to services and products like value proposition.

In our research, we selected four elements from the conceptual framework of the strategic scope of a business model of Abell (1980) and Allaire & Firsirotu (1993) to investigate the components of a business model. According to this model, the components of a business model could be operationalized as being the choices regarding four elements: products and services scope, market scope (distribution channels), the scope of competencies (including technology), and the geographic scope. These components define the scale and scope of the components of a business model.

## Blockchain Technology and Management transformation of Business Models

Blockchain represents a strategic opportunity for the management transformation of financial institutions such as banks. On this topic, Wirtz *et al.* (2016) mentioned that the financial technology of blockchain appears to influence the transformation of several constituent elements of a business model. Firstly, they argue that blockchain technology represents a significant change in the value chain of a bank ecosystem. Secondly, blockchain might review or eliminate the role of technology suppliers and distributors (such as platforms) of a bank. Thirdly, in case of correspondent banking, blockchain technology has been able to transform the cooperation mechanisms among banks (Nowiński & Kozma, 2017).

Among the core functions where blockchain is leading to a management transformation is the matter of cross border payments. For instance, lately, Ripple created an application to offer interbank payments using blockchain engineering, involving many banks, like Santander, CIBC, ReiseBank, UniCredit, UBS, National Bank of Abu Dhabi (NBAD), and ATB Financial (Businesswire, 2016).

Another case of blockchain transformation could be found within the system of correspondent banks. Blockchain technology is about to replace the present system of correspondent SWIFT banking by real-time payments between the involved parties (Holotiuk, Pisani, and Moorman, 2017). In October 2016, in a first trial, R3 and Ripple introduced a blockchain consortium backed by several significant banks to complete cross border transactions using blockchain technology of Ripple's XRP electronic currency (Roberts, 2016).

Management transformation of business models could also be found when blockchain impacts a company or a financial institution through the implementation of smart contracts; programmable contracts that may enforce themselves upon the occurrence of predefined problems (Capgemini Consulting, 2016). Based on Capgemini's article (2016), the possibility of these smart contracts leading to a management transformation is significant when financial activity lags in terms of processes, speed of settlement, risk of fraud, operational risks, or back-office costs and operational risk.

However, management transformation of business models remains a complex topic. For example, blockchain development is largely yoking under the influence of regulation. Since the mid-1990s, regulators and financial institutions have been working towards the implementation of blockchain engineering of payments, including leading global stock exchanges, notable among which are London Stock Exchange, CME, Deutsche Borse, NYSE, and Nasdaq (Rizzo, 2016). In October 2015, Nasdaq introduced Linq, "a solution enabling private businesses to electronically represent share ownership utilizing blockchain-based technology" (Nasdaq, 2016). However, the national regulatory framework will have to be harmonized globally and remain a critical source of uncertainty for banks when deploying blockchain.

### Strategic Intent

Owing to uncertainties of technology and occluded regulatory framework, the retooling of business models by banks to incorporate, test and deploy blockchain still seem a good distance away. Therefore, to study the impact of blockchain on bank business models, the research generally relies on the strategic intent of the banking industry as whole to investigate emergent strategies of banks to design and deploy a business model integrating a technology such as blockchain.

Strategic intent is the guiding sylloge of tactical decision and policy-making to reach or maintain a goal in the future (Prahalad & Hamel, 1989). Strategic intent represents the aspirational plans, overarching purpose, or intended direction of growth needed to reach an organizational vision. Beneficial change results from the strategic intent, ambitions, and needs of an organization." (Metzlar, 2017). Strategic intents are intentions orienting decision-making to reach or maintain a goal in the future (Prahalad & Hamel, 1989). In practice, the study of the strategic intent of corporations is generally based on the content analysis of official and legal corporate documents such as annual reports that make it possible to study the objectives of a corporation.

## RESEARCH STATEMENT, OBJECTIVES, METHODOLOGY AND DATA

### Research Problems Statement

For several years, researchers, as well as practitioners, have been concentrating on the promise of digitalization and have worked diligently to better understand how to leverage digital technologies (Porter & Heppelmann, 2015). The research on business models took an interdisciplinary perspective by researchers only ten years ago (Teece, 2010). It became diffused mainly by consultants and practitioners after the Internet Bubble (DaSilva & Trkman, 2016). As indicated before, FinTech has been mentioned to represent a disruptive technology that is introducing revolutionary business models that might lead to new competitive advantages (Chesbrough, 2010; Haefliger & Baden-Fuller, 2013).

The literature has argued that FinTech, such as blockchain, represents a disruptive technology that could transform the management of business models and represents a valuable research question. For instance, Nowinsky & Kozma (2017) have mentioned that blockchain technology disrupts business models and may affect several components of business models and that it needs to be studied.

In this context, the research has indicated that the different types of business models used by banks to develop and deploy this technology of blockchain are not well understood. For instance, Nowinsky & Kozma (2017) have argued blockchain technology can affect and disrupt business models in three ways: a) by authenticating traded goods, b) by facilitating financial disintermediation, and c) by lowering transaction costs.

However, the research did not indicate how the disruption of blockchain on business models applied specifically to banks. They did not describe either the management transformation provided by these business models of banks.

In this regard, the research underlines the need for a better understanding of the management transformation of the different components of business models. Several topics could be identified, such as the deployment of the blockchain for technology development and the transformation of digital competencies, new product bundling with digital functions, and new market channels such as platforms for the financial services industry. This corresponds to what Foss & Saebi (2017) have indicated as the need to study business model innovation as: "designed, novel, non-trivial changes to the key elements of a company's business model and the architecture linking these elements."

Given this latest enabling development of financial technology on business models in the financial industry, the research underlines the importance of recognizing the similarities as well as differences among business models that egress from FinTech (Eickhoff *et al.*, 2017).

A more immersive study might facilitate the categorization of business models approach brought by the blockchain technology. In this regard, research suggests that the development of the taxonomy of FinTech business models can be used to analyze the landscape of established and emergent companies more directly (Eickoff *et al.*, 2017).

In general, the review of literature indicates that the research on digitalization and new business models needs to be addressed with more depth and acumen to grasp the viewpoint of the sub-components in order to accurately understand the implications of digitalization for all its facets and actors (Parida *et al.*, 2019). Among these facets and actors,, there is a special incumbency to understand the business model and bring its different components to align with the needs and functions of digitalization.. According to Ritter & Lettl (2018), business model alignment is critical to ensure that all the components work in concert to accomplish the complete business logic of the business.

In summary, the study of blockchain in lieu of business models for the banks is essential to precisely trace the management transformation provided by this technology and could be considered as a relevant research question.

## Research Objectives

Our research objective was to complete a descriptive study of the strategic intent of banks to understand better the design and deployment of their business models for the blockchain technology. More specifically, our objectives constituted;

(i) studying and describing the strategic intent of banks regarding blockchain technology when deploying a business model.
(ii) categorizing the bank's strategic intent into a taxonomy based on the strategic scope of its business model for blockchain technology based on the four components of Abell (1980) and (Allaire & Firsirotu, 1993).
(iii) suggesting hypotheses for pursuing additional empirical research on management transformation of business models by blockchain for banks.

# METHODOLOGY

This section presents the procedural aspects of our methodology.

## Descriptive Research

Our research methodology is descriptive in nature as it attempts to describe the strategic intent of banks. Therefore, we did not conduct empirical analysis. The empirical analysis would have necessitated a more symmetrical research question and a different scope. Doyle *et al.* (2019) have argued that qualitative and descriptive research is useful for applied fields of study, such as management. According to Doyle *et al.* (2019), descriptive research is justified when the research topic to investigate questions could be found before the structuring phases of the research process.

Consequently, in this case, researchers have to articulate the research perspective with descriptions. Others have indicated that when structuring a research question with an emergent topic, descriptive research is relevant (Sandelowski, 2010). It is also relevant for building a taxonomy for a specific context (Bradshaw *et al.*, 2017).

## Sample

In our research, we surveyed 45 banks. Our sample of 45 represents a sample of convenience. Convenience sampling is defined as a nonprobability, or nonrandom sampling justified when the sample population meets specific practical criteria, for example, easy accessibility, geographical proximity, availability in a specific time, or perhaps the willingness to participate are integrated for the intent behind the study (Dörnyei, 2007). The research indicates that the use of a sample of convenience is justified when the population is just about finite (Explorable, 2009). Based on Etikan *et al.* (2015), a convenience sample could also be justified for exploring new topics and a limited population (Henry, 1990). More specifically, in our research, we exhausted the population of our sample and did not find more than 45 banks with a mention for blockchain directly in their annual report or indirectly through official corporate press communique.

## Data Collection

We used Google to search bank corporate annual reports on the topic of the blockchain. All of the 45 banks are registered on the stock exchange with the legal and fiduciary responsibility to provide reliable and adequate financial information and clear strategic intent for shareholders and regulators. Annual reports and complementary corporate documents provided an explicit divulgation of the bank's strategic intent regarding investment such as FinTech and the deployment of blockchain technology.

Google, being the most frequently used search engine to collect information on companies (Hubspot, 2020), was our choice for collecting data from all 45 banks.

Our sample excluded smaller private banks not traded on the stock exchange. We also restricted our search to corporate annual reports available in English since most banks' annual reports are available in English and are publicly available for stakeholders and regulators.

## Data Categorization

The next step of our methodology was to document the information available on each bank on the topic of blockchain and business models. The categorization was completed based on four components of a business model of Abell (1980) and (Allaire & Firsirotu, 1993) as defined before:

1. The products and services offered in terms of scope. Did the bank offer a broad selection or a narrow selection of products and services? Blockchain products were defined as product functionalities.

2. The market scope and pricing are defined as the channel of distribution and the pricing policy. Did the bank offer its products and services through a platform or its existing distribution channels?
3. The geographical scope of the initiatives. Did the bank deploy blockchain in a single country or multiple countries?
4. The scope of competencies and technology. Was the blockchain initiative managed internally based on in-house development or outsourced externally to third parties and external suppliers?

### Taxonomy Development

Finally, a taxonomy of business models was developed and described using the commonalities for banks, and a label was given to each group. Before labeling the business model, it was necessary to correctly identify the characteristics of the model with the four components of a business model mentioned previously. A brief description of each business model was then completed.

The business models were categorized according to three levels: the low, medium, and high intensity of management transformation. When the integration of technology was restricted to the accommodation of technology without transforming the core competencies of traditional banking intermediation, it was labeled as a low-intensity management transformation.

When the integration of blockchain technology mandated in-depth alterations and upgradation for transformation leading to new digital competencies, it was labeled as high-intensity management transformation.

Finally, when the integration of the blockchain technology was done partially for some aspects and not for others or/and on a selective basis without an in-depth transformation of the banking intermediation function, it was labeled as an intermediate-intensity management transformation.

## RESULTS AND DISCUSSION

### Results

In this section, we present the findings of our survey of strategic intent for 45 banks regarding their blockchain initiatives. We developed a taxonomy of five groups with different business models. They were labeled as the following: the coordinators, the integrators, the solution providers, the disrupters, and the explorers. Each business model led to a different management transformation.

In terms of relative importance, we found the following distribution among the business models. The explorers came first (27%) followed by the coordinators (24%), and the integrators (21%) The disrupters and the solution providers stood last with 17% and 11% respectively(and with only 4% if we exclude Chinese banks).

## Business Model #1: The Coordinators

With the first business model of coordinators, banks outsource the management of their blockchain to companies and startups. They develop a model based on a network of external technology providers and partners for platforms distribution. Subcontractors and partners work in straight collaboration. These banks prefer not to integrate vertically by acquitting the assets of their suppliers (technology development) and distributors (platforms). This first business model gathers banks of large scale and scope with an intermediate vertical integration of technology for suppliers and distributors. Technology development and the integration of blockchain technology is achieved through consortiums and partnerships with high-tech companies and startups. The deployment of this business model consists of creating partnerships with high-tech companies and startups with significant know-how in the field of blockchain. This enables them to focus on their core banking intermediation business while benefiting from the opportunities offered by the technology of blockchain by relying on external players.

We found that this business model represents a medium-intensity management transformation since the integration of blockchain technology is only partially completed. The business model is based on one hand, at the stretch of existing core competencies to develop a new center of gravity but, on the other hand, rely mainly on the addition of new digital skills provided by external technology providers and technology platforms.

This business model regarding blockchain is adopted by large international banks such as BNP Paribas, DBS Bank, Spain's BBVA, UBS Group, JP Morgan, and Barclays. For example, BNP Paribas, in partnership with other banks, is developing a coordinated approach with a new blockchain platform finance eTrade Connect. BNP Paribas has become the third bank to conduct a live trade transaction on the Voltron blockchain platform[1]. Voltron is a platform aimed at making the exchange of trade finance documentation digital and more efficient. Built on R3's blockchain framework, the initiative is run by a consortium of eight founding members[2].

DBS Bank has partnered with a group of vendors and government bodies to develop a new open-source trade finance blockchain platform, the ICC TradeFlow. The platform's pilot trade of $20 million worth of iron-ore will be shipped from Africa to China in November[3]. The platform is built on IMDA's TradeTrust network infrastructure and powered by Perlin's blockchain technology. It has been designed to be interoperable with existing and future digital trade platforms[4].

Spain's BBVA has become the first global bank to issue a loan using the distributed ledger technology that underpins cryptocurrencies and has the potential to revolutionize banking processes. In its corporate communique, the bank claims that "the BBVA platform uses blockchain distributed ledger technology to perform the entire process from conditional negotiation of loans to contract to sign, including notifying banks and borrowers of all loan progress"[5].

The Swiss bank, UBS declared in its annual report that it coordinated with a group of financial firms and plan to start using a bitcoin-like token to settle cross-border trades; one of the most significant developments yet in the effort to make use of nascent blockchain technology[6].

JP Morgan has claimed to have initiated in-house development and partnerships with leading technologists to bring about sector-leading enterprise-grade blockchain on a collaborative platform[7]. They claim that this will enable strategic relationships and investments with critical vendors and consortia such as Digital Asset, Axoni, Enterprise Ethereum Alliance, and Hyperledger, a Linux Foundation Project[8].

Another example is the Barclays PLC. Barclays is building a large-scale scope platform based on blockchain technology. Barclays is coordinating with a set of innovative startup companies as a platform and geared to become the first organization to execute a global trade transaction using blockchain technology[9].

Finally, according to Forbes, Wells Fargo & Company, became the seventh-largest world company in blockchain, using blockchain technology to track home mortgages[10]. Based on this business model, partnerships via a collaborative platform allow banks to focus on their core competencies, plan for the long term, and share the risk with other partners.

In sum, this model promotes collaborative innovation and thus enables the development of new products, processes, management systems based on risk-sharing. Delegating of activities to specialized partners allows the bank to avoid complexity costs. However, it forces the bank to depend on its technology suppliers and platform developers. Thus, the latter does not fully control certain aspects of the value chain, such as the operations of platforms or the supply of technologies. This business model can be problematic in disputes and could lead to transaction costs because of a lack of fully vertical integrated approach of the bank's chain of activities.

## Business Model #2: The Integrators

This second business model is based on a more complete vertical integration of critical activities to lower transaction costs with the help of blockchain market. In this case, technology development is not delegated to subcontractors. The objective is to ensure that technology providers and platforms developers have virtually no impact on value production and are therefore easily replaceable. Even if this business model relies on vertical integration, it could be classified as a medium intensity in terms of management transformation for the following two reasons. Firstly, the integration of supply technology is completed by adding center of gravity upstream but without transforming thc traditional bank center of gravity based on financial intermediation between depositors and lenders. Secondly, the addition of platforms for distribution of blockchain products is achieved by adding new distribution channels without transforming existing distribution channels such as branches, call centers, or internet banking.

This business model is used by banks such as the Bank of America, American Express, Citigroup, Goldman Sachs, Capital One and Royal Bank of Scotland (RBS).

For example, Bank of America can be considered an integrator is gathering more than fifty interrelated applications within the blockchain field[11]. According to Forbes, The Bank of America is the sixth-largest holder of blockchain patents, with sales up to $102.98 billion. It has been leading in the blockchain patent race with huge investments, sidestepping such players as IBM and Alibaba[12]. The bank has cumulated 82 blockchain-related patents, more than any other financial firm, including payment companies, Mastercard and PayPal. Under tech and operations, the giant bank has accumulated the most patents for the technology of any financial services company for inventions ranging from blockchain-powered ATMs to storage for cryptocurrency keys[13].

For its part, American Express incorporated blockchain in its products by integrating blockchain into its Membership Rewards program[14]. American Express made a huge high-tech investment of $8.7 billion in 2017 for blockchain in this reward program. It developed and integrated an indigenous blockchain solution, from scratch to simulation. The proposed system will automate proof-of-payments by encrypting payment payload data with a public key on an initial node of the blockchain – the data in question comprising the merchant's identifying information and the transaction amount. The encrypted data could then securely be propagated to a second blockchain node.

Citigroup is yet another exemplary organization: the organization invested mostly in blockchain-based trade finance startups to incorporate blockchain initiative hence modernizing from paper-based trade finance. The collaboration was launched in 2018 in partnership with ConsenSys and intends to streamline trade financing in the commercial market. The platform 'Komgo' allows ease of communication between equity traders, financial institutions, and trade service providers across blockchain technology.

In sum, the benefits of this business model is to provide a high level of control and vertical integration of the bank chain value activities. It keeps the technological know-how within the bank and reduces transaction cost with technology providers and platform developers.

However, this business model requires significantly high costs in both infrastructure and human capital. These investments might lead to a lack of flexibility to adapt to changes in new technological development. For example, Bank of America tech and operations chief mentioned that the bank grew doubtful that blockchain and it's the distributed ledger software behind cryptocurrencies like bitcoin will amount to anything in the near future in terms of financial returns[15].

## Business Model #3: The Solution Providers

This business model gathers smaller players with a narrow market focus in comparison with the members of the two previous groups. While the technology development and turnkey solutions are fabricated in-house, they might often end-up working for third parties as technology providers and platform developers Because of their limited scale and scope, these banks may develop a blueprint for blockchain development and deployment but are unable to integrate it within their system and hence invest in blockchain to develop solutions for other banks. This kind of business model is reliant on business to business (B2B) model rather than business to consumers (B2C) model. These banks have a strong orientation for technology development but lack the scope and resources. They may foster the learning curve of the technology, develop turnkey solutions, but finally act like a distributor for third parties. All the charges of innovation, such as product development or platforms, are conferred to the bank. Solution providers get relevant data and can extract solutions using big data and artificial intelligence algorithms. The bank is then able to provide technological solutions to other banks that don't possess skills and technical knowledge.

They represent the case of a high-intensity management transformation with the assimilation of technology and a radical integration of new blockchain technological competencies. In this case, blockchain technology is radically transforming the banking intermediation function and introducing a disintermediation function as a third party.

We have a few examples for this type of business model: Westpac piloted a proof-of-concept in 2018, combining four emergent technologies to trade; Data Analytics, Artificial Intelligence (A.I.), Internet of Things (IoT), and Blockchain[16]. Their solution successfully digitizes important areas of inventory management, procurement and trade that could potentially transform global business.

Additionally, ASB Bank has invested in TradeWindow, a blockchain startup, to speed up the trading platform of its Distributed Ledger Technology (DLT). "TradeWindow is a technological solution that allows all relevant documents – from certificates to invoices – to be exchanged digitally using one touchpoint".[17] As per the CEO, the DLT solution has the potential to become a supplier across Australia, being the first companies to have received funds from New Zealand banks.

Meanwhile, many Chinese banks are leveraging technological solution providers. One such bank, The Industrial and Commercial Bank of China, has patented blockchain innovations for digital certificates. In contrast, China Construction Bank (CCB) is outsourcing sales channels to IBM blockchain platform. Berkshire Hathaway Inc. is exploring the technology to improve its supply chain[18].

Agricultural Bank of China, a state-owned bank, is striving to decentralize its network for unsecured agricultural loans, whereas, the Bank of China has registered blockchain patents and is affiliating with IT. company Tencent to develop blockchain technology[19].

In sum, the benefits of this business model are to support the development of technological solutions to play a leading role in financial ecosystems. However, this strategy faces several risks. All the sunk costs in developing a solution are conferred to the bank. Furthermore, the share of technological skills might lead to an involuntary knowledge transfer to clients and suppliers and a replication of the solutions provided by competitors.

## Business Model #4: The Disrupters

This fourth group attracts generally smaller banks in comparison with larger international banks. Their objective is to disrupt the market and accelerate the market substitution for blockchain technology. They accept riskier profiles and pilot advanced blockchain initiatives to move early and ahead in the market. They are early technology adopters entering the market at the beginning of the blockchain market growth. The strategy is to adopt as quickly and as positively to the blockchain technology in quest for disrupting the market. These disruptive banks often face a deficit in asset size relative to the dominant financial institutions in the market. They strive to speed up and pilot blockchain products. In this context, smaller and younger banks tend to be in a better position to disrupt the market. The players' ideal success strategy is to introduce the blockchain product in the market to get a significant market share. Santander Bank, EQIBank, Axis Bank and Cuallix Bank are following this strategy.

This fourth business model represents a high-intensity management transformation with the assimilation of the technology. However, the management of technology disruption is a risky business. Since these banks move at an early stage of the market phase, they face high technology uncertainty. The lack of norms and standards, and on top of it the lack of regulatory framework represent strategic uncertainty on the development of this business model.

Several examples could be found. For instance, Santander became the 31st largest public-owned company that invested in Ripple and piloted payment applications using Ripple technology. It became the first bank to introduce blockchain technology via the application for international transactions (Forbes; July 3, 2018).

Another example is the Aelf Bank that developed an ecosystem called the Aelf Innovation Alliance. This bank has built up successful partnerships with several players from the financial services industry such as Arrington and Arrington XRP Capital, Huobi Labs, and FBG Capital[20]. They enable blockchain technology to be adopted and integrated into mainstream organizations, large and small[21].

EQIBank has also adopted this business model. This bank became the world's first licensed and regulated bank for national currencies, crypto, and digital assets. For the first time, customers will be able to manage traditional and crypto assets within a single banking relationship while accessing a comprehensive suite of services, including trading, custody, lending, clearing, and settlement[22]. EQIBank is the first licensed bank to deliver services based on the potential of blockchain.

Another example is the case of Axis Bank. India's third-largest private sector bank Axis Bank has launched instant international payment services using their enterprise blockchain technology solution. The bank has launched a service for its retail customers in India to receive payments from RAKBANK in UAE while its corporate customers in India can receive payments from Standard Chartered Bank in Singapore[23].

A final example is the case of Cuallix Bank, which became the first institution worldwide to use xRapid solution that utilizes XRP as a liquidity tool to reduce the cost of sending cross-border payments from the U.S. to Mexico. Cuallix moved to the forefront of digital payments by using digital assets to remove the inefficiencies and red-tape associated with processing and sourcing liquidity[24].

In short, this business model is advantageous due to its pioneering spirit and thereby reaps from first-mover advantage and public awareness. Nevertheless, it is risky and might not be non-sustainable in the long run. With the fast pulse of blockchain technology's evolution, the banks might be unable to keep up with the pace of technology development.

## Business Model #5: The Explorers

This business model gathers banks of smaller scope, of two types. We have international banks of smaller scope such as Credit Suisse or purely regional banks such as National Bank of Canada operating in a single regional market. This fifth business model consists of introducing new products and services on the market incrementally without a pre-established strategy. Prudent and conservative technology development is achieved to minimize risk and sunk costs. The bank evaluates the market and client reactions to fine-tune and adjust its prospective strategy. It is achieved so by carefully undertaking projects after thoroughly reviewed pilots, and tests with a new blockchain product or service. The objective is to move gradually in the market rather than slap-dash tactics.

In terms of management transformation intensity, they represent a case of low-intensity management transformation. The objective is to integrate the blockchain and to minimize technology disruption which entails a conservative and defensive strategy. The whole strategy, hence, is geared towards treading with caution and to minimize the management transformation process.

Banks such as SBI Holdings, HSBC, Sberbank CIB, CIMB Group, Credit Suisse, Singapore's, National, Bank of Canada are following this strategy.

An example is the case of Credit Suisse. Credit Suisse Asset Management Branch that used this business model to test blockchain with investment fund transactions. Credit Suisse's asset management arm claims "to have successfully tested blockchain to process investment fund trades becoming the latest financial institution to show an interest in technology that could speed up transactions and keep them secure"[25]. Their business model had a scope limited to investment fund trades.

Another case is SBI Holdings; a Japanese financial group completed a pilot project in a financial partnership with Ripple in 2019. Japanese SBI Holdings trials blockchain-based virtual currency Ripple enables banks, payment providers, digital asset exchanges, and corporations to send money globally using blockchain technology. In 2018, SBI Holdings, Orb, and Glory Corporation announced they would test the new S-Coin blockchain platform for smartphone transactions[26].

HSBC has also tested its blockchain-based trade finance platform Voltron and arranged a partnership with major retail organization Landmark Group. HSBC processed a pilot Letter of Credit on the Voltron blockchain trade finance platform that demonstrated interoperability with a second blockchain[27].

A similar claim has been attested to Royal Bank of Canada for being in the top 50 Companies exploring blockchain technology with its CAD 40.49 billion ($ 52 billion) with its position as the 42nd largest company in the world and 25th largest company in the world using distributed ledger technology solutions[28]. As of March 2018, RBC has patented blockchain technology for credit scoring within its market as well as commercial and capital markets, as per the patent application released by the US Patent and Trademark Office[29]. Additionally, USPTO introduced a shadow ledger of cross-border payments between the U.S. and Canada based on the same technology that is currently being reviewed by RBC management and auditing its release[30].

Finally, we have the case of several regional banks such as the National Bank of Canada that have launched a pilot program that uses blockchain technology to enable its business customers to arrange financing by teaming up with tech firms CGI Group Inc. and Skuchain. The pilot aims to streamline the process for negotiating trade finance arrangements, such as standby letters of credit and guarantees, by enabling customers to initiate and conclude negotiations on smart contracts.[31].

However, the wait-and-see approach of this business model might lead to a deterioration of the position and the reliability of a bank entering the market too late. If the blockchain market moves at the current pace to getting structured and regulated, it might leave only a small window of opportunity leading to a smaller market share.

In sum, this business model relies on a defensive and conservative strategy with an incremental and gradual entry in the market with blockchain technology. It allows the bank to keep its flexibility and minimize its sunk cost investments. However, this business model might offer limited opportunities and has several constraints when the market will be getting structured to reach the full potential of the market. The bank might become a laggard and lose its technology leadership with its clients if it does not move when the market timing is right.

The following Table 1 summarize our findings.

## DISCUSSION

Our research brings some potential contributions to the topic of blockchain technology, business models, and management transformation. It could lead to the formulation of the following hypotheses for future research on the topic:

**Hypothesis #1:** the selection of a business model for the blockchain technology would be explained to a considerable extent, by the timing of entry into the blockchain market.

Our research suggests that the timing of entry into the blockchain market would significantly influence the selection of business models for banks. For instance, the timing of entry has been associated with the fact that companies that commit themselves early with their business models are capable of capitalizing on digital opportunities and outperform competitors (IBM, 2015).

In our research, we found that the revenue potential and risks could explain the timing of entry in the blockchain market. The literature has argued that strategic entry in digital technologies such as FinTech and blockchain represent an opportunity in terms of revenue streams but require an adequate business model (Cheah, 2017; Rachinger *et al.*, 2018). An early entry in the blockchain market would represent a high risk but might lead to higher revenues. We could argue that banks deploying a business model based on an early entry with a high-intensity management transformation would require an in-depth assimilation of blockchain technology and could access revenues more quickly. This is the case for instance, of solution providers and disrupters.

*Table1. Categorization of Bank Business Models for the Blockchain Technology and Bank Business Models for the Blockchain Technology*

| Business Models | Characteristics | Technology | Management Transformation | Examples |
|---|---|---|---|---|
| 1. Coordinators | Large scale and scope players with an intermediate vertical integration of suppliers and distributors | Technology development through consortiums and partnerships with high-tech companies and startups | Medium-intensity management transformation based on a stretch of existing of competencies | BNP Paribas, Wells Fargo, Barclays, JP Morgan, UBS Group, AG, CaixaBank, Banco Bilbao Vizcaya Argentaria (BBVA), DBS Bank, and Commonwealth Bank of Australia (CBA). |
| 2. Integrators | Large scale and scope players with a completed vertical integration of suppliers and distributors | Technology development is done predominantly in-house to minimize risks and integrate processes | Medium-intensity management transformation with accommodation of the technology in their core competencies. Development of an integrated value chain with technology providers and platform developers | Bank of America, American Express, Citigroup, Goldman Sachs, Capital One, the Royal Bank of Scotland (RBS). Mitsubishi UFJ Financial Group (MUFG), UnionBank, Capital One. |
| 3. Solution providers | Smaller players with a limited market focus often working for third parties | In-house development of technological turnkey solutions | High-intensity management transformation with the assimilation of the technology | Westpac, ASB Bank, Industrial and Commercial Bank of China, China Construction Bank, Agricultural Bank of China. |
| Disrupters | Smaller banks moving early into the market with a high-risk profile piloting advanced blockchain initiative | Early technology adopters at the beginning of the market growth phase | High-intensity management transformation and assimilation of the technology | Santander Bank, EQIBank, Aelf Bank, Axis Bank, Cuallix Bank, UnionBank, National Bank of Dubai. |
| 5.Explorers | Smaller scope international banks such as Credit Suisse or purely regional banks such as National Bank of Canada | Incremental technology development to minimize the risk and sunk costs | Low-intensity management transformation and defensive approach toward blockchain integration | Credit Suisse, HSBC, Royal Bank of Canada, SBI Holdings, Sberbank Russia, CIB, National Bank of Canada. |

In contrast, a late entry might represent a lower risk and but also less attractive revenue streams. The cost to acquire market share in the blockchain market would be higher. The business models, such as coordinators, integrators, and explorers that correspond more to late market entry, would access a more stable potential, but maybe lower revenue stream at a much lower risk.

Regarding the risk associated with a blockchain deployment and business models, the research on FinTech has indicated that the value creation is best achieved via radical rather than incremental digitalization but that such a radical innovation might impact the company's financial performance (Parida, 2014). The research argues that the increased technological uncertainty of the deployment of a radical innovation has to be managed, and that a management approach is needed to focus on value creation and creating an adaptable management system (Dellermann & Fliaster, 2017; Ehret & Wirtz, 2017).

Regarding the topic of value creation of revenues and risk, our research seems to indicate that for banks relying on a business model of disrupters or solution providers, entering early in the market might lead to a pre-emptive competitive advantage with a pioneering advantage in the blockchain market. Moving early in the market might represent a structural competitive advantage. However, as mentioned before, this would require a high-intensity management transformation when integrating the blockchain technology.

In contrast, the business model of explorers with a late entry might represent a lower risk in terms of sunk cost investment but with less of a competitive advantage when moving in the market. It would be more of a defense strategy to preserve the existing market share and would require a lower intensity management transformation. It would rely on an imitative strategy to replicate the learning curve of blockchain technology of competitors.

Finally, in our research, we found that in the case of a coordinator, the business model would represent an intermediary approach with a market entry in the second majority of entrants and a moderate risk. In this case, the lower risk might be explained by the propensity of some banks to transfer technology risk to suppliers through alliances and shared platforms.

**Hypothesis #2:** the level of technology maturity would influence the selection of a business model for a bank when deploying a blockchain technology.

Another underlying question is the correspondence between the maturity of blockchain technology, business models, and management transformation. The research on FinTech and business models has indicated that the success of financial technology is, to a large extent, explained by the maturity of the technology. For instance, Kauffman & Nault (2018) indicated that in the FinTech revolution, the adoption of technologies such as big data but also the emergence of pattern recognition, data mining, machine learning (ML), and other digital-sensing tools could be explained by the increasing maturity level of the data infrastructures and integrated systems. Furthermore, Brogaard *et al.* (2014) have argued that the FinTech sector is likely to experience significant adjustments and evolution as time passes, as technology matures into a specific industry sector. A high level of technology maturity with less uncertainty and established norms and standards might facilitate the introduction of new business models and the management transformation of a bank.

More specifically, our findings suggest a correspondence between the maturity of blockchain technology and the deployment of specific business models. As blockchain technology mature, business models such as integrators, coordinators, and explorers will be privileged. It would become possible to move ahead as compared to later entrants with more extensive scale and scope business models that require technology with established norms and standards that lower the risk of sunk costs investments.

As the blockchain technology mature, it would attract a smaller proportion business models of smaller scale and scope such as disrupters or the of solution providers. With an established set of norms and standards for the blockchain technology, it would reduce strategic windows of opportunities to enter on a smaller scale with new solutions and applications. It would then become more difficult to disrupt the blockchain market in a defined regulatory framework and standard operating procedures (SOP).

**Hypothesis #3:** Large established banks are moving with a business model with low-intensity management transformation, a larger scale, and scope with a vertical integration to control suppliers and platforms.

Regarding the intensity of the management transformation, the research has indicated that factors such as product and service development and infrastructure plays a critical role in FinTech (Dijkman *et al.*, 2015; Kiel *et al.*, 2017). According to Visnjic *et al.* (2018), these business models would require different management transformation because of the risks. They gave the example of digital technologies such as artificial intelligence, digital platforms and big data analytics of technologies that would require a more in-depth management transformation to be exploited.

Our findings suggest that larger banks would prefer the deployment of business models with a lower intensity of management transformation. This is the case of the business model, such as coordinators and integrators. In this case, the banks are searching to fully integrate the blockchain but adding new competencies without transforming their traditional intermediation banking activities with their suppliers and distribution channels such as branches.

In our research, we found that larger banks seem to prefer a low-intensity management transformation but are looking to keep a high control of blockchain technology development. They would prefer a business model that does not require a transformation of their traditional banking skills but are searching to lower transaction cost with a controlling hand on the value chain over technology providers and also over platform developers.

In contrast, the solution providers and the disrupters would be ready to adopt a high management transformation process by introducing radically new digital competencies. This high-intensity management transformation might destroy the value of their traditional intermediation banking skills such as collecting deposits and lending money with a spread. This high level of management transformation would be more easily achieved by banks with a smaller scope.

Our findings are aligned with resource-based theories (Varga, 2017) that argue that there should be a perceived opportunity and benefits to motivate companies to allocate resources and experiment with innovative digital business models (Baines *et al.*, 2017) and start an important management transformation. This is also consistent with the work of Eloranta & Turunen (2016) and Cenamor *et al.* (2017) that have used the platform theory to explain the development of digital technologies. To paraphrase the seminal work of Williamson (1981), they would prefer to control markets with hierarchies versus transaction costs. The vertical integration of the blockchain technology platform with in-house development is an example of a bank mechanism to keep control over the distribution of its products and services and minimize transaction costs with technology providers and distributors.

**Hypothesis #4:** We found that banks that are moving massively into the blockchain technology market need a significant sunk investment and resources not available to smaller bank business models.

In our findings, we found that integrators and coordinators would need access to considerable external financial resources to develop and deploy blockchain technology in the market. In the case of integrators, we found several large American banks such as Bank of America, American Express, Citigroup, Goldman Sachs, and Capital One correspond to this approach since they have excellent access to the financial market. This hypothesis is concurrent with the findings of Gomber *et al.* (2018) that conclude that it might become difficult for smaller entrepreneurial banks searching to create value with FinTech applications to compete with large, well-capitalized banks.

Our hypothesis indicates that the deployment of this business model would be facilitated by access to the financial market to procure optimal financial resources. This is the case with the business model of coordinators and integrators. Banks such as BNP Paribas, Wells Fargo, Barclays, JP Morgan and UBS Group would also be able to access the financial market to leverage resources and develop their blockchain technology.

**Hypothesis #5:** Radical innovation with the blockchain technology would be predominant for smaller banks' positions as a technology specialist for specific solutions and applications.

Our hypothesis is that radical innovation with blockchain technology would be predominant for smaller banks' positions as a technology specialist offering specific solutions and applications. In our research, we found that this was the case of the business model of disrupters with banks such as Bank, EQIBank, Aelf Bank, Axis Bank, and Cuallix Bank. It was also the case of solution providers with banks such as Westpac, ASB Bank, Industrial and Commercial Bank of China, China Construction Bank, Agricultural Bank of China These banks have selected a smaller scale and scope business model and a strong technology development to compete with larger banks.

In the case of disrupters, for instance, this could necessitate an innovative management transformation with different core competencies than a traditional bank. In the case of solution providers, the management transformation would be even more challenging by proposing an entirely new turnkey technological solution to the financial ecosystem. This would lead to a high-intensity management transformation in both cases.

The risk factor in terms of radical innovation of business models based on technology has been discussed in the research by several authors such as Kauffman & Nault (2018). In this regard, Kauffman & Nault (2018) highlighted the risk associated with radically new business models and technology. They argue that for smaller innovative banks in financial technology, entrepreneurship often led to a negative experience. They gave the example of the failure of Mondex in the UK for cash alternative list transactions, and also financial technology for pension fund portfolio that was a failure. They also give the case of Optimark for institutional trading by price-time-quantity bids for large blocks of shares, which did not survive despite its major innovation of a three-dimensional order book. Hess & Kemerer (1994), using the concept of transaction costs, suggest that banks relying on hierarchy versus the market (technology outsourcing) would face the risk of several failures when adopting the blockchain technology. Malone *et al.* (1987) mentioned that several cases of failure had been identified with some of the leading innovative players such as First Boston Corporation's Shelternet, Citicorp's Mortgage Power Plus, American Financial Network's Rennie Mae, Prudential's CLOS, and PRC's Loan Express that have faced failure when integrating financial technology.

**Hypothesis #6:** Explorers that are not specialized would outsource in a more meaningful manner their blockchain technology development.

Our findings suggest that smaller regional banks, such as explorers, would outsource in a large proportion, their blockchain technology development. In this group of banks that are explorers, we have Credit Suisse, HSBC, Royal Bank of Canada, SBI Holdings, Sberbank Russia, CIB, National Bank of Canada gather.

More specifically, we found that this business model gathers two types of banks.

First, we have purely regional banks such as the National Bank of Canada operating mainly in Eastern Canada. In the first case, our findings suggest that these banks would outsource a significant part of their technology developments. For example, the National Bank of Canada has for several years, outsourced its technology development to IBM. This would represent a low-intensity management transformation. Our research suggests that regional banks would in a higher proportion, outsource their blockchain technology development to external providers. In the case of smaller regional banks, these players would not be able to make such significant investments to develop their blockchain solution internally. This has also been argued by Brodsky & Oates (2017) that have indicated that it is more suitable for smaller companies to outsource their financial technologies, rather than attempting to develop them in house.

In the second case, we have specialized and conservative banks such as Credit Suisse. They have smaller scope than others international banks. They would be more tempted to follow a segmentation strategy (such as Credit Suisse in private banking). In contrast with larger banks relying on the business model of integrators and coordinators, these smaller banks would not benefit from economies of scope and a sharing of cost for technology development in multiple markets.

In sum, this is consistent with the business literature that has indicated that banks are known as being conservative regarding new technology development.

## Research Limitations

Our research has several limitations. We have identified three:

Firstly, our research studied management transformation only based on the strategic intent of banks. Several authors, such as Mintzberg & Water (1985) have shown that strategic intents and deliberate strategies might lead to a different strategy when implemented. In other words, blockchain might, in a few years, lead to failure or a completely emergent and different strategy than the initial intent.

Secondly, our research focused predominantly on larger international and national banks and did not focus on the different contexts of FinTech in the financial industry. For example, we did not study FinTech startups or sectors of financial services such as insurance and financial brokerage. In the case of startups, it would have necessitated a different sample and a different focus to investigate the role of capital venturing when financing FinTech startups. However, we identified that startups appear to play a strategic role in the specific case of the business model of coordinators.

Thirdly, our research was primarily descriptive and did not provide any empirical validation. The lack of empirical validation limits the generalization of our findings and their external validity to other sectors of the financial service industry. However, we suggested hypotheses that might lead to further empirical validation.

## Implications for Management

The research has indicated that there is increasing evidence that most incumbent firms across industries are ill-prepared to benefit from the promise of digitalization, such as financial technology (Porter & Heppelmann, 2015; Lanka *et al.*, 2017). For instance, Rachinger *et al.* (2018) argued that organizational capacity and employee competence are significant obstacles in the deployment of new business models in the digital context.

Our research highlights potential implications for management. We proposed three implications for banks when deploying a business model based on blockchain:

Firstly, timing appears to play a critical strategic role when entering the blockchain market. Entering the blockchain market early presents a significant risk since the norms and standards are continually evolving. Norms and standards might be radically transformed by regulators, by technology development or by the preference of users. Entering early in the market with a blockchain market is a risky business. However, entering late in the blockchain market might require significant capital resources and huge sunk costs investments only available to large established banks. Our findings suggest that larger banks such as the ones playing the role of Coordinators might be interested in transferring the business risk of technology deployment to their suppliers with platform alliances and consortiums.

Secondly, we suggest that platforms by providing economies of scope to distribute multiple products and services and by facilitating the formation of a bundle of strategic competencies could play a strategic role in the structuring of product engineering and digital distribution channels. For instance, blockchain technology platforms might impede the strategic entry of smaller banks when entering the blockchain market.

Thirdly, adopting a high-intensity management model such as one of the solution providers or disrupters might require an in-depth transformation of the core competencies of the traditional financial intermediation bank function. In other terms, a high-intensity transformation might require a divestment in traditional banking functions based on omni channels such as branches and call centers that would have to be replaced by a new disintermediated digital function provided by the blockchain, such as being a third party player.

## Future Research Direction

Our research puts in perspective three future research directions for additional research on the topic:

Firstly, our research underlines the importance of additional research to better understand the management transformation of the business models based on blockchain. We need empirical data to improve the internal validity of our findings based on strategic intent. Additional work will be necessary to study strategies and understand their factors of success with case studies and empirical analysis.

Secondly, additional work is also necessary to generalize the external validity of our findings by researching other non-banks sectors. We need to document the impact of blockchain on other financial sectors such as insurance and stock brokerage. The question arises that are the business models of the banking industry found for blockchain, unique, or could it be generalized to other sectors of the financial services industry?

Finally, startups and the financial ecosystem should require a special attention. This is important since startups are disruptive players that might replace established banks as dominant players in the financial services industry. This substitution of financial providers requires specific consideration to better understand how FinTech could disrupt and transform the core competencies of financial institutions by introducing processes leading to financial disintermediation. As mentioned in the literature, we could argue that additional research on emergent financial ecosystem is needed to better understand the impact of FinTech (Schmidt *et al.*, 2018). Emergent and growing technologies like blockchain have been mentioned as a particularly crucial role in changing the value capture mechanisms by enabling improved transparency in the exchange among many actors (Parida *et al.*, 2019).

## CONCLUSION

In conclusion, our research illustrates the critical role played by the blockchain technology for designing and deploying business models in the case of banks. It also highlights how the management transformation of these business models has different intensity regarding the depth of their management transformation. We found that the resource commitment for blockchain technology development and the timing of entry into the blockchain market would explain to a large extent, the selection of a business model for deploying blockchain technology in the banking industry.

Our research indicates that in general, banks are pursuing a relatively conservative strategy when deploying blockchain technology by relying on a business model minimizing the business risk. For example, business models such as coordinators and explorers, and to a lesser extent, integrators were found to be more conservative. This might be explained by the technology uncertainty and the lack of a regulatory framework of the blockchain technology at this moment of the market development.

We found that the design and deployment of a business model for blockchain requires a strategic decision for technology development with in-house technology development, on the one hand, or and the outsourcing to external providers of technology, on the other hand. We have also found that the existence of intermediary approaches such as platforms and alliances for blockchain technology development with the business model of coordinators are configurations combining both approaches.

Regarding the management transformation, we devised three levels of intensity for management transformation of business models for the blockchain technology (high, medium, and low intensity). We found that most banks are trying to accommodate the integration of technology by stretching or extending their traditional core competencies in financial intermediation (low-intensity management transformation) rather than by integrating the disruptive technology of blockchain by developing radically new competencies (high-intensity management transformation).

However, as explained earlier, additional research will be necessary to generalize our findings to better understand the process of management transformation following the deployment of a business model based on the technology of blockchain.

## REFERENCES

Abell, D. F. (1980). *Defining the business: The starting point of strategic planning*. Prentice Hall.

Allaire, Y., & Firsirotu, M. E. (1993). Strategy and Performance Drivers (French) Theories of organizational culture. *Organization Studies*, *5*(3), 193–226. doi:10.1177/017084068400500301

Alt, R., & Zimmermann, H. D. (2001). Preface: Introduction to special section–business models. *Electronic Markets*, *11*(1), 3–9.

Anonymous. (2015). The Fintech revolution: A wave of startups is changing finance—For the better. *The Economist*.

Baines, T., Bigdeli, A. Z., Bustinza, O. F., Shi, V. G., Baldwin, J., & Ridgway, K. (2017). Servitization: Revisiting the state-of-the-art and research priorities. *International Journal of Operations & Production Management*, *37*(2), 256–278. doi:10.1108/IJOPM-06-2015-0312

Bradshaw, C., Atkinson, S., & Doody, O. (2017). Employing a qualitative description approach in health care research. *Global Qualitative Nursing Research*, *4*, 2333393617742282. doi:10.1177/2333393617742282 PMID:29204457

Businesswire. (2016). *More Financial Institutions Join Ripple's Global Network.* https://www.businesswire.com/news/home/20160622005370/en/Financial-Institutions-Join-Ripple%E2%80%99s-Global-Network

Cant, B., Khadikar, A., Ruiter, A., Bronebakk, J. B., Coumaros, J., Buvat, J., & Gupta, A. (2016). Smart contracts in financial services: Getting from hype to reality. *Capgemini Consulting*, 1-24.

Capgemini Consulting. (2016, October 11). *Smart Contracts in Financial Services: Getting from Hype to Reality*. Author.

Cenamor, J., Sjödin, D. R., & Parida, V. (2017). Adopting a platform approach in servitization: Leveraging the value of digitalization. *International Journal of Production Economics*, *192*, 54–65. doi:10.1016/j.ijpe.2016.12.033

Cheah, S., & Wang, S. (2017). Big data-driven business model innovation by traditional industries in the Chinese economy. *Journal of Chinese Economic and Foreign Trade Studies.*

Chesbrough, H. W. (2010). Business Model Innovation: Opportunities and Barriers. *Long Range Planning*, *43*(2-3), 354–363. doi:10.1016/j.lrp.2009.07.010

Courbe, J. (2016). Financial services technology 2020 and beyond: Embracing disruption. PWC.

DaSilva, C. M., Trkman, P., Desouza, K., & Lindič, J. (2013). Disruptive technologies: A business model perspective on cloud computing. *Technology Analysis and Strategic Management*, *25*(10), 1161–1173. doi:10.1080/09537325.2013.843661

DaSilva, C. M., & Trkman, P. (2016). Business Model: What It Is and What It Is Not. *Long Range Planning*, *47*(6), 379–389. doi:10.1016/j.lrp.2013.08.004

Dellermann, D., Fliaster, A., & Kolloch, M. (2017). Innovation risk in digital business models: The German energy sector. *The Journal of Business Strategy*, *38*(5), 35–43. doi:10.1108/JBS-07-2016-0078

Dijkman, R. M., Sprenkels, B., Peeters, T., & Janssen, A. (2015). Business models for the Internet of Things. *International Journal of Information Management*, *35*(6), 672–678. doi:10.1016/j.ijinfomgt.2015.07.008

Dorfleitner, G., Hornuf, L., Schmitt, M., & Weber, M. (2017). The fintech market in Germany. In *FinTech in Germany* (pp. 13–46). Springer. doi:10.1007/978-3-319-54666-7_4

Dornyei, Z. (2007). Research Methods in Applied Linguistics. Oxford University Press.

Doyle, L., McCabe, C., Keogh, B., Brady, A., & McCann, M. (2019). An overview of the qualitative descriptive design within nursing research. *Journal of Research in Nursing*.

Economist. (2015). *Blockchain: The Next Big Thing or Is It?* Special Report.

Ehret, M., & Wirtz, J. (2017). Unlocking value from machines: Business models and the industrial internet of things. *Journal of Marketing Management, 33*(1-2), 111–130. doi:10.1080/0267257X.2016.1248041

Eickhoff, M., Muntermann, J., & Weinrich, T. (2017). *What do FinTechs actually do? A taxonomy of FinTech business models*. Academic Press.

Eloranta, V., & Turunen, T. (2016). Platforms in service-driven manufacturing: Leveraging complexity by connecting, sharing, and integrating. *Industrial Marketing Management, 55*, 178–186. doi:10.1016/j.indmarman.2015.10.003

El Sawy, O. A., & Pereira, F. (2013). *Business modelling in the dynamic digital space: An ecosystem approach*. Springer. doi:10.1007/978-3-642-31765-1

Etikan, I., Musa, S. A., & Alkassim, R. S. (2016). Comparison of convenience sampling and purposive sampling. *American Journal of Theoretical and Applied Statistics, 5*(1), 1–4. doi:10.11648/j.ajtas.20160501.11

Foss, N. J., & Saebi, T. (2017). Fifteen years of research on business model innovation: How far have we come, and where should we go? *Journal of Management, 43*(1), 200–227. doi:10.1177/0149206316675927

Geissdoerfer, M., Vladimirova, D., & Evans, S. (2018). Sustainable business model innovation: A review. *Journal of Cleaner Production, 198*, 401–416. doi:10.1016/j.jclepro.2018.06.240

Gomber, P., Kauffman, R. J., Parker, C., & Weber, B. W. (2018). On the fintech revolution: Interpreting the forces of innovation, disruption, and transformation in financial services. *Journal of Management Information Systems, 35*(1), 220–265. doi:10.1080/07421222.2018.1440766

Gozman, D., Liebenau, J., & Mangan, J. (2018). The innovation mechanisms of fintech start-ups: Insights from SWIFT's innotribe competition. *Journal of Management Information Systems, 35*(1), 145–179. doi:10.1080/07421222.2018.1440768

Han, K., Kauffman, R. J., & Nault, B. R. (2008). Relative importance, specific investment, and ownership in inter-organizational systems. *Information Technology Management, 9*(3), 181–200. doi:10.100710799-008-0039-9

Hatch, E. M., & Lazaraton, A. (1991). *The research manual: Design and statistics for applied linguistics*. New York, NY: Newbury House Publishers.

Hatzakis, E. D., Nair, S. K., & Pinedo, M. (2010). Operations in financial Services—An overview. *Production and Operations Management, 19*(6), 633–664. doi:10.1111/j.1937-5956.2010.01163.x

Henry, G. T. (1990). *Practical sampling* (Vol. 21). Sage. doi:10.4135/9781412985451

Hess, C. M., & Kemerer, C. F. (1994). Computerized loan origination systems: An industry case study of the electronic markets hypothesis. *Management Information Systems Quarterly, 18*(3), 251–275. doi:10.2307/249618

Holotiuk, F., Pisani, F., & Moormann, J. (2017). *The impact of blockchain technology on business models in the payments industry*. Academic Press.

Hubspot. (2020). *The Top 7 Search Engines, Ranked by Popularity*. https://blog.hubspot.com/marketing/top-search-engines

IBM Report. (2017). Leading the pack in blockchain banking. IBM. Innovative Analytics (GBE03664-USEN-02).

IFLR. (2016). *Blockchain: Regulating the future of finance*. https://www.iflr.com/article/b1lsps8kgddhbq/blockchain-regulating-the-future-of-finance

Kiel, D., Arnold, C., & Voigt, K. I. (2017). The influence of the Industrial Internet of Things on business models of established manufacturing companies–A business-level perspective. *Technovation, 68*, 4–19. doi:10.1016/j.technovation.2017.09.003

Kothari, M., & Moolani, S. (2015). Reliability of "Google" for obtaining medical information. *Indian Journal of Ophthalmology, 63*(3), 267. doi:10.4103/0301-4738.156934 PMID:25971176

Lee, D. K. C., & Teo, E. G. S. (2015). Emergence of FinTech and the LASIC Principles. *Journal of Financial Perspectives, 3*(3), 1. doi:10.2139srn.2668049

Lenka, S., Parida, V., & Wincent, J. (2017). Digitalization capabilities as enablers of value co-creation in service firms. *Psychology and Marketing, 34*(1), 92–100. doi:10.1002/mar.20975

Liebenau, J., & Elaluf-Calderwood, S. (2016). *Blockchain innovation beyond bitcoin and banking.* Available at SSRN 2749890

Lin, T. C. (2015). Infinite financial intermediation. *Wake Forest Law Review, 50,* 643.

Lucas, H. Jr, Agarwal, R., Clemons, E. K., El Sawy, O. A., & Weber, B. (2013). Impactful research on transformational information technology: An opportunity to inform new audiences. *Management Information Systems Quarterly, 37*(2), 371–382. doi:10.25300/MISQ/2013/37.2.03

Magnuson, W. (2017). The next crisis will start in Silicon Valley. *Bloomberg View, 18.*

Malone, T. W., & Crowston, K. (1987). J. Yates, RI Benjamin. 1987. *Electronic markets and electronic hierarchies. Communications of the ACM, 30*(6), 484–497. doi:10.1145/214762.214766

Mearian, L. (2017). What is blockchain? The most disruptive tech in decades. *Computerworld,* 1–8.

Metzlar, A. (2017). Strategic intent and the strategic position of smallholders: A case study of a smallholders' organization in the Ghanaian cocoa industry. *Review of Social Economy, 75*(3), 371–387. doi:10.1080/00346764.2017.1299202

NASDAQ. (2016). *Building on the Blockchain.* https://www.nasdaq.com/articles/building-blockchain-2016-03-23

Nofer, M., Gomber, P., Hinz, O., & Schiereck, D. (2017). Blockchain. *Business & Information Systems Engineering, 59*(3), 183–187. doi:10.100712599-017-0467-3

Nowiński, W., & Kozma, M. (2017). How can blockchain technology disrupt existing business models? *Entrepreneurial Business and Economics Review, 5*(3), 173–188. doi:10.15678/EBER.2017.050309

Osterwalder, A., Pigneur, Y., & Tucci, C. L. (2005). Clarifying business models: Origins, present, and future of the concept. *Communications of the Association for Information Systems, 16*(1), 1. doi:10.17705/1CAIS.01601

Parida, V., Sjödin, D., & Reim, W. (2019). *Reviewing the literature on digitalization, business model innovation, and sustainable industry: Past achievements and future promises.* Academic Press.

Parida, V., Sjödin, D. R., Wincent, J., & Kohtamäki, M. (2014). Mastering the transition to product-service provision: Insights into business models, learning activities, and capabilities. *Research Technology Management*, *57*(3), 44–52.

Popper, N. (2015). *Digital gold: Bitcoin and the inside story of the misfits and millionaires trying to reinvent money*. Harper.

Porter, M. E., & Heppelmann, J. E. (2015). How smart, connected products are transforming companies. *Harvard Business Review*, *93*(10), 96–114.

Prahalad, C. K., & Hamel, G. (1989, May). Strategic Intent. Harvard Business Review, 63–76.

Puschmann, T. (2017). Fintech. *Business & Information Systems Engineering*, *59*(1), 69–76. doi:10.100712599-017-0464-6

PwC. (2016). *Blurred lines: How FinTech is shaping financial services.* PwC.

Rachinger, M., Rauter, R., Müller, C., Vorraber, W., & Schirgi, E. (2019). Digitalization and its influence on business model innovation. *Journal of Manufacturing Technology Management*, *30*(8), 1143–1160. doi:10.1108/JMTM-01-2018-0020

Ritter, T., & Lettl, C. (2018). The broader implications of business-model research. *Long Range Planning*, *51*(1), 1–8. doi:10.1016/j.lrp.2017.07.005

Roberts, D. (2016). *Walmart to team with IBM (IBM) and Tsinghua University to track the pork supply chain in China using blockchain.* Academic Press.

Sandelowski, M. (2010). What's in a name? Qualitative description revisited. *Research in Nursing & Health*, *33*(1), 77–84. doi:10.1002/nur.20362 PMID:20014004

Schmidt, J., Drews, P., & Schirmer, I. (2018). *Charting the emerging financial services ecosystem of fintech and banks: Six types of data-driven business models in the fintech sector*. Academic Press.

Sia, S. K., Soh, C., & Weill, P. (2016). How DBS Bank Pursued a Digital Business Strategy. *MIS Quarterly Executive*, *15*(2).

Swan, M. (2015). *Blockchain: Blueprint for a new economy*. O'Reilly Media, Inc.

Swartz, N. D. (2014). Bursting the Bitcoin bubble: The case to regulate digital currency as a security or commodity. *Tul. J. Tech. & Intell. Prop.*, *17*, 319.

Teece, D. J. (2010). Business models, business strategy, and innovation. *Long Range Planning*, *43*(2-3), 172–194. doi:10.1016/j.lrp.2009.07.003

Timmers, P. (1998). Business models for electronic markets. *Electronic Markets, 8*(2), 3–8. doi:10.1080/10196789800000016

Underwood, S. (2016). *Blockchain beyond bitcoin*. Academic Press.

Varga, D. (2017). Fintech, the new era of financial services. *Vezetéstudomány-Budapest Management Review, 48*(11), 22–32. doi:10.14267/VEZTUD.2017.11.03

Visnjic, I., Neely, A., & Jovanovic, M. (2018). The path to outcome delivery: Interplay of service market strategy and open business models. *Technovation, 72*, 46–59. doi:10.1016/j.technovation.2018.02.003

Williamson, O. E. (1981). The Economics of Organization: The Transaction Cost Approach. *American Journal of Sociology, 87*(3), 548–577. doi:10.1086/227496

Wirtz, B. W., Pistoia, A., Ullrich, S., & Göttel, V. (2016). Business models: Origin, development, and future research perspectives. *Long Range Planning, 49*(1), 36–54. doi:10.1016/j.lrp.2015.04.001

Yap, B. (2017). India's new payment banks need a regulatory boost. *International Financial Law Review*.

Zott, C., Amit, R., & Massa, L. (2011). The business model: Recent developments and future research. *Journal of Management, 37*(4), 1019–1042. doi:10.1177/0149206311406265

Zhao, J. L., Fan, S., & Yan, J. (2016). *Overview of business innovations and research opportunities in blockchain and introduction to the special issue*. Academic Press.

## ENDNOTES

1 https://www.gtreview.com/news/fintech/bnp-paribas-becomes-latest-bank-to-pilot-voltron-blockchain-platform/

2 https://www.forbes.com/sites/michaeldelcastillo/2020/02/19/blockchain-50/#75cbde977553

3 https://www.fintechfutures.com/2019/11/dbs-bank-unveils-trade-finance-blockchain-project/#:~:text=DBS%20Bank%20has%20partnered%20with,project%2C%20the%20ICC%20TradeFlow%20platform.&text=The%20platform%20is%20built%20on,powered%20by%20Perlin's%20blockchain%20technology.

4 https://www.ctrmcenter.com/news/perlin-singaporean-companies-govt-to-launch-open-source-blockchain-commodity-trade-platform/

5 https://www.bbva.com/en/bbva-indra-deliver-worlds-first-blockchain-supported-corporate-loan/

6 https://www.fnlondon.com/articles/ubs-and-others-to-use-bitcoin-like-token-for-trade-settlement-20190603

7 https://www.jpmorgan.com/global/technology/blockchain

8 https://www.jpmorgan.com/global/research/blockchain-next-steps

9 https://www.barclayscorporate.com/insights/innovation/what-does-blockchain-do/

10 https://www.reuters.com/article/us-wells-fargo-blockchain/wells-fargo-tests-cryptocurrency-for-internal-transactions-idUSKBN1W22D3

11 https://www.cnbc.com/2019/03/25/bank-of-america-skeptical-on-blockchain-despite-having-most-patents.html#:~:text=Menu-,Bank%20of%20America%20tech%20chief%20is%20skeptical%20on%20blockchain%20even,the%20most%20patents%20for%20it&text=Still%2C%20the%20bank%20has%2082,payment%20companies%20Mastercard%20and%20PayPal.

12 https://www.forbes.com/sites/tedknutson/2018/10/08/blockchain-ai-not-ready-for-primetime-financial-leaders-told/#7c5908ce316c

13 https://www.cnbc.com/2019/03/25/bank-of-america-skeptical-on-blockchain-despite-having-most-patents.html

14 https://toshitimes.com/american-express-will-adopt-blockchain-technology/

15 https://www.cnbc.com/2019/03/25/bank-of-america-skeptical-on-blockchain-despite-having-most-patents.html

16 https://www.cio.com/article/3493094/westpac-proof-of-concept-wins-tech-buzzword-bingo.html

17 https://www.finextra.com/newsarticle/34240

18 https://www.chgtoday.com/top-corporations-exploring-blockchain/

19 http://www.chinabankingnews.com/2018/08/18/bank-china-leads-chinese-banks-blockchain-patents-11-applications/

20 https://medium.com/aelfblockchain/aelf-announced-the-inauguration-of-the-innovation-alliance-38c178f7a69#:~:text=aelf%20Innovation%20Alliance%20is%20aimed,on%20Blockchain%20technology%20and%20applications.&text=Mappo%20has%20been%20investing%20and%20trading%20in%20fiat%20currencies%20since%202013.

21 https://medium.com/aelfblockchain/aelf-announced-the-inauguration-of-the-innovation-alliance-38c178f7a69#:~:text=aelf%20Innovation%20Alliance%20is%20aimed,on%20Blockchain%20technology%20and%20applications.&text=Mappo%20has%20been%20investing%20and%20trading%20in%20fiat%20currencies%20since%202013.

22 https://www.finanznachrichten.de/nachrichten-2018-10/44979797-eqibank-the-world-s-first-licensed-and-regulated-offshore-bank-for-national-currencies-crypto-and-digital-assets-has-launched-008.htm

23 https://www.fintechfutures.com/2019/08/schroders-personal-wealth-troubled-by-it-issues/

24 https://www.pymnts.com/blockchain/2018/ripple-kuwait-finance-house-cross-border-payments/

25 https://www.credit-suisse.com/se/en/articles/asset-management/blockchain-se-201909.html

26 https://cointelegraph.com/news/sbi-virtual-currencies-the-bank-backed-japanese-exchange-with-big-plans

27 https://www.ledgerinsights.com/blockchain-interoperability-hsbc-voltron-landmark/

28 https://news.coinsquare.com/blockchain/royal-bank-of-canada-only-canadian-firm-exploring-blockchain-forbes/

29 https://news.coinsquare.com/blockchain/royal-bank-of-canada-only-canadian-firm-exploring-blockchain-forbes/

30 https://www.bai.org/globalinnovations/awards/2018-finalists/internal-process-innovation/royal-bank-of-canada/

31 https://thepaypers.com/e-invoicing-supply-chain-finance/cgi-national-bank-of-canada-pilot-blockchain-guarantee-and-standby-negotiation-platform--775480

# Chapter 2
# Commodity Trading in the Blockchain Technology Era:
## An Investigation on Global Companies

**Sonia Arsi**
https://orcid.org/0000-0002-2238-7723
*Carthage Business School, University of Tunis, Carthage, Tunisia*

## ABSTRACT

*The emergence of Blockchain technology is gradually disrupting the traditional way of trading commodities. To go beyond the theory to the practical cases, this chapter provides an overview of the Blockchain-based digital transformation process behind and the pre-requisites for its inclusion in the commodity industry. A reality check through vivid examples of global companies highlights the increasing attention drawn to the Blockchain. Furthermore, this chapter discusses the impact of Blockchain technology's use in improving commodity finance trades at different levels and optimizing the transactions' effectiveness. Finally, future challenges and useful perspectives for managers and commodity firms are spotlighted.*

## INTRODUCTION

Over the last decade, digital technologies, such as the blockchain technology are increasingly attracting managers and media attention. Particularly, the introduction of the blockchain is about to metamorphose industries management, and it is disrupting businesses from their traditional customs to the digitalized era more than ever. To

DOI: 10.4018/978-1-7998-7110-1.ch002

briefly pin down the denomination of "blockchain", it refers to a decentralized database that records a registry of assets and transactions through a Peer-to-Peer network (Taylor et al., 2019).

Faced with a plethora of benefits and innovations, many companies across different sectors are considering the implementation of the blockchain technology among their regular business and are in the process of a gradual transformation of their ways of management. This is mainly due to the additional visibility on transactions offered by this novel technology, the ability to handle an open and global platform where to store information, the availability of a worldwide network system, among other advantages. Within this context, several reports, like those of Belt & Kok (2018), ConsenSys (2020), and Forbes (2020), highlighted the progressive development of blockchain technology across commodity industries. Straying from the gory details, examples are manifold, while each case is unique. TradeCloud is a supply chain platform, created by a Singaporean start-up and intended to bring traders together, provide market liquidity for metals and minerals commodities (S&P Global Platts, 2018). Royal Dutch Shell launched its blockchain platform Vakt in November 2018 and designated to treat "post-trade transactions of Brent crude" (Payne, 2018). Louis Dreyfus Co. implemented the first blockchain trading platform designated to connect between commodity traders and negotiate and conclude online deals (Terazono, 2018). This leads to a key point: how does the blockchain technology reform the way of trading commodities?

Here, one shall stall and think through the rationale for commodity trading within this digital framework. The blockchain technology is being implemented at different steps of the commodity transaction life cycle and with the collaboration of financial technology solutions offered by banks and financial services (like supply chain management, networking, insurance, forecasting, and crowdfunding platforms, etc.). The future seems to be promising; however, it's necessary to bring to the limelight additional matters on how the blockchain technology drove a radical revolution to commodity trading. What are the aspects of migration to the digitalization age? How commodity industries coped with their management brush up? And, what are the key implications and challenges that commodity industries are effectively exposed to?

The purpose of this chapter is to highlight how the implementation of the blockchain technology has shaped a new way of trading commodities for global companies. This chapter provides relevant examples extracted from the real world, as it tracks records on their experiences in order to properly understand the influence of the blockchain technology on the commodities' business. Specifically, it mainly handles the perceived renovation on each step of the physical commodity transaction life cycle, through the negotiation of the contract terms to the delivery to final clients' companies. Equally, this chapter offers insights on the role of FinTech in transforming the means of trading commodities in the financial markets at different strands: a network of worldwide payment systems, easing and security of payments, a timely search for new financing sources, opportune data for investors, an enhancement of derivatives products' trading, and so on.

This chapter aims to help professionals to understand the role of blockchain technology in the commodity trading industries. Besides, it gives handy inferences for managers to rethink their traditional way of management and the urge reconsideration of the blockchain-based commodity's use in their current businesses.

The remainder is as follows. The first section backtracks the digitalization and blockchain technology. Then, the transition decision towards blockchain technology is studied through a SWOT analysis and details on its pre-requisites. Beyond that, real-world applications of blockchain in commodity trading are highlighted. Finally, this chapter sums up with current challenges and future perspectives.

## LITERATURE REVIEW

### Exploring Digitalization and Blockchain

Numerous definitions of digitalization have been put forward. According to Gartner® IT Glossary, digitalization refers to "*the use of digital technologies to change a business model and provide new revenue and value-producing opportunities; it is the process of moving to a digital business*[1]". (Muro et al., 2017, p. 17) stated that digitalization deals with "*transforming the nation's job rolls both by expanding the digital content of hundreds of existing jobs and shifting the overall job mix toward more digitally intensive occupations*". Hence, digitalization is about bringing into play digital technology. This tends to shift the traditional way businesses are undertaken and consider the digital adoption into the workplace.

However, a difference with the term "digitization" has to be considered as it adds confusion within this context. Gartner® IT Glossary reported that "*digitization is the process of changing from analog to digital form (…) digitization takes an analog process and changes it to a digital form without any different-in-kind changes to the process itself*". (Loebbecke & Picot, 2015) and (Proeger & Runst, 2019) highlighted that digitization consists of the automation process through "digitizing information". In sum, digitization is a key prerequisite for digitalization and "digital disruption".

The digitalization process is drastically expanding across industries. Beyond that, different and sophisticated tools/technologies are designed, such as the blockchain technology. Indeed, blockchain, designated as a "Distributed Ledger Technology" (DLT), refers to a decentralized database that records a registry of assets and transactions through a Peer-to-Peer network (Taylor et al., 2019). The transaction history is stored and locked in blocks of data, that is then "chained" together and secured *via* cryptography. Such an infrastructure has the specific feature of being immutable and hard to tamper with, *i.e.* all transactions are in an unforgeable record and cannot be modified (Ernest &Young, 2017). Thus, going beyond this "new technology of trust"[2] is a must to understand.

## Blockchain and Commodity Trading

The debate on the use of blockchain technology and "the dematerialization of commodity business process" is still inconclusive (Ávila & Teixeira, 2019). How does it work with commodity trading?

(Camarda, 2018) reported that "*blockchain establishes a digital ledger of transactions that can be shared across large, decentralized networks of computers. Cryptographic techniques enable each participant in a blockchain to add new transactions that are verified by other computers on the network using specialized algorithms. Once these transactions are verified and recorded, they become extremely difficult to change or remove. A blockchain network has no central point of control, and participant computers must reach consensus on verifying new entries.*"

Yet much integrating blockchain within commodity trading is of great advantages as each component of the commodity trading cycle is considered. Further details are provided later on; particularly, a reality check on the use of blockchain technology in commodity trading is highlighted at diverse levels.

# THROUGH THE DECISION OF BLOCKCHAIN INCLUSION

## Prerequisites of an Efficient Strategy

The digital transformation process towards blockchain technology involves a roadmap, or what is called "digital information strategy". It implies "*planning, mapping, and prioritizing for the future*". It is a long-term view to sustain the relationship between innovation and technology. To which extent can the company keep going towards digital transformation and which costs to bear? Will it have the ability and capability to continue performing knowing the speed of IT changes?

"Building bridges" is the solution. It's about future perspectives and handling diverse interactions with internal and external factors. Indeed, commodity trading companies must fulfil at least the following characteristics (among others):

- Higher flexibility and agility to changes, *i.e.* 'change-aware' capacity.
- Deep understanding of blockchain technology.
- Capacity for the digitization of information[3] and its management.

- Ability to forecast accurately.
- Self-criticism.
- Self-control.
- Capability of thinking about internal collaboration ("*hyper-connectedness*").

Furthermore, the road to digitalization is an "ongoing journey". It is a continuous transformation process of permanent innovation. Pillar tactics are underlined:

- Detection of strengths, weaknesses, opportunities, and threats (SWOT).
- Evaluate of current and emerging IT evolutions.
- Prioritization of which way to undertake.
- Tracking of its position following current IT evolution status.
- Evaluation of its resources (HR skills, extra-cash for investing, relations with customers among others).
- Conception of a roadmap and elaborate future directions.
- Bridge gaps between current data and technology.
- Focus on end-relationship with customers.
- Set of final short, intermediate, and long run goals.
- Final assessment.
- Forecast on a starting way.
- Understanding, measurement, gain of skills, correction of errors, start of innovation.

## SWOT Analysis

Each commodity trading company, willing to shift toward blockchain technology, has to conduct a SWOT[4] analysis (Strengths Weaknesses Opportunities Threats). Table 1 presents a draft example of a potential SWOT analysis that should be conducted.

The strengths and opportunities are considered as *enhancers*. Through such analysis, the company would sustain and readjust its internal competences or resources and focus on its external positive possibilities. This would *enhance* the future performance of the commodity trading company eager to implement blockchain. The *inhibitors* consist of weaknesses and threats, since a careless handling would create barriers toward achieving better results.

*Table 1. Example of SWOT Matrix*

| Performance Factors | Enhancers | Inhibitors |
|---|---|---|
| Internal | Strengths<br>• paperless process.<br>• decrease in the exchange period.<br>• new sources of financing.<br>• safe electronic payment.<br>• cost savings.<br>• transparency in the supply chain management.<br>• decrease in the storage costs | Weaknesses<br>• sophisticated technology.<br>• expensive implementation costs.<br>• lack of regulatory framework.<br>• Excessive power consumption. |
| External | Opportunities<br>• network effect.<br>• eagerness to learn/adopt. | Threats<br>• risk of fraud.<br>• country legislation.<br>• difficult control of embargo countries.<br>• rejection due to unfamiliarity.<br>deep root in traditions (conservatism).<br>• Size of ledgers (or storage) |

## IN THE AFTERMATH OF BLOCKCHAIN INCLUSION: REAL-WORLD PRACTICES

Considering the fast-paced IT change, large corporations, as well growing/small IT firms or startups are redrawing their ways of doing commodity trading. Features of such a revolution are pointed out.

### Commodity FinTech Solutions

The ongoing digitalization, and Blockchain technology in particular, contributed to redress the role of financial and non-financial institutions in commodity finance trades. This requires erasing the traditional way of deals and consider innovation in financial services, referred to as "*financial technology*" or "*FinTech*". In other words, fintech involves "*innovative financial solutions enabled by IT*" (Puschmann, 2017, p. 70).[5] Within this milieu, (Gomber et al., 2017, p. 540) split FinTech into two categories; "*sustaining FinTech*" and "*disruptive FinTech*". The former refers to "*established financial services providers that try to protect their market position by the use of information technologies*", while the latter applies to "*new companies and start-ups that challenge established providers by offering new products and services*". In the following, the author describes how institutions are prone to deliver diverse Blockchain-based fintech solutions.

## Blockchain-Based "Know-Your-Customer" Process

As a step of the customer due diligence, financial institutions have to verify the identity of their customers and their possible involvement in any illegal/criminal activity *via* the "Know-Your-Customer" process (KYC). (Camarda, 2018) underlined that it uses to be generally a "*time-consuming, costly, and frustrating*" process. (FinTech Network, 2018) mentioned that regular KYC process can "*cause delay to banking transactions, typically taking 30 to 50 days to complete to a satisfactory level*". To overcome such shortcomings, "Blockchain-based KYC" solution emerge.

How this works? As a bank has a new customer, it detains his ID and KYC's documents' summary, which will be stored on the Blockchain[6]. The other institutions can have access only if they are *accredited* and detain the private key. In such a case, the customers and their corresponding institutions would not waste time in launching the KYC process once again thanks to the irreversibility feature of the Blockchain. Following (Goldman Sachs, 2016, p. 75), Case Study 7, the inclusion of Blockchain in the KYC process leads to a 10 percent decline in customer onboarding headcount, equivalent to cost savings of around 160 million of dollars.

## Collaboration with FinTech Startups

(Puschmann, 2017, p. 69) underlined that digitalization changed the overall ecosystem and contributed to "*entirely new ecosystems including incumbents and fintech startups but also to the inclusion of companies from outside the financial services industry*". Mainly such partnership aims to decrease the risk of scams and improve commodity trading (Burton, 2017). Examples of outputs in the form of blockchain solutions are highlighted here below.

## R3 Corda Blockchain Platform

In May 2018, the banks HSBC India and ING Brussels executed the first "live finance trade transaction" through Blockchain. The transaction involved soybeans shipped from Argentina to Malaysia for the benefit of Cargill Inc. The output was incredible since the delivery took only 24 hours, instead of a period ranging between 5 to 10 days.

## komgo Platform

In December 2018, the Swiss company komgo SA, resulting from a joint venture of 15 leading banks and corporations[7], was the first to officially launch a Blockchain-based open platform for commodity trade finance banks, using the Ethereum Blockchain infrastructure. This was preceded by trials in soft and energy commodities *via* the Easy Trading Connect[8] of ING (Wass, 2019). The main difference with the other Blockchain-based platforms, like Voltron, Marco Polo, Wilson, and we.trade among others, is that komgo SA encompasses "*a mix of banks and corporates*".

(ConsenSys, 2020) highlighted that the implemented "enterprise ethereum solution" involved Anti-Money Laundering (AML) checks to enhance trustworthiness in the Blockchain-based KYC.

## "Network of Networks"

The UK-based IT firm Quant Network launched the Overledger Network on September 26th, 2019. This blockchain solution allows to interconnect blockchain networks and thus solves the problem of "interoperability" (Wragg, 2019). Diverse solutions are provided, like for supply chain (trade finance), smart contracts agreements, complex searches (*i.e.* for the KYC process), among others.

## Kratos™ Platform

In 2017, the Singaporean IT company Triterras began the development of Kratos platform, a "*blockchain-enabled trading and trade finance platform*". Officially launched in 2019, it provides customized financing options for traders (*i.e.* buyers, suppliers, insurers, lenders, borrowers, etc.), such as supply chain financing, insurance, loan financing, ARP financing[9], and logistics[10].

The supply chain financing consists of facilitating the financing for suppliers, through allowing them additional cash, with taking the outstanding invoice as warranty in return. Equally, buyers or producers can "extend their days payable outstanding". It is one of the largest blockchain-based commodity trading and trade finance platform. By June 30th, 2020, "Triterras generated over $6.6 billion in volume on Kratos"[11].

## Others Blockchain-based Platforms/Solutions

*TradeCloud* is specialized in supply chain management for manufacturers and miners.

*LiquidX* aims to "*digitize illiquid assets*"[12], like invoices, insurance contracts, purchase orders, among others, and ensure delivery in a timely and effective way.

## Smart Contracts

Instead of paper agreements, the emergence of "smart contracts" represents a revolution. These contracts are distinguished as they are based upon blockchain technology. To borrow the words of (Hazik & Hassanian, 2018), the main characteristics of smart contracts consist of "*programmability, multisignature (or multisig), authentication, escrow capability, and oral inputs*".

### Smart Letter of Credit L/C

BNP Paribas developed Smart L/C, which consists on a Blockchain-based L/C instead of the conventional one. This solution allows to substitute paper flows with digital transfers.

### Payment

The Bank Payment Obligation (BPO) was firstly used in April 2015 by Cargill and BHP Billiton. This new banking payment ensures a paperless process within the supply chain. Equally, it guarantees a binding payment commitment between parties, whether for exporters or importers.

### Commodity Flows

The effect on blockchain technology on commodities differs following specific factors. (Belt & Kok, 2018) underlined that this technology is suitable for power markets. As these markets involve standardized and homogenous products, blockchain allows to improve the transaction's settlement. From another part, the authors showed that the adoption of blockchain is convenient for oil, iron ore, and diamonds' markets in order to enhance transparency within the supply chain and track quality of goods.

### Derivatives Markets

Financial innovation in terms of new *digital derivatives*. (S&P Global Platts, 2018) underlined that blockchain-based commodity trading helped in increasing liquidity within derivatives markets, improved transactions' transparency, and even provided "*attractive prices for traders based on a large liquidity pool*".

## CHALLENGES AND PERSPECTIVES

### Future Challenges

The blockchain technology is increasingly adopted or set into production by many corporations. However, ach new technology represents new threats. And, challenges still persist and they they have to face it. The remaining draws attention of potential tackles:

*Limited users:* The previous examples involve large commodity trading corporations (or ABDC[13]) and international banks that seek "*larger players with bigger balance sheets who are chasing larger deals*" (e.g. (Burton, 2017)). Faced with intensive IT investments, decisive constraints emerge for SMEs.

*Path dependency:* companies are reluctant to make changes. It's a "resistance to change". This can be due to regulation or policy complexity, among others. (Loderer et al., 2017) showed that as companies are getting older, they become more rigid and are inclined to miss growth opportunities, which declines their innovation abilities.

*The disruption effect:* For SMEs, the current KYC process can be time-wasting and burden their existing tasks in turn (e.g. (Camarda, 2018)), especially while faced with their inability to transit towards digitalization and integrate the various stakeholders.

*Party/country inconveniency:* As stated by (Goldman Sachs, 2016), Blockchain technology is not about business intermediaries, but can totally shift industries. This implies a drastic decrease in labor force and efforts. Could it be an issue in emerging and poor markets, where physical commodities are abundant? Could the Blockchain technology suitable for such markets?

*Social dimension:* It is a crucial issue. Indeed, the Blockchain technology requires "massive scale adoption", referred to as "network effects" ((Ahl et al., 2019)). In other words, the growth of such digital solutions entails a growth of its users ((Alabi, 2020)).

*IT skills:* The complexity of this nascent technology requires high qualification in the IT fields (*i.e.* Blockchain, big data, artificial intelligence, etc.).

## COVID-19: A Stark Awakening

The current COVID-19's crisis is changing the ways "dots are connected". An entire reshape of the traditional ways commodity finance trades are made. This pandemic crisis is the real proof.

For example, as commented by (Goh, 2020), the food and beverage industry is witnessing a disrupt in the supply chain during the COVID-19 pandemic crisis. Even the automation and machinery markets witnessed a shutdown during the coronavirus crisis in China (Wang, 2020) or elsewhere (Omdia Technology, 2020), but strong rebounds are expected. Firms, consumers, and individuals are conscious of the urge to move towards digitalization.

Bright spots come out and encouragements to invest in innovative technologies are massive. Although that COVID-19 is blowing a wind of change on commodity trade finance, but barriers are there on the short term (Wang, 2020). Following this debate, data privacy and digital security emerges at the forefront. It is a key priority, especially within this accelerated shift and companies are demonstrating additional resilience towards digitalization (Omdia Technology, 2020, p. 22).

## CONCLUSION

This chapter is designed in such a way to respond to how blockchain technology impacted commodity industry management.

In this respect, despite the costly achievement of the migration process to blockchain, commodity trading companies needed to tackle the implications of their interest in such innovative technology. Such a digital transformation requires additional resources, *i.e.* entailing financial (to implement the blockchain-based platform), human (to identify technological and managerial talents embedded in) functions, amongst others. Nevertheless, the results show up that this new-fangled epoch is undoubtedly not without advantages that are emphasized for each example of case companies treated.

Then, a series of challenges for managers and investors is provided. The latter has to anticipate the next IT battle and be the "architects of change" through designing adequate and efficient strategies in order to transform their business models and organizational management. Within this same path, different defies to cope with and overcome by commodity industries willing to implement the blockchain technology among their businesses in the near future have to be considered. Furthermore, the ongoing COVID-19 pandemic crisis is an enabler of innovation. Thus, companies have to tackle opportunities and prepare the post crisis period.

Needless to highlight, blockchain-based solutions are popping up. In the meanwhile, non-blockchain and even hybrid alternatives are competing on a level playing field and putting money on the table (e.g. (Camarda, 2018). Ultimate questions are of concern. Whose would prevail? Is the evolution effect of commodity finance trading only limited to technology?

## REFERENCES

Ahl, A., Goto, M., Yarime, M., Tanaka, K., & Sagawa, D. (2019). Practical Challenges and Opportunities of Blockchain in the Energy Sector: Expert Perspectives in Germany. *International Conference on Applied Energy*.

Alabi, K. (2020). A 2020 perspective on "Digital blockchain networks appear to be following Metcalfe's Law.". *Electronic Commerce Research and Applications, 40,* 40. doi:10.1016/j.elerap.2020.100939

Ávila, L., & Teixeira, L. (2019). The Main Concepts Behind the Dematerialization of Business Processes. In M. Khosrow-Pour (Ed.), *Advanced Methodologies and Technologies in Business Operations and Management* (pp. 508–519). IGI Global. doi:10.4018/978-1-5225-7362-3.ch037

Belt, A., & Kok, S. (2018). A Reality Check for Blockchain in Commodity Trading. *Bonston Consulting Group*. https://www.bcg.com/publications/2018/reality-check-blockchain-commodity-trading.aspx

Burton, M. (2017). Blockchain Booster: Singapore Eyes Commodity Fintech Firms. *Reuters*. https://www.reuters.com/article/us-commodities-fintech/blockchain-booster-singapore-eyes-commodity-fintech-firms-idUSKCN1C10ZZ

Camarda, B. (2018). *Improving "Know Your Customer" Processes for Trade Finance and Other Purposes*. American Express.

ConsenSys. (2020). *komgo: Blockchain Case Study for Commodity Trade Finance*. https://consensys.net/blockchain-use-cases/finance/komgo/

Ernest & Young. (2017). *Overview of Blockchain for Energy and Commodity Trading*.

FinTech Network. (2018). *Four Blockchain Use Cases for Banks*. https://germanyfintech.org/wp-content/uploads/2018/01/fintech_blockchain_report_fintech_network.pdf

Forbes. (2020). *2020 Forbes Blockchain 50 List*. Author.

Goh, T. C. (2020). A Production Crossroads: The Food and Beverage Conundrum. *Omdia Technology*. https://technology.informa.com/625247/a-production-crossroads-the-food-and-beverage-conundrum

Goldman Sachs. (2016). Blockchain: Putting Theory into Practice. *Profiles in Innovation*. https://www.finyear.com/attachment/690548/

Goldman Sachs. (2020). *Blockchain - The New Technology of Trust*. https://www.goldmansachs.com/insights/pages/blockchain/

Gomber, P., Koch, J.-A., & Siering, M. (2017). Digital Finance and FinTech: Current Research and Future Research Directions. *Journal of Business Economics, 87*(5), 537–580. doi:10.100711573-017-0852-x

Hazik, M., & Hassanian, A. (2018). Blockchain and the Digital Economy. In M. Hazik & A. Hassanian (Eds.), *Blockchain, Fintech, and Islamic Finance: Building the Future in the New Islamic Digital Economy* (pp. 111–138). Walter de Gruyter GmbH & Co KG.

Irish Tech News. (2019). *How has FinTech Revolutionised Commodities Trading?* Academic Press.

Loderer, C., Stulz, R., & Waelchlig, U. (2017). Firm Rigidities and the Decline in Growth Opportunities. *Management Science, 63*(9), 1–20.

Loebbecke, C., & Picot, A. (2015). Reflections on Societal and Business Model Transformation Arising from Digitization and Big Data Analytics: A Research Agenda. *The Journal of Strategic Information Systems, 24*(3), 149–157. doi:10.1016/j.jsis.2015.08.002

Madir, J. (2019). *FinTech: Law and Regulation*. Edward Elgar Publishing. doi:10.4337/9781788979023

Muro, M., Liu, S., Whiton, J., & Kulkarni, S. (2017). Digitalization and the American Workforce. Metropolitan Policy Program.

Murphy, S., Burch, D., & Clapp, J. (2012). Ceral Secrets: The World's Largest Grain Traders and Global Agricuture. *Oxfam Research Reports*.

Omdia Technology. (2020). *Connecting the Dots: Key Strategic Opportunities in a Post-COVID-19 World*. Author.

Payne, J. (2018). Blockchain Platform Goes Live for North Sea Crude Oil Trading. *Reuters*. https://www.reuters.com/article/us-blockchain-oil-trading/blockchain-platform-goes-live-for-north-sea-crude-oil-trading-idUSKCN1NY0X6

Plume, K. (2018). ABCD Quartet of Grain Traders Partner to Digitilize Global Trades. *Reuters*. https://www.reuters.com/article/us-global-grains-traders/abcd-quartet-of-grain-traders-partner-to-digitize-global-trades-idUSKCN1MZ2E8

Proeger, T., & Runst, P. (2019). Digitization and Knowledge Spillover Effectiveness - Evidence from "German Mittelsland.". *Journal of the Knowledge Economy*. Advance online publication. doi:10.100713132-019-00622-3

Puschmann, T. (2017). Fintech. *Business & Information Systems Engineering, 59*(1), 69–76. doi:10.100712599-017-0464-6

S&P Global Platts. (2018). *Blockchain for Commodities: Trading Opportunities in a Digital Age*. Author.

Taylor, P. J., Dargahi, T., Dehghantanha, A., Parizi, R. M., & Choo, K. K. R. (2019). *A Systematic Literature Review of Blockchain Cyber Security*. Digital Communications and Networks. doi:10.1016/j.dcan.2019.01.005

Terazono, E. (2018). Commodities Trader Louis Dreyfus Turns to Blockchain. *Financial Times*. https://www.ft.com/content/22b2ac1e-fd1a-11e7-a492-2c9be7f3120a

Wang, L. (2020). Post–COVID-19: China's Machinery Production and Automation Equipment Market Cannot be Immune to the Global Pandemic. *Omdia Technology*. https://technology.informa.com/624995/postcovid-19-chinas-machinery-production-and-automation-equipment-market-cannot-be-immune-to-the-global-pandemic

Wass, S. (2019). komgo Unwrapped: Financing Commodity Trade on Blockchain. *GTR Global Trade Review, 17*(1). https://www.gtreview.com/magazine/volume-17-issue-1/komgo-unwrapped-financing-commodity-trade-blockchain/

Wragg, E. (2019). Tech Company Unveils 'Network of Networks' to Solve Blockchain's Interoperability Issue for Trade. *GTR Global Trade Review*. https://www.gtreview.com/news/fintech/tech-company-unveils-blockchain-network-of-networks-to-solve-interoperability-issue/

## KEY TERMS AND DEFINITIONS

**Blockchain Technology:** It refers to a decentralized database that records a registry of assets and transactions through a peer-to-peer network.

**Digital Disruption:** It consists of the business/process transformation generated by a migration to digitalization.

**Digitalization:** It is the transformation of business activities and processes due to digital technologies.

**Digitization:** It refers to the automation of the business process/information through the incorporation of technology.

**FinTech Solution:** It consists of the use of technology to provide financial services.

## ENDNOTES

1 Gartner® IT Glossary defined digital business as "the creation of new business designs by blurring the digital and physical worlds".

2 This term was used by (Goldman Sachs, 2020).

3 Digitization of information consists of "build bridge between the business and the information/process".

4 SWOT is the acronym of Strengths Weaknesses Opportunities, and Threats.

5 An additional definition of "FinTech" is provided by (Madir, 2019); it "refers to the use of technology in providing financial services that could result in new business models, application, processes or products with an associated material effect on financial markets and institutions and the provision of financial services".

6 (FinTech Network, 2018; Hazik & Hassanian, 2018) highlighted that Chris Huls of Rabobank was the first to suggest to store the "KYC statements" on a Blockchain.

7 (FinTech Network, 2018; Hazik & Hassanian, 2018) highlighted that Chris Huls of Rabobank was the first to suggest to store the "KYC statements" on a Blockchain.

8 The platform was based upon prior experiments known as Easy Trading Connect. While unpacking it, two main trials were carried out, i.e. Easy Trading Connect 1 and Easy Trading Connect 2 in February 2017 and January 2018, respectively. The former was handled by ING, Société Générale, and Mercuria in 2017 and covered an oil cargo shipment to China. The latter included Louis Dreyfus Company, Société Générale, ING, and ABN Amro and consisted of soybeans shipment from the United States to China, involving an overall paperless process.

9 The ARP solution is defined as follows: "account receivables are purchased by lenders to provide short-term financing to suppliers". Cf. https://triterras.com/kratos.

10 The solution regarding logistics is scheduled to be launched by the 3rd quarter of 2020.

11 Source: https://triterras.com/triterras-generated-over-6-6-billion-in-transaction-volume-on-its-kratos-platform-through-june-30th-despite-covid-19.

12 Cf. www.liquidx.com.

13 "ABCD companies" refer to the quartet of the dominant commodity traders (grains and agricultural commodities), composed of Archer Daniels Midland (ADM), Bunge, Cargill and Louis Dreyfus ((Murphy et al., 2012; Plume, 2018)).

# Chapter 3
# Regulatory Standards and Measures:
## Panacea for Blockchain Technology Acceptability

**Bilal Ahmad Ali Al-khateeb**
https://orcid.org/0000-0001-8708-0709
*Department of Business Administration, Imam Mohammad Ibn Saud Islamic University, Saudi Arabia*

## ABSTRACT

*Blockchain technology is an emerging technology which has caught the attention of practitioners, governments, business enterprises including the academic researchers in this present century. Its attraction is mainly due to its potential to enhance the human way of doing things including service delivery and consequently leading to happier consumers and stakeholders and providing an edge over competitors, resulting in an improved brand image. Unfortunately, the adoption of a new technology is not all other easy, it takes time and effort. The major issue of the technology is the lack of regulatory measure framework to boost its acceptability among many countries of the world. Both practitioners and scholars have agreed that the technology needs to be validated, regulated, and adopted. Unfortunately, this is yet to be achieved. The chapter examined regulatory standard measures of blockchain technology as a panacea for blockchain technology acceptability. It adopts a literature review approach with a content analysis technique where several but selected views and opinions of countries on the regulatory positions were analysed. Evidence shows that the absence of regulatory measure standard is fear to non-acceptability and accessibility of blockchain technology. It also revealed that a specific regulatory*

DOI: 10.4018/978-1-7998-7110-1.ch003

*standard is needed to drive the acceptability and accessibility of blockchain technology not only in Saudi Arabia but also in the globe. This paper therefore concludes that a specific regulatory measure and standard is a panacea to the acceptability and accessibility of blockchain technology.*

## 1. INTRODUCTION

Blockchain technology being a new and emerging area in the field of research has attracted global attention including practitioners, governments, business enterprises even academic researchers in this present century (Jesus Leal Trujillo, Steve Fromhart, & Val Srinivas, 2017; Zambrano, 2017). Even since its emergence, very few researchers have made attempts to investigate its importance and how it is related to the improvement of human way of doing things including service delivery and consequently leading to happier consumers and stakeholders and providing an edge over competitors, resulting in an improved brand image (Jesus Leal Trujillo et al., 2017). Despite the attempts, it is observed that the majority of the studies mainly focused on the conceptualization of the concept of blockchain technology. For example, studies (Boujemi, 2017; Compliance, 2017; Mearian, 2019) such as appear to be interested in the description of the concept rather than looking into the adoption and acceptance of the new technology and how the technology can be best regulated across the globe. Unfortunately, the adoption of a new technology is not all other easy, it takes time and effort. This is the current position of blockchain technology.

Another major issue with blockchain technology is that of lack of regulatory measure framework to boost its acceptability among many countries of the world (Boujemi, 2017; Compliance, 2017). For example, the Federation of Indian Chambers of Commerce and Industry (Baru, 2018) state that blockchain technology needs to be validated, regulated and adopted. Unfortunately, this is yet to be achieved. Studies pointing to this direction are yet to arrive at a consensus on a single unified framework for its regulations. For example, Yeoh (2017) presented the regulatory issues in blockchain technology. The paper's findings provide support for blockchain technology to advance with minimum regulatory brakes for greater value-adding and efficiency advancement, especially for financial services, thereby expanding accessibility and therefore financial inclusiveness. However, the study failed to advance a unified single regulatory framework for the acceptance of blockchain technology.

Furthermore, the lack of regulatory measure framework to boost its acceptability is equally a major issue of concern among the countries of the world as the international community is yet to agree on the single unified regulatory framework for the adoption and acceptance of the technology. For example, countries differ in terms of approach on blochchain technology regulations and measures. For example, some countries have made attempts to introduce specific regulatory and policy frameworks to promote innovation and growth, while preventing systemic risk, ensuring financial stability, and protecting consumers and entrepreneurs against economic harm and illegal activity. But on the other hand, other countries even although they are aware of its promised economic boost, have taken different direction by placing a ban on it completely until adequate rules are introduced. Thus, *"regulators have been slow to respond to the questions surrounding the application of existing regulations or the introduction of new ones"* (Compliance, 2017). Boujemi (2017) observed in his study on policy and regulatory challenges to deploying blockchain technologies that blockchain has no specific policy and regulatory directions as it operates without a central bank or single administrator. The study argued that blockchain technology omits the central authorities of any country because there are no concrete products to validate its use beyond the financial sector. Attempt by Compliance (2017) *"to provide lists of relevant measures with regard to blockchain regulation only focused on financial service and related areas. Thus, neglecting other areas where blockchain technology is being applied"*. Also, studies e.g (Boujemi, 2017) *"have noted the paucity of research that defines the policy challenges of this technology as a key emerging issue in public policy. Thus, it is now very crucial to understand if the existing policy ecosystem takes care of such technology and if the current approaches and regulations can be applicable in the face of the present environment upon which the technology operates"*.

In Saudi Arabia for example, the issue of blockchain technology, its adoption, acceptance and regulatory is critical as the government is yet to take a standing position concerning the technology particularly how the technology is to be regulated. Blockchain is a technology that can be created by any individual from any part of the world using their own blockchain-powered application without the need to fulfill any regulatory obligations from any centralized authorities. This is due to the fact that there is no regulating practical software that can predict how it will be used. It is global perceived acceptability, accessibility and distributed nature have given birth to the questions of which jurisdiction will be regulating them? Which law applies, and how feasible it is to impose defensive regulation on a technology of which we are not yet aware of its full potential? These questions also generated the same concerns about how it should be governed, and whether or not it should be regulated using existing laws or left completely intact. In all these, it is clear that blockchain technology requires a regulatory framework for effective acceptability, accessibility and operations across the globe. In fact, the Saudi government believes that the country is not matured for the adoption of the technology. For example, the Saudi Central Bank states that blockchain technology *"Cryptocurrency Industry is "Not Mature Enough" to Warrant Regulation"* (Haig, 2017), indicating that there is an issue with the regulatory of blockchain technology. This paper, therefore, argued on the need for the regulatory framework as a standard and measure for blockchain accessibility and accessibility around the world including country such as Saudi Arabia. Thus, the major objective of this study is to examine blockchain technology and its acceptance with regulatory measure standards as a panacea in Saudi Arabia. Also, the paper tends to provide a holistic regulatory framework that would encompass all areas of blockchain technology applicability and accessibility particularly in Saudi Arabia.

## 2. LITERATURE REVIEW

### 2.1 Blockchain Technology-Definitions

Generally, blockchain technology is simply described as a distributed, decentralized, public ledger." Yeoh (2017) described blockchain as that which deals with a collaborative generation of digital distributed ledgers characterized by properties and capabilities beyond those of traditional paper-based ledgers. This implies that blockchain technology is mainly concerned with digital distributed ledgers. For Modgil and Sonwaney (2019), blockchain technology is concerned with governance, internet of things, health sector, education sector, privacy and security, data management, financial and integrity verification (Casino, Dasaklis, & Patsakis, 2019; Drosatos & Kaldoudi, 2019). Similary, Benchoufi and Ravaud (2017) of the view that blockchain technology is that technology that powers the Bitcoin, as an open, distributed public ledger that records all the Bitcoin transactions in a secure and verifiable way, without the need for a third party to process payments. In an attempt to relate blockchain technology to healthcare, Wong, Yee, and Nohr (2018) argued that blockchain technology is a radical concept based on a distributed ledger concept. Y. Wang, Singgih, Wang, and Rit (2019) believe that blockchain technology which is also called distributed ledger technology is mainly a peer-to-peer distributed asset database that can be shared across a network of multiple sites, geographies or institutions. From the definition, it is clear that blockchain technology has the ability to publicly validate records and distribute transactions in immutable, encrypted ledgers. Subsequent definitions from Thiruchelvam, Mughisha, Shahpasand, and Bamiah (2018) acknowledged that blockchain technology focuses on a decentralised database, encrypted tamper-proof digital ledger technology that allows all network participants to trust each other and interact. In a different direction, Litvin, Korenev, Knyazeva, and Litvin (2019) referred to blockchain technology as "future Internet" includes the invention of the steam engine, discovery of electricity, and the development of information technologies. This view demonstrates that blockchain technology possesses certain characteristics such as immutability, transparency, and reliability of all operations performed using blockchain technology.

Nowiński and Kozma (2017) described blockchain technology using cryptocurrency (bitcoin). They claimed that blockchain technology powers both cryptocurrency and bitcoin. Thus, cryptocurrency and bitcoin are developed based on blockchain technology. They argued that blockchain technology is nothing but another just another type of database for recording transactions – one that is copied to all computers in a participating network" (Deloitte, 2016). Similar to Nowiński and Kozma (2017) is the study by Seebacher and Schüritz (2017) that described blockchain technology as the underlying basis of Bitcoin. For them, it is a technology that altered the way we interact and transact over the Internet, resulting in the dawn of a new economy. In the construction engineering management, J. Wang, Wu, Wang, and Shou (2017) defined blockchain technology as a decentralised transaction and data management technology. In order to understand, Sarmah (2018) is a technology that tends to supervise records of all transactions through a large community rather than a single central authority such as the bank. By this definition, it shows that no single individual person has control over the technology. Thus, control, supervision and authority are essential in this case.

Furthermore, Ainsworth and Viitasaari (2017) described it as a decentralized distributed ledger technology that gives room to create, validate and encrypt any transaction digital assets to happen and get recorded in an incorruptible way. The technology is behind both Bitcoin and Cryptocurrencies. As noted by Jesus Leal Trujillo et al. (2017), it is one of the emerging technologies currently in the market attracting a lot of attention from enterprises, start-ups and media. It is equally defined as a decentralized, distributed ledger technology that records the provenance of a digital asset. Reiff (2020) referred to it as the technology behind the record-keeping technology behind the Bitcoin network. Further explanation by Blockchain.com connotes the technology as the transparent, trustless, publicly accessible ledger that allows us to securely transfer the ownership of units of value using public-key encryption and proof of work methods. It notes that the technology applies decentralized consensus to maintain the network, suggesting that the technology is not centrally controlled by a bank, corporation, or government. In fact, the larger the network grows and becomes increasingly decentralized, the more secure it becomes. In an attempt by Mearian (2019) to describe blockchain technology referred it as the "much-hyped distributed ledger technology (DLT) has the potential to eliminate huge amounts of record-keeping, save money, streamline supply chains and disrupt IT in ways not seen since the internet arrived". It is also a public e-larger created around a P2P system that can be shared by the disparate users to create an unchangeable record of transactions, each time-stamped and linked to the previous one (Mearian, 2019). Therefore, in summary, blockchain technology is nothing but a kind of system concerned with distributed ledger technology (DLT) which allowed global data storage on thousands of servers, and this makes it possible for anyone on the network to see everyone else's entries in near real-time. For this single reason, it becomes very difficult if not impossible for one user to gain control of, or game, the network. From the above descriptions, it is clear that blockchain technology potential is not limited to bitcoin and cryptocurrencies. The technology is even receiving more attention in a variety of industries including: financial services, charities and nonprofits, the arts, and e-commerce.

## 2.2 Fear of Blockchain Technology

Despite the huge potential benefits of blockchain technology to the business organization as well as to the government, there are still some fears attempting to hamper or slow down its advancement, key among these are regulatory measures and security. Generally, there is an issue of lack of awareness among all the stakeholders in blockchain technology. As stated by Jesus Leal Trujillo et al. (2017), lack of awareness is a major hindrance to Blockchain adoption. Jesus Leal Trujillo et al. (2017) argued that there is a need for business houses including the government for an internal team that will be a focus on understanding what the technology is all about, its impact, and areas of usage. In some situations, it is observed that employees were sent for external conferences and industry working groups or internal knowledge sessions and Hackathons were conducted. Apart from that, some firms even included blockchain as part of their strategic investment without an adequate understanding of the technology.

Furthermore, the government being the major player in blockchain technology has been nursing fear on how it would be able to control blockchain technology. The technology operates in the cyberspace, in other words, it operates in what is called extraterritorial, meaning without boundaries. It implies that the regulatory practices which are supposed to exist and operate in the ordinary world are missing (Weatherston, Brooks, & Wilkinson, 2010). The prime example of how this situation can impact upon the business can be seen in the relation to an attempt to fraud by the Sicilian Mafia in October 2002. Governments' fears of blockchain technology including tax evasion, traditional currencies displacement, prevention and monitoring of dubious activities. Therefore, since there are no current regulations and specific standard measures, it would be very difficult for governments to just allow such emerging technology into the economy. Thus, governments need to provide these missing regulatory measures upon which blockchain technology can be able to operate effectively. Country such as Saudi Arabia must work towards providing regulatory standards and measures for the effective operation of the technology (Crosby, Nachiappan, Pattanayak, Verma, & Kalyanaraman, 2017).

The second one is the issue of security. blockchain technology imposes huge security challenges since it operates in the cyberspace via the internet. The business community and the world's governments that support and encourage the technology are yet perhaps dealt appropriately with the security issues associated with blockchain. For example, some of them are assuming that the electronic environment is simply an extension of the actual business environment where things are done as business as usual. Unfortunately, it is not so. The security and safety of blockchain are yet to be determined and verified. Even though, some of these can be reduced or eradicated with extra precautions, very few governments and business organizations can boost of securing their internet against intruders, hackers, viruses and other dubious activities. Due to this, there have been lengthy delays in the adoption of blockchain technology in many countries of the world including Saudi Arabia. This is also similar to the adoption of the internet during the initial dot.com boom (Weatherston et al., 2010).

Finally, transparency issue is equally of concerned with the government and this has imposed fear on the government. For example, the government is fearful of transparency in handling the business operations of blockchain technology. Since the technology works through a decentralized consensus to maintain the network, it becomes very difficult for a central control by a bank, corporation, or government. However, blockchain holds the promise of transactional transparency for businesses because it has the ability to create secure, real-time communication networks with partners around the globe to support everything from supply chains to payment networks to real estate deals and healthcare data sharing (Mearian, 2019). This is the fear of the government as it lacks the regulations to track the transparency of these activities. Thus, the issue of transparency becomes very crucial.

## 2.3 Blockchain Technology and Regulatory Standards and Measures

It has been observed that there is always a gap between new innovation and regulations, and this has often led to lengthy delays in the adoption of the new innovation. If governments are to follow the same archaic rational to regulate blockchain technologies, the clash between innovation and regulation will persist since the essence of blockchain is code-generating, programmable logic, while regulation is usually broad and vague and, in many instances, does not fit the purpose of technological innovation. Without a doubt, this is the current position of regulations of blockchain technology in many countries across the world. Therefore, practically speaking, one major fear about blockchain technology is the absence of a regulatory body that tends to determine the standards and measures upon which cryptocurrencies are transacted (Wright & De Filippi, 2015). As observed by (Crosby et al., 2017) blockchain technology must deal with a number of regulatory issues involving national governments and financial institutions. They argued that regulatory standard measures would go a long way in making blockchain technology acceptable by people, government and financial institutions across the globe. To establish the relationship between regulatory and effective blockchain technology, the Chambers of Commerce and Industry (Baru, 2018) argued that there is a need for the technology to be validated and regulated by the concerned authorities in any country that is hoping to adopt blockchain technology. For example, there should be regulation on parties' share data. That is, on data sharing among multiple parties, and there should be a requirement for verification of participants because participants need to trust that the actions that are recorded are valid. However, it has been claimed that the advantages of blockchain technology outweigh the regulatory issues and technical challenges. Finally, Baru (2018) advocated for a structured approach with a policy and regulatory framework for an effective blockchain technology. This paper, therefore, proposed a strong relationship between regulatory standards and measures and blockchain technology.

## 2.4 Theoretical Framework

The issue being investigated by this study is majorly rooted in technology. Today, technology plays a crucial role and has continued to advance to many areas of human lives. The advancement of technology has even extended to what is now called blockchain technology, which digital economy literature defines as essentially a distributed database of records or public ledger of all transactions or digital events that have been executed and shared among participating parties. Blockchain is a technology that allows creation, validation and encrypted transaction of digital assets to happen and get recorded in an incorruptible way. There are several theories in the area of technology. Some of these theories are technology acceptance model (TAM); social technological theory, Diffusion of Innovation (DOI) Theory, the unified theory of acceptance and use of technology (UTAUT), The Theory of Planned Behavior etc. However, all technological theories are tailored towards explaining the factors that shape technological innovation as well as the impact of technology on society and culture. This study adopts two main relevant theories; the Technology Acceptance Model (TAM) and 'Social' theories. The technology acceptance model (TAM) is adopted to underpin and explain the acceptance of blockchain technology. TAM is one of the notable theories in the academic field technology and information and communication technology (ICT). The theory is often accredited to Fred Davis in

1989. It is a theory that tends to model how users come to accept technology. In other words, it is the extent to which people believe that using a particular technology would enhance their performance. According to Silva and Dias (2007), it is highly impossible in the present situation to manipulate information without the assistance of technology. In other words, high technical performance will be good for nothing if the user, for any reason, does not adopt and do not accept the available technology (Davis, 1989). Thus, there is a need for people to understand why users do not adopt, accept, or reject technology particularly the latest technology like blockchain. In the same vein, it may be interesting to know why country such as Saudi Arabia has failed to adopt blockchain technology just like other countries. blockchain technology is one of the latest technologies currently trending the globe. It is part of the digital technology which is shaping the economy particularly the global financial economy. Ainsworth and Viitasaari (2017) acknowledged that factors such as supporting ecosystem, the whole of government' approach, the widespread use of blockchain technologies and the introduction of standards and measures of a regulatory nature must be considered when talking about blockchain acceptability and accessibility

Furthermore, the social theory is equally relevant in this study. The theories focus on how humans and technology affect each other. For example, the theories focus on how decisions are made with humans and technology: humans and technology are equal in the decision, humans drive technology, and vice versa. In other words, the social theories emphasis on individual human's interactions with technology including group interaction. For example, Social presence theory advocates for more text-based forms of interaction that include e-mail, instant messaging which involves recording and documentation. The theory argues that the social impact of a communication medium depends on the social presence it allows communicators to have. Since blockchain technology is all about creating, validating and encrypting any transaction digital assets to happen and get recorded in an incorruptible way. Thus, social theory is essential to link human interaction with modern technology like blockchain technology. Thus, the social theory would promote and propagate the usefulness and importance of blockchain technology, that is, by a way of awareness of the technology.

Based on the above literature review, Figure 1 presents a conceptual framework depicting the link between the regulatory standard measure, and blockchain technology acceptability. The arrow demonstrates that the two variables are possibly related. It shows that regulatory standards and measures have a way of affecting blockchain technology acceptability, suggesting that the acceptability and accessibility of blockchain-dependent on whether the technology is effectively regulated and validated in terms of its content, transparency, taxes, sales, payment verification and effective monitoring of transactions. The governments, business enterprises including the customers will accept and access blockchain technology at ease as

*Figure 1. presents a conceptual framework depicting the link between the regulatory standard and measure, and blockchain technology acceptability*

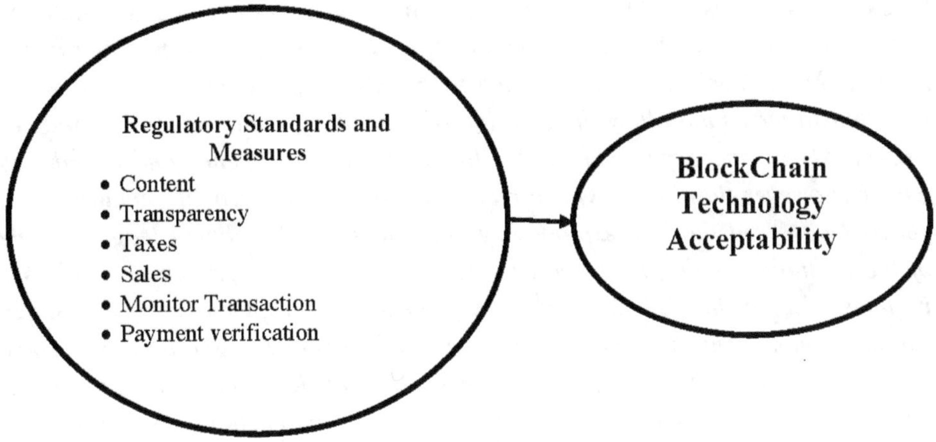


soon as a regulatory standard and measure framework is put in place. Therefore, bringing the fear of everyone to a hurt.

## 3. METHOD

It adopts a content analysis were secondary data was collected from the available literature through the internet on issues concerning the regulation and measures of blockchain technology across the globe. Here, the documented content of views, opinions and written published comments on blockchain technology regulation and measures are collected and analysed textually as discussed in the preceding section. The study also relies on a literature review called systematic review as employed by Nowiński and Kozma (2017).

## 4. EVIDENCE ON THE STATE OF REGULATIONS (STANDARDS AND MEASURES) OF BLOCKCHAIN TECHNOLOGY

This study obtained some evidence on the state of blockchain technology regulations and standards among key countries of the world.

## 4.1 In Russia, Regulatory Issue is of Concern

It has been well observed that almost the countries across the globe entertain one fear or the other about blockchain technology. "*In Russia for example, the Prime Minister Mikhail Mishustin as reported by Baydakova (2020) noted that Russian government may soon allow the creation of regulatory sandboxes for companies working on cutting-edge technologies like artificial intelligence and distributed ledgers, however, the plan does not directly mention blockchain or cryptocurrencies, yet it is observed that the explanatory note mentions distributed ledger as one of the technologies that could be explored in the new "experimental regulatory regimes. Also, the blockchain technology in the form of cryptocurrencies is used in Russia in many contexts including for payment for goods and services or as some instrument analogous securities. Yet the Russian authorities continue to stand against cryptocurrencies due to the fear of generally non-transparent nature of transactions with cryptocurrencies and the associated compliance and similar risks. In fact, at present, there is no law that tends to specifically allows cryptocurrencies, and there are no legal definitions of cryptocurrencies"*.

## 4.2 In UK, Blockchain Technology Suspended

"Blockchain technology and its antecedent bitcoins or cryptocurrencies have generated a lot of controversies among professionals and Central banks of many countries. For example, the UK government through its Central Bank has directed that blockchain technology including its elements such as bitcoin and cryptocurrency transactions should be suspended".

## 4.3 In U.S, Regulatory Uncertainty

It is being observed that after some regulatory uncertainty, the U.S. has started its journey to the regulated space for blockchain and the DLT industry (Ozelli, 2020). For example, U.S. law enforcement and regulatory agencies are now responding through continued law enforcement efforts, such as the establishment of a Cryptocurrency Intelligence Program and the proposing of new regulations and tax reporting requirements to open the way for the widespread adoption of blockchain technology. However, "*some states in the US have proposed and/or pass laws relating to cryptocurrencies and blockchain technology with most of the activity taking place in the legislative branches. Some of the areas of regulations include sales, security, money transmission laws, anti-money laundry, tax, etc.*". This implies that not all states in the US have accepted the adoption of blockchain technology.

## 4.4 In China, Regulatory Adoption

It is reported by Tassev (2020) on China Adopts Security Standards for Blockchain Applications in the Financial Sector, China through its central bank has adopted a new regulation to improve blockchain technology in all sectors in china most especially the financial sector. The regulation covers improving information security of distributed ledger technology (DLT) applications. The regulation would act as a standard and measure. In that, blockchain technology developers and blockchain technology service providers would conform to certain standards as set up by the central authority. In totality, it is all about security standards for blockchain applications in all areas of its applicability.

## 4.5 In India, Regulatory Preparation

As reported by Pan (2019), *"the Indian government is preparing a national framework to support the wider deployment of blockchain use cases. For example, the minister of state for electronics and IT (MeitY) Sanjay Dhotre"* said that the government is drafting an approach paper on the National Level Blockchain Framework which discusses the potential for distributed ledger technology and the need for a shared infrastructure for different use cases". There should be a proof-of-existence framework that guides the activities of blockchain technology. From the tone, it is obvious that the government is working on a regulatory framework that would make blockchain technology adoption effective among the people.

## 4.6 The United Arab Emirates (UAE)-Proposes Regulations

In UAE, the government is at the verge of completing a regulatory framework for blockchain technology in particular cryptoassets. In fact, its agency, UAE Securities and Commodities Authority (SCA) has published draft regulations governing cryptoassets, which tends to set standards for a range of market participants. According to SCA, *"the regulatory measure framework is expected to cover all aspects of the crypto-asset industry, such as safekeeping practices and compliance with financial crime prevention measures"*. In view of this, the body is currently asking for responses on the draft by the end of October 2019 (Bicknell, 2019). This shows that efforts have been made towards regulating blockchain technology. In their effort, the country wants to become a pioneer in blockchain technology by launching the UAE Blockchain Strategy 2021. It aims at conducting at least 50% of all its transactions using blockchain technology in 2021. To solidify it vision, regulations on the use of crypto assets, including cryptocurrencies have recently been issued (Adil Shafi & Kajal Patel, 2018). The Financial Services Regulatory Authority (FSRA) has claimed to be the first regulator in the UAE to issue comprehensive guidance and regulations on carrying out activities relating to cryptocurrencies.

## 4.7 Saudi Arabia-Not Mature Enough

Unlike other countries that are making an effort to see how blockchain technology through cryptocurrencies and bitcoin can be regulated, Saudi Arabia has claimed that both cryptocurrencies and bitcoin are not mature enough to be regulated. As noted by Abdulmalik Al-Sheikh, senior advisor at the Saudi Arabian Monetary Agency (SAMA), *"cryptocurrencies are not something the body is looking to regulate right now"* (Kharpal, 2017). He stated that the government being the regulator is taking a wait and to see approach to initial coin offerings (ICOs). Similarly, the Saudi Central Bank states that *"Cryptocurrency Industry is "Not Mature Enough" to Warrant Regulation"* (Haig, 2017). The simple analysis here is that Saudi Arabia is not ready for blockchain technology yet the economy including its financial sector is fast growing to accommodate the new technology.

## 4.8 In Africa-Nigeria, No Regulatory Mechanism

*"The Nigerian National Assembly has equally directed the Central Bank of Nigeria and the Nigerian Stock Exchange to stop all blockchain transactions most especially the Bitcoin. The CBN in line with that directive however stated that it has no mechanism to stop bitcoin business since there are no regulations and standards for doing that"*. Obviously, the country has no any former regulations towards blockchain technology.

# 5. CONCLUSIONS AND IMPLICATIONS

The paper examined the regulatory standard measures as a panacea for blockchain technology acceptability particularly in Saudi Arabia. It aims to provide a regulatory standard framework that would promote the acceptability and accessibility of blockchain technology activities. The paper then examined literature which provides an insight on blockchain technology through expert's views. Blockchain is a potentially transformational technology that could have as much impact as the arrival of the Internet in the 1990s. The paper argued on the issue of a lack of a regulatory framework for effective blockchain technology across the globe. The paper found through the literature that due to a lack of regulatory measure framework to guide the activities of blockchain technology, its accessibility and acceptance have been slowed down. (Boujemi, 2017) argued that blockchain technology has outpaced the regulatory capacities of law and legislation, which prompts a close examination of current public policy approaches to establish if they are sufficient or if there is a need to catalyse new thinking. The study further argued that rather than the government through several regulatory bodies forming task forces and working groups to identify the capabilities of blockchain technologies since they are keen to promote technology that lowers costs and increases transparency, it is better for them to allow the market decide the rules that would guide blockchain technology. In this case, the lawmakers have no choice. It is argued in Japan that it is important to legalise trading cryptocurrencies rather than allowing it to circulate in an unregulated environment (Barsan, 2017; Young, 2017). In fact, Japanese Financial Services Authority (FSA) became the first regulator in the world to issue licenses authorising cryptocurrency exchanges. The overall, it shows that key major world economies are yet to adopt a regulatory measure to dealing with blockchain technology. For example, available evidence revealed that countries such as Russia, UK, US, UAE, China, India, Nigeria and a host of others are yet to establish a specific regulatory framework for the acceptability and accessibility of blockchain.

Countries, individual as well as institutions wanting to adopt blockchain technology must address the issue of fear through the establishment of regulatory standard measures that can be a check to all the stakeholders involved in blockchain technology. Thus, Saudi Arabia needs to eliminate fear by creating a regulatory framework that promotes trust and ensuring adequate monitoring of all contents and transactions on the technology platform.

Finally, what is the future of blockchain technology for cryptocurrencies in the world including Saudi Arabia? Will it survive the present criticism from experts, practitioners, academic and government? Answers to these questions are not farfetched, as the understanding of blockchain technology for bitcoin and cryptocurrencies require the implementation of a specific regulatory measure framework for the benefits of all major players in the global economy. By implication, this paper has the tendency and ability to eliminate fear among the anti-blockchain technology (bitcoin and cryptocurrencies) through the information provided, and this would improve the acceptability and accessibility of the technology particularly by the governments. Also, the government would use the information provided to formulate the needed regulatory measure to legalise and direct the activities of blockchain for acceptability and accessibility.

## 6. RECOMMENDATIONS

From the findings obtained from this study, the study recommends as follows:

First and foremost, there should be a very serious awareness about blockchain technology among all the stakeholders particularly on how the technology works and how it affects everybody that is involved. In so doing, the issue of fear can be avoided. Also, the issue of transparency should be strengthened in order to avoid fear among all the players involves in blockchain technology. Finally, a unified regulatory measure framework is needed for the adoption and acceptance of blockchain technology. This regulatory framework would promote trust and transparency among the key players of the technology. Thus, the panacea for the adoption and acceptance of blockchain technology is rooted in the development, acceptance and adoption of a unified regulatory framework which promotes trust and transparency, thus, eliminating fear.

Finally, the issue of security needs to be strengthened. The business community and the world's governments that support and encourage the blockchain technology should find the best approach to dealing with security issues such as the internet against intruders, hackers, viruses and other dubious activities. It is only when these security issues are well taken care of that blockchain technology adoption and acceptance would be boosted.

## 7. DIRECTIONS FOR FUTURE RESEARCH

First and foremost, this study lacks quantitative data, however, it is more or less a content analysis where secondary data was collected from the available literature through the internet on issues concerning the regulatory measures of blockchain technology across the globe. Thus, it appears qualitative in nature because the content of views, opinions and written published comments on blockchain technology regulation and measures are collected and analysed textually. Therefore, future studies should extend this study through the use of quantitative data for additional robust findings.

Secondly, a study of this nature with a face-to-face interview or focus group is highly encouraged in a further attempt to investigate the issue raised by this study. Although sample size problems could arise in this respect however, it could provide additional insight into the issue being studied. Thus, the qualitative approach to this issue is highly advocated.

## REFERENCES

Adil Shafi, P., & Kajal Patel, A. (2018). *Blockchain technology and cryptocurrencies: regulatory framework in the UAE*. Retrieved from https://ach-legal.com/blog/Blockchain-technology-cryptocurrencies-regulatory-framework-UAE

Ainsworth, R. T., & Viitasaari, V. (2017). Payroll Tax & the Blockchain. *Tax Notes International, 13*, 1007-1024.

Barsan, I. M. (2017). Legal challenges of initial coin offerings (ICO). *Revue Trimestrielle de Droit Financier,* (3), 54-65.

Baru, S. (2018). Blockchain: The next innovation to make our cities smarter. Academic Press.

Baydakova, A. (2020). *Russian Prime Minister Introduces Bill to Allow Fintech Sandboxes, Blockchain Included*. Retrieved from https://www.coindesk.com/russian-prime-minister-introduces-bill-to-allow-fintech-sandboxes-blockchain-included

Benchoufi, M., & Ravaud, P. (2017). Blockchain technology for improving clinical research quality. *Trials, 18*(1), 1–5. doi:10.118613063-017-2035-z PMID:28724395

Bicknell, T. (2019). *Cryptoasset regulations*. Retrieved from https://www.pinsentmasons.com/out-law/news/uae-outlines-proposed-cryptoasset-regulations

Boujemi, H. (2017). *Policy and Regulatory Challenges To Deploying Blockchain Technologies*. Faculty of Arts, University of Malta.

Casino, F., Dasaklis, T. K., & Patsakis, C. (2019). A systematic literature review of blockchain-based applications: Current status, classification and open issues. *Telematics and Informatics, 36*, 55–81.

Compliance, P. (2017). *An Overview of Blockchain Legislation and Regulatory Measures*. Retrieved from https://www.planetcompliance.com/2017/07/04/overview-blockchain-regulation-legislation/

Crosby, Nachiappan, Pattanayak, Verma, & Kalyanaraman. (2017). *Blockchain Technology: Beyond Bitcoin*. Retrieved from https://j2-capital.com/blockchain-technology-beyond-bitcoin

Davis, F. D. (1989). Perceived usefulness, perceived ease of use, and user acceptance of information technology. *Management Information Systems Quarterly, 13*(3), 319–340. doi:10.2307/249008

Drosatos, G., & Kaldoudi, E. (2019). Blockchain applications in the biomedical domain: A scoping review. *Computational and Structural Biotechnology Journal, 17*, 229–240. doi:10.1016/j.csbj.2019.01.010 PMID:30847041

Haig, S. (2017). *Saudi Central Bank Says Cryptocurrency Industry is "Not Mature Enough" to Warrant Regulation.* Retrieved from https://news.bitcoin.com/saudi-central-bank-says-cryptocurrency-industry-is-not-mature-enough-to-warrant-regulation/

Kharpal, A. (2017). *Cryptocurrencies 'not mature enough' to assess impact: Saudi Arabia regulator.* Retrieved from https://www.cnbc.com/2017/10/23/cryptocurrencies-not-mature-enough-to-assess-impact-saudi-arabia-regulator.html

Litvin, A., Korenev, S., Knyazeva, E., & Litvin, V. (2019). The Possibilities of Blockchain Technology in Medicine. *Современные технологии в медицине, 11*(4).

Mearian, L. (2019). *What is blockchain? The complete guide.* Retrieved from https://www.computerworld.com/article/3191077/what-is-blockchain-the-complete-guide.html

Modgil, S., & Sonwaney, V. (2019). Planning the application of blockchain technology in identification of counterfeit products: Sectorial prioritization. *IFAC-PapersOnLine, 52*(13), 1–5. doi:10.1016/j.ifacol.2019.11.080

Nowiński, W., & Kozma, M. (2017). How can blockchain technology disrupt the existing business models? *Entrepreneurial Business and Economics Review, 5*(3), 173–188. doi:10.15678/EBER.2017.050309

Ozelli, S. (2020). *US Takes Regulatory Steps for Blockchain Technology Adoption.* Retrieved from https://cointelegraph.com/news/us-takes-regulatory-steps-for-blockchain-technology-adoption

Pan, D. (2019). *India Plans to Issue a National Blockchain Framework.* Retrieved from https://www.coindesk.com/india-plans-to-issue-a-national-blockchain-framework

Reiff, N. (2020). *Blockchain explained.* Retrieved from https://www.investopedia.com/terms/b/blockchain.asp

Sarmah, S. S. (2018). Understanding blockchain technology. *Computing in Science & Engineering, 8*(2), 23–29.

Seebacher, S., & Schüritz, R. (2017). *Blockchain technology as an enabler of service systems: A structured literature review.* Paper presented at the International Conference on Exploring Services Science. 10.1007/978-3-319-56925-3_2

Silva, P. M., & Dias, G. A. (2007). Theories About Technology Accepentace: Why The Users Accept Or Reject The Information Technology? *Brazilian Journal of Information Science: Research Trends, 1*(2), 69–91. doi:10.36311/1981-1640.2007.v1n2.05.p69

Tassev, L. (2020). *China Adopts Security Standards for Blockchain Applications in the Financial Sector.* Retrieved from https://news.bitcoin.com/china-adopts-security-standards-blockchain/

Thiruchelvam, V., Mughisha, A. S., Shahpasand, M., & Bamiah, M. (2018). Blockchain-based technology in the coffee supply chain trade: Case of burundi coffee. *Journal of Telecommunication, Electronic and Computer Engineering, 10*(3-2), 121-125.

Trujillo, Fromhart, & Srinivas. (2017). *Evolution of blockchain technology.* Retrieved from https://medium.com/@crowdmachine/evolution-of-blockchain-technology-9ee208c000e2

Wang, J., Wu, P., Wang, X., & Shou, W. (2017). The outlook of blockchain technology for construction engineering management. *Frontiers of Engineering Management,* 67-75.

Wang, Y., Singgih, M., Wang, J., & Rit, M. (2019). Making sense of blockchain technology: How will it transform supply chains? *International Journal of Production Economics, 211,* 221–236. doi:10.1016/j.ijpe.2019.02.002

Weatherston, J., Brooks, I., & Wilkinson, G. (2010). *The international business environment: challenges and changes.* Prentice Hall.

Wong, M. C., Yee, K. C., & Nohr, C. (2018). Socio-technical consideration for blockchain technology in healthcare. *Studies in Health Technology and Informatics, 247,* 636–640. PMID:29678038

Wright, A., & De Filippi, P. (2015). *Decentralized blockchain technology and the rise of lex cryptographia.* Available at SSRN 2580664

Yeoh, P. (2017). Regulatory issues in blockchain technology. *Journal of Financial Regulation and Compliance.*

Young, J. (2017). *Bitcoin and Ethereum Price Recover From Korea ICO Ban as Japan Licenses Exchanges.* Retrieved from https://www.ccn.com/bitcoin-ethereum-price-recover-korea-ico-ban-japan-licenses-exchanges/

Zambrano, E. (2017). The 'troubling tradeoffs' paradox and a resolution. *Review of Income and Wealth, 63*(3), 520–541. doi:10.1111/roiw.12235

## ADDITIONAL READING

Modgil, S., & Sonwaney, V. (2019). Planning the application of blockchain technology in identification of counterfeit products: Sectorial prioritization. *IFAC-PapersOnLine*, *52*(13), 1–5. doi:10.1016/j.ifacol.2019.11.080

Sarmah, S. S. (2018). Understanding blockchain technology. *Computing in Science & Engineering*, *8*(2), 23–29.

Seebacher, S., & Schüritz, R. (2017). Blockchain technology as an enabler of service systems: A structured literature review. Paper presented at the International Conference on Exploring Services Science. 10.1007/978-3-319-56925-3_2

Yeoh, P. (2017). Regulatory issues in blockchain technology. *Journal of Financial Regulation and Compliance*.

## KEY TERMS AND DEFINITIONS

**Blockchain Technology:** Means decentralised database, encrypted tamperproof digital ledger technology that allows all network participants to trust each other and interact. It also covered cryptocurrency and bitcoin.

**Regulatory Standard Measures:** Means a framework of regulatory measures or a system, including institutions or agencies, established to secure compliance with regulatory measures.

**Technology Acceptability:** Is an information systems theory that models how users come to accept and use a technology.

# Section 2
# Managerial and Cultural Transformations in the Era of FinTech

# Chapter 4
# Instilling FinTech Culture in a Digitalized World:
## Defining, Issuing, and Opening Up

**Wassim J. Aloulou**
https://orcid.org/0000-0003-2144-6805
*Imam Mohammad Ibn Saud Islamic University, Saudi Arabia & University of Sfax, Tunisia*

## ABSTRACT

*FinTech has revolutionized the financial industry by its disruptive innovations and emergent technology-enabled business models. After defining the concept of FinTech, the chapter sheds the light on its drivers, features, and challenges, and discusses the elements and attributes of the FinTech ecosystem and the diversity of FinTech models operating in the sector. Then, the chapter emphasizes the role of a FinTech culture as a vibrant digital, agile, customer-centric, creative technology-driven, and entrepreneurial culture in a digitalized and changing world. Such culture is needed for enterprising individuals and startups, incumbents, and established financial and technology firms and for the economy and the society as a whole to nurture a FinTech community and benefit from the ecosystem's resources and opportunities. The chapter suggests certain recommended future research directions for the emerging field of FinTech at individual, corporate, incumbent, and institutional levels to be investigated in countries developing the FinTech industry.*

DOI: 10.4018/978-1-7998-7110-1.ch004

## INTRODUCTION

The digital economy has growing rapidly since the last two decades, and has become a dominant force in the world economy by its contribution to the GDP of most important developed countries. The use of digital-to-disruptive technologies has become more frequent to achieve more disruptive innovation, competitiveness and growth (Aloulou, 2019). As the fourth industrial revolution is getting underway, this new era of digitalization has disrupted most of sectors and organizations challenging them to move towards a digital transformation (Mezghani & Aloulou, 2019).

The digitization of financial services industry is a true example that is impacting the nature of financial product and service provision. Advanced and digital-to-disruptive technologies and innovative business models are leveraged by new entrants to meet customers' interests and preferences (Arner et al., 2015; Tanda & Schena, 2019; Zetzsche et al., 2017). This offering of customer-centric services is capable of combining speed and flexibility (Nicoletti, 2017). Consequently, the financial sector is witnessed the arrival of a new industry sector – FinTech, but also, the entry of BigTech and other technology firms into finance. This financial technology is transforming finance and challenging its regulation at an unprecedented rate (Zetzsche et al., 2017).

With the digitalization, most heritage financial firms will be irrelevant, cease to exist, become commoditized or achieve zombie or dinosaur status by 2030 (Gartner, 2018; Tanda & Schena, 2019). The challenges posed of the two different kind of tech firms (FinTech and BigTech) are quite different. Nonetheless, one common goal shared by these firms is to improve the efficiency of financial markets and systems through the use of emergent and disruptive technology such as Big Data analytics, Blockchain, Robotics, Internet of Things (IoT), Artificial Intelligence, Cloud Computing (Imerman & Fabozzi, 2020).

For instance, the FinTech industry has been assisting an exponential growth. According to the market survey of Ernst & Young (2019), the global adoption rate of FinTech services has reached 64% in 2019, up from 33% in 2017 and 16% in 2015. Global investments in FinTech companies has totaled US$57.9 billion across 875 deals in the first half of 2018 (KPMG, 2018). According to the CB Insights 2019 FinTech trends report, 2018 was a stellar year for FinTech startups with over 1,700 deals worth nearly US$40 billion (CB Insights, 2019). Therefore, the global venture capital (VC) FinTech investment in 2018 has already reached $30.8 billion, up from $1.8 billion in 2011, according to a McKinsey & Company's report (Galvin et al., 2018).

Traditional financial institutions are now taking FinTech phenomenon seriously and are trying to narrow the technology gap between them and the FinTech startups (Nicoletti, 2107). They are developing new strategies by investing in external

FinTech startups through collaboration, and in internal FinTech projects in hopes of leapfrogging FinTech innovation and gaining competitive advantage (Lee & Shin, 2018). It becomes imperative for them to think and act entrepreneurially, review their business models and rebuild their technological capabilities to regain the trust of customers. In so doing, they will evolve and offer the same or higher level of interactivity and profitability as their FinTech rivals (Nicoletti, 2107).

In the chapter, we will define what do we mean by "FinTech", then, examine how FinTech is likely to affect the future of incumbent financial institution activities, and understand the challenges and opportunities posed by them in the business ecosystem. This chapter sheds the light of why a FinTech culture is needed for all players and how incumbents respond to FinTech phenomenon as they seek to preserve their position.

The rest of the chapter is organized as follows. Section 2 examines the definition of a FinTech company, its (r)evolution in the financial industry, its typology and diverse areas of activities, its drives, features and challenges, and introduces the FinTech ecosystem with its elements and attributes. In section 3, the chapter focuses on the diversity of FinTech models, the importance of instilling a FinTech culture with new standards and value of digital culture, agility, corporate entrepreneurialism and creative technology-enabled movement. This culture will be helpful for incumbents to decide the strategic choices of collaboration with FinTech startups and companies. Finally, the chapter recommends new future research directions towards the adoption of FinTech innovations and services by individual and corporate customers, the dynamics of emergence of FinTech startups, the potential collaboration between incumbents and FinTech companies and the managerial challenges of that collaboration, the potential development of dynamic capabilities of incumbents in-house, and the ways of nurturing a new FinTech community among future FinTech leaders. At the end, the chapter concludes with the promising of FinTech after global crises (e.g, COVID-19 pandemic) and the thriving of FinTech in other industries similar to the financial sector.

## BACKGROUND

### Defining FinTech

As a portmanteau of the words "financial" and "technology", Financial technology, also known as FinTech, has been defined as "a line of business based on using software to provide financial services. FinTech companies are generally startups founded with the purpose of disrupting incumbent financial systems and corporations that rely less on software." [1] Ernst & young (2016) set a working definition of the term FinTech by defining it in its boarder sense as "high-growth organisations combining innovative business models and technology to enable, enhance and disrupt financial services".

FinTech are providing or facilitating financial services by using technology (Ventura et al., 2015). They are aiming at improving the user experience and optimizing the operation costs. They refer to innovators and disruptors in the financial sector that make use of Internet and launch innovative services and/or create new business models and processes (Puschmann, 2017). FinTech companies can be either a start-up or a new entrant including a scale-ups, maturing companies; an established technology company, an established service provider, and even non-financial services companies such as telecommunication providers and e-retailers (Ernst & young, 2016; Gomber et al., 2017). Similarly, Nicoletti (2017) considered that FinTech initiatives fall into one of the following: startup; traditional/well-established financial institution; technological or retail companies moving into financial services, or advanced startup with a mixed ownership. These FinTech are not only covering by their offerings the banking sector, but also, they distribute insurance and other financial instruments or provide third party services (Dorfleitner et al., 2017). They are making the financial system more efficient using information technology.

## FinTech: A Paradigm Shifting or an Ongoing Process?

The FinTech phenomenon involves a change of paradigm that is revolutionizing the financial sector and disrupting the ways financial services are being offered, promising to provide access to underserved markets in new ways (Arner et al., 2015; Ventura et al., 2015). It has significantly spurred numerous incremental and disruptive innovations impacting on customer experience (Schueffel, 2016; Puschmann 2017).

Arner et al., (2015) stated that the interlinkage of finance and technology has a long history and has evolved over three distinct eras: FinTech 1.0; from 1866 to 1987, was the first period of financial globalization supported by technological infrastructure such as transatlantic transmission cables. This was followed by FinTech 2.0, from 1987-2008, during which financial services firms increasingly digitized their processes. Since 2008 a new era of FinTech has emerged in both the developed and developing world. However, this latest evolution of FinTech, led by start-ups, poses challenges for regulators and market participants alike and is referred as a FinTech revolution since the use of a large number of technologies (Ashta & Biot-Paquerot, 2018; Imerman & Fabozzi, 2020). The 2008 Global Financial Crisis represents a turning point and has catalyzed the growth the FinTech 3.0 era and democratization of digital financial services for both enterprises and individuals. In emerging markets (e.g., Asia, Africa…), recent FinTech developments have been prompted within a regulatory framework and have been characterized by a new era called FinTech 3.5 (Ratecka, 2020; Arner et al., 2015).

Most of researchers have reported the impact of FinTech on the future outlook for individuals, startups, incumbent financial institutions (Anagnostopoulos, 2018; Ventura et al., 2015; Arslanian & Fischer, 2019). More specifically, the major changes are seen of the domains: payments; insurance; deposits and lending; retail and SME capital raising; investment and wealth management (Anagnostopoulos, 2018).

The drivers of the FinTech revolution as described by Arslanian & Fischer (2019) are concerned with a changing economic/regulatory landscape to increase the availability of funding for FinTech entrepreneurs and facilitate their emergence; a rapidly evolving technology environment helping the new entrants to explore new trading strategies enabled by artificial intelligence; and shifting customer expectations to digital experiences to be timely, personalized and on-demand.

The foundation of the FinTech revolution as explained by Gomber et al., (2018) rest on the following pillars of innovation: the availability of capital for technology innovation for financial services; new transformed services designed for the financial industry; and transformed processes and operations.

Cortina & Schmukler (2018) provided, for example, the latest FinTech developments as well as their potential effects on global banks, and the financial system in general as alternative lending systems and online platforms (e.g., peer-to-peer lending; equity crowdfunding…); innovations in payments and transfers leveraging on mobile devices (person-to-person payment app) and blockchain technology for cryptocurrency (bitcoin…). For instance, FinTech companies become game changers for individuals and businesses for better efficiency (Liu, 2019b; Mackenzie, 2015; Ventura et al., 2015).

## FinTech Innovations: Types and Areas

Now, incumbent institutions in the financial sector were found themselves to compete not only with other banks or insurance firms, but also, by new other direct competitors coming from FinTech companies as financial intermediaries, and from TechFin or BigTech companies starting as technology and data intermediaries and adding financial services to their value-chain (Stulz, 2019; Tanda & Schena, 2019; Zetzsche, et al., 2017). There are derivatives and extensions of financial technology companies found in literature and in practice: FinTech startups; WealthTech; InsurTech; TechFin; BigTech (GAFAA as referred to Google, Apple, Facebook, Amazon, and Alibaba, and others BigTech like Tencent and Paypal…); BankTech (hybrid model of bank); RegTech; SupTech as subsets of FinTech (Accenture, 2016a; Anagnostopoulos, 2018; Arslanian & Fischer, 2019; Chishti & Puschmann, 2018; Tanda & Schena, 2019; Zetzsche, et al., 2017; Vanderlinden et al., 2018).

Following several scholars, leaders and executives from global financial institutions, the FinTech industry comprises major areas, considered as business models covering the financial intermediation activities, technological, functional or instrumental activities. Some of them are disrupted and historically have been offered by incumbents (insurance). Some others are invented and become possible with technology and alternative business models (peer-to-peer platform lending, mobile phone payments) (Anagnostopoulos, 2018; Arner et al., 2015; Arslanian & Fischer, 2019; Chen et al., 2019; Dorfleitner et al., 2017; Gosman et al., 2018; Haddad & Hornuf, 2019; Lee & Shin, 2018; Nicoletti, 2017; Ratecka, 2020; Tanda & Schena, 2019; Tsang, 2018; World Economic Forum, 2017; Yan et al., 2018).

These areas are explored below:

1. Payment services: providing new and innovative payment solutions such as money transfers/remittances, mobile payment solutions, e-billing, alternative payment methods, e-wallets, blockchain and cryptocurrencies, digital, peer-to-peer networks…
2. Financing and investment solutions: providing equity-based financing; debt financing, crowdfunding, crowdinvesting and crowdlending via peer-to-peer software, systems, networks or platforms; microcredit, factoring solutions and information services to investors;
3. Wealth and asset management: WealthTech offering services in the field of wealth management using robo-advising; social trading; personal financial management apps, or software that enable financial education and literacy through gamification.
4. Insurance and risk management services: InsurTech or firms that broker peer-to-peer insurance, spot insurance, usage-driven insurance, insurance contract management, and provide brokerage services as well as claims and risk management services.
5. Banking itself: digital banking, mobile banking, challenger banks as alternatives to traditional banking (retail and commercial) services mainly with the use of mobile apps.
6. Technology services: search engines and comparison sites, IT, infrastructure, API integration between data, applications and devices, cybersecurity and protection, monetization, big data analytics for loyalty programme services, and customer interface…
7. Other activities (regulation, supervision…): RegTech or technology-enabled regulatory solutions in the context of compliance burdens, regulatory monitoring, reporting benefitting the finance industry; SupTech or technology-enabled supervisory solutions and applications used by financial supervision agencies; and PropTech or property technology applied to various activities in the real estate sectors.

The FinTech industry is related to three types of innovation: service innovation that structures information flows at the intersection between FinTechs and its consumers (e.g., digital banking); business infrastructure innovation including technologies, extending the functionality, improving the performance or facilitating the provision of core services (data governance and privacy); and component innovation as building blocks from which the two innovation types (services and business infrastructure) are constituted (e.g., big data technologies, blockchain). These types are central to the construction of the FinTech business model. The value is created through the mix or synthesis of services, business infrastructure and component innovation, and through the underlying of technological mechanisms that act to coordinate the distribution of financial information (Gozman et al., 2018).

The development of FinTech has witnessed the adoption of increasingly innovative and competitive business models and the multiplicity of innovations related to the range of financial products/services, the different business processes, and the emergent technology as integral part in the FinTech offering (Tanda & Schena, 2019). Emergent technologies as having full impact on customer journeys and covering multiple areas of concerns: Data-focused technologies (Analytics, artificial intelligence), front-end interface (gamification, intuitive user interface), operational excellence (chabots, Distributes Ledger Technology), and infrastructure enablers (open APIs, platformification, cloud) (World FinTech Report, 2018).

## FinTech Innovations: Drivers, Features and Challenges

We continue to see the emergence of FinTech companies that seek to directly compete with, look to partner with or sell their services to incumbent financial institutions. FinTech companies that are becoming more mature can both disrupt incumbents in certain areas or markets and also collaborate in others (Pollari, 2016).

Pollari (2016) mentioned the drivers of FinTech innovations to emerge in the financial industry. What drives them is related, first, to changing consumer behavior and preferences when embracing new technology and demanding great level of personalization, convenience and immediacy. Second, to the proliferation and widespread adoption of mobile devices and digital platforms. Third, to the accelerating pace of change and the lesser time that new technology took to reach higher level of penetration. Fourth, to the declining levels of trust and its shift from top-down (financial institution) to a world of distributed and connected communities (opinion of strangers). Fifth, to the falling of barriers to entry for digital disruptors. Sixth, to the attractive profit pools which are accessible due to the digital transformation. And seventh, to the supporting policy and regulatory environment for the FinTech sector and their ability to address issues of financial inclusion, affordability and literacy.

This new reality imposed by the FinTech industry is characterized by the adoption of technology and innovation as a source of competitive advantage, dynamic business model, innovative communication channels, and customer orientation. In fact, in analyzing 1500 new FinTech companies (Drummer et al., 2016), McKinsey identified the following features:

- FinTech are lean, agile and innovative by attracting digital talent, using agile processes and greater customer orientation, and accelerating their speed of innovation to fulfill customer expectations;
- FinTech focus on individual segments of the value chain (e.g., payment transactions) to substantially undercut the fees charged by incumbents;
- FinTech have so far primarily targeted private customers (SMEs sector) that are not being receiving financial services or not being served sufficiently.

Furthermore, in their report on the evaluation of the international FinTech sector, Ernst & Young (2016) associate FinTech companies with several common characteristics like costumer centric (specific customer propositions, designed around pain points, user experience and engagement); legacy-free (systems designed around digital channels, free from the burdens of legacy systems and platforms), asset light (of fixed-asset base and balance sheet light), scalable (ability to increase in scale without increasing costs or compromising the efficiency of the technology), simple (customer proposition and transparent business processes), innovative (in their business models, products, services and delivery) and compliance light (based on simple and unbundled models that are often designed so as to avoid the need for authorization).

However, FinTech companies are facing serious obstacles challenging them to resist to the competition and assure their positioning in the market. According to Arslanian & Fischer (2019), six obstacles can be identified next. First, FinTech companies may lack the needed talent people with requisite technical skills. The access to talent becomes challenging because of the competition to hire such talent people. Large technology firms and incumbent financial institutions are also searching for similar talent. Second, FinTech companies need more supportive regulatory compliance to assure a good start and test their new products and experiment new technologies in such controlled market (e.g., regulatory regimes: sandbox, licensing…)[2]. Third, FinTech companies are searching for gaining and sustaining customer trust by deploying a large marketing budget. Fourth, they need to secure their clients in order to achieve profitability. Acquiring and scaling the base of customer (end customer B2C, large institutions B2B) is another challenge that FinTech companies need to face. Fifth, like any startups, FinTech companies need to secure capital from venture capitalists. To raise the necessary capital, they have to be sure that their offerings in terms of digital services and technologies are tested and refined with success (proof of concept…) before their launch to avoid any supplementary operating cost at startup stage.

## FinTech Ecosystem as a Growing and Fast-Moving Ecosystem for Success

FinTech ecosystems are critical to nurturing technology innovations necessary to make financial markets and systems more efficient and improve the overall customer experience (Diemers et al., 2015). They are formed by government and regulators (financial regulation and legislature), incumbent financial institutions (retail banks, insurance firms, asset management firms, venture capitalists), FinTech entrepreneurs and companies with different segments and domains (startups and mature FinTechs, BigTech, TechFin), technology developers (big data analytics, cloud computing, mobile services, infrastructure and platform…), and consumers (individuals users, corporates, SME…) (Hendrikse et al., 2019; Imerman & Fabozzi, 2020; Lee & Shin, 2018; Riasanow et al., 2018; Sironi, 2016).

Other elements/players can be found in a FinTech ecosystem. Their presence is important for the sustainability of the ecosystem, its FinTech during their stages of development (starting up, scaling up and maturity) and FinTech entrepreneurship. First, investors, venture capital, incumbent's incentives, and government support are the most important partner for FinTech startups. Second, other complementary supports are necessary for the development of FinTech companies. They concern incubation centers and accelerators in cooperation with universities or private sector, and Sandbox environment from government regulators as an effective and safe environment of experimentation and innovation.

Figure 1 presents the different elements and attributes of a FinTech ecosystem following Lee & Shin (2018) and Ernst & Young (2016).

For a FinTech ecosystem to function, it is imperative that each ecosystem actor clearly understands its role, as well as the benefits it stands to gain from involvement. Knowledge, inter-firm connections and talents permit the sustainability of FinTech ecosystem's competitive advantage in global markets and networks. The ecosystem dynamics will be understood through the symbiotic, competitive or collaborative actions and mechanisms between actors (Hendrikse et al., 2019; World FinTech Report, 2018). The power of a FinTech ecosystem is dependent on its players and the synergy that exists between them. Subsequently, a stable symbiotic FinTech ecosystem is contributory to the disruptive innovation, growth of FinTech industry, and consumers' satisfaction (Lee & Shin, 2018). Every actor in this ecosystem is trying to develop its strategies and reevaluate its existing business model to embrace FinTech innovation.

Ernst & Young (2016) analyzed the quality of FinTech ecosystems and viewed that a well-functioning FinTech ecosystem is built on four attributes:

- Talent: the availability of technical, financial services and entrepreneurial talent;
- Capital: the availability of financial resources for startups and scale-ups
- Policy: government policy across regulation, tax and sector growth initiatives
- Demand: end-client demand across consumers, corporates and financial institutions.

These four categories are carefully assessed to facilitate a benchmarking of the FinTech ecosystems. Hence, to operate more efficiently, it is important, for a FinTech ecosystem, to make sure that all these categories are fully developed and that ecosystem' stakeholders network and produce synergy by cooperating, competing or even by coopeting. To realize its full potential for financial inclusion, FinTech ecosystem has to operate within a strategic framework of underlying infrastructure and supportive policy and regulatory environment to support digital financial transformation (Arner, et al., 2018).

*Figure 1. Elements of the FinTech Ecosystem*
*Source: Adapted and modified from Lee & Shin, 2018; Ernst & Young (2016)*

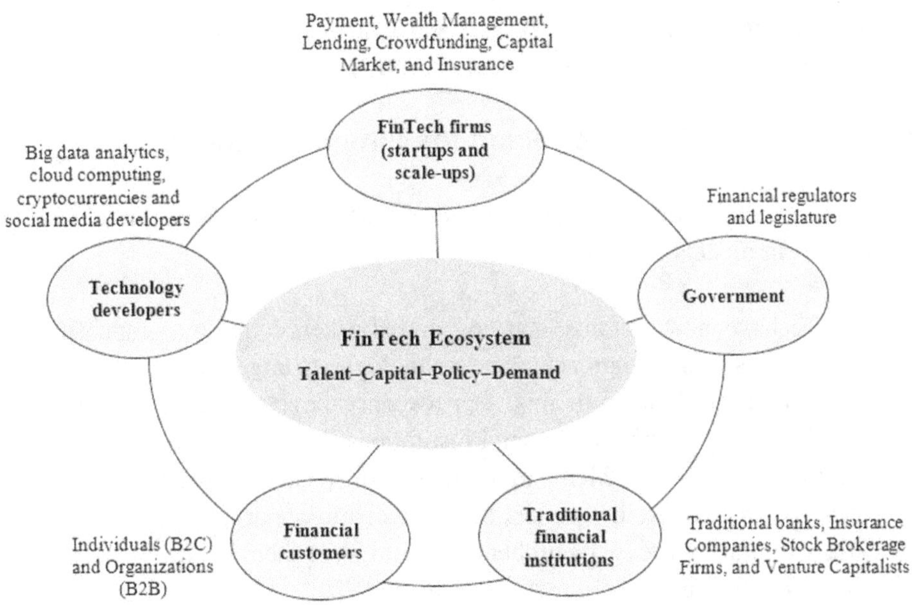

The FinTech ecosystem can be understood as an entrepreneurial ecosystem since it provides new (digital) opportunities enabled by the digital transformation to its stakeholders for (digital) entrepreneurship and business model experimentation and innovation (Autio et al., 2018). In order for the FinTech ecosystem to flourish, it has to support a culture of innovation and entrepreneurship, enabling policies, an adequate supply of financing to support startup firms, ready access to well-educated human capital and talents, access to markets for the products or services that the ecosystem provides, and a range of necessary institutional and infrastructure supports (Arner et al., 2018; Isenberg, 2011; van Winden, 2017).

Scholars, practitioners and policy makers are paying greater attention to the FinTech ecosystems, hubs and spaces to understand better their dynamics and the interactions between key players (Hornuf et al., 2020; Berdak et al., 2018).

## FOCUS OF THE CHAPTER

The digital transformation era has changed the financial industry and the financial consumption and behavior of customers. As financial disruptor, FinTech has built new figure for the industry (e.g., retail banking; online banking) and it has completely changed the way individuals and businesses (and especially the digital natives) are handling the money (Weichert, 2017; Wewege & Thomsett, 2019). The FinTech success is due to the fact that it is catering to customer changing and unmet needs by quickly and creatively harnessing emerging digital technologies. FinTech is setting up new and innovative services that are changing what customers expect over time. Its offerings are responsive, able to serve and adapt to emerging customer financial needs (Bhardwaj et al., 2019; Riemer et al., 2017).

### Diversity of FinTech Models in the Financial Industry

Galvin et al., (2018) identified four variants of FinTech operating in different niches with different models of operations:

* FinTechs as new entrants, startups, and attackers looking to enter financial services using new approaches and technologies to target a niche or a particular product. Their challenge is about how to reduce the cost of customer acquisition.
* FinTechs as incumbent financial institutions that are investing significantly in technology and in talents to improve performance, respond to competitive threats, and capture investment and partnership opportunities. To succeed in their digital journeys, incumbents have to shift their mindsets and cultural values to the culture of a real FinTech.

* FinTechs as ecosystems orchestrated by large technology companies (Tech Giants, BigTech) which offer financial services both to enhance existing platforms and to monetize current user data or relationships. They have no problem of the acquisition of customers, but their challenge is mostly regulatory.
* FinTechs as infrastructure providers (platform service) selling services to financial institutions to help them digitize their technology stacks and improve risk management and customer experience.

These varying types of FinTechs will be developed in different ways in the future, and then, will face very different obstacles for succeeding. Obstacles are related to the lack of talent and skills; resources and funding for investing in technology or people; FinTech mindset and culture; or compliance.

## FinTech as a New Organizational Model and Culture

Nowadays, well-established financial institutions are exposed to digital disruption by the entrepreneurial actions and the aforementioned common characteristics of FinTech companies. "How can they survive disruption" becomes a recurrent and worthy asked question. The answer to this question has engaged several scholars to argue that:

1. Incumbents need to set a "FinTech culture", a new vibrant and creative technology-driven entrepreneurial culture, customer-centric design and an aggressive desire to explore new opportunities are some of the traits that are commonly associated with FinTech (Accenture, 2013; Oshodin et al., 2017). FinTech is more than just a startup company that provide financial services. It's a new culture that needs to be instilled in the financial ecosystem.
2. Incumbents like Banks or insurance firms that still struggle with culture and legacy systems need to shift to new set of standards and values of digital culture, open innovation, agility, flexibility, offering adaptability and customer centricity as a DNA of FinTech companies (MacKenzie, 2015; PwC, 2016; Riemer et al., 2017). Incumbents need to transform their cultures, develop new capabilities and clarify their strategies (Mention, 2019)
3. Incumbents consider FinTech startup not as a threat, but also as opportunity to gain a competitive advantage over competitors. Incumbents have to take FinTech seriously and develop strategies to compete, coexist, and collaborate with FinTech startups (Lee & Shin, 2018).
4. Incumbents need to assess, adapt and adopt continuously these new technologies most quickly in order to be best positioned to achieve their desired position in the new industry structure (Accenture, 2016b).

The issue for incumbent financial institutions is how to foster an organizational culture as a key enabler to (disruptive) innovation beyond technology. As FinTech industry is accelerating, it is high time to consider the expected "FinTech culture" in the financial sector and break with the assumption being that anything but a "traditional" banking or insurance culture. When observing the impacts of paradigm shifts caused by FinTech industry, it becomes clear that FinTech is not just a technological shift disrupting an industry, it is also a cultural shift with shared values such as accessibility of customers to services and resources, accessibility and of innovators to personal preferences and data, hyper-connected community of peers for financial support and transparency during service provision and for gaining customer loyalty (Malone, 2020).

## Strategic Options Available for Incumbents to Respond to FinTech Innovations

Until recently, FinTech companies have posed threats and challenges to incumbents (banks and other financial companies) engaging customers with new experiences and with high level of trust, loyalty and centricity. Still, many incumbents are resisting to them and trying to preserve their market share. However, with the arrival of BigTech giants like facebook to cryptocurrency (CNBC, 2018), Amazon to launch a bank (W.UP, 2019), and the others to cover other financial activity in the sector (Detrixhe, 2017), incumbents are rethinking the rules of competition to sustain their market share. They have to act quickly!

Several strategic options available for incumbents were identified based on previous works. Several scholars, consultants and reporters consider that incumbents have to collaborate, compete or close (Accenture, 2016b; Ashta & biot-Pauerot, 2018; Berdak et al., 2018; Bömer & Maxin, 2018; Chishti & Barberis, 2016; Ernst & Young, 2017; Mills & McCarthy, 2017; Narsalay & Patrao, 2016; Zalan & Toufaily, 2017). Incumbents need to think collaboration with FinTech startups (as partners) or think coopetition rather than competition to boost innovation (Berdak et al., 2018). They have to engage startups in an ad hoc (time-limited programs and events: meetups, Hackathons, proof of concept, Startupbootcamp…) or in a structured way (structured incubation and acceleration programs, FinTech/InsurTech innovation labs and programs, ongoing partnerships and venture funds) (e.g., Accenture, NESTA, 2014; Nicoletti, 2017; Oracle, 2018; Sinha, 2017; Vanderlinden et al., 2018; World FinTech Report, 2018). Incumbents can build alliance strategies with FinTech startups as a source of organizational legitimacy and to take advantage of each other's strengths or they can proceed to mergers & acquisitions strategies (M&A) or to incubation actions as innovation-enhancing form of cooperation to acquire the needed know-how and staff (Anand & Mantrala, 2019; Drasch et al., 2018; Svensson et al., 2019).

Each partner will profit from the cooperation to develop new customer segments, products, and services, expand into new markets, develop new capabilities, and access new technologies (incumbents) or look for the financial resources, infrastructures, access to customers, and security reputation (FinTechs).

In the collaboration/partnership strategy, the challenge for incumbents is related to their organizational culture's ability to adopt such approach with new innovators and startups. According to the World FinTech Report (2018), FinTechs and incumbents need to understand the importance of having the right cultural fit. For the collaboration to be productive, both parties need to be flexible and look to find the middle ground between a highly hierarchical incumbent and a very horizontally-managed startup. Through collaboration, mutual needs are identified and strengths swapped for a mutually beneficial win-win situation for industry players. Commitment and agility from FinTechs and incumbents are required for a successful collaboration.

Other suggest that incumbents have to build their dynamic capabilities and talented people by themselves (in-house programs) to meet the challenges of FinTech startups or by copying the key organizational technologies of their challengers (Hendrikse et al., 2018; Muthukannan & Gozman, 2019; Oshodin et al., 2017). They have to reimagine their business model by supporting early-stage FinTech innovators and putting the necessary investments (venture investing; corporate venture). Big incumbents (like Big and challengers Banks) are using their FinTech brands by creating or acquiring them specifically in response to new FinTech challengers (FT Partners FinTech industry Research, 2020).

To successfully seize the opportunities presented by the digital revolution, incumbents can use other mechanisms for collaborating and acting openly with open innovation, open banking, integrated platform aggregation; or for collaborating with FinTech partners with co-innovation, co-creation, co-production, co-specialization to combine efforts and sources and co-create value (Hendrikse et al., 2018; Muthukannan & Gozman, 2019; Omarini, 2018; Schueffel & Vadana, 2016; Vanderlinden et al., 2018).

## RECOMMENDING FUTURE RESEARCH DIRECTIONS

Future research will interest at five recommended directions: User behavior and experience towards the adoption of FinTech disruptive innovations from the user's perspective (Chishti & Barberis, 2016; Gomber et al., 2017); emergence of the FinTech phenomenon and its dynamics in the ecosystem (Eickhoff et al., 2017); the value co-creation and proposition of industry incumbents with FinTech startups and tech giant players (Breidbach et al., 2019; Kavuri & Milne, 2019); the development of their dynamic capabilities, the building and management of their talented leaders;

and the synergetic efforts of the financial and technology players in nurturing a FinTech community and reshaping the financial services ecosystem locally and globally (Chishti & Barberis, 2016; Hendrikse et al., 2018; 2019).

## FinTech Adoption

Future research will investigate the new culture of financial consumption and the user behavior and experience towards the adoption of FinTech disruptive innovations (mobile payments, p2p landing apps…) (Chishti & Barberis, 2016; Gomber et al., 2017). Millennials, or Gen Y are usually the target market of FinTech startups and the early adopters of their services (Gulamhuseinwala et al., 2015; Lee & Shin, 2018; Pollari, 2016). Having lost the faith in the traditional financial services, this tech-savvy generation demands convenient access to financial accounts, assets and services. A comparison between generations could identify the generational gap in the adoption behavior of such FinTech services (Bhardwaj et al., 2019; Ernst & Young, 2019; HBS Digital Initiative, 2017; Rooney, 2018). Also, future research could focus on corporate consumer (SMEs, business or corporate firms) as the next wave of FinTech companies to investigate their behavior of adopting FinTech innovations and services. For them, FinTech companies will be the game changer in the financial industry (Fuscaldo, 2019; Ghazali & Yasuoka, 2018; Liu, 2019a). FinTech innovation and services will be adopted for revitalizing SMEs from alternative funding sources for the easiness of access to finance.

## Starting Up and Scaling FinTech Firms

Future research will examine on how the FinTech companies have emerged and their business models are built, then, which of them are becoming more relevant, are playing crucial role in the financial industry or are needing for new forms of regulation. Future research could address this questioning of how FinTech firms are configuring resources and capabilities to achieve innovative outcomes (Gimpel et al., 2018; Oshodin et al., 2019). The dynamic foundation and development of FinTech to occupy a niche of a market or to reach beyond niche offering, creates a need for future investigation (Brandl & Hornuf, 2017; Eickhoff et al., 2017; Leong et al., 2017). FinTech firms have to evolve into significant competition in the financial ecosystem. To grow and scale up, they need to secure venture capital. Their strategy of attracting investor and venture capital community also needs to be understood in the future.

## Value Proposition and Dynamic Capabilities of Incumbent Financial Institutions

Future research will explore the digital transformation of financial service systems through FinTech innovations initiated by new market entrants or by digitalized incumbent financial institutions. Future research will investigate how to improve the value proposition of industry incumbent (bank, insurance…) with FinTech and how to orchestrate the value co-creation processes with and between customers from different perspectives (incumbent vs. FinTech) (Breidbach et al., 2019; Kavuri & Milne, 2019). It could also investigate how financial institutions and FinTechs can cooperate and work together to develop their dynamic capabilities (flexibility, agility, innovativeness) (Drasch et al., 2018; Hornuf et al., 2020). Similarly, Breidbach et al., (2019) launched a call for researchers to address managerial challenges associated with FinTech and the digital transformation of financial services to improve the value proposition of industry incumbents by understanding customers through big financial data; open data for value co-creation; and finally changing role of traditional financial intermediaries.

## Building and Managing Talented Leaders

For building the dynamic capabilities, financial institutions need to fill in the gap in terms of talent shortage (technology, financial, and entrepreneurial talents) by offering to their talented employees the opportunity to be trained to become future agile transformers in incumbents. Future research will investigate the preparedness of financial institutions to build new FinTech leaders and disruptive innovation capabilities to succeed the agile transformation (Arslanian & Fischer, 2019; Mei et al., 2018; Utoyo et al., 2019). The changes in technological capabilities involved by new entrant FinTech invite incumbent's managers to reconsider their portfolio of capabilities by acquiring, matching or attracting the missing capabilities or talents (Anand & Mantrala, 2019). The choice of appropriate response strategy to fill in the talent gap can be studied by future researchers to understand how incumbents could respond to these new entrant FinTechs.

## Nurturing FinTech Community and Ecosystem

All players in the economy (e.g., entrepreneurs, investors, venture capitals, governments, developers, and customers) are turning to FinTech innovations to drive forward the reinvention of banking, finance, insurance, and commerce. Clusters are emerging all over the world and offering innovators access to engaged communities and combined members providing opportunities to collaborate and grow. Future research will examine how to nurture a new FinTech community in a country and how to benefit from the resources and opportunities of a FinTech ecosystem and from the use of incubators, accelerators, platforms, and regulators' sandboxes (Bardawil, 2018; Chishti & Barberis, 2016; Cumming & Schwienbacher, 2018; Findexable, 2020; Gazel & Schwienbacher, 2020; Hendrikse et al., 2018; 2019).

For building a new generation of FinTech entrepreneurs and talent people, university policymakers are now opening the doors to the FinTech startups and their entrepreneurs and providing facilities to potential entrepreneurs (business hubs, spaces, incubation and acceleration programs, university curriculum). Future research will consider the role of universities in teaching FinTech and entrepreneurial finance and promoting the FinTech culture among students as FinTech startuppers and innovators of the future (Arslanian & Fischer, 2019; Aloulou, in press).

## CONCLUSION

This chapter was developed to explore the phenomenon of FinTech as a disrupted innovation in the financial services based on emergent technologies. The coming of FinTech companies, Tech fin and BigTech companies in the financial sector with incumbents is making the landscape more competitive, more efficient and more responsive to customer expectations. The incumbent financial institutions are facing big challenges to resist in this landscape, they need to acquire, distribute FinTech capabilities or invest in FinTech initiatives to seize opportunities. They have to instill FinTech culture of innovation, agility, co-creation, customer centricity… in their businesses. They also have to undertake the digital transformation of their entire value chain themselves, realize the value of digitalization and launch their own products and services by utilizing their huge customer base.

The chapter offered a better understanding of the opportunities and challenges of the rise of FinTech companies in the financial sector and the strategic choices for incumbent financial institutions. It identified some recommended future research directions for scholarship and practitioners.

However, the mindset towards FinTech will be irrevocably changed amid and after the COVID-19 pandemic. Many companies will be facing several problems of fundraising, regulations, credibility, profitability, consolidation, merging & acquisition deals, and will be seizing opportunities of democratization of more sophisticated financial services (Fu & Mishra, 2020; Sahay et al., 2020). What will be the "new normal" for key players, such as FinTech, banks, insurers in the digital financial sector? Will the wave of digital transformation accelerated by the pandemic crisis help individual and business consumers to adopt digital financial services and incumbent financial institutions to adopt emergent digital technologies for their business processes? Will the FinTech be the promising tool for developed and developing countries to achieve the financial inclusion in the post COVID-19 era?

In the future, FinTech culture and ecosystem will influence and disrupt other sectors of activities in the economy (World FinTech Report, 2018). What will be the emergent FinTech ecosystem surrounding other sectors that preparing the digital transformation and new entrant FinTech players? Will, for example, the automotive sector witness disruptive innovation in auto FinTech lending, insurance and payments?

## REFERENCES

Accenture. (2013). *Corporate Innovation Is Within Reach: Nurturing and Enabling an Entrepreneurial Culture*. https://www.accenture.com/t20150523T052044__w__/us-en/_acnmedia/Accenture/Conversion-Assets/DotCom/Documents/Global/PDF/Strategy_2/Accenture-Survey-Enabling-Culture-Innovation-Entrepreneurialism.pdf

Accenture. (2016a). *Beyond the everyday bank: How a GAFA approach to digital banking transformation will increase revenues, improve customer engagement, while reducing the cost base*. https://www.accenture.com/t20160502T051308Z__w__/us-en/_acnmedia/PDF-10/Accenture-Banking-Beyond-Everyday-Bank-pdf.pdf#zoom=50

Accenture. (2016b). *FinTech and the evolving landscape: landing points for the industry*. https://www.accenture.com/t20161011T031409Z__w__/pl-en/_acnmedia/PDF-15/Accenture-FinTech-Evolving-Landscape.pdf

Aloulou, W.J., (2019). Entrepreneurship and innovation in the era of digitalization: Exploring uncharted territories. In *Business Transformations in the Era of Digitalization*. IGI Global.

Aloulou, W. J. (in press). Mapping incubation mechanisms in Saudi Arabia: State-of-the-art and challenges for the future. In International Handbook of Research on Business and Technology Incubation. Edward Elgar Publishing.

Anagnostopoulos, I. (2018). FinTech and Regtech: Impact on Regulators and Banks. *Journal of Economics and Business*, *100*, 7–25. doi:10.1016/j.jeconbus.2018.07.003

Anand, D., & Mantrala, M. (2019). Responding to disruptive business model innovations: The case of traditional banks facing FinTech entrants. *Journal of Banking and Financial Technology*, *3*(1), 19–31. doi:10.100742786-018-00004-4

Arner, D. W., Barberis, J., & Buckley, R. P. (2015). The evolution of FinTech: A new post-crisis paradigm. *Geo. J. Int'l L.*, *47*, 1271. doi:10.2139srn.2676553

Arner, D. W., Buckley, R. P., & Zetzsche, D. A. (2018). *Fintech for financial inclusion: A framework for digital financial transformation. AFI special report*. https://www.cnbs.gob.hn/wp-content/uploads/2020/01/AFI_FinTech_Special-Report_AW_digital.pdf

Arslanian, H., & Fischer, F. (2019). *The Future of Finance: The Impact of FinTech, AI, and Crypto on Financial Services*. Springer. doi:10.1007/978-3-030-14533-0

Ashta, A., & Biot-Paquerot, G. (2018). FinTech evolution: Strategic value management issues in a fast changing industry. *Strategic Change*, *27*(4), 301–311. doi:10.1002/jsc.2203

Autio, E., Nambisan, S., Thomas, L. D., & Wright, M. (2018). Digital affordances, spatial affordances, and the genesis of entrepreneurial ecosystems. *Strategic Entrepreneurship Journal*, *12*(1), 72–95. doi:10.1002ej.1266

Bardawil, N. (2018). FinTech and the Accelerator Culture. *Int'l Fin. L. Rev.*, *37*, 101.

Berdak, O., Ensor, B., Ng, Z. Y., Giudice, D. L., & Causey, A. (2016). *How to work with FinTech startups. Partner with financial technology startups to boost innovation*. Forrester.

Bhardwaj, G. N., Sinha, G., & Pal, S. (2019). FinTech and the Younger Generation. *IUP Journal of Information Technology*, *15*(1), 16–33.

Bömer, M., & Maxin, H. (2018). Why FinTechs cooperate with banks—evidence from Germany. *Zeitschrift für die gesamte Versicherungswissenschaft*, *107*(4), 359-386.

Brandl, B., & Hornuf, L. (2020). *Where did FinTechs come from, and where do they go? The transformation of the financial industry in Germany after digitalization. In Frontiers in Artificial Intelligence*. Artificial Intelligence in Finance. doi:10.3389/frai.2020.00008

Breidbach, C. F., Keating, B. W., & Lim, C. (2019). FinTech: Research directions to explore the digital transformation of financial service systems. *Journal of Service Theory and Practice*, *30*(1), 79–102. doi:10.1108/JSTP-08-2018-0185

Chen, M. A., Wu, Q., & Yang, B. (2019). How valuable is FinTech innovation? *Review of Financial Studies*, *32*(5), 2062–2106. doi:10.1093/rfs/hhy130

Chishti, S., & Barberis, J. (2016). *The FinTech book: The financial technology handbook for investors, entrepreneurs and visionaries*. John Wiley & Sons. doi:10.1002/9781119218906

Chishti, S., & Puschmann, T. (2018). *The Wealthtech book: The FinTech handbook for investors, `entrepreneurs and finance visionaries*. John Wiley & Sons. doi:10.1002/9781119444510

CNBC. (2018). *Facebook will reportedly use cryptocurrency for transferring money through WhatsApp*. www.cnbc.com/2018/12/21/facebook-reportedly-working-on-a-cryptocurrency-for-transfering-money-through-whatsapp-.html

Cortina, J. J., & Schmukler, S. L. (2018). The FinTech Revolution: A Threat to Global Banking? *World Bank Research and Policy Briefs*, (125038).

Cumming, D. J., & Schwienbacher, A. (2018). FinTech venture capital. *Corp. Gov. International Review*, *26*, 374–389. doi:10.1111/corg.12256

Detrixhe, J. (2017). Big tech firms like Amazon are eager to eat the banking industry's lunch. *Quartz*. https://qz.com/1112460/banks-are-under-threat-from-big-tech-firms-like-apple-amazon-and-facebook-according-to-mckinsey/

Diemers, D., Lamaa, A., Salamat, J., & Steffens, T. (2015). *Developing a FinTech ecosystem in the GCC*. Dubai: Strategy. https://www.strategyand.pwc.com/media/file/Developing-a-FinTechecosystem-in-the-GCC.pdf

Dorfleitner, G., Hornuf, L., Schmitt, M., & Weber, M. (2017). Definition of FinTech and Description of the FinTech Industry. In G. Dorfleitner, L. Hornuf, & M. Schmitt (Eds.), *FinTech in Germany* (pp. 5–10). Springer. doi:10.1007/978-3-319-54666-7_2

Drasch, B. J., Schweizer, A., & Urbach, N. (2018). Integrating the 'Troublemakers': A taxonomy for cooperation between banks and FinTechs. *Journal of Economics and Business*, *100*(March), 26–42. doi:10.1016/j.jeconbus.2018.04.002

Drummer, D., Jerenz, A., Siebelt, P., & Thaten, M. (2016). *FinTech: Challenges and Opportunities -How digitization is transforming the financial sector*. McKinsey.

Eickhoff, M., Muntermann, J., & Weinrich, T. (2017). What do FinTechs actually do? A taxonomy of FinTech business models. *ICIS 2017 Proceedings*.

Ernst & Young. (2016). *UK FinTech On the cutting edge an evaluation of the international FinTech sector*. https://FinTechauscensus.ey.com/2018/Documents/EY-UK-FinTech-On-the-cutting-edge.pdf

Ernst & Young. (2017). *Unleashing the potential of FinTech in banking*. https://www.ey.com/Publication/vwLUAssets/ey-unleashing-the-potential-offin-tech-in-banking/$File/ey-unleashing-the-potential-of-fin-tech-in-banking.pdf

Ernst & Young. (2019). *Global FinTech Adoption Index 2019*. https://FinTechauscensus.ey.com/2019/Documents/ey-global-FinTech-adoption-index-2019.pdf

Findexable. (2020). *The global FinTech index 2020. The global FinTech index city ranking report*. https://findexable.com/wp-content/uploads/2019/12/Findexable_Global-FinTech-Rankings-2020exSFA.pdf

FT Partners FinTech industry Research. (2020). *The rise of Challenger Banks. Are the apps taking over?* https://ftpartners.docsend.com/view/suxcjc4

Fu, J., & Mishra, M. (2020). *The Global Impact of COVID-19 on FinTech Adoption*. Swiss Finance Institute Research Paper No. 20-38. Available at SSRN: https://ssrn.com/abstract=3588453

Fuscaldo, D. (2019). Small Businesses Are The Next Wave Of FinTech Focus. *Forbes*. https://www.forbes.com/sites/donnafuscaldo/2019/02/12/small-businesses-are-the-next-wave-of-FinTech-focus/#53783afb8663

Galvin, J., Han, F., Hynes, S., Qu, J., Rajgopal, K., & Shek, A. (2018). *Synergy and disruption: Ten trends shaping FinTech*. McKinsey & Company. https://www.mckinsey.com/industries/financial-services/our-insights/synergy-and-disruption-ten-trends-shaping-FinTech

Gartner. (2018). *Digitalization will make most heritage financial firms irrelevant*. https://www.gartner.com/en/doc/337197-innovation-insight-for-insurance-cios-analyzing-the-digital-maturity-of-insurtechs

Gazel, M., & Schwienbacher, A. (2020). Entrepreneurial FinTech clusters. *Small Business Economics*, 1–21.

Ghazali, N. H., & Yasuoka, T. (2018). Awareness and Perception Analysis of Small Medium Enterprise and Start-up Towards FinTech Instruments: Crowd funding and Peer-to-Peer Lending in Malaysia. *International Journal Of Finance and Banking Research*, *4*(1), 13–24. doi:10.11648/j.ijfbr.20180401.12

Gimpel, H., Rau, D., & Röglinger, M. (2018). Understanding FinTech start-ups–a taxonomy of consumer-oriented service offerings. *Electronic Markets*, *28*(3), 245–264. doi:10.100712525-017-0275-0

Gomber, P., Kauffman, R. J., Parker, C., & Weber, B. W. (2018). On the FinTech revolution: Interpreting the forces of innovation, disruption, and transformation in financial services. *Journal of Management Information Systems*, *35*(1), 220–265. doi:10.1080/07421222.2018.1440766

Gomber, P., Koch, J., & Siering, M. (2017). Digital Finance and FinTech: Current research and future research directions. *Journal of Business Economics*, *87*(5), 537–580. doi:10.100711573-017-0852-x

Gozman, D., Liebenau, J., & Mangan, J. (2018). The innovation mechanisms of FinTech start-ups: Insights from SWIFT's innotribe competition. *Journal of Management Information Systems*, *35*(1), 145–179. doi:10.1080/07421222.2018.1440768

Gulamhuseinwala, I., Bull, T., & Lewis, S. (2015). *FinTech is gaining traction and young, high-income users are the early adopters*. https://www.ey.com/Publication/vwLUAssets/ey-FinTech-is-gaining-traction-and-young-high-income-users-are-the-early-adopters/$FILE/ey-FinTech-is-gaining-traction-and-young-high-income-users-are-the-early-adopters.pdf

Haddad, C., & Hornuf, L. (2019). The emergence of the global FinTech market: Economic and technological determinants. *Small Business Economics*, *53*(1), 81–105. doi:10.100711187-018-9991-x

HBS Digital Initiative. (2017. December 18). *Why millennials flock to FinTech for personal investing*. Harvard Business School. https://digital.hbs.edu/FinTech-digital-currencies/millennials-flock-FinTech-personal-investing/

Hendrikse, R., Bassens, D., & Van Meeteren, M. (2018). The Appleization of finance: Charting incumbent finance's embrace of FinTech. *Finance and Stochastics*, *4*(2), 159–180.

Hendrikse, R., van Meeteren, M., & Bassens, D. (2019). Strategic coupling between finance, technology and the state: Cultivating a FinTech ecosystem for incumbent finance. *Environment and Planning A: Economy and Space*.

Hornuf, L., Klus, M. F., Lohwasser, T. S., & Schwienbacher, A. (2020). How do banks interact with FinTech startups? *Small Business Economics*, 1–22. doi:10.100711187-020-00359-3

Imerman, M. B., & Fabozzi, F. J. (2020). Cashing in on innovation: A taxonomy of FinTech. *Journal of Asset Management*, *21*(3), 167–177. doi:10.105741260-020-00163-4

Insights, C. B. (2019). *FinTech trends to watch in 2019*. https://www.cbinsights.com/research/report/FinTech-trends-2019/

Isenberg, D. J. (2011). The Entrepreneurship Ecosystem Strategy as a New Paradigm for Economic Policy: Principles for Cultivating Entrepreneurships. *The Babson Entrepreneurship Ecosystem Project, 1*(781), 1–13. doi:10.1093/rfs/hhr098

Kavuri, A. S., & Milne, A. (2019). *FinTech and the future of financial services: What are the research gaps?* CAMA Working Paper No. 18/2019. Available at SSRN: https://ssrn.com/abstract=3333515

KPMG. (2018). The pulse of FinTech. Global report on FinTech investment trends. *H1' 2018.*

Lee, I., & Shin, Y. J. (2018). FinTech: Ecosystem, business models, investment decisions, and challenges. *Business Horizons, 61*(1), 35–46. doi:10.1016/j.bushor.2017.09.003

Leong, C., Tan, B., Xiao, X., Tan, F. T. C., & Sun, Y. (2017). Nurturing a FinTech ecosystem: The case of a youth microloan startup in China. *International Journal of Information Management, 37*(2), 92–97. doi:10.1016/j.ijinfomgt.2016.11.006

Liu, C. (2019a). Finance strategies for medium-sized enterprises: FinTech as the game changer. In Strategic Optimization of Medium-Sized Enterprises in the Global Market (pp. 162-184). IGI Global.

Liu, C. (2019b). FinTech and its disruption to financial institutions. In A. Guerra Guerra (Ed.), *Organizational Transformation and Managing Innovation in the Fourth Industrial Revolution* (pp. 104–124). IGI Global. doi:10.4018/978-1-5225-7074-5.ch006

Mackenzie, A. (2015). The FinTech revolution. *London Business School Review, 26*(3), 50–53. doi:10.1111/2057-1615.12059

Malone, V. (2020). *Fintech culture is here to stay. Horizon Fintex.* https://medium.com/@horizonfintex/fintech-culture-is-here-to-stay-207657a533e0

Mei, S., Peiguang, L., & Xiushan, N. (2018). Research on FinTech Industry Development and Talent Training Status. In *2018 13th International Conference on Computer Science & Education (ICCSE)* (pp. 1-4). IEEE. 10.1109/ICCSE.2018.8468796

Mention, A. L. (2019). The future of FinTech. *Research Technology Management, 62*(4), 59–61. doi:10.1080/08956308.2019.1613123

Mezghani, K., & Aloulou, W. (2019). Business Transformations in the Era of Digitalization. Hershey, PA: IGI Global. doi:10.4018/978-1-5225-7262-6

Mills, K., & McCarthy, B. (2017). How banks can compete against an army of FinTech startups. *Harvard Business Review*. https://hbr.org/2017/04/how-banks-can-compete-against-an-army-of-FinTech-startups

Muthukannan, P., & Gozman, D. (2019). Meeting the Challenge of FinTech Startups: The Development of Dynamic Capabilities at Incumbent Banks. *ICIS 2019 Proceedings*. https://aisel.aisnet.org/icis2019/blockchain_FinTech/blockchain_FinTech/6

Narsalay, R., & Patrao, M. (2016). Thriving with FinTechs: Strategies for Large Indian Banks. *Vinimaya*, *37*(1), 5.

NESTA. (2014). *Startup Accelerator Programmes: A Practice Guide*. www.nesta.org.uk

Nicoletti, B. (2017). *The Future of FinTech: Integrating Finance and Technology in Financial Services*. Springer. doi:10.1007/978-3-319-51415-4

Omarini, A. E. (2018). Banks and FinTechs: How to develop a digital open banking approach for the bank's future. *International Business Research*, *11*(9), 23–36. doi:10.5539/ibr.v11n9p23

Oracle. (2018). *Bank and insurance innovators to benefit from European Oracle FinTech innovation program with B-Hive Europe*. Press Release. www.oracle.com/corporate/pressrelease/oracle-FinTech-innovation-program-062818.html

Oshodin, O., Karanasios, S., Molla, A., & Ong, C. E. (2019). How do FinTech Start-ups Develop Capabilities? Towards a FinTech Capability Model. *Twenty-Third Pacific Asia Conference on Information Systems*.

Oshodin, O., Molla, A., Karanasios, S., & Ong, C. E. (2017). Is FinTech a disruption or a new eco-system? An exploratory investigation of Banksr response to FinTech in Australia. In *Proceeding of Australasian Conference on Information Systems* (pp. 1-11). Academic Press.

Pollari, I. (2016). The rise of FinTech opportunities and challenges. *Jassa The Finsia Journal of Applied Finance*, (3), 15.

Puschmann, T. (2017). FinTech. *Business & Information Systems Engineering*, *59*(1), 69–76. doi:10.100712599-017-0464-6

PwC. (2016). *Blurred lines: How FinTech is shaping Financial Services – Global FinTech Report*. New York. https://www.pwc.com.au/pdf/pwc-FinTech-global-report-2016.pdf

Ratecka, P. (2020). FinTech—Definition, taxonomy and historical approach. *Zeszyty Naukowe Małopolskiej Wyższej Szkoły Ekonomicznej w Tarnowie, 1*(45), 53–67.

Riasanow, T., Flötgen, R. J., Setzke, D. S., Böhm, M., & Krcmar, H. (2018). The Generic Ecosystem and Innovation Patterns of the Digital Transformation in the Financial Industry. *22nd Pacific Asia Conference on Information Systems (PACIS).*

Riemer, K., Hafermalz, E., Roosen, A., Boussand, N., El Aoufi, H., Mo, D., & Kosheliev, A. (2017). *The FinTech Advantage: Harnessing digital technology, keeping the customer in focus*. University of Sydney, Business School and Capgemini.

Rooney, K. (2018). *After the crisis, a new generation puts its trust in tech over traditional banks*. https://www.cnbc.com/2018/09/14/a-new-generation-puts-its-trust-in-tech-over-traditional-banks.html

Sahay, R., Allmen, U., Lahreche, A., Khera, P., Ogawa, S., Bazarbash, M., & Beaton, K. (2020). *The Promise of FinTech: Financial Inclusion in the Post COVID-19 Era New*. Journal Issue.

Schueffel, P. (2016). Taming the beast: A scientific definition of FinTech. *Journal of Innovation Management, 4*(4), 32–54. doi:10.24840/2183-0606_004.004_0004

Schueffel, P., & Vadana, I. (2016). Open Innovation in the Financial Services Sector – A global literature review. *Journal of Innovation Management, 3*(1), 25–48. doi:10.24840/2183-0606_003.001_0005

Sinha, S. (2017). A Glimpse into the World of FinTech Accelerators? The Open Vault at OCBC. *IEEE Potentials, 36*(6), 20–23. doi:10.1109/MPOT.2017.2737238

Sironi, P. (2016). *FinTech Innovation: From Robo-Advisors to Goal Based Investing and Gamification*. Wiley. doi:10.1002/9781119227205

Svensson, C., Udesen, J., & Webb, J. (2019). Alliances in Financial Ecosystems: A Source of Organizational Legitimacy for FinTech Startups and Incumbents. *Technology Innovation Management Review, 9*(1).

Tanda, A., & Schena, C. M. (2019). *FinTech, BigTech and Banks: Digitalisation and Its Impact on Banking Business Models*. Springer. doi:10.1007/978-3-030-22426-4

Tsang, C. Y. (2018). A Tentative Analytical Framework and Developing Roadmap for SupTech. *Management Review, 37*, 105–120.

Utoyo, I., Fontana, A., & Satrya, A. (2019). The role of entrepreneurial leadership and configuring core innovation capabilities to enhance innovation performance in a disruptive environment. *International Journal of Innovation Management*, *24*(06), 2050060. doi:10.1142/S1363919620500607

van Winden, W. (2017). Boosting The Entrepreneurial Local Scene. *Maximizing The Ecosystem Approach. Thematic Workshop*, Torino, Italy.

Vanderlinden, S. L., Millie, S. M., Anderson, N., & Chishti, S. (2018). *The INSURTECH Book: The Insurance Technology Handbook for Investors, Entrepreneurs and FinTech Visionaries*. John Wiley & Sons.

Ventura, A., Koenitzer, M., Stein, P., Tufano, P., & Drummer, D. (2015, October). *The Future of FinTech: A paradigm shift in small business finance*. World Economic Forum, Global Agenda Council on the Future of Financing and Capital. https://www.weforum.org/reports/future-FinTech-paradigm-shift-small-business-finance

Weichert, M. (2017). The future of payments: How FinTech players are accelerating customer-driven innovation in financial services. *Journal of Payments Strategy & Systems*, 23-33.

Wewege, L., & Thomsett, M. C. (2019). *The Digital Banking Revolution: How FinTech Companies are Transforming the Retail Banking Industry Through Disruptive Financial Innovation*. Walter de Gruyter GmbH & Co KG. doi:10.1515/9781547401598

World Economic Forum. (2017). *Beyond FinTech: A pragmatic assessment of disruptive potential in financial services*. http://www3.weforum.org/docs/Beyond_FinTech_-_A_Pragmatic_Assessment_of_Disruptive_Potential_in_Financial_Services.pdf

World FinTech Report. (2018). https://www.capgemini.com/news/capgeminis-world-FinTech-report-2018-highlights-symbiotic-collaboration-as-key-to-future-financial-services-success/

W.UP. (2019). *Tech Giants in Banking: Will Amazon Launch a Bank?* https://wup.digital/blog/tech-giants-banking-amazon-in-banking/

Yan, T. C., Schulte, P., & Chuen, D. L. K. (2018). InsurTech and FinTech: banking and insurance enablement. In Handbook of Blockchain, Digital Finance, and Inclusion, Volume 1 (pp. 249-281). Academic Press. doi:10.1016/B978-0-12-810441-5.00011-7

Zalan, T., & Toufaily, E. (2017). The promise of FinTech in emerging markets: Not as disruptive. *Contemporary Economics*, *11*(4), 415–431.

Zetzsche, D. A., Buckley, R. P., Arner, D. W., & Barberis, J. N. (2017). From FinTech to TechFin: The regulatory challenges of data-driven finance. *NYUJL & Bus., 14*, 393. doi:10.2139srn.2959925

## ADDITIONAL READING

Autio, E., & Thomas, L. D. W. (2014). Innovation ecosystems: Implications for innovation management? In M. Dodgson, D. M. Gann, & N. Phillips (Eds.), *The Oxford Handbook of Innovation Management* (pp. 204–228). Oxford University Press.

Block, J. H., Colombo, M. G., Cumming, D. J., & Vismara, S. (2017). New players in entrepreneurial finance and why they are there. *Small Business Economics*, 112.

Christensen, C. M., McDonald, R., Altman, E. J., & Palmer, J. E. (2018). Disruptive Innovation: An Intellectual History and Directions for Future Research. *Journal of Management Studies, 55*(7), 1043–1078. Advance online publication. doi:10.1111/joms.12349

Del Vecchio, P., Ndou, V., Passiante, G., & Vrontis, D. (2020). *Innovative Entrepreneurship in Action: From High-Tech to Digital Entrepreneurship*. Springer International Publishing AG.

Fasnacht, D. (2018). *Open Innovation Ecosystems*. Springer. doi:10.1007/978-3-319-76394-1

Knewtson, H. S., & Rosenbaum, Z. A. (2020). Toward understanding FinTech and its industry. *Managerial Finance, 46*(8), 1043–1060. Advance online publication. doi:10.1108/MF-01-2020-0024

Navaretti, G. B., Calzolari, G., Mansilla-Fernandez, J. M., & Pozzolo, A. F. (2017). FinTech and Banking. Friends or Foes? *European Economy – Banks, Regulation, and the Real Sector, 2017.2.* https://european-economy.eu/2017-2/FinTech-and-banks-friends-or-foes/?did=2045

Romānova, I., & Kudinska, M. (2016). Banking and FinTech: a challenge or opportunity? In *Contemporary issues in finance: Current challenges from across Europe*. Emerald Group Publishing Limited. doi:10.1108/S1569-375920160000098002

Teigland, R., Siri, S., Larsson, A., Puertas, A. M., & Bogusz, C. I. (2018). *The rise and development of FinTech*. Routledge. doi:10.4324/9781351183628

Zhang, X., Zhang, J., & He, Z. (2018, August). Is FinTech Inclusive? Evidence from China's Household Survey Data. In *35th IARIW General Conference, Copenhagen* (pp. 20-25).

## KEY TERMS AND DEFINITIONS

**Coopetition:** A form of collaboration between two competitive companies in the hope of mutually beneficial results.

**Disruptive Innovation:** Is an innovation that creates a new market and eventually disrupts an existing market. It is produced by outsiders rather than market-leading firms.

**Emerging Technologies:** New digital technology that shakes up the industry or a ground-breaking product/service that creates a completely new industry, change dramatically the costumer expectation and reshape the marketplace.

**FinTech:** Is a financial technology firm that is providing or facilitating financial services by using emergent technology.

**FinTech Ecosystem:** Refers to the factors—individuals, groups, firms, organizations, and institutions (micro ecosystem); and cultural, social, and material attributes (macro ecosystem)—outside the individual FinTech entrepreneur—that are conducive to, or inhibitive of, the choice and decision of a person or group of persons to become FinTech entrepreneur or enterprising.

**Incumbent:** A well-established firm in a defined sector. Bank or insurance is an incumbent firm in the financial industry.

## ENDNOTES

1. Source: Wikipedia, at https://en.wikipedia.org/wiki/Financial_technology, Accessed 29 May 2020.
2. Sandbox: is a framework used to allow some (fintech) firms to test their innovations in a controlled environment under the supervision of the financial sector regulator.

# Chapter 5
# Big Data Management in the Era of FinTech:
## Insights From a Literature Review

**Mona Fourati Ennouri**
*University of Sfax, Tunisia*

**Karim Mezghani**
https://orcid.org/0000-0002-9404-405X
*Imam Mohammad Ibn Saud Islamic University, Saudi Arabia*

## ABSTRACT

*Within the 4th industrial revolution, disruptive technologies spread along the financial value chain giving rise to FinTech phenomenon. In this context, more digitized and useful big data about customers and their transactions are generated. Managers need big data tools in order to get meaningful insights from the huge volumes of such data. Managing this vast amount of data can represent both an opportunity and a challenge for FinTech. This chapter investigates the big data management issues in the context of FinTech and proposes a framework for big data management tools adoption based on expected benefits and challenges.*

DOI: 10.4018/978-1-7998-7110-1.ch005

## 1 INTRODUCTION

Researches in the economic and managerial literature don't agree on a single definition of Fintech (Nicoletti, 2017). Fintech could be understood as novel technologies adopted by the financial service institutions (Gai et al., 2018), financial services which leverage on modern technologies (Dapp et al. 2014) or companies (startups) which serve as enablers of such kinds of services (Zavolokina et al., 2016).

Zavolokina et al. (2016) argue that Fintech is a very broad phenomenon and that shedding light on the term and its understanding will help both practitioners to identify potentials and threats of the phenomenon, and researchers to unveil new possibilities for research regarding all aspects of Fintech (e.g., technologies behind, ecosystems, organizational matters, etc.).

The phenomenon of Fintech is supported by the development and the diffusion of modern information and communication technologies. At the same time, these technologies allowed the development of a digital environment in which we are confronted with an "information overload" (Dapp et al.,2014) from various sources and in different formats, often referred to as big data (Alharthi et al., 2017). Managing this vast amount of data can represent both an opportunity and a challenge for firms (Alharthi et al., 2017; Almeida, 2017), notably in Fintech context. Indeed, firms can take full advantage of the potential of these data to predict changes in customers' needs (Dubey et al., 2018) and to improve decision making (Mezghani, 2019; Ignatyuk et al., 2020) and firm's competitiveness (Gupta and George, 2016; Alharthi et al., 2017). For Fintech, this allows a greater personalization of services (Dapp et al., 2014) and the improvement of customer experience and innovation (Nicholetti, 2017; Palmié et al., 2020). Nevertheless, working with big data, in Fintech era, poses some challenges related to data quality, security and privacy or customer management (Lee and Yong, 2018). These challenges are not only at a technical level (Almeida, 2017), but include also managerial concerns (Alharthi et al., 2017; Vassakis et al., 2018) related to leadership, talent management or organizational culture (Shamim et al., 2019).

Based on previous theoretical and managerial studies linking big data with the development of Fintech, this chapter attempts to investigate the big data management issues in the context of Fintech.

The first section deals with the main transformations of the financial sector in a digital revolution context permitting the emergence and the development of the Fintech phenomenon. The second section discusses the main challenges of big data management with a focus on managerial issues. The importance of big data management in the era of Fintech is then considered. In the third section, we attempt to develop a framework of big data management tools adoption in the Fintech context combining expected benefits and challenges.

# 2 FINTECH AND DIGITAL TRANSFORMATIONS

## 2.1 The Essence of FinTech

The term Fintech, an abbreviation of financial technology, comes from the application of technological innovation in the financial sector. Despite the obvious meaning of the term, the researchers did not have a consensus on its definition.

The vagueness and the broadness of the term seems to be related to novelty and rapid tremendous rise of Fintech industry (Zavolokina et al., 2016), to the overall diversity of the business (Nicholetti, 2017) and to the manner the researchers characterize this phenomenon (Gimpel et al., 2018).

Many researchers consider Fintech as technological innovation or new technologies providing financial services (Dapp et al., 2014; Gai et al., 2018; Gimpel et al., 2018; Gomber et al., 2018, Thakor, 2020). Other researchers used the term as financial services and products or innovative financial solutions (Kim et al., 2015; Zavolokina et al., 2016; Puschmann, 2017). The term Fintech is also used for startup companies which enable such services (Zavolokina et al., 2016; Puschmann, 2017; Gimpel et al., 2018) or for the whole financial technology sector or industry made up of these organizations (Kim et al., 2015, Vasiljeva and Lukanova, 2016; Nicholetti, 2017; Gai et al., 2018). Furthermore, we can distinguish between Fintech as startups and Fintech as innovative use of digital technologies to create new financial products and services sector (Gimpel et al., 2018). So, novel technologies serve as a catalyst for the development of such innovations that respond to the changing consumer behavior and needs regarding the use of digital tools in their financial transactions. Generally, the application of IT in finance, startups, and services are the three top discussed elements of Fintech definitions (Zavolokina et al., 2016).

Kerényi et Müller (2019, p.8) believe that "technology creates the possibility to dramatically reshape finance as we know it". Thus, Fintech can result in new business models, processes, applications, or products (Zavolokina et al.,2016; Gimpel et al., 2018; Thakor, 2020) and Fintech solutions will differ regarding these diverse financial innovation objects (Puschmann, 2017).

**Fintech products and services:** Fintech offers to potential customers' alternatives to traditional products and services provided by the financial industry (Vasiljeva and Lukanova, 2016). Gimpell et al.(2018) summarize the major groups of financial products and services offered by Fintech. They list the following functional domains of financial services: account management, asset management, crowdfunding / crowdinvesting, cryptocurrencies, financial planning, insurance, lending and financing, payment and money transfer, peer-to-peer lending and trading. But researchers classify generally differently the Fintech products and services

(Gulamhuseinwala et al., 2017; El-Masri et al., 2019; Thakor, 2020). The Basel Committee on Banking Supervision (BCBS) also specified the innovations and new technologies (open source, big data analysis, blockchain, cloud computing, internet of things, mobile technology, artificial intelligence ...) that could support the Fintech service development (BCBS, 2018). Some classifications highlight the fact that Fintech offer more than traditional financial services. Vasiljeva et Lukanova (2016) suggest a division of activities in the Fintech area that includes service-oriented activities which are traditionally provided by financial institutions; data-oriented solutions and technologies devoted to collecting, processing and analyzing information; and process-oriented activities enabling banks to re-define their operating models and to work on increasing efficiency and process automation. Palmié et al. (2020) propose; in addition to banking and payment applications, crowdfunding, InsurTech (insurance technology) and RegTech (regulatory technology) applications.

**Fintech ecosystem:** When we talk about Fintech, we note the presence of new actors in the financial industry from outside the banking sector, both in the developed (e.g. United States, United Kingdom) and in the developing markets (e.g. India, China) (Dapp, 2017; Shmeljov, 2017; Kerényi et Müller, 2019; Palmié et al., 2020). These actors compose with the traditional financial institutions and the financial customers the Fintech ecosystem (Lee and Shin, 2018). Lee and Shin (2018) identified 3 other elements of the Fintech ecosystem. At the center of the ecosystem, there are Fintech startups, which have driven major innovations in different financial areas. Technology developers offer digital platforms and create favorable environment for Fintech startups to launch innovative service rapidly and government provide favorable regulatory environment for Fintech (Lee and Shin, 2018).According to Palmié et al. (2020), this Fintech ecosystem benefits from technological advancements (in online payments, cryptocurrency, artificial intelligence...) to provide new financial solutions that increase efficiency in financial markets and banking transactions for consumers, banks, businesses, and all ecosystem members. These new solutions are changing the way financial service firms operate as well as the way consumers save, transfer, borrow, spent and manage their wealth and assets (Lee and Shin, 2018; Palmié et al., 2020). This implies a transformation or disruption in the business model of traditional banks and the emergence of new business models in the financial market (Llorca, 2017; Shmeljov, 2017, Gomber et al., 2018; Kerényi et Müller, 2019).

**Fintech business models:** The business models implemented by the new generation of Fintech startups and companies concern generally payments, wealth management, crowdfunding, peer-to-peer lending, capital market and insurance services(Lee and Shin, 2018; Gomber et al., 2018). These Fintech business models are characterized by an extended consumer access outside branches and beyond normal banking business hours; a higher level of service personalization based on digital technologies; new ways of delivering traditional banks services, etc. (Gomber et al., 2018). This leads to a more customer centric companies (Nicoletti, 2017; Shmeljov, 2017, Alt et al., 2018; Gomber et al., 2018)that rethink their customer relationships and serve their target markets as no traditional organizations did in the past(Nicoletti, 2017). Shmeljov (2017) talks about a new spiral of innovation in which new technologies and products are taking a more prominent space in the financial business models, citing examples of Fintech credit, use of artificial intelligence in advice giving, big data analytics, use of distributed ledger technology like blockchain in payments or customer identification, expansion of internet-only or mobile-only banks and payments, etc.

## 2.2 FinTech as a Driver of Digital Transformations

It is argued that the emergence of Fintech is only the latest wave of innovation affecting the banking industry (BCBS, 2018).

Many researchers use a historical perspective to describe the digital transformation of the financial sector leading to the emergence and the evolution of the Fintech phenomenon (Alt et al., 2018; Lee and Shin, 2018; Thakor, 2020). According to Lee and Shin (2018), the emergence of Fintech is linked to the internet revolution of the 1990's. This revolution led to the rise of e-finance. With the growth of Smartphone use in the mid 2000's, one could note the development of internet banking, mobile payment and mobile banking. Fintech innovation emerged then after the worldwide financial crisis in 2008 by "combining the e-finance, internet technologies, social networking services, social media, artificial intelligence and big data analytics" (Lee and Shin, 2018, p.36).

Kerényi and Müller (2019, p.7) talk about the 4th industrial revolution during which the digital transformation associated with innovation in the field of digital technology impacted all aspects of society and the economy, notablythe financialand banking sector. In the financial sector,3 waves of technological changes can characterize the emergence of Fintech: Electronic payments, blockchain and cryptocurrency and Artificial intelligence (Palmié, 2020).The digital technologies spread along the banking value chain (customers, channels, financial service providers and interbank providers) (Alt et al., 2018) and are combined with a profound change in the demand and uses of financial customers (especially the youngest) in terms of consumption of financial services (Llorca, 2017). In fact, it has been suggested that the digital transformation is not a pure technological revolution (Omarini, 2017), it includes technologies, Management/processes and people (Verina and Titko, 2019).

Four digital transformation drivers are proposed by Puschmann (2017) and Alt et al., (2018): The diffusion and changing role of IT, allowing not only business process automation but providing entirely new services and business models (like crowdfunding or peer-to-peer insurance platforms); changing consumer behavior to more customer self-services and multi-bank-relations; developing new ecosystems including incumbents, Fintech startups and companies from outside the financial services industry; and finally regulatory and competitive consequences of the 2008 financial crisis increasing the pressure on traditional financial services providers and supporting the development of Fintech start-ups.

Accelerated technological developments brought solutions both for the production side (databases, decision-making tools) and for distribution (digital channels, knowledge of customers, good customer experience, and flexibility of customer offerings) (Nicoletti, 2017). They allow new disruptive players to find a place in the sector by delivering the same value a traditional player provides without having to reproduce the conventional value chain and at a much lower cost (Llorca, 2017; Omarini, 2017).

The digital transformation in the Fintech era implies also a set of challenges for the financial sector:

- Placing the customer at the center of the process: The objective is to better respond to the new customer needs that become "digitally highly advanced" (Shmeljov, 2017). This implies changing the interaction approach with the customers to become more customer-centric (Nicoletti, 2017; Puschmann, 2017; Shmeljov, 2017, Alt et al., 2018; Gomber et al., 2018).

To do that, financial companies need to "listen to the voice of the customer" (Nicholetti, 2017) in order to reduce the gap between customer's satisfaction and expectations of the banking experience (Omarini, 2017). Then, they should adjust their strategies to maintain their existing customers, by adapting to the changing customers' expectations, or to attract new customers, searching for more diversified, customized and digitalized products. In doing so, banks can embrace recent Fintech trends and may become Fintech leaders (Shmeljov, 2017, Gomber et al., 2018).

- Fundamental reorganization of financial services value chain:According to Pushmann (2017), the digital transformation "is not only leading to an increasing automation of processes, but to a fundamental reorganization of the financial services value chain with new business models (e.g., robo-advisors) and new actors entering the market (e.g., Apple). (p. 69). This leads to reconsidering the role of banking and finance more as enabler than a provider of products and services (Omarini, 2017, Shmeljov, 2017).

Fintech revolution implies changes and transformations in many key areas of the financial services industry: operations management, payments, lending and funding, etc. (Omarini, 2017; Gomber et al., 2018). More and more financial activities are available online; business models, offerings, and value chains are digitized to the maximum extent, blurring so the lines between industries (Omarini, 2017).

Furthermore, the decrease in launch costs of technology startups allowed the access of new entrants into the market (Gomber et al., 2018). Fintech startups are offering a variety of platforms serving new and/or complementary products to both B2C and B2B segments. These startups are able to link themselves with different market players of the digital ecosystems (Dapp, 2017). Other new entrants in the financial sector, particularly the giants of the web, are able to win over customers, young people in particular, and to support them throughout the value chain. Their financial solidity even allows them to acquire Fintech startups and to compete very quickly with banks (Llorca, 2017). The challenge for the financial sector is to understand that the pace of changes in financial services value chain is increasing and that new technologies and competitors will change its competitive arena (Omarini, 2017).

Fintech and traditional players' relationship: Nicholetti (2017) noted the growing attention of the financial service sector toward Fintech initiatives. Banks and traditional financial organizations adopted different types of solutions to deal with the threats posed by Fintech companies. According to Ashta and Biot-Paquerot (2018), different strategic options are offered to banks and traditional players: freezing, competing, closing or collaborating. Many researchers consider that the solutions adopted are more and more often oriented toward collaboration with Fintech startups: Buying or taking shares in startups, creating or participating in innovation incubators dedicated to the development of these startups, carrying out external partnerships (Llorca, 2017; Nicholetti, 2017), creating Fintech shared platforms (Shmeljov, 2017), etc.

Llorca (2017) consider that banks are in a direct situation of coopetition (both cooperation and competition) with Fintech startups. According to Dapp (2017) the Fintech scene is more interested in Collaboration than Confrontation because collaboration represents more benefits than disadvantages for the two parts. Karagiannaki et al. (2017) find that this is a win-win situation for both incumbents and new players; each of them having strengths, that can be combined, and weaknesses, that can be fought. This permits to create value for both established banks and Fintech startups (Shmeljov, 2017). The established banks could be assisted by Fintech startups in developing shared platforms (Shmeljov, 2017) and using emerging technologies, thereby increasing their awareness of new market trends, their agility in the development of products and services (Karagiannaki et al., 2017) and the resilience and cost effectiveness of banking and payment systems (Shmeljov, 2017). On the other hand, collaboration allows Fintech startups to take advantage of specific financial bank's expertise and experience, to access to customer data and payment systems, etc. (Karagiannaki et al., 2017; Omarini, 2017; Shmeljov, 2017). Obviously, there are some barriers, like mutual trust and unclear decision-making model, to collaboration between incumbents and Fintech startups (Karagiannaki et al., 2017).

## 3 BIG DATA: FROM MANAGEMENT TO ANALYTICS

### 3.1 Why Firms Need Big Data Tools

Terms as "Industry 4.0", "artificial intelligence" or "machine learning" are becoming common within firms in all sectors. Managers are more and more concerned by the use of disruptive technologies as the digital transformations become an ultimate issue to deal with competition and to promote innovations.

Consequently, one can note the explosion of data in different formats from various digital sources (Louati and Mekadmi, 2019). Every year, thousands of exabytes of new data are generated from the use of numerous digital platforms such as social media and mobile devices (Feki, 2019). Vassakis et al. (2018) guess that the generation of data is expected to reach 180 zettabytes in 2025, giving data a leading role in a new "digital universe". Louati and Mekadmi (2019) affirm that "data are produced extensively every day in many forms and from many different sources. Accordingly, firms in several industries are increasingly interested in how to leverage on these "big data" to draw valuable insights from the various kinds of data and to create business value".

Managers need big data tools in order to get meaningful insights from the huge volumes of data which covers hidden patterns that could be useful for decision making (Mezghani, 2019). Indeed, "it is big data that is heralded as the next big thing for organizations to gain the competitive edge" (Gupta and George, 2016). Besides useful to predict the rapid evolution of the competition and the continuous changes in the customers' needs, big data are largely considered to predict the effects of natural disasters (Dubey et al., 2018) as well as to successfully prevent outbreaks in pandemic periods as the case of Covid-19 (Chen et al., 2020).

However, big data are not easily extracted due to their volume and various formats (structured, semi-structured and unstructured). That is why such "data" require specific tools in terms of management and analysis. It is commonly known that getting insights from big data requires two phases: data management and data analytics (Vassakis et al., 2018). While data management "involves processes and supporting technologies to acquire and store data and to prepare and retrieve it for analysis", data analytics "refers to techniques used to analyze and acquire intelligence from big data" (Gandomi and Haider, 2015).

## 3.2 The Challenges of Big Data Management

Besides volume, big data are defined in reference to additional characteristics known as "Vs". When some authors define big data in terms of 3 Vs (Gandomi and Haider, 2015), others prefer to extend the definition to 5 Vs (Wamba et al., 2015; Feki, 2019).

Wamba et al. (2015) present the 5 Vs of big data as follow:

- Volume: large volume of records that consume huge storage.
- Variety: various types (structured, semi-structured and unstructured) of data collected from variety of sources.
- Velocity: "refers to the rate at which data are generated and the speed at which it should be analyzed and acted upon" (Gandomi and Haider, 2015).
- Veracity: "represents the unreliability inherent in some sources of data" (Gandomi and Haider, 2015).
- Value: "The extent to which big data generates economically worthy insights and or benefits through extraction and transformation" (Wamba et al., 2015).

By analyzing such Vs, one can note that big data management is a challenging issue. Indeed, extracting and preparing data that are not only huge, but also presented in different formats, usually informal and continuously changing require specific tools and considerable efforts. These Vs are considered as the "dimensions of challenges in data management" as they make it difficult to deal with big data using traditional data management technologies (Gandomi and Haider, 2015).

The challenges are also linked to the management process itself. According to Gandomi and Haider (2015), in the overall process of 'insight extraction' from big data, big data management is a sub-process in which three main stages can be identified:

- Acquisition and recording: as some data sources may provide huge amounts of raw data, much of this data can be of no interest and should be filtered, which represents a challenging issue since useful information could be lost (Labrinidis and Jagadish, 2012).
- Extraction and cleaning: inside big data we will find "erroneous data" which makes it crucial to proceed to extraction "that pulls out the required information from the underlying sources and expresses it in a structured form suitable for analysis" (Labrinidis and Jagadish, 2012).
- Integration, aggregation and representation that need to be processed automatically to facilitate different types of data analyses as it is useless to save extracted big data as bunch of data sets (Labrinidis and Jagadish, 2012; Nasser and Tariq, 2015).

Every stage will require specific technologies which increase the big data management concerns.

Besides technological challenges, recently Shamim et al. (2019) identified the challenges of big data management from a managerial perspective. Based on McAfee et al. (2012), they presented these challenges as follow:

- Leadership focus on big data: "Companies succeed in the big data era not simply because they have more or better data, but because they have leadership teams that set clear goals, define what success looks like, and ask the right questions. Big data's power does not erase the need for vision or human insight" (McAfee et al., 2012). In order to develop an effective use of big data in decision-making, leaders need to adapt their styles and behaviors according to the work environment in a way to encourage more collaboration and knowledge sharing (Shamim et al., 2019).
- Talent management for big data: Although a knowledge of statistics is important, big data management requires complex skills that are more than traditional statistical skills. In fact, in order to perform large data sets cleaning and visualization, firms need specific skills generally possessed by the new generation of computer scientists that who are not largely available (Shamim et al., 2019). The lack of employees with big data-linked skills is one of the major challenges which may increase confuse data interpretation, lead to lose valuable information and prevent business from getting benefits from big data (Alharthi et al., 2017; Moktadir et al., 2019). This suggests that firms need to develop best practices in term of talent management regarding big data specialists.
- Organizational culture of big data: Several studies showed that most reasons for big data initiative failures are related to the absence of a data-driven culture within firms rather than to data characteristics and technological factors (LaValle et al., 2011; Shamim et al., 2019). These authors argue that, in many firms, managers continue to "make their decisions using traditional approaches and then justify them by spicing them up with lots of data". This means that getting big data tools does not mean necessarily that any firm would succeed in big data management. An organizational culture of knowledge exchange and data science is required in order to develop positive attitudes toward big data and then be able to take benefits from such data (Shamim et al., 2019).

Such challenges would be more significant as disruptive technologies like Fintech are more and more deployed.

## 3.3 Importance of Big Data Management in the Era of FinTech

One can see that the era of Fintech is associated with the large use of disruptive technologies to provide financial services, especially online. Digital platforms allow providers and consumers to interact with each other and to create and exchange value (Omarini 2017). These platforms permit to collect an exponentially rising data volume (Dapp, 2017). This means more digitized and useful big data about customers and their transactions. Companies, like the GAFA companies entering the financial sector, for which data and data analysis represent a core activity, are using these digital platforms for collecting data from their billions of users all over the world (Dapp, 2017, Lorca, 2017). In line with the growth in the volume of such data, more big data tools are developed (Verma, 2019).

A set of services based on big data are also offered by Fintech. These solutions are devoted to collecting, processing and analyzing information (Vasiljeva and Lukanova, 2016). The collection and the analysis of very large amounts of valuable data possessed by banks can offer a deep insight into customer habits (Vasiljeva and Lukanova, 2016) helping so refining customer relationship management (purchasing and savings behavior, customer experience, solvency) (Lorca, 2017).According to Miskam and Eksan (2018), big data "can be used to anticipate customer behavior, but also to create protective strategies and policies for alternative banks and financial institutions from all around the world". Big data and predictive analytics can be used to extract useful patterns and knowledge, which can be applied to improve financial services and provide unique personalized services to customers, such as private financial advice and management (Lee and Shin, 2018; Verma, 2019). Hence, they offer the opportunity to explore new ways of addressing customer needs and a perfect targeting of offers made to customers (Dapp, 2017, Lorca, 2017).

Unlike traditional banks that still use traditional and simplistic indicators of credit risk, peer-to-peer lending platforms, as an example, are also involving analytical skills in order to examine a wide range of dynamic data from public websites and public records to evaluate credit risk (Yan et al., 2015). These authors argue also that big data can provide "a more complete picture of a borrower".

Moreover, from a law perspective, big data tools are very helpful to improve cybersecurity by detecting the fraudulent transactions in real time from unusual behaviors or by encrypting sensitive data (Lorca, 2017; Verma, 2019).

Providing such personalized and unique services to customers requires gathering heterogeneous metadata from many sources, like the online social networks, that "provide useful/distinctive information in terms of features based on which the data analysis/data mining models are generated" (Verma, 2019).

Regarding the reasoning part above, we can associate the importance of big data management in the era of Fintech to two main points. First, Fintech data are linked to financial issues, which means higher risk regarding data use and storage. Decisions makers need "clean" data in order to make effective decisions and provide suitable advice to customers. Second, Fintech data are integrated from various sources and can be presented in different and unstructured formats. Thus, the stages of big data management sub-process presented earlier in this chapter are crucial in terms of filtering, cleaning and integration of big data in order to prepare the analytics phases.

## 4 A FRAMEWORK FOR BIG DATA MANAGEMENT TOOLS ADOPTION IN THE ERA OF FINTECH

Regarding the benefits and challenges linked to big data management tools from one side, and those of Fintech as disruptive technologies from another side, it is crucial to assess both benefits and challenges of such tools in Fintech context. Indeed, from a two-factor theory perspective, adoption of IT innovations can be explained in reference to dual-factored constructs, the inhibitors (expected challenges) and the enablers (expected benefits), that can act separately and simultaneously on adoption issues (Smaoui Hachicha and Mezghani, 2018).

Regarding benefits, most previous studies focus on the big data benefits in general (Schaeffer et al., 2016; Almeida, 2017; Feki, 2019), or let's say the outcomes of using big data tools (in terms of costs saving, tracking customers' behaviors, improving decisions making…). This can be noted also when analyzing the big data benefits in Fintech. Indeed, according to Dorfleitner and Hornuf (2019), big data tools can help in anticipating customers' behaviors, detecting frauds, managing credit risk, provide personalized services…

Such benefits are closely linked to the "analytics" sub-process which provides the big data process outcomes. Nevertheless, analytics could not be effectively performed if "management" sub-process is not suitably done in term of data preparation. Thus, one can link the direct benefits of big data management to the effective execution of itsmain stages(acquisition, cleaning and extraction).

Vis-à-vis challenges, it is possible to adopt the framework developed by Shamim et al. (2019) who presented the main challenges of big data management. Considering the specificities of Fintech, it is possible to propose the big data management challenges in the era of Fintech as follow:

- Leadership focus on big data: In finance industry, when big data are not appropriately managed, governance problems arise and constitute a real challenge related to big data and Fintech (Miskam and Eksan, 2018). As presented earlier, Fintech involve dynamic data from multiple sources. This would require more efforts from leaders in terms of what Shamim et al. (2019) proposed as styles and behaviors flexibility toward more collaboration and knowledge sharing in order to manage effectively the huge and dynamic Fintech data.
- Talent management for financial big data: Dealing with big data in the era of Fintech may face a double challenge in term of skills. Indeed, in addition to financial skills required to perform the different and advanced financial analyses, Fintech are facing the challenge of big data management skills required to perform large data sets cleaning and visualization. Such skills are more than traditional statistical skills and are not largely available (Shamim et al., 2019).
- Data-driven culture: As mentioned earlier, one of the most reasons for big data initiative failures is related to the absence of a data-driven culture within firms rather than to data characteristics and technological factors (LaValle et al., 2011; Shamim et al., 2019). This data-linked concern seems to be more crucial in the Fintech context in which personalized financial services should be provided. Hence, decisions makers are faced to develop a culture that favors data-based decisions unless data management tools would not be too fruitful. Indeed, Lack of a data-driven culture within the firm can hinder the adoption of big data tools (Mezghani, 2019).
- Technology-linked challenges: The most largely used frameworks in IT innovations adoption support the idea according to which the technological issues represent a real challenge. The "complexity" presented in the Technology-Organization-Environment (TOE) framework and the "ease of use" presented in the Technology Acceptance Model (TAM) inform about the necessity to consider the technology-linked challenges when to decide about an IT innovation adoption and use. Since the big data management process is viewed as requiring specific tools and skills that are not largely available, one can argue that technological issues represent a real challenge when to deal with Fintech data management. From the infrastructure perspective, using big data tools requires big investment in hardware and software (Mezghani, 2019).

The reasoning part above leads to the following framework:

*Figure 1. The proposed framework*

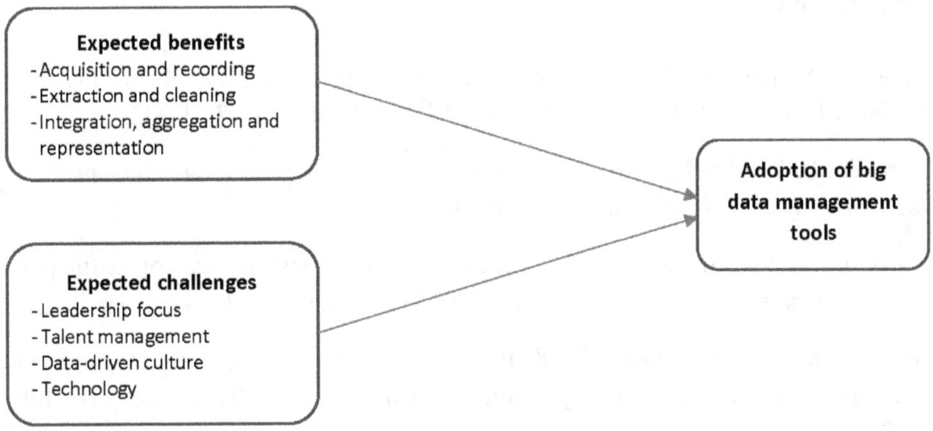


## 5 CONCLUSION

This chapter aimed to explore the main issues linked to big data management in the era of Fintech. In fact, with the development of disruptive technologies use in the financial sector and the growth of Fintech, more digitizedand useful big data about customers and their transactions are accumulated. This means that financial actors are requiring more tools to deal with such huge volume of data.

Through a literature review, we tried first to understand the roles of Fintech in the digital transformations occurring in the financial sector. Then, we discussed the main concerns linked to big data in terms of benefits and challenges with a focus on management issues. Indeed, while several studies already discussed the analytics concerns, we attempted to explore the big data management sub-process as a crucial element in the big data process.

By combining Fintech with big data management concerns, we proposed a framework for big data management tools adoption. Based on a dual-factored perspective, we argue that big data management is more than a technology-linked issue. Hence, besides the expected benefits of big data tools, the organizational and cultural aspects could play a crucial role when selecting such tools in order to guarantee the best way of their use.In other words, even if big data management tools provide technical benefits in term of data preparation, the literature review showed that decision makers in Fintech should develop suitable leadership, talent management practices and a data-driven culture to ensure an effective adoption and use of such tools.

The proposed framework should be strengthened and contextualized in further empirical research as the Fintech market is more and more expanding.

## REFERENCES


Alharthi, A., Krotov, V., & Bowman, M. (2017). Addressing barriers to big data. *Business Horizons*, *60*(3), 285–292. doi:10.1016/j.bushor.2017.01.002

Almeida, F. L. (2017). Benefits, challenges and tools of big data management. *Journal of Systems Integration*, *8*(4), 12–20.

Alt, R., Beck, R., & Smits, M. T. (2018). Fintech and the transformation of the financial industry. *Electronic Markets*, *2018*(28), 235–243. doi:10.100712525-018-0310-9

Ashta, A., & Biot-Paquerot, G. (2018). FinTech evolution: Strategic value management issues in a fast changing industry. *Strategic Change*, *27*(4), 301–311. doi:10.1002/jsc.2203

BCBS (Basel Committee on Banking Supervision). (2018). *Sound Practices-Implications ofFintech Developments for Banks and Bank Supervisors*. Bank for International Settlements.

Chen, F. M., Feng, M. C., Chen, T. C., Hsieh, M. H., Kuo, S. H., Chang, H. L., & Chen, Y. H. (2020). (in press). Big data integration and analytics to prevent a potential hospital outbreak of COVID-19 in Taiwan. *Journal of Microbiology, Immunology, and Infection*. Advance online publication. doi:10.1016/j.jmii.2020.04.010 PMID:32327328

Dapp, T., Slomka, L., & Hoffmann, R. (2014). Fintech–The digital (r) evolution in the financial sector. Deutsche Bank Research.

Dapp, T. F. (2017). Fintech: the digital transformation in the financial sector. In *Sustainability in a Digital World* (pp. 189–199). Springer. doi:10.1007/978-3-319-54603-2_16

Dorfleitner, G., & Hornuf, L. (2019). Fintech Business Models. In *Fintech and Data Privacy in Germany* (pp. 85–106). Springer. doi:10.1007/978-3-030-31335-7_5

Dubey, R., Luo, Z., Gunasekaran, A., Akter, S., Hazen, B. T., & Douglas, M. A. (2018). Big data and predictive analytics in humanitarian supply chains. *International Journal of Logistics Management*, *29*(2), 485–512. doi:10.1108/IJLM-02-2017-0039

El-Masri, M., Al-Yafi, K., & Sherif, K. S. (2019). The Digital Transformation of Fintech: Disruptions and Value Paths. *Twenty-Third Pacific Asia Conference on Information Systems*.

Ernst and Young. (2016). *UK Fintech-On the cutting edge*. Ernst and Young Report. Retrieved from https://Fintechauscensus.ey.com/2018/Documents/EY-UK-Fintech-On-the-cutting-edge.pdf

Feki, M. (2019). Big Data Analytics Driven Supply Chain Transformation. In K. Mezghani & W. Aloulou (Eds.), *Business Transformations in the Era of Digitalization* (pp. 106–124). IGI Global. doi:10.4018/978-1-5225-7262-6.ch007

Gai, K., Qiu, M., & Sun, X. (2018). A survey on Fintech. *Journal of Network and Computer Applications*, *103*, 262–273. doi:10.1016/j.jnca.2017.10.011

Gandomi, A., & Haider, M. (2015). Beyond the hype: Big data concepts, methods, and analytics. *International Journal of Information Management*, *35*(2), 137–144. doi:10.1016/j.ijinfomgt.2014.10.007

Gimpel, H., Rau, D., & Röglinger, M. (2018). Understanding Fintech start-ups–a taxonomy of consumer-oriented service offerings. *Electronic Markets*, *28*(3), 245–264. doi:10.100712525-017-0275-0

Gomber, P., Kauffman, R. J., Parker, C., & Weber, B. W. (2018). On the Fintech revolution: Interpreting the forces of innovation, disruption, and transformation in financial services. *Journal of Management Information Systems*, *35*(1), 220–265. doi:10.1080/07421222.2018.1440766

Gulamhuseinwala, I., Hatch, M., & Lloyd, J. (2017). *EY Fintech Adoption Index 2017: The rapid emergence of Fintech*. Retrieved from https://www.ey.com/Publication/vwLUAssets/ey-Fintech-adoption-index-2017/$FILE/ey-Fintech-adoption-index-2017.pdf

Gupta, M., & George, J. F. (2016). Toward the development of a big data analytics capability. *Information & Management*, *53*(8), 1049–1064. doi:10.1016/j.im.2016.07.004

Karagiannaki, A., Vergados, G., & Fouskas, K. (2017). The impact of digital transformation in the financial services industry: insights from an open innovation initiative in Fintech in Greece. *Mediterranean Conference on Information Systems (MCIS). Association For Information Systems*.

Kerényi, Á., & Müller, J. (2019). Brave New Digital World? Financial Technology and the Power of Information. *Financial and Economic Review, 18*(1), 5–32. doi:10.33893/FER.18.1.532

Kim, Y., Park, Y. J., Choi, J., & Yeon, J. (2015). An empirical study on the adoption of "Fintech" service: Focused on mobile payment services. *Advanced Science and Technology Letters, 114*(26), 136–140. doi:10.14257/astl.2015.114.26

Labrinidis, A., & Jagadish, H. V. (2012). Challenges and opportunities with big data. *Proceedings of the VLDB Endowment International Conference on Very Large Data Bases, 5*(12), 2032–2033. doi:10.14778/2367502.2367572

LaValle, S., Lesser, E., Shockley, R., Hopkins, M. S., & Kruschwitz, N. (2011). Big data, analytics and the path from insights to value. *MIT Sloan Management Review, 52*(2), 21–32.

Lee, I., & Shin, Y. J. (2018). Fintech: Ecosystem, business models, investment decisions, and challenges. *Business Horizons, 61*(1), 35–46. doi:10.1016/j.bushor.2017.09.003

Llorca, M. (2017). Les banques aux prises avec les Fintech [Banks grappling with FinTech]. *Economics and Politics*, (3), 43–58.

Louati, R., & Mekadmi, S. (2019). Toward a Conceptualization of Big Data Value Chain: From Business Problems to Value Creation. In K. Mezghani & W. Aloulou (Eds.), *Business Transformations in the Era of Digitalization* (pp. 76–92). IGI Global. doi:10.4018/978-1-5225-7262-6.ch005

McAfee, A., Brynjolfsson, E., Davenport, T. H., Patil, D. J., & Barton, D. (2012). Big data: The management revolution. *Harvard Business Review, 90*(10), 60–68. PMID:23074865

Mezghani, K. (2019). On the Need for Big Data Analytics in the Era of Digitalization. *Proceedings of the 34th conference of "International Business Information Management Association"*.

Miskam, S., & Eksan, S. H. R. (2018). Big Data and Fintech In Islamic Finance: Prospects and Challenges. *4th Muzakarah Fiqh & International Fiqh Conference.*

Moktadir, M. A., Ali, S. M., Paul, S. K., & Shukla, N. (2019). Barriers to big data analytics in manufacturing supply chains: A case study from Bangladesh. *Computers & Industrial Engineering, 128*, 1063–1075. doi:10.1016/j.cie.2018.04.013

Nasser, T., & Tariq, R. S. (2015). Big data challenges. *J Comput Eng Inf Technol, 4,* 3. doi: http://dx.doi.org/,9307(2) doi:10.4172/2324

Nicoletti, B. N., & Weis. (2017). Future of Fintech. Basingstoke, UK: Palgrave Macmillan.

Omarini, A. (2017). *The digital transformation in banking and the role of Fintechs in the new financial intermediation scenario.* MPRA Paper. Retrieved from https://mpra.ub.uni-muenchen.de/85228/

Palmié, M., Wincent, J., Parida, V., & Caglar, U. (2020). The evolution of the financial technology ecosystem: An introduction and agenda for future research on disruptive innovations in ecosystems. *Technological Forecasting and Social Change, 151*, 119779. doi:10.1016/j.techfore.2019.119779

Puschmann, T. (2017). Fintech. *Business & Information Systems Engineering, 59*(1), 69–7. doi:10.100712599-017-0464-6

Schaeffer, C., Haque, A., Booton, L., Halleck, J., & Coustasse, A. (2016). Big data management in United States hospitals: benefits and barriers. *Proceedings of the Business and Health Administration Association Annual Conference.*

Shamim, S., Zeng, J., Shariq, S. M., & Khan, Z. (2019). Role of big data management in enhancing big data decision-making capability and quality among Chinese firms: A dynamic capabilities view. *Information & Management, 56*(6), 103135. doi:10.1016/j.im.2018.12.003

Shmeljov, O. (2017). Banking in the Digital Age-Impact of Fintech on Banks' Business Models. *The Journal for Money and Banking, 66*(11), 22–28.

Smaoui Hachicha, Z., & Mezghani, K. (2018). Understanding Intentions to Switch Toward Cloud Computing at Firms' Level: A Multiple Case Study in Tunisia. *Journal of Global Information Management, 26*(1), 136–165. doi:10.4018/JGIM.2018010108

Thakor, A. V. (2019). Fintech and banking: What do we know? *Journal of Financial Intermediation.*

Vasiljeva, T., & Lukanova, K. (2016). Commercial banks and FINTECH companies in the digital transformation: Challenges for the future. *Journal of Business and Management*, 11.

Vassakis, K., Petrakis, E., & Kopanakis, I. (2018). Big data analytics: applications, prospects and challenges. In *Mobile Big Data* (pp. 3–20). Springer. doi:10.1007/978-3-319-67925-9_1

Verina, N., & Titko, J. (2019, May). Digital transformation: conceptual framework. In *International Scientific Conference Contemporary Issues in Business, Management and Economics Engineering.*

Verma, M. (2019). Data-oriented and Machine Learning Technologies in Fintech. *Fintechs and an Evolving Ecosystem*, 1.

Wamba, S. F., Akter, S., Edwards, A., Chopin, G., & Gnanzou, D. (2015). How 'big data' can make big impact: Findings from a systematic review and a longitudinal case study. *International Journal of Production Economics*, *165*, 234–246. doi:10.1016/j.ijpe.2014.12.031

Yan, J., Yu, W., & Zhao, J. L. (2015). How signaling and search costs affect information asymmetry in P2P lending: The economics of big data. *Financial Innovation*, *1*(1), 19. doi:10.118640854-015-0018-1

Zavolokina, L., Dolata, M., & Schwabe, G. (2016). Fintech–What's in a Name? *Thirty Seventh International Conference on Information Systems.*

## KEY TERMS AND DEFINITIONS

**Data-Driven Culture:** Organizational culture based on knowledge exchange within the firm and the data-based decision making.

**FinTech:** Innovative use of digital technologies in the financial sector. The term Fintech includes innovative financial solutions enabled by IT and start-up companies who deliver these solutions (Puschmann, 2017; Gimpel et al., 2018).

# Chapter 6
# The Transformation of Payments Industry:
## The European Regulatory Perspective

**Yasmin Ahmed Mahgoub**
*Department of Industrial Economics and Management, KTH Royal Institute of Technology, Sweden*

## ABSTRACT

*Mobile payment is an innovative area, which will speedily grow in the coming years. The mobile payments in the European vision stresses as payment industry transformation to the digital economy. This management transformation applied via seamless availability for the users and business in an open cross-country platform, to meet the user requirements and will not hinder the mobile payments industry transformation. Several regulations and directives have been made on the European Union context to realize this vision; however, there is still a challenging road ahead. Directives and regulations legislated to increase the confidence payment transformation and users by instructive the rights and obligations of all mobile payments parties, providing the requirements for transformation such as interoperability, likewise users requisites such as security and customer protection. This chapter provides a brief overview of these directives and raises to some critical matters that have to be taken into consideration for successful management transformation of a pan-European mobile payment service in the Fintech context.*

DOI: 10.4018/978-1-7998-7110-1.ch006

## 1. INTRODUCTION

Due to evolution in digitalization, various financial technologies are being innovated, such as financial technologies (Fintech) solutions. Notably, digitization of Fintech and using mobile devices is driving expectation for fast, convenient and borderless payments between users and providers in Fintech context, ecosystems, retail purchases and business transactions (Swift, 2018). Although the digitalization in the financial industry, mobile payments are still limited used in a limited area, due to numerous regulations and introducing to the market(Swift,2018).However, as high adoption of the mobile device in global and electronic shopping is activated, the mobile payments market has expanded largely (Humbani & Wiese,2019).

According to Juniper Research 2019, almost 2.1 billion consumers globally will be using mobile payments to pay or transfer money. According to Capgemini's World Payments, Report transaction-related non-cash conducted via mobile payments were estimated to 41.8 billion globally. About 71% (or 29.7 billion) were conducted via the payment apps and e-wallets provided by Fintech Techs to their customers (The Paypers, 2019).

The European Union, including 28 member states, has made steps concerning harmonization for cross-border payments within the Union (European Commission, 2015). Currently, 19 member states have the Euro as their local currency and the Payment Services Directives established the Single European Payments Area (SEPA), which enables euro payments between consumers and businesses under the same conditions member states. In this context, regulation can provide secure and interoperable payments services to provide value to consumers and businesses (Single euro payments area (SEPA), 2018). Besides, regulation can provide member states with the opportunity to enhance financial services and play a role in the transformation of the payment industry. In this context, transformation leads to network externalities among consumers and businesses (Union, 2015).

Digitalization is driving the transformation in the payment industry in Europe. The drivers of the transformation are including customer expectations, technology; competition. This driver is a challenging process for the financial institutions as banks, mobile network operators (MNOs), technology providers, merchants. The challenges remain in designing and provide interoperable mobile payments, include customer protection. Moreover, starting a universal open service rather than a closed payments solution, which organized and managed under restrict regulation for country level, regional level, and international level.

Regulation is the main driver for payment transformation in Europe. The main objective of current EU regulation established a single, competitive market to drive the payments transformation globally. The implementation of the Payment Services Directives (PSD 1, PSD2), and the introduction of pan-European direct payments services, and SEPA as a platform for euro-denominated transactions are challenging payments industry landscape to transform their business models (Swift, 2018; Bank, 2018).

Existing research in mobile payments trends is focusing on exploring t how mobile payments services platform developed from a technological perspective or business models and providers cooperation. However, there is a limit of studies that researchers have presents the role of regulations in mobile payments platform (Harris & Beasley, 2019).

This chapter objectively studies the phenomenon of European mobile payments in the Fintech context through analytical existing European legal frameworks (PSD2 and SEPA). The framework studied and examined to determine whether they can provide transformation to the rapidly evolving Fintech.

Therefore, this chapter aims to provide an overview of exploring the European regulation aspect to enable the transformation of mobile payments. The chapter perceived that the mobile payments are a promising area for the innovation of Fintech solutions, which will further contribute to economic incorporation of the European member states, and their inhabitants through providing a secure economical settle through convenient, open, secure transactions among business and users. Chapter similarly results identify the innovation that has occurred, through the cooperation among platform providers but can be a hinder cause of the regulation. Therefore, this chapter will explore the following essential questions:

***How does regulation stimulate the transformation of mobile payments in the Fintech context?*** This chapter organized as follows. "Mobile payments as Fintech trend" discusses it comparing traditional payments service, and "Mobile payment as a tool for management transformation" then **"**The driver for transformation: EU Regulation**"** analyzes and categorizes it with their framework. "Trends of recent European mobile payments as Fintech tool" explains "Regulation driven or delay transformation" and chapter finally finishes the work by "Conclusion".

## 2. MOBILE PAYMENTS AS FINTECH TREND

Mobile payments have existed since the early 2000s. Hundreds of mobile payments solutions, including access to electronic payments and Internet banking introduced in the EU such as Blue code from Austria, Swish from Sweden, Vipps from Norway, Portuguese Sibs; however, still introducing the service to the market is limited(Dahlberg et al., 2015). However, the current implementations of mobile payment service have many challenges that prevent the service from realizing their full prospective (Obaid et al., 2019). The rate adoption of the service is lower than estimated because of Risk, Trust, Security, and Privacy (Harris & Beasley, 2019).

A post-failure analysis (Gannamaneni et al., 2015)has developed an elaborate case (Paybox in Germany, Mobipay in Spain, Postfinance in Switzerland) to show that the failure factors of mobile payment platforms were lack of cooperation among the stakeholders, limited of technology standard, and low value-added for users and merchants compared to existing payment services

Likewise, M-maestro in Switzerland, Bart in Sweden, and O2 Wallet in the UK were failed (Ondrus et al., 2009; SvD, 2014). With the first of introducing of the Diners Club card in 1950 as a credit card, the electronic payments industry emerged to resemble into the now universal electronic money (Swift, 2018). Recently, mobile payments are solution enables customers to pay for products in retails, E-commerce, and invoice with a mobile device such as mobile phone, smart-phone, and tablets (Dahlberg et al., 2015). Technically, using payment services requires a bank account and card to pay for the sellers online or off-line (Kang, 2018). The process must exchange payment information with the bank in order to receive money.

The payment information sends to acquirer securely through the payment processor without sending directly to the bank subsequently that the payment made to merchants in the forthcoming. In addition, upon it, mobile payment service could be directly linked to banks and Fintech payment service that links with banks through IT companies (Kang, 2018). The rapid innovation in the financial technology and the rapid diffusion and adoption of smart-phones have enabled innovative mobile services that are transforming the mobile payments industry to Fintech environment (Iman, 2018). In this chapter, consider mobile payments as *'payments for a transaction with a mobile device, smart-phone, or bank account* debit/credit card *or* technological provider or mobile wallet (Dahlberg et al., 2015; Swift, 2018).In the context of mobile payments, Regulators cannot ignore the role of Fintech; one of the main challenges facing the Fintech service is the extensive and strict regulation to approve the service licences this emphasize that financial services are the most regulated industry (Lu, 2018;Dahlberg et al., 2015). Thus, this burdensome regulation played a significant role in slow the growth of mobile payments compared to further technological innovation (Evans & Pirchio, 2015; Liu et al., 2015).

Since the last decade, there is a movement of the launching of mobile payments platforms; the aim of these platforms provides mobile payments as mediators between consumers and business to achieve the Fintech service (Iman, 2018). Furthermore, Fintech has developed to be an inevitable area in the payment industry. In this context, regulators aim to design regulation to provide secure, portable, interoperable, off-line capable, accessible, reliable, valid, efficiently and privacy services to all parties (Gannamaneni et al., 2015; Dahlberg al., 2015). However, many mobile payments platforms have challenged to meet business and customer expectations, searching process about business models and the framework that may be required for an innovative transformation to achieve successful Fintech (Swift, 2018). Therefore, regulation, market situation, user's conceptions and existing financial access are the most obstacles are existing (International Finance Corporation, 2020).

## 3. MOBILE PAYMENT AS A TOOL FOR MANAGEMENT TRANSFORMATION

Certainly, the technology paly a significant role in changing the dynamics of financial business, to some extent because the digital technologies users became powerful in management transformation. Recently, the consumers have no obstacles such as geography, time, and price to purchasing service. Consequently, there has been a significant change in consumer behaviour and expectations in the financial industry, with consumers becoming extremely demanding (Best, 2020).

Considering the role the consumer now plays in management transformation' success. Digital transformation is an essential part of management transformation in financial technology (Fintech) developing. It is a great challenge for policymakers to stay on track by understanding and accepting the new change of payments industry transformation; the main challenges of Fintech to meet the update transformation are security and customer protection. The possible disruption of Fintech impact on the business of traditional financial intermediaries fixed to face the disruption of financial services (Pantielieieva et al., 2018).

The trends of Fintech in the areas of payments is mobile payments. Since Mobile payments have a high impact as a communication channel between business and customer, the companies, banks and retailers used this channel for the transformation to enter the digital transformation process (Liébana-Cabanillas et al., 2020). The transformation processes from traditional payments to mobile payments are reducing queues and waiting times, which is play a great role potential to compromise the consumers purchasing experience (Liébana-Cabanillas et al., 2020).

Mobile payments have been discussed for several years past with many tries to play a role in payments industry transformation. The need to regulate mobile payments emerges when mobile technology developed much further and disrupted financial services (Dahlberg et al., 2015). Therefore, Banks, MNOs, other non-bank institutions such as Fintech providers have cooperated to develop payment platform services that connect customers and retailers to meet the updated industry transformation.

In the European context, the main aim of the regulation is placing the transformation of European payments at the cutting edge. In this context, several challenges arise relating to interoperability, security, consumer protection and the status of non-banking institutions. The PDS2 and related regulations work to set rules renewal market infrastructure (ECB, 2020).

## 4. THE DRIVER FOR TRANSFORMATION: EU REGULATION

The Payment Service rule declares that payment services are transactions processed via direct debit, payment card or account-based payments, withdrawals or deposits of cash from a debit account. Similarly, payments through digital technology, telecommunication, or information are categorized as payment services. The Payment Service Act applied for the payment services in the European Economic Area (EEA) processed in Euro or national currencies EEA (Riksbank, 2015).

The European Commission set directives and regulations directly related to payment services. These directives drafts to be less detailed and allow some degrees of resilience in national legislation. The Directive tries to create a modern framework for the EU Member States on the foundation of national concern and particular characteristics of each EU Member States to offer rigorous rules. The aim is that the regulations have to be equal during the application in all Member States.

### 4.1 Payment Services Directives (PSD1 and PSD2)

The Payment Services Directive (PSD, Directive 2007/64/EC) substituted by PSD 2, Directive (EU) 2015/2366) is an EU Directive, controlled to regulate payment services and providers throughout the European Union (EU) and European Economic Area (EEA). The Directive aimed to increase pan-European competition and contribution in the payments industry from non-banks organizations and to provide payments by harmonizing customer protection and the rights and obligations for payment providers and users.

The necessity to regulate electronic money occurred when technology rapidly advanced to a level where electronic money was not only in payment cards. Recently technology continues innovating and establishing several payment systems such as Fintech and mobile payments. Here, the EU present the "electronic money" expression with the Directive 2000/46/EC and work to provide a single market setting (Gürkaynak & Yilmaz, 2015).

Probably, EU legislator faces challenges process to achieve equal opportunities and adequate security while avoiding hindering technological innovation. The legislator considers how the Payment Services Directive implemented in the national legislation of the different EU Member States. In the Payment Service Act (2010:751), the legislator aims to harmonize regulations for all retail-payment markets in the EU. This legal framework pursues the users' the accessibility, security, cheaper and effective payment services. Notably, the Payment Services Directive intentions to harmonize consumer protection rules and business accuracy. The Payment Service Act covers comprehensive rules and regulations relating to transaction fees, process and the speed of transaction between customers and business. Therefore, regulations establish confidence between consumers the payment service providers.

On October 8, 2015, the European Parliament proposed to create safer and more innovative European payments (PSD2, Directive (EU) 2015/2366). The new Directive aims to improve consumer protection during pay online, and promote the innovation of mobile payments through Fintech firms and establish digital single European market for safer payment services. In 2017, the EU Member stated incorporated the Directive into their national laws and regulations.

The EU banks are assertive this change with the new Payments Service Directive 2 (PSD2), which has come into force in January 2018 and more expansions came into application on September 2018. PSD2 brings several changes to the banks. The aim is to open banking that enables financial institutions to allow access to customer data to third party providers. This openness brings several technical challenges, however also brings many strategic opportunities, such as cooperating with Fintech providers, for the future of the payment industry.

The objectives of the PSD2 can be summarised as follows:

- Allow non-banks to offer payment services thereby opening the market up for competition
- Making market entry for payment institutions subject to license requirements
- Provide an adequate regulatory framework in which these non-banks would operate
- Currently, any payments institution that works at a European scale now needs a regulatory license for every single country. Under PSD regulation, only one license needed to serve all European areas.

Increases consumers' rights by reducing users' liability for unauthorized payments. In September 2019, updates in Directive for online purchasing Introduced strong security, privacy and users protection for all payments operators for the enhancement of consumer confidence. Banks, Fintech and third-party payment service providers regulated under to be able to initiate payments on behalf of customers.

## 4.2 Single Euro Payments Area (SEPA)

Parallel with the Payment Services Directive, in 2002, a comprehensive project initiated by the EU institutions called SEPA (Single Euro Payments Area) to synchronize the European retail-payment market structure. The differences between the Payment Services Directive and SEPA is that Directive aims to harmonize consumer protection regulations for conducting payment service activities, despite the fact SEPA aims to harmonize infrastructure and technical standards in the retail-payment market(SEPA, 2018).

Therefore, the Single Euro Payments Area (SEPA), the European payments-integration initiative applied through SEPA. The SEPA regulation regulated by the European Commission has established a single payment market in Europe. SEPA aims to enhance the efficiency of cross-border payments, as national payments within one country, therefore, will enable all cashless payments across the Euro area (European Commission, 2020). This regulation brought together all Euro electronic payments, including direct debit, debit card, credit card and bank transfer and acted as one platform. Through applying to SEPA standards enables to send and receive EUR-designated payments, both nationally and across EU borders, simply as the same terms and conditions in the home country (Single euro payments area (SEPA, 2018).

SEPA initiated based on self-regulation of the market and, the European banking sector has formed a European Payments Council (EPC) to manage and operate the work of SEPA. SEPA is mainly contained of three parts: SEPA Credit Transfer, SEPA Direct Debits and SEPA card payment. SEPA Credit Transfer is a EUR-denominated credit transfer's service that is simple to pay EUR-denominated invoices to another country in Europe as in the home country. SEPA Direct Debit assist that the payer authorizes firm in other countries in Europe to debit their account in the home country. All EUR denominated direct debit services are under the authority of SEPA Direct Debit. Direct debit services in other currencies are not affected.

To conclude that the Directives and SEPA work to create harmonization through cooperation among the exciting actors such as traditional banks and the new entrant's such as new' third-party provider and Fintech companies because of this lead to the innovation and sustainability of the electronic euro payments. Therefore, the Directives and SEPA has facilitated the setting-up of a collaboration between the payments stakeholder (Single euro payments area (SEPA, 2018).

## 5. TRENDS OF RECENT EUROPEAN MOBILE PAYMENTS AS FINTECH TOOL

The above section shed light on mobile payments framework under the regulation issued by the European Commission. On the other hand, it essentials to be recognized that mobile payments are rapidly innovating with lots of new entrants in the European market, such as innovative Fintech solutions. This section will present the current European mobile payments as Fintech trends. As shown in Figure 1, there is a top50 European mobile payment Fintech by Valuation. Briefly, this section will present the top three Fintech trends in Europe. Still, Europe remains a varied region with a wide range of payments systems and customer favourites. For instance, in transaction value in the mobile payments in the EU accounted for 85 million euros across the EU in 2019, expecting to reach 707millin Euros by 2024, as shown in Figure 2. However, in Germany, cash is still desired for payments 74% of all consumer payment transactions by volume compared to Sweden is widely considered Europe's most cashless economy; more than 70% survive without cash (Swift, 2018). On the other hand, still, the number of mobile payments users increased in Europe, as shown in Figure 3.

*Figure 1. The Recent mobile Fintech payment services (Fintech, 2019)*
*Source: Fintech, 2019*

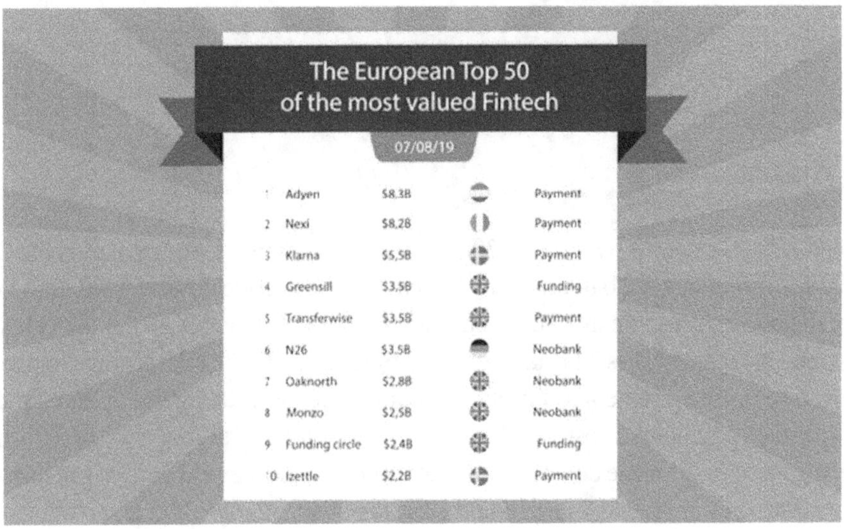


*Figure 2. Total Transaction Value in the Mobile Payments in EU*
*Source: Mobile POS Payments in Europe, 2020*

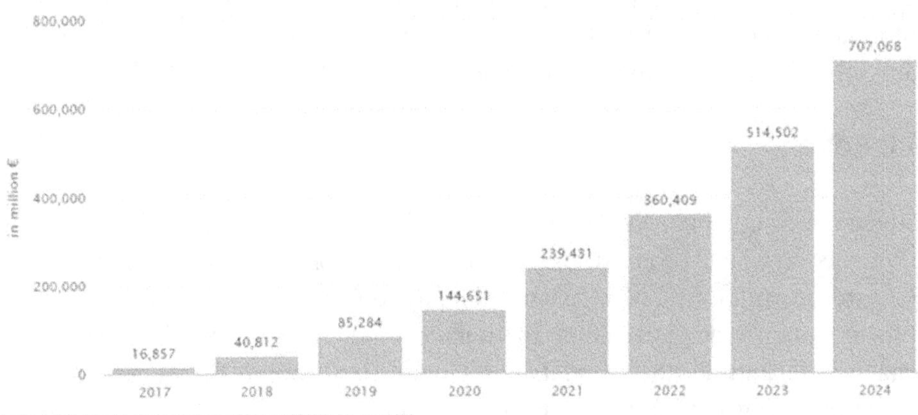

*Figure 3. Mobile Payments number of users in the EU*
*Source: Mobile POS Payments in Europe, 2020*

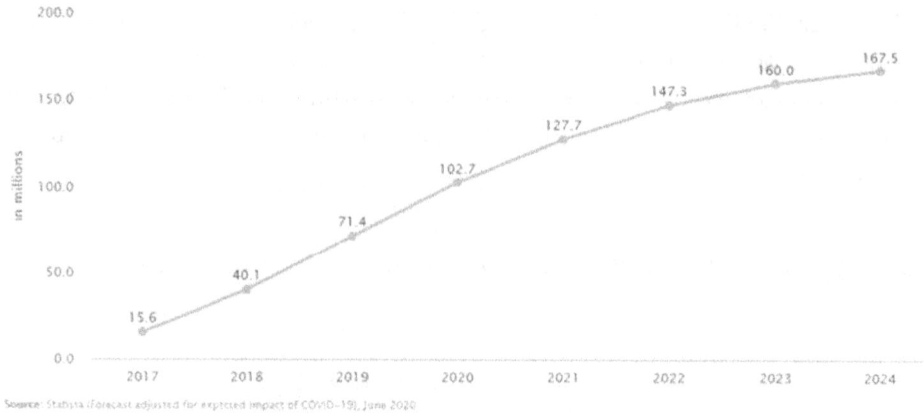


## 5.1 Klarna

Klarna was founded in Sweden in 2005 as Fintech payment service and since 2017 became a fully licensed bank that can be used of the mobile device or off-line in the store. Klarna is available in 17 markets and in 2019-estimated post-money valuation of 5.5bn USD that makes Klarna the largest Fintech globally. Klarna aims to provide innovative online payment solutions for consumers and merchants online, and in-store, direct payments, post-purchase payments and the uniqueness of Klarna is offering an option for the consumers is paying later. The central core of the business is to make shopping easy, simple and smarter; also, it considers as an alternative to credit cards. Klarna has a partnership choice with more than 200,000 merchants globally. For instance, IKEA, NIKE, ZARA, SAMSUNG. Through 2020, Klarna expects to earn one billion leads to the merchants across markets through these channels and brands. From Klarna annual report published in 2019, the financial information shows that Klarna has total operating revenue, net – USD 753m and Gross merchandise volume – USD 35bn (Klarna, 2019).

## 5.2 Adyen

Adyen is a Single Fintech platform founded in 2006 in the Netherlands to accept payments anywhere, on any device. The central core of their business is connecting the card network (Visa, MasterCard) globally to the local payments through new infrastructure. Ayden is enabling the joined commerce and providing customer's data to merchants. Furthermore, it allows merchants to accept payments in a single system, allowing revenue evolution online on mobile and at the point of sale, in 2017, obtaining purchasing licenses for Singapore, Hong Kong, Australia, and New Zealand. In 2020, Adyen obtained purchasing licenses for Malaysia also has a partnership with more than 4,500 businesses globally. For instance, Facebook, Spotify, Uber, Netflix, Spotify and L'Oréal. From Net income report of Adyen 2015-2019, the financial information shows that Ayden has currently valued at around 2.3 billion, and the revenue of 2019 reached 204 million Euro (Best, 2020).

## 5.3 Nexi

The Nexi is the biggest Italian payment service launched in 1939 as a bank then in November 2017 shifted their business to Nexi Payments. Nexi payments provide solutions for Merchant with authorization services, Insurance Companies, ATM Management, and Public Administration Interbank Corporate Banking, Clearing and Settlement and customer protection to prevent fraud. The core business of Nexi is to transfer money between companies and private companies. Likewise, Recently Nexi has outsourcing services and considered as the most prominent payment service that valued at €8.2 billion, including €1.7 billion of debt. Likewise, Nexi has 60% market share in card issuing and partnerships with about 150 Italian bank to provide innovative services for new purchasing technologies (e-commerce, NFC, mobile, contactless). (NEXI, 2020)

# 6. GENERAL DISCUSSION

This section will discuss how the EU regulations play a role transformation of payments and how mobile payments applied as a tool for Fintech. Regulation is challenging due to the complexity in dealing with differing requirements in various EU countries. Cooperation with financial intermediaries or independent service providers with an established global mobile payment platform could help banks and mobile network operators to make the entrance in the global remittance market. However, offering this service is still only interesting if the starting point of the payment transfer is in a country with significant adoption of mobile payments (Swift white paper, 2018).

Regulation considered as the most crucial factor to transfer the payment industry, in this context regulators has the mission to understand the environment of the industry also realize the challenges face the whole industry actors such as banks and MNOs. Afterwards, regulate frameworks to meet the management transformation through clear rules to promote the development of innovative mobile payments.

The main aim of policymakers is to encourage the expansion of mobile payments through cooperation among existing actors to bring economic and social benefits. Moreover, ensure the users protection and secure the payment process (European

Commission, 2019). Likewise, the higher in customer expectations, digital innovation in mobile apps, and the new entrance such as Alipay drive the changing EU regulatory, for instance, Payment Services Directive 2 (Paypers, 2019).

Mobile payments providers realized the cooperation strategy as an innovative process to the business transformation also realize how managing cooperation among competitors in the same market (Dahlberg et al., 2015; Barrett 2015; de Reuver et al., 2015). At this point, the regulation plays an essential role for interoperable mobile payment services through SEPA. In 2017, SEPA Credit Transfers and SEPA Direct Debited played a significant role in adding value to the Retail payments, which represents 73% of the EU total by value. Through SEPA, around 57 billion transactions handled through retail payment systems with an amount of €44 trillion.

In November 2018, the Euro system introduced Target Instant Payment Settlement (TIPS) as a new market infrastructure service launched. (TIPS) infrastructure enables payment and transferring fund in real-time 24/7. TIPS motivated the adoption of mobile payment at the pan-European level (Jessé, 2018). In April 2020, for example, the Swedish Central Bank settled agreement on the settlement of electronic payments in Swedish krona on the TIPS platform. However, application of instant payments in the pan European level offerings both a challenge and an opportunity for banks, it is predictable that TIPS platform, scope and use of central bank liquidity, will be a game-changer. (ECB, 2020)

Here we can observe SEPA and PSD governs security, data protection, competition, standardization and interoperability in the Fintech context. These factors are essential to ensure interoperability among mobile payments and Fintech providers. The most challenging mission for regulators is to achieve full security while avoiding hindering technological innovation. In this context, Payment service Directive that released in January 2018, flagged the way for much innovative mobile payment services with more supervisory authorities and technical standards, as well as being more in line with the secure consumer rights.

Approximately, of European countries such as Sweden, Spain and the Netherlands have adopted "payment service" regulations based on PDS Directives. As the rules are almost identical to the PDS Directives except for minor differences, National laws regarding payment services raise the same questions and concern the Directives raise. While the new Directives flagged the way for more ecosystem stockholders to create a platform for payment service and more Fintech solutions since Sweden and Spain are part of European economic integration.

## 7. REGULATION DRIVEN OR DELAY TRANSFORMATION

The body of the Single Euro Payments Area (SEPA), the European payments-integration initiative is relevant here. The SEPA regulation by the European Commission has established a single payment market in Europe. SEPA aims to improve the interoperability of cross-border payments, as payments within one country, therefore, will enable all cashless payments across the Euro area. This regulation brought together all Euro electronic payments, including direct debit, debit card, credit card and bank transfer and acted as one platform. Moreover, SEPA body aims to increase consumer choice and reduce transaction costs of the payment services, by facilitating that third parties may offer payment solutions. Furthermore, the new Payment Services Directive - PSD 2, aims to renovate the payment services area, by promoting a friendly solution, which affects significant challenges to the traditional banking model. For instance, Nordea bank in Denmark provides its customers with several options of payments such as Apple Pay, Samsung Pay and invoicing via Facebook Messenger.

The call of SEPA and PSD 1 and PSD 2 to harmonized interoperability standards provide an opportunity to cooperation among mobile payments stockholders for developing platforms. On of succeeding case in Sweden "SWISH" established in 2012 to provide Person to person payment. This platform involved the major Swedish banks, through a jointly owned clearing system for mass payments that developed payment in real-time. As of February 2019, Swish users have completed 1,000,000,000 payments, and 33315002 payments were made in February 2019. Additional succeed case Visa Europe was launched in 2014 to deliver Europe's largest commercial mobile contactless payments service in Spain and managed by CaixaBank, Orange, Telefónica and Vodafone. This platform covers more than 80 per cent of the Spanish market.

Regulations hinder innovation happens when regulators limit cooperation between firms for and therefore impede innovation activities. Besides, market-entry regulations delayed innovators to enter a particular market. Regulators' actions also may change the settings in the market, consciously or unintentionally. Thus, it becomes unattractive for firms to adopt or practice specific technological innovations (Blind, 2012; Aghion et al., 2005). After these regulatory restrictions lower the stimulus for technological evolution (Averch & Johnson 1962), delay innovation in financial services, and slow their accomplishment.

Typically, the intention of regulation is not to openly interfere with innovations and hinder their evolvement. As an alternative, it is to decrease potential negative influence related to disruptive technology innovation and to ensure security, equality in the market, efficiency and stability. At this point, where many uncertainties are existing, regulatory asymmetry is not reflected as a negative issue of the invention payments platforms.

## 8. CONCLUSION

This chapter addressed two fundamental issues. Firstly, to explore the role played by EU regulation in evolution, the transformation of mobile payments. The Directive on Payment Services (PSD) establishes a modern and comprehensive legal framework, which based on establishing a single market for payments in the EU. These rules aim to provide accessible, secure and efficient cross-border payments as 'domestic' payments among EU states. Moreover, the Directive on Payment Services (PSD) pursues to improve competition through open the payment markets to new players, therefore, enhancing better efficiency and cost-reduction. The Payment Services (PSD) offers an important legal platform for the Single Euro Payments Area (SEPA). However, implementation and authority are the responsibilities of each Member States.

Considering at the significant increase in electronic payments institutions and EU states being more in conformity with each new Directive and regulation concerning electronic payments, the EU shows to be on the right track in many ways to stimulate the innovate transformation to a single market for electronic payments services. However, the issue regarding the applicability of EU regulations to each member states payments remains a challenge.

Regulating with widely cases and definitions considered a step towards stimulating the transformation. Looking at the recent Fintech, the EU still notarize that take on a detailed and specific process for regulation might be a practical choice. However, the EU is still facing challenges of the new technologies and new business models that emerge. The EU might adopt a different approach, such as issuing broader definitions and conditions, as judging by the high amount of adjustments regarding electronic payment regulation.

Regulators should develop regulation on enhancing transformation, interoperability, data privacy and customer security. Thensued through regulatory frameworks such as the Payment Services (PSD 2) and the Euro payment single market (SEPA) regulation that assist competition via opening retail payments to third-party providers and new technologies such as Fintech. Also, via fostering the implementation of real-time payment solutions and develop infrastructures and platforms. Regulators have to balance the necessity for limiting risks with the desire to encourage innovation, protect customer privacy and reduce mobile payments and electronic commerce fraud, with the maximize goal of developing new mobile payment services ate the lower cost. The concentrate on enhancing competition and innovation may drive to a fragmentation of the retail payment market and customer experiences. Even recent innovations, such as Fintech solutions, tokenization are still in the deployment phase.

Mobile payments have been under evolution for years, though few initiatives by the single actor or cooperating actors have reached critical mass and market-broad adoption. This chapter suggests that establishing a clear perception of the direction of payments ecosystem competition and related regulation can accelerate services innovation and facilitate successful adoption of the Fintech components and business platforms. Cooperation involving central banks, commercial banks and mobile payments services stockholders related to the reducing of risks, platform costs and uncertainties are important for fostering a new business model for mobile payments without damaging the payments ecosystem, as it currently works. New competition regulatory policies are important for enabling new entrants to compete with large existing players such as banks.

EU countries should have the same objectives as the EU and try to achieve a high level of interoperability with adequate privacy and data security while welcoming Fintech solutions and new actors in electronic payment services and step forward with the transformation of the digital economy. Therefore, European states should invite new actors, instead of keeping obstacles of creating shared Europeans payment platform. This study encourages payments providers from different European states to shift the current niche of digital payment market to other domains involve several Europeans countries. Finally, the last stage of the development of EU payments regulation has witnessed a critical shift of goals. From establishing an integrated payments market to "regulation for transformation", through market infrastructure renewal.

## 9. FUTURE RESEARCH DIRECTIONS

The significance of this chapter is to derive from the intense pressure in the mobile payments platform in the Fintech context to play a role in management transformation. Management transformation via interoperable infrastructure, marketability, and decrease transaction cost. This chapter expected to provide an in-depth understanding to assist the transformation of mobile payments with a holistic regulatory perspective. Since this chapter, assumed that transformation could obtain value through cooperation among actors in the Fintech context. This chapter has a limitation that might be addressed in a future study. Future study can address the emerging trend of the strategic opportunities for innovative Fintech opened up by EU payments regulations. Then analyses several European countries Fintech and compare how they implemented EU Directives.

## REFERENCES

Aghion, P., Bloom, N., Blundell, R., Griffith, R., & Howitt, P. (2005). Competition and innovation: An inverted-U relationship. *The Quarterly Journal of Economics*, *120*(2), 701–728.

Averch, H., & Johnson, L. L. (1962). Behaviour of the firm under regulatory constraint. *The American Economic Review*, *52*(5), 1052–1069.

Bank, E. C. (2018). *Annual Report of the Euro Retail Payments Board 2017 /2018.* Retrieved October 13, 2001, from https://eur-lex.europa.eu/legal-content/EN/TXT/PDF/?uri=CELEX:32015L2366&from=EN

Barrett, M., Davidson, E., Prabhu, J., & Vargo, S. L. (2015). Service innovation in the digital age: Key contributions and future directions. *Management Information Systems Quarterly*, *39*(1), 135–154. doi:10.25300/MISQ/2015/39:1.03

Best, R. d. (2020, April 22). *Total net income of payments company Adyen from 2015 to 2019.* Retrieved August 22, 2020, from Statista: https://www.statista.com/statistics/870088/net-income-of-adyen/

Blind, K. (2012). The influence of regulations on innovation: A quantitative assessment for OECD countries. *Research Policy*, *41*(2), 391–400. doi:10.1016/j.respol.2011.08.008

Commission, E. (2019). *European Commission. Retrieved from Frequently Asked Questions: Making electronic payments and online banking safer and easier for consumers.* https://ec.europa.eu/commission/presscorner/detail/en/QANDA_19_5555

Dahlberg, T., Guo, J., & Ondrus, J. (2015). A critical review of mobile payment research. *Electronic Commerce Research and Applications*, *14*(5), 265–284. doi:10.1016/j.elerap.2015.07.006

de Reuver, M., Verschuur, E., Nikayin, F., Cerpa, N., & Bouwman, H. (2015). Collective action for mobile payment platforms: A case study on collaboration issues between banks and telecom operators. *Electronic Commerce Research and Applications*, *14*(5), 331–344. doi:10.1016/j.elerap.2014.08.004

ECB, t. E. (2020). *Sweden joins ECB's instant payments settlement platform.* Academic Press.

European Commission. (2015). Retrieved October 13, 2001, from https://europa.eu/rapid/press-release_IP-15-5792

Evans, D. S., & Pirchio, A. (2014). An empirical examination of why mobile money schemes ignite in some developing countries but flounder in most. *Review of Network Economics, 13*(4), 397–451. doi:10.1515/rne-2015-0020

Fintech, T. E. (2019). Retrieved from https://insights.invyo.io/europe/mapping/the-european-top-50-ofthe-most-valuedfintech

Gannamaneni, A., Ondrus, J., & Lyytinen, K. (2015, January). A post-failure analysis of mobile payment platforms. In *2015 48th Hawaii International Conference on System Sciences* (pp. 1159-1168). IEEE. 10.1109/HICSS.2015.141

Gürkaynak, G., & Yilmaz, I. (2015). Regulating payment services and electronic money: A comparative regulatory approach with a specific focus on Turkish legislation. *Computer Law & Security Review, 31*(3), 401–411. doi:10.1016/j.clsr.2015.03.009

Harris, M. A., Chin, A. G., & Beasley, J. (2019). *Mobile payment adoption: An empirical review and opportunities for future research. Southern Association of Information Systems*. SAIS.

Humbani, M., & Wiese, M. (2019). An integrated framework for the adoption and continuance intention to use mobile payment apps. *International Journal of Bank Marketing, 37*(2), 646–664. doi:10.1108/IJBM-03-2018-0072

Iman, N. (2018). Is mobile payment still relevant in the fintech era? *Electronic Commerce Research and Applications, 30*, 72–82. doi:10.1016/j.elerap.2018.05.009

International Finance Corporation. (2020). *IFC Mobile Money Scoping Reports 2020*. Author.

Jessé, M. B. D. (2018). TARGET Instant Payment Settlement: The Euro system's response to an evolving payments landscape. *Journal of Payments Strategy & Systems, 12*(4), 322–327.

Kang, J. (2018). Mobile payment in Fintech environment: Trends, security challenges, and services. *Human-centric Computing and Information Sciences, 8*(1), 1–16. doi:10.118613673-018-0155-4

Klarna. (2019). *Annual report*. Retrieved August 20, 2020, from https://www.klarna.com/assets/2020/04/Klarna_Bank_AB_publ_Annual_Report_2019_EN.pdf

Liébana-Cabanillas, F., García-Maroto, I., Muñoz-Leiva, F., & Ramos-de-Luna, I. (2020). Mobile Payment Adoption in the Age of Digital Transformation: The Case of Apple Pay. *Sustainability, 12*(13), 5443. doi:10.3390u12135443

Lu, L. (2018). Decoding Alipay: mobile payments, a cashless society and regulatory challenges. *Butterworths Journal of International Banking and Financial Law*, 40-43.

Mobile POS Payments in Europe. (2020). Retrieved August 20, 2020, from Statista: https://www.statista.com/outlook/331/102/mobile-pos-payments/europe#market-revenue

NEXI. (2020). *The Nexi Group*. Retrieved August 20, 2020, from NEXI: https://www.nexi.it/en/about-us/brand/group.html

Nordea. (2020). *Mobile payments*. Retrieved June 13, 2020, from https://www.nordea.com/en/our-services/cashmanagement/oursolutions/mobile-payments/

Obaid, M., Bayram, Z., & Saleh, M. (2019). Instant secure mobile payment scheme. *IEEE Access: Practical Innovations, Open Solutions*, *7*, 55669–55678. doi:10.1109/ACCESS.2019.2913430

Ondrus, J., Lyytinen, K., & Pigneur, Y. (2009). Why mobile payment fail? Towards a dynamic and multi-perspective explanation. In *The 42nd Hawaii International Conference on System Science (HICSS'09)*. IEEE.

Pantielieieva, N., Krynytsia, S., Khutorna, M., & Potapenko, L. (2018, October). FinTech, transformation of financial intermediation and financial stability. In *2018 International Scientific-Practical Conference Problems of info communications. Science and Technology (PIC S&T)* (pp. 553-559). IEEE. 10.1109/INFOCOMMST.2018.8632068

Paypers, T. (2019). *European payments council*. Retrieved August 20, 2020, from https://www.europeanpaymentscouncil.eu/sites/default/files/inline

Sood, A., James, G. M., Tellis, G. J., & Zhu, J. (2012). Predicting the path of technological innovation: SAW vs. Moore, Bass, Gompertz, and Kryder. *Marketing Science*, *31*(6), 964–979. doi:10.1287/mksc.1120.0739

Stewart, L. A. (2010). The impact of regulation on innovation in the United States: A cross-industry literature review. *Information Technology & Innovation Foundation, 6.*

SvD. (2014). *Swedbank lägger ned betallösningen Bart* [Swedbank closes down the payment solution Bart]. Retrieved June 20, 2020, from www.svd.se/naringsliv/swedbank-lagger-ned-betallosningen-bart_8913772

Swift White Paper. (2018). Retrieved August 20, 2020, from https://www.swift.com/sites/default/files/documents/swift_whitepaper_transformation_european_payments_landscape.pdf

The History of Electronic Payments. (n.d.). http://blog.e-money.com/the-history-of-electronic-payments-part-1/

Union, O. J. (2015). *Directives.* Retrieved June 13, 2020, from https://eur-lex.europa.eu/legal-content/EN/TXT/PDF/?uri=CELEX:32015L2366&from=EN

# Section 3

# Empirical Experiences and Applications

# Chapter 7
# Managerial Challenges Under FinTech:
## Evidence From Zimbabwean Commercial Banks

**Mufaro Dzingirai**
*Midlands State University, Zimbabwe*

## ABSTRACT

*FinTech has become an increasingly important phenomenon around the world in recent times. This is substantiated by a growing interest from researchers, academicians, and policymakers. While the adoption of FinTech appears to be widely regarded as a strategic priority for financial institutions worldwide, the empirical evidence on the managerial challenges under FinTech is very scant, especially from the perspective of developing countries. With this in mind, this chapter aims at providing empirical evidence on the managerial challenges emanating from FinTech within the context of Zimbabwean commercial banks. The study establishes seven challenges, namely, customer retention, regulatory compliance, technology risk, increased competition, cyber-attacks, the inadequacy of IT employees, and system downtimes. The recommendations to deal with these challenges are proffered and the suggestions for further study are captured.*

DOI: 10.4018/978-1-7998-7110-1.ch007

## INTRODUCTION

During the past three decades, the financial sectors of both developed and developing countries have witnessed a paradigm shift whereby the Information and Communication Technology (ICT) is driving digital transformation (Zhao, Tsai, & Wang, 2019). This has led to the manifestation of the concept of FinTech which is widely accepted as a game-changer in the financial sector. FinTech as a phenomenon has pressured the management of financial institutions to relentlessly pursue digital transformation more aggressively than before (Kotarba, 2016). In fact, new business models are being adopted by strategic managers of financial institutions as a response to FinTech. This is not surprising given that strategic managers must constantly monitor the changes in technology so that they can keep abreast of technological advancement. Accordingly, it appears that the future of the financial institutions of the 21st century is based on the adoption of FinTech. It is necessary to note that FinTech is an abbreviation of finance technology.

In light of the above, according to Gomber, Kauffman, Parker, & Weber (2018), FinTech refers to an integration of finance technologies. The technologies include robo-advice, crowdfunding, mobile payments, social trading, cryptocurrency, blockchain, and insurance just to mention a few. In light of recent developments in FinTech, it is becoming extremely hard to ignore the existence of the managerial challenges related to the adoption of FinTech. Admittedly, it is salient to observe that mobile payments, as a form of FinTech service, are growing at an exponential rate since they provide more accessibility of payment services (Kim, Choi, Park, & Yeon, 2016). Moreover, the banks are embracing social media which is forcing the management of banks to adopt new operation procedures (Hennig-Thurau, Hofacker, & Bloching, 2013). Therefore, managers are confronted with a plethora of challenges under FinTech.

The disruptive market innovations are now increasingly transforming the financial sectors of many countries. Technological innovations in the finance sector can lead to operational efficiency, controlling risks, and lowering the costs of transactions. (Zhao et al., 2019). This means that FinTech is the need of the hour. The banks are experimenting with FinTech through digitalizing and modernizing their systems and processes. Technological advancement has spurred distinct financial innovations that have transformed many banking services, products, organizational structures, and production processes. For instance, technological advancement has easily facilitated the shift from human judgment towards automation of consumer data. Nonetheless, FinTech is posing unique managerial challenges for banks, microfinance institutions, finance companies, and insurance institutions.

Going forward, it is worth mentioning that the finance sector is associated with cut-throat competition. In this regard, the financial institutions that have a high propensity to innovate are more likely to enjoy a sustainable competitive advantage in the market. Given this information, it appears that the commercial banks of the 21st century are embracing FinTech so as to outsmart competitors. Despite the potential benefits of embracing FinTech by banks, not much is known about the managerial challenges associated with FinTech. This means that there is an urgent need to conduct empirical studies in order to advance our understanding of FinTech.

The developments and debates surrounding the suitability of FinTech in the banking sector had supported the fact that strategic managers can be confronted by a plethora of challenges under FinTech especially at the implementation stage. Nonetheless, to the author's best knowledge, little is known about managerial challenges under FinTech. The qualitative methodology was adopted in this study. The chapter's objectives are to capture worldwide controversies associated with managerial challenges under FinTech and to review the importance of FinTech in the banking sector as well to capture how the management of commercial banks perceive the managerial challenges associated with FinTech. Accordingly, the current study provides evidence to practice and policy, and sets out the future research agenda.

## BACKGROUND

FinTech is a topical phenomenon when it comes to the financial sector in recent times but its concept is old since the concept is linked to Trans-Atlantic transmission cable (Sung & Leong, 2018). In the existing body of literature concerning FinTech, there are mainly two stages, namely, The First Wave and Second Wave. During the First Wave, the supporting technologies were including mainframe computers and Trans-Atlantic transmission cable of 16 August 1958 just to mention a few. Going forward, the Second Wave is characterized by technologies like the internet and the Internet of Things (IoT) (Sung & Leong, 2018). With this in mind, it is apparent that FinTech plays a crucial role in the financial sector as it redefines the business models of financial institutions across the globe. It is worth noting that traditional banking has been transformed significantly. Undoubtedly, traditional technologies have been overridden by new types of financial technologies which received much attention from researchers, academicians, and practitioners (Gomber, Koch, & Siering, 2017; Puschmann, 2017).

Drawing from the existing literature on FinTech, it is apparent that there is a plethora of definitions of FinTech. In this regard, different scholars have managed to define FinTech from different perspectives and therefore, there is no consensus on the definition of FinTech. According to Micu & Micu (2016), FinTech refers to a plethora of innovations and technologies adopted by financial institutions so as to facilitate trading, corporate business transactions, and interaction with consumers. In a broad sense, Shim & Shin (2016) defined FinTech as new technology that encompasses peer to peer (P2P) lending, third-party payment, risk management, authentication, and insurance products. On the other hand, Cizinska, Krabec, & Venegas (2016) defined FinTech as an emerging economic sector that is constituted of firms that use technology in a manner that fosters efficiency in the provision of financial services. Although there is ambiguity associated with the concept of Fintech, it can be deduced that FinTech is closely linked to a combination of technologies and innovative business models that disrupt financial services.

Going forward, it is salient to observe that technology has transformed how the financial sector operates. In this regard, it is widely recognized that disruptive technology has enabled financial institutions to broaden access to products and services, serve customers more efficiently and effectively, augment partnerships with external innovators, and introduce new products and services. It is of great importance to highlight that the financial sectors of both developed and developing countries are witnessing online banking, digital data exchange platforms, e-commerce, mutual lending sites, high-frequency trading, robo-advice, and digital currencies owing to technological advancement in the context of financial services. Thus, this state of affairs demands the strategic managers to have a deeper understanding of the managerial challenges associated with FinTech.

It is widely accepted that the United States of America (USA) has the largest number of FinTech adopters and then followed by United Kingdom (UK), Canada, India, and Germany (Haddad & Hornuf, 2016). The UK is widely recognized in the world as one of the leading nations when it comes to the development of FinTech as the government is very ambitious to make it the global capital of FinTech (Ernst & Young, 2016). In this regard, London is the pioneer in terms of FinTech regulation as substantiated by the fact that more than 1 600 FinTech companies were registered as at 30 April 2019 and it is expected that this number will double by end of 2030 (Helm, Low, & Townson, 2019). Given this development in the UK, it is estimated that an additional 100 000 jobs will be created in the FinTech sector by the end of 2020 (Oakley, Hughes, Gulati, & Miscampbell, 2018).

In the case of India, the adoption of FinTech has increased at a faster rate. It is interesting to observe that the scope for growth of FinTech services in India has had redefined the way firms and customers transact business on a daily basis. Moreover, investment in FinTech services has increased at a faster rate. For instance, the investment in FinTech increased from US$4.05 billion as of 2013 to US$12.2 billion as of 2014 and then increased to US$19.1 billion as of 2015 (Kandpal & Mehrotra,

2019). This suggests that the investment in FinTech has increased by 371% as from 2013 to 2014. It is within this context that India has witnessed the highest expected return on investment of 29% when it comes to FinTech which is above the global average of 20% (Nishmitha, 2018).

Furthermore, there is a huge market for FinTech services in India provided that cash payment constitutes 87% of all payments, 40% of the total population is not yet linked to banks, 90% of small business are not yet connected to formal financial institutions, internet penetration is steadily increasing, and mobile usage increased from 53% in 2017 to 64% in 2018 (Kandpal & Mehrotra, 2019). It is interesting to note that the Indian government is playing a crucial role in promoting the usage of FinTech products and services through educating and encouraging consumers to move towards digitalized business transactions. However, the finance sector in India is still facing a plethora of challenges with respect to new business models that are supported by FinTech like P2P transactions, data security, and crowdfunding (Nishmitha, 2018).

Within the context of Sub-Saharan Africa, the adoption of FinTech has increased at an exponential rate. The FinTech in Sub-Saharan Africa is led by three countries, namely, South Africa, Kenya, and Nigeria (Ernst & Young, 2019). It is of great importance to highlight that these three countries are shaping financial innovation in the finance industry. Given the fact that FinTech in Sub-Saharan Africa is at the infant stage, there is a plethora of challenges being faced by managers when it comes to the successful implementation of FinTech. These challenges include among others cyber risk, scalability, big data use, employee retention, customer retention, use of artificial intelligence, and regulatory compliance (International Monetary Fund, 2019).

In light of the above, Zimbabwe is trying very hard to invest in FinTech so as to improve the consumer experience. Admittedly, the total monthly value of digital payment transactions has increased by 18% as from January 2019 to May 2019 whereas corresponding monthly volumes increased by an average of 23% (RBZ, 2019a). During the same period, electronic payments worth of RTGS$ 87 billion were transacted. Moreover, mobile transactions are increasing in Zimbabwe owing to high mobile penetration in Zimbabwe. However, a lot is needed to be done so as to perform better in terms of FinTech adoption as compared to other countries in Sub-Saharan Africa like Kenya. It is within this context that Bara & Mudzingiri (2016) recommended that the government of Zimbabwe must promote financial innovation through heavy investment in infrastructure and technology that supports financial innovation in the banking sector.

## Need for FinTech in Banking Sector

It is evident that banks across the globe are embracing FinTech. There is no doubt that the banking sector of the 21st century is experiencing rapid development and expansion of technology as the traditional banking business is experiencing noticeable changes (Vasiljeva & Lukanova, 2016). Notably, the majority of banks are moving away from traditional banking systems to FinTech in an attempt to create a sustainable competitive advantage in the banking sector. In this regard, it is widely known that the banking sector is mainly associated with the cut-throat competition since all banks offer similar products and services. It is within this context that some banks are making collaboration arrangements with FinTech firms so as to easily gain trust from their consumers (Juengerkes, 2016). For instance, one of the largest banks in the US, namely, Capital One has managed to acquire Level Money which was a FinTech start-up (Li, Spigt, & Swinkels, 2017). It is interesting to observe that FinTech companies are investing more in the banking sector so as to make financial services more customized and accessible (Dorfleitner, Hornuf, Schmitt, & Weber, 2017). In this regard, many consumers are shifting their preferences and needs from face-to-face transactions to online financial transactions (Thompson, 2017).

Despite the emerged pattern of FinTech wave in the banking sector worldwide, traditional banks have a very limited digital footprint as they are not transforming or adjusting their business models. It is of great importance to mention that traditional banks are still sticking to the brick-and-mortar banking approach which is too costly when compared to the adoption of FinTech. More so, it is discouraging to note that these banks are constrained when it comes to responding to new customer needs and preferences since such banks pursue non-digital initiatives. Nonetheless, some consumers are still showing a high level of affinity for face-to-face financial transactions rather than digital financial transactions (Konigsheim, Lukas & Noth, 2017). To this end, these banks are more likely to be negatively affected by the rapid growth in digitalization in the banking sector.

Going forward, banks that have managed to embrace FinTech or re-designing their business models can formulate their business strategies in a sustainable competitive way as compared to traditional banks. Drawing from the extant literature on FinTech in the banking sector, banks that are effectively embracing FinTech are widely recognized as transformational banks or digital banks (King, 2014). Many banks around the world are embracing FinTech in order to enjoy the benefits that are associated with the effective implementation of FinTech. Firstly, the effective implementation of FinTech permits the bank to customized financial services. It is within this context that Bugrov, Dietz, & Poppensieker, (2017) suggested that FinTech allows the customers to enjoy better financial services as they gain access to state-of-art software and technology. The young generation appears to be digital natives who have a high propensity for technology. Therefore, it is of great importance for the banks of the 21st century to respond to their needs and preferences through effective implementation of FinTech that leads to customized financial services. In a similar vein, Skan, Dickerson, & Masood (2015) accentuated that FinTech ensures the provision of good quality financial services.

Secondly, digital innovations like mobile money can stimulate financial inclusion. Disruption digital innovation has broadened access to financial products and services. It is imperative to note that Sy, Maino, Massara, Perez-Saiz, & Sharma (2019) documented that FinTech can allow the unbanked population to have access to finance thereby fostering financial inclusion in both more-developed and less-developed countries. This implies that FinTech can enable the banking sector to reach unserved poor people who account for a large portion of the total population in developing countries like Kenya and Zimbabwe. More strikingly, Ahamed & Mallick (2019) underscored that FinTech ensures financial inclusion of Small and Medium Enterprises (SMEs) which can reduce their limited access to financial resources. This suggests that banks can adapt FinTech like mobile money as a strategic move to capture the new segments of customers (poor people and SMEs). Therefore, banks can foster financial inclusion through FinTech.

Thirdly, cost-cutting is another benefit that can be enjoyed by banks after successfully implementing FinTech. Drawing from the available mainstream literature on FinTech, it is widely accepted that the adoption of FinTech in the banking sector can result in innovative and cost-effective ways of conducting business like allowing customers to access financial service on the comfort of their homes and allowing 24/7 access to financial services (Ahamed & Mallick, 2019; Drasch, Schweizer, & Urbach, 2018; Philippon, 2018). In a similar vein, Hirt & Willmott (2014) documented that the successful implementation of FinTech can pressurize banks to embrace new business models in an attempt to reduce costs. This suggests that the banks can easily formulate cost-cutting strategies such as reducing the loan approval process since some manual steps can be done electronically.

Fourthly, advancements in new technologies permit banks to improve their operational efficiency. In this regard, Dorfleitner et al., (2017) highlighted that FinTech can improve efficiency owing to the automatization of their services. This implies that automatization of the operations of banks can result in efficiency when it comes to processes such as lending process. Given the automatization of the bank's operation, it is very easy to reduce operation costs by processing every transaction online. Notably, banks can re-design their business models, modernize their systems, and digitalize their process in a manner that improves operational efficiency.

Fifthly, shorter turnaround time is another benefit that can be enjoyed by banks after successfully implementing FinTech. Drawing from the extant mainstream literature on FinTech, it is widely accepted that the adoption of FinTech in the banking sector can result in speeding up otherwise time-consuming operations such as loan processing (Idowu, Ngumi, & Muturi, 2016). This suggests that the problems associated with manual banking like long turnaround time have justified the need for FinTech in the banking sector. It is within this context that Domeher, Frimpong, & Appiah (2014) recommended that the banks should adopt modern banking technologies in order to save time for customers. It is necessary to highlight that FinTech supports real-time transactions in the banking sector. With the adoption of FinTech in the banking sector, customers can have real-time access to information concerning loan eligibility, account balances, interest rates, transfer of funds between accounts, and online bill payment.

## CHALLENGES UNDER FINTECH

This part covers the challenges or risks associated with FinTech. The challenges are explained in detail as follows:

### Cybersecurity Challenge

Cybersecurity is one of the challenges which is mainly associated with FinTech. In this regard, it is widely accepted that the adoption of FinTech has led to a rapid increase in cyber and financial crime. The issue of cybersecurity is a great concern for both the largest global financial institutions and the smallest financial institutions (Prescott & Larose, 2016; Vardi, 2017). The integration of traditional banking systems and FinTech companies can raise great concerns about data privacy since FinTech companies gather voluminous customer data that can be targeted by hackers (Kandpal & Mehrotra, 2019). Moreover, some new bank customers are more exposed to hackers since they may have little awareness of cybersecurity risk. Drawing from the existing literature on FinTech, the issues like threats to cybersecurity, and infringement of customer's data privacy are related to the challenge of cybersecurity (Prescott & Larose, 2016). Surprisingly, some issues are linked to the usage of FinTech for illegal purposes such as tax evasion, contraband transactions, and money laundering (Campenon, 2016; Nakaso, 2016).

### Regulation Challenge

Regulation is another formidable challenge under FinTech. According to Kaveri (2014), there is a public outcry about a sharp increase of frauds that seems to reveal a weak regulation of FinTech when it comes to data privacy and security. In a similar vein, a lack of clear regulation appears to encourage a high affinity for risky behavior in the financial sector (Munteanu, 2016). Although customers are willing to embrace cryptocurrencies and blockchain, there are potential threats to these FinTech elements since there is a lack of an appropriate legal framework that is linked to cryptocurrencies and blockchain.

## High Operational Risk

It is of great importance to mention that FinTech is mainly associated with the introduction of innovative products and services that may lead to an increase in operational risk owing to the complexity of financial services delivery. For instance, the implementation of banking information technology systems may be ineffective due to the ineffective change management process. Moreover, there is also another operational risk associated with the adaptability of the banking information technology systems. In this regard, the bank can depend on the Robo-advisers but can also encounter technical dilemmas linked to overly complex algorithms, static client information, overly simplistic algorithms, and errors in algorithms. Admittedly, some of the operational risks are linked to information technology outages owing to unreliable provision of internet service and electricity especially in developing countries like Zimbabwe. To this end, there is no doubt that the effectiveness of digital modes of offering financial services relies on reliable internet and electricity.

## Liquidity Challenge

It is salient to observe that the adoption of technology and innovations in the financial sector creates avenues of opportunities for customers to instantly change between different savings accounts in order to earn a better return. Although this can promote efficiency, it may increase the volatility of deposits and affect customer loyalty negatively. This state of affairs can lead to an increase in liquidity risk for banks.

## Strategic Risk

The banks may suffer stiff competition from big FinTech firms. In this regard, the unbundling of banking services to FinTech companies reduces the profitability of banks. This suggests that the existing financial institutions can lose sales provided that the new entrants can utilize digital technology more efficiently and effectively. It is within this context that Al-Ajlouni & Al-Hakim (2018) underscored that there is a decline in profit margin and sales of banks since the banks are under competitive pressure from FinTech firms that are luring a substantial portion of their customers.

## Customer Management Challenge

The financial sector is dominated by cut-throat competition for customer acquisition and retention. Notably, many customers may use several financial services from FinTech companies for different needs which creates a big challenge when it comes to customer management. With the adoption of FinTech, the issue of double-dipping creates a formidable challenge for ensuring effective customer management in the financial sector.

## Technology Integration Challenge

Technology integration is another great challenge that can be faced under FinTech. Given a plethora of FinTech products and services, it is not surprising to observe that combining the FinTech software packages with the existing banking systems is challending. Although banks may focus on internally developed FinTech, there is also a dire need to create a joint venture or partnership with FinTech start-ups. It is also worth mentioning that banks may face challenges when they want to integrate with new FinTech companies because some FinTech firms are not willing to comply with regulatory requirements (Gomber et al., 2017). Additionally, Al-Ajlouni & Al-Hakim (2018) suggested that FinTech firms have a high IT risk because some of the new FinTech companies have a limited ability to control IT risks.

# COMMERCIAL BANKS IN ZIMBABWE

It is deemed necessary to look at the overall performance of the banking sector in Zimbabwe. In this regard, it is interesting to note that the Zimbabwean banking sector has performed satisfactorily as from January 2019 to December 2019. The indicators of performance in the banking sector such as earnings performance, asset quality, capital levels, and liquidity were satisfactory. Notably, some of the indicators of financial soundness are captured in the table below:

As indicated in Table 1, the overall performance of the banking sector in Zimbabwe was satisfactory. In this regard, it is interesting to note that the Zimbabwean banking sector remained adequately capitalized since the average adequacy (39.56%) and tier 1 ratio (27.87%) were above the minimum requirement of 12% and 8% respectively.

Going forward, the Zimbabwean banking sector has not been spared from technological innovations, which are disrupting the financial landscape (Chirima & Chikochi, 2016). The banking sector of Zimbabwe is comprised of 19 banking institutions. In this respect, 13 are commercial banks, 5 are building societies, and 1 saving bank. In the context of Zimbabwean commercial banks, it is imperative to

*Table 1. Financial soundness indicators*

| Key Indicators | Benchmark | Dec-18 | Jun-19 | Sep-19 | Dec-19 |
|---|---|---|---|---|---|
| | | | | | |
| **Total Assets ($ bn)** | - | 13.98 | 23.54 | 40.99 | 60.64 |
| **Total Loans & Advances ($ bn)** | - | 4.22 | 6.17 | 8.35 | 12.63 |
| **Net Capital Base ($ bn)** | - | 1.83 | 3.31 | 5.35 | 9.75 |
| **Total Deposits ($ bn)** | - | 10.32 | 16.92 | 21.51 | 34.50 |
| **Net Profit ($ bn)** | - | 0.43 | 0.93 | 2.09 | 6.41 |
| **Return on Assets (%)** | - | 4.57 | 5.11 | 7.91 | 8.99 |
| **Return on Equity (%)** | - | 20.59 | 20.95 | 26.85 | 33.02 |
| **Capital Adequacy Ratio(%)** | 12.00 | 30.27 | 32.64 | 41.24 | 39.56 |
| **Tier 1 Ratio (%)** | 8.00 | 23.84 | 27.24 | 27.92 | 27.87 |
| **Loans to Deposits (%)** | 70.00 | 40.71 | 36.49 | 38.82 | 36.6 |
| **Non-Performing LoansRatio (%)** | 5.00 | 6.92 | 3.95 | 3.23 | 1.75 |
| **Liquidity Ratio (%)** | 30.00 | 70.66 | 64.77 | 76.54 | 72.42 |

Source: RBZ, (2020).

note that they are utilizing digital innovations such as digital finance, psychometric credit scoring models, mobile banking, and biometric technology (RBZ, 2020). Admittedly, commercial banks in Zimbabwe are taking into account the significant role of FinTech in promoting efficient and effective service delivery as they are currently harnessing and leveraging technology in order to offer a wide range of products and services. More interestingly, Commercial Bank of Zimbabwe (CBZ) which is the largest commercial bank is Zimbabwe has signed a Memorandum of Association (MoA) with an American firm, namely, Apollo Fintech (Zwinoira, 2020). In this respect, Apollo Fintech will create and operate three national FinTech solutions in Zimbabwe (Dumont, 2020). In an attempt to reduce the additional risks associated with FinTech, RBZ has managed to come up with the National Fintech Steering Committee (NFSC) (RBZ, 2019a).

Even though the financial performance of commercial banks in Zimbabwe is satisfactory, the uptake of digital banking services is at a slow rate. It is discouraging to note that only 13% of banking customers in Zimbabwe are using e-banking products (Maswaure & Choga, 2016). On the other hand, the provision of cyber-security is a big challenge which is faced by banks in Zimbabwe (RBZ, 2020). This may be the reason why banking customers in Zimbabwe are hesitant when it comes to the usage of digital technology. There is no doubt that the customers are more worried about the security of their personal information when making online business transactions. Nonetheless, some scholars like Mavaza (2019) are of the opinion that there is a greater chance for FinTech growth in the banking sector given the introduction of new digital technologies and improvement of internet connectivity in Zimbabwe.

## RESEARCH METHODOLOGY

### Research Philosophy

The author employed interpretivism as a philosophical lens that supports this study on managerial challenges under FinTech with a particular focus on Zimbabwean commercial banks. It is widely known that interpretivism is usually used in qualitative research in which the phenomenon is being investigated within its distinctive context (Bryman & Bell, 2011; Creswell, 2014). With this in mind, the interpretivism was the most appropriate philosophical lens for qualitative methods that were adopted in this study (Saunders & Rojon, 2014). Interpretivism was justified by its appropriateness for the creation of a new, in-depth, and richer understanding of the managerial challenges under FinTech through the gathering of multiple opinions and experiences of managers of commercial banks in Zimbabwe.

### Research Design

In line with the philosophical assumptions of interpretivism, this study applied exploratory research design in an attempt to explore the challenges under FinTech in the unique context of Zimbabwean commercial banks. Research design is a general plan of the researcher that can be used to answer his or her research question(s) (Saunders, Lewis, & Thornhill, 2012). In this regard, an exploratory research design was most appropriate in this study as it allowed the author to explore the challenges under FinTech within the context of Zimbabwean commercial banks.

### Sampling Procedure

The author believed that it is more fascinating to explore the challenges under FinTech with a specific focus on commercial banks in Zimbabwe. Six managers from six commercial banks in Gweru were purposively selected as they were in a better position to unleash in-depth insights related to managerial challenges under FinTech (Patton, 2015). Notably, willingness to participate and the availability of participants were taken into account when it comes to sample selection process in this study. Within the context of the sample size for qualitative research, Creswell (2014) stressed that two participants can constitute a sample size for qualitative research.

## Data Collection Techniques

In this study, two data collection techniques were employed, namely in-depth personal interviews and observations. In this respect, in-depth semi-structured interviews were conducted with managers of commercial banks. Additionally, the collected data from observations were used for triangulation with the purpose of ensuring the reliability and validity of the research findings. It is worth noting that each interview session with management lasted about 35 minutes on average.

## Data Analysis

Data analysis was done using thematic analysis which is a qualitative method of analyzing data according to emerged themes from the data (Braun & Clarke, 2012). Notably, thematic analysis's six stages suggested by Braun & Clauke (2006) were observed in order to ensure methodological rigor in this study on the challenges under FinTech with particular focus to Zimbabwean commercial banks.

# RESULTS AND DISCUSSION

This section captures the key findings related to the challenges under FinTech. In this regard, seven major key themes emerged from the data, that is, *Customer retention, Regulation compliance, Technology risk, Increased competition, Cyber-attacks, Inadequacy of Information Technology (IT) employees,* and finally *System downtimes* as captured below:

## Customer Retention

The study sought to identify the challenges under FinTech with a particular focus on commercial banks in Zimbabwe. Notably, customer retention was highlighted by interviewees as one of the challenges faced by bankers with respect to FinTech as captured in the following responses:

*"In this digital transformation era of the 21st century, the concept of customer retention is not dead in the context of the banking sector but it is unquestionably on life support because it is very difficult to gain customer trust." (R1)*

*"I believe that the finance technology is very dynamic which makes it cumbersome to retain customers for a year as they can easily switch to FinTech companies with the purpose of experiencing the latest digital financial services at a particular time." (R3)*

*"The customers are practicing double-dipping and then, as bankers, we are faced with customer retention challenges because customers can utilize digital financial services from various FinTech firms at any point in time." (R5)*

As captured in the above responses, it is apparent that interviewees highlighted that, with the advent of FinTech, customer retention was a formidable challenge faced by bank managers. This implies that it is now difficult to gain customer trust since customers can access various digital financial services from numerous banks and FinTech start-ups at a given time. This is supported by research outcomes of Kaushal & Balaini (2016) who found that customer trust is the biggest challenge faced by financial institutions when it comes to e-banking.

## Regulatory Compliance

It emerged from the thematic analysis that many interviewees identified regulation compliance as another tough challenge associated with FinTech. Notably, the quotes of the interviewees are recorded as follows:

*"Although it is evident that digital financial services are transforming the banking sector of Zimbabwe, tightening of regulatory requirements is a major challenge that we are facing as bankers since more financial resources are needed to meet regulatory compliance standards." (R2).*

*"We are demanded, as bankers, to adapt to increasingly stringent regulatory requirements that consume a sizeable amount of time and effort of the management. However, new FinTech start-ups are not complying with such regulatory requirements which lead to unfairness" (R4)*

*"With respect to national payment systems like Real Time Gross Settlement System (RTGS) and Zimbabwe Electronic Transfer Settlement System (ZETSS), volume and complexity of available regulatory compliance requirements remained a big challenge which we are facing in the banking sector."(R5)*

Based on the above quotes, it is noticeable that the interviewees were facing stringent regulatory compliance as a challenge. This suggests that the complexity and volume of regulatory requirements require bank managers to invest more money, effort, and time into regulatory compliance. This consistent with the views of Kaveri (2014) and Munteanu (2016) who suggested that regulation risk is a formidable challenge faced by financial institutions when it comes to FinTech. Moreover, the author observed that the regulatory authorities in the banking sector were devising stringent regulatory requirements in an effort to ensure financial stability. However, such requirements were consuming more time of management of banks.

## Technology Risk

Technology risk emerged from the collected data as one of the challenges that were faced by banks with respect to FinTech. The majority of the respondents expressed that technology risk is an urgent concern in the banking sector as indicated in the following quotes:

*"Of all the biggest challenges concerning finance technology, obsolete core IT systems is a very urgent challenge for global bankers since it is exposing the banks to technology risk. Some of the current IT systems are out-of-date when compared to systems of the banks in developed countries." (R3)*

*"In some cases, as bankers, we are exposed to technology risk due to failure to invest in suitable, agile, and secure systems that can enhance mobile and digital banking." (R5)*

In line with the above quotes, technology risk is one of the challenges faced by bankers when it comes to the successful implementation of FinTech. This suggests that banks are struggling with core legacy systems that are not capable to facilitate the delivery of expected kinds of digital financial services and experiences. Similarly, it is also worth mentioning that banks may face challenges when they want to integrate with new FinTech companies because some FinTech companies are not willing to comply with regulatory requirements (Gomber, Koch, & Siering, 2017).

## Increased Competition

The interviewees were of the opinion that increased competition was one of the biggest challenges under FinTech. Most of the interviewees lamented that FinTech start-up was exposing their organizations to strategic risk owing to increased competition. With this challenge in mind, one of the responses is recorded as follows:

*"As you may know, the challenge of increased competition from new FinTechs is of great concern in this sector. The FinTech start-ups are focusing on most lucrative niches in financial services which then expose our business to strategic risk." (R1)*

As apparently illustrated in the above response, bankers are facing increased completion as one of the biggest challenges faced by banks with respect to FinTech. The researcher also observed that the banks were facing a formidable challenge in the form of increased competition from several disruptive innovators who are offering seamless and cheap experiences especially is the most profitable areas such as card payments. This is in line with the opinion of Jaksic & Marinc (2015) who echoed that banks are facing a big challenge because some FinTech firms are offering new digital financial services like P2P and FinTech start-ups are rapidly increasing in mobile payments.

## Cyber Attacks

Another challenge that emerged from data analysis was cyber-attacks. The majority of the interviewees expressed that the banking sector was regarded by hackers as a lucrative avenue for cyber-attacks in Zimbabwe. In this regard, some of the quotes from interviewees are captured below:

*"With the dominance of mobile banking and technological transformation in our sector, we are experiencing a challenge in terms of cyber-attacks. In fact, banks, as you know, are highly exposed to sophisticated cyber-attacks from fraudsters and hackers who keep on formulating sophisticated strategies and tactics to hack into our numerous types of online banking platforms." (R1)*

*"In spite of the fact that my organization is working so hard to implement an advanced security system to deal with cyber-attacks, vulnerabilities in relation to cyber-attacks occur but not frequently." (R6)*

Based on the above quotes, it is apparent that cyber-attacks are a great concern for bankers given a high uptake of financial technology. This implies that commercial banks are exposed to multiple sources of cyber risks which posed a challenge to their reputations. Harmoniously, this issue of cybersecurity is an increasing great concern for both the largest global financial institutions and the smallest financial institutions (Prescott & Larose, 2016; Vardi, 2017).

## Inadequacy of IT employees

Another challenge that emerged from data analysis was the inadequacy of IT employees. The majority of the interviewees lamented that they were experiencing a serious challenge of lack of well-qualified IT employees due to brain drain as indicated in the quotes recorded underneath:

*"In the current digital age, we are lacking well-qualified IT personnel due to a massive brain drain that has been witnessed in our sector. Precisely, the lack of IT employees is a serious challenge for the successful adoption of digital financial services." (R3)*

It is noted that the interviewees expressed that they were faced with a lack of IT employees which hinders the effective adoption of financial services. This is in line with the research finding of Prasanth & Sudhamanthi (2018) who found that scarcity of human resources was the biggest which limits the effectiveness of the latest finance technology tools and applications in the banking sector of India.

## System Downtimes

The interviewees were of the opinion that system downtimes were constraining the operation of banks as captured in responses recorded below:

*"We are experiencing disruptions linked to system downtimes caused by power outages that last for a long period of time." (R1)*

*"System downtimes are constraining our operation because we don't have reliable electricity and internet connectivity in our country. In most cases, these disruptions are rectified after a long period of time." (R5)*

Based on the above quotes, it is noticeable that system downtimes were constraining the operation of banks which then negatively affected the provision of digital banking services. In this regard, it is widely known that there is no reliable electricity and internet in Zimbabwe which causing unnecessary economic disruptions (RBZ, 2019).

# SOLUTIONS AND RECOMMENDATIONS

The study focused on the managerial challenges under Fintech with particular attention on commercial banks and the previous section has presented the empirical evidence in this regard. The following solutions and recommendation were suggested on the basis of the results of this study:

**Conducting Customer Awareness Campaigns:** It is hereby recommended that the managers of commercial banks in Zimbabwe should sensitize more the use of digital banking services. Given that Zimbabwe has a high literacy rate, this could help the management of commercial banks to augment customer retention.

**Embrace Modern Digital Business Models:** Although there is empirical evidence that commercial banks are adapting to the digital world brought about by the 4$^{th}$ industrial revolution, the pace is too slow. Consequently, it is recommended that banks must embrace modern digital business models through the utilization of finance technology to transform their current business models.

**Training and Development:** As the research findings of this study revealed that the banks were facing a challenge of the inadequacy of IT employees, it is suggested that the managers of banks should embark on training and development programs related to financial technology.

**Cooperation:** As the research findings of this study revealed that the banks were facing a challenge of increased competition from FinTech companies, it is recommended that the commercial banks must collaborate with both local and international FinTech companies in an attempt to protect their existence and adapt with volatility in the financial milieu.

**Establishment of FinTech Hubs:** The government of Zimbabwe through RBZ should establish FinTech hubs in Zimbabwe in an effort to foster innovation and creativity culture in the financial sector. The FinTech Hubs could ensure effective interaction among academicians, government authorities, FinTech companies, and financial institutions.

## FUTURE RESEARCH DIRECTIONS

In the future, more research work is welcomed in order to advance our understanding of FinTech. This qualitative study has focused on the banking sector only; therefore, more qualitative studies are recommended on managerial challenges under FinTech in the insurance sector as a comparative study. Furthermore, more qualitative studies are recommended in the financial sector using brokerage companies in an effort to capture how they are affected by FinTech firms as new entrants.

## CONCLUSION

This chapter aims to contribute to scarce empirical evidence on FinTech with a particular focus on commercial banks in Zimbabwe. Interestingly, this study intends to fill this gap by developing insights into the challenges under FinTech in the banking sector. Notably, seven challenges emerged from this exploratory study, that is, customer retention, regulation compliance, technology risk, increased competition, the inadequacy of IT employees, and system downtimes. Recommendations were proffered with respect to these challenges and the avenues for future research have been suggested in this chapter. The empirical evidence from this study aid decision making process engaged by policymakers and practitioners concerning FinTech. Managers of banks can be guided by the empirical evidence from this study when it comes to the formulation of strategies to address the challenges identified in this study. It is, therefore, concluded that the management of banks is confronted with a multiplicity of challenges given an exponential growth of FinTech firms in this digital epoch.

## REFERENCES

Admati, A. R., & Hellwig, M. (2013). *The bankers' new clothes*. Princeton University Press.

Ahamed, M. M., & Mallick, S. K. (2019). Is financial inclusion good for bank stability? International evidence. *Journal of Economic Behavior & Organization*, *157*, 403–427. doi:10.1016/j.jebo.2017.07.027

Al-Ajlouni, A. T., & Al-Hakim, M. (2018). *Financial technology in banking industry: Challenges and opportunities*. Paper presented at International Conference on Economics and Administrative Sciences. Applied Sciences University, Jordan. 10.2139srn.3340363

Anagnostopoulos, I. (2018). Fintech and regtech: Impact on regulators and banks. *Journal of Economics and Business*, *100*, 7–25. doi:10.1016/j.jeconbus.2018.07.003

Arner, D. W., Barberis, J. N., & Buckley, R. P. (2015). *The evolution of fintech: A new post-crisis paradigm?* Retrieved May 10, 2020, from https://core.ac.uk/download/pdf/38088713.pdf

Auta, E. M. (2010). E-banking in developing economy: Empirical evidence from Nigeria. *Journal of Applied Quantitative Methods*, *5*(2), 212–222.

Bara, A., & Mudzingiri, C. (2016). Financial innovation and economic growth: Evidence from Zimbabwe. *Investment Management and Financial Innovations, 13*(2), 65–75. doi:10.21511/imfi.13(2).2016.07

Beck, T., Chen, T., Lin, C., & Song, F. M. (2016). Financial innovation: The bright and the dark sides. *Journal of Banking & Finance, 72*, 28–51. doi:10.1016/j.jbankfin.2016.06.012

Braun, V., & Clarke, V. (2006). Using thematic analysis in psychology. *Qualitative Research in Psychology, 3*(2), 77–101. doi:10.1191/1478088706qp063oa

Braun, V., & Clarke, V. (2012). Thematic analysis. In H. Cooper (Ed.), *APA Handbook of research methods in psychology: Research design: Quantitative, Qualitative, Neuropsychological and Biological* (Vol. 2, pp. 57–71). American Psychological Association. doi:10.1037/13620-004

Bryman, A., & Bell, E. (2011). *Business research methods* (3rd ed.). Cambridge University Press.

Bugrov, D., Dietz, M., & Poppensieker, T. (2017). *A brave new world for global banking. McKinsey Global Banking Annual Review 2016*. McKinsey and Company.

Campenon, B. (2016). Fintech and the future of securities services. *Journal of Securities Operations and Custody, 8*(2), 107–112.

Cetorelli, N., McAndrews, J., & Traina, J. (2014). Evolution in bank complexity. *Economic Policy Review, 20*(2), 85–106.

Chirima, D. T., & Chikochi, K. (2016). The impact of electronic banking on the competitiveness of commercial banks in Zimbabwe (2014–2015). *International Journal of Case Studies, 5*(1). Retrieved May 12, 2020, from https://www.academia.edu/30268731/The_Impact_of_Electronic_Banking_on_the_Competitiveness_of_Commercial_Banks_in_Zimbabwe_2014-2015

Cizinska, R., Krabec, T., & Venegas, P. (2016). FieldsRank: The network value of the firm. *International Advances in Economic Research, 22*(4), 461–463. doi:10.100711294-016-9604-x

Creswell, J. W. (2014). *Research design: Qualitative, quantitative, and mixed-method approaches* (4th ed.). Sage Publication.

Dodgson, M., Gann, D., Waldawsky-Berger, I., Sultan, N., & George, G. (2015). Managing Digital Money. *Academy of Management Journal, 58*(2), 325–333. doi:10.5465/amj.2015.4002

Domeher, D. J., Frimpong, M., & Appiah, T. (2014). Adoption of financial innovation in Ghanaian banking industry. *African Review of Economics and Finance*, *6*(2), 207–243.

Dorfleitner, G., Hornuf, L., Schmitt, M., & Weber, M. (2017). *FinTech in Germany*. Springer International Publishing. doi:10.1007/978-3-319-54666-7

Drasch, B. J., Schweizer, A., & Urbach, N. (2018). Integrating the 'Troublemakers: A taxonomy for cooperation between banks and fintechs. *Journal of Economics and Business*, *100*, 26–42. doi:10.1016/j.jeconbus.2018.04.002

Dumont, M. (2020). *Apollo signs MoA with Zimbabwean bank*. Retrieved May 10, 2020, from https://medium.com/@apollocurrency/apollo-signs-mou-with-zimbabwean-bank-d0fde9e61431

Ernst & Young. (2016). *UK fintech on the cutting edge: An evaluation of the intentional fintech sector*, EY. Retrieved May 16, 2020, from https://www.ey.com/Publication/vwLUAssets/EY-UK-FinTech-On-the-cutting-edge/$FILE/EY-UK-FinTech-On-the-cutting-edge.pdf>

Ernst & Young. (2019). *FinTechs in Sub-Saharan Africa: An overview of market developments and investment opportunities*. Retrieved March 01, 2020, from https://hollandfintech.com/wp-content/uploads/2019/02/ey-fin-tech-market-opportunities-2019.pdf

Gomber, P., Kauffman, R. J., Parker, C., & Weber, B. W. (2018). On the fintech revolution: Interpreting the forces of innovation, disruption and transformation in financial services. *Journal of Management Information Systems*, *35*(1), 220–265. doi:10.1080/07421222.2018.1440766

Gomber, P., Koch, J. A., & Siering, M. (2017). Digital finance and fintech: Current research and future research directions. *Journal of Business Economics*, *87*(5), 537–580. doi:10.100711573-017-0852-x

Haddad, C., & Hornuf, L. (2016). *The emergence of the global Fintech market: Economic and technological determinants*. Retrieved March 01, 2020, from https://papers.ssrn.com/sol3/papers.cfm?abstract_id=2830124

Helm, T., Low, A., & Townson, J. (2019). *UK fintech: State of the nation*. Department for International Trade.

Hennig-Thurau, T., Hofacker, C. F., & Bloching, B. (2013). Marketing the pinball way: Understanding how social media change the generation of value for consumers and companies. *Journal of Interactive Marketing*, *27*(4), 237–24. doi:10.1016/j.intmar.2013.09.005

Hirt, M., & Willmott, P. (2014). *Strategic principles for competing in the digital age*. Retrieved May 15, 2020, from https://www.mckinsey.com/business-functions/strategy-and-corporate-finance/our-insights/strategic-principles-for-competing-in-the-digital-age

Idowu, A. A., Ngumi, P., & Muturi, W. (2016). Financial innovation adoption and turnaround time. *Journal of Research in Economics and International Finance*, *5*(2), 14–28.

International Monetary Fund. (2019). *FinTech in Sub-Saharan African countries: A game changer?* Retrieved March 01, 2020, from https://www.imf.org/en/Publications/Departmental-Papers-Policy-Papers/Issues/2019/02/13/FinTech-in-Sub-Saharan-African-Countries-A-Game-Changer-46376

Jakšič, M., & Marinč, M. (2015). *The future of banking: The role of information technology*. Bancni vestnik: Banking Sector at the Crossroads: Challenges For The Future. Retrieved May 15, 2020, from https://ssrn.com/abstract=2656388

Juengerkes, B. E. (2016). FinTechs and banks: Collaboration is key. In S. Chishti & J. Barberis (Eds.), *The FinTech book: the financial technology handbook for investors, entrepreneurs and visionaries* (pp. 179–182). Wiley. doi:10.1002/9781119218906.ch47

Kandpal, V., & Mehrotra, R. (2019). Financial inclusion: The role of fintech and digital financial services in India. *Indian Journal of Economics and Business*, *19*(1), 85–93.

Kaushal, V., & Balaini, A. (2016). E-banking: Challenges and issues. *Hill Quest*, *3*(3-4), 69–73.

Kaveri, V. S. (2014). Bank frauds in India: Emerging challenges. *Journal Of Commerce and Management Thought*, *5*(1), 14–26. doi:10.5958/j.0976-478X.5.1.002

Kim, Y., Choi, J., Park, Y. J., & Yeon, J. (2016). The adoption of mobile payment services for "FinTech.". *International Journal of Applied Engineering Research*, *11*(2), 1058–1061.

King, B. (2014). *Breaking Banks*. Wiley. doi:10.1002/9781118958247

Konigsheim, C., Lukas, M., & Noth, M. (2017). Financial knowledge, risk preferences, and the demand for digital financial services. *Schmalenbach Business Review*, *18*(4), 343–375. doi:10.100741464-017-0040-0

Kotarba, M. (2016). New factors inducing changes in the retail banking customer relationship management (CRM) and their exploration by the FinTech industry. *Foundations of Management*, *8*(1), 69–78. doi:10.1515/fman-2016-0006

Li, Y., Spigt, R., & Swinkels, L. (2017). The impact of fintech start-prices. *Financial Innovation*, *3*(1), 26. doi:10.118640854-017-0076-7

Maswaure, F., & Choga, F. (2016). Electronic banking uptake in Zimbabwe. *Journal of Business and Management*, *18*(4), 80–82.

Mavaza, T. (2019). E-Banking adoption by Zimbabwe banks: An exploratory study. *PM World Journal*, *8*(11), 1–10.

Micu, I., & Micu, A. (2016). Financial technology (fintech) and its implementation on the Romanian non-banking capital market. *SEA-Practical Application of Science*, *11*, 379–384.

Munteanu, B. (2016). Shadow banking – developments in times of financial crisis. *"Ovidiu s" University Annals. Economic Sciences Series*, *16*(2), 43–47.

Nakaso, H. (2016). *FinTech and the future of money*. Retrieved May 16, 2020, from https://www.bis.org/review/r161214a.htm

Nishmitha, N. (2018). *Financial technology implications: Indian context* (Master thesis). National Institute of Technology, Surathkal.

Oakley, M., Hughes, S., Gulati, S., & Miscampbell, G. (2018). *Supporting UK fintech: Accessing a global talent pool*. Innovate Finance.

Patton, M. Q. (2015). *Qualitative research and evaluation methods: Integrating theory and practice* (4th ed.). Sage.

Philippon, T. (2018). *The fintech opportunity*. Retrieved May 15, 2020, from http://pages.stern.nyu.edu/~tphilipp/papers/FinTech.pdf

Prasanth, S., & Sudhamathi, S. (2018). Challenges faced by banking sector on digital innovation. *Journal of Technologies and Innovative Research*, *5*(10), 964–967.

Puschmann, T. (2017). Fintech. *Business & Information Systems Engineering*, *59*(1), 69–76. doi:10.100712599-017-0464-6

Reserve Bank of Zimbabwe. (2019a). *2019 Midterm monetary policy statement: Transition to normalcy*. Retrieved May 10, 2010, from https://www.rbz.co.zw/documents/mps/MPS-September-2019-.pdf

Reserve Bank of Zimbabwe. (2019b). *Financial stability report June 2019*. Retrieved May 15, 2020, from https://www.rbz.co.zw/documents/BLSS/2020/Zimbabwe-Financial-Stability-Report-as-at-30-June-2019.pdf

Reserve Bank of Zimbabwe. (2020). *Monetary policy statement 2020: Focusing on price and exchange rate stability*. Retrieved May 16, 2020, from https://www.rbz.co.zw/documents/mps/Monetary-Policy-Statement-17-February-2020.pdf

Saunders, M. N. K., & Rojon, C. (2014). There's no madness in my method: Explaining how your research findings are built on firm foundations' coaching. *An International Journal of Theory. Research and Practice*, *7*(1), 74–83.

Saunders, M. N. K., Lewis, P., & Thornhill, A. (2012). *Research methods for business students* (6th ed.). Pearson Education Ltd.

Shim, Y., & Shin, D. H. (2016). Analyzing China's fintech industry from the perspective of actor–network theory. *Telecommunications Policy*, *40*(2–3), 168–181. doi:10.1016/j.telpol.2015.11.005

Skan, J., Dickerson, J., & Masood, S. (2015). *Future of fintech and banking – Accenture*. Retrieved May 14, 2020, from https://www.accenture.com/us-en/insight-future-fintechbanking

Sung, A., & Leong, K. (2018). FinTech (Financial Technology): What is it and how to use technologies to create business value in Fintech way? *International Journal of Innovation, Management and Technology*, *9*(2), 74–78.

Sy, A. N. R., Maino, R., Massara, A., Perez-Saiz, H., & Sharma, P. (2019). *FinTech in Sub-Saharan African countries: A game changer?* IMF, Departmental Papers. No. 19/04. Retrieved May 16, 2020, from https://www.imf.org/en/Publications/Departmental-Papers-Policy-Papers/Issues/2019/02/13/FinTech-in-Sub-Saharan-African-Countries-A-Game-Changer-46376

Thompson, K. (2017). Wealth management advice in the digital age. *Journal of Securities Operations and Custody*, *10*(1), 6–11.

Vardi, M. (2017). Cyber insecurity and cyber libertarianism. *Communications of the ACM*, *60*(5), 5. doi:10.1145/3073731

Vasiljeva, T., & Lukanova, K. (2016). Commercial banks and fintech companies in the digital transformation: Challenges for the future. *Journal of Business and Management, 11*, 25–33.

Zavolokina, L., Dolata, M., & Schwabe, G. (2016). The FinTech phenomenon: Antecedents of financial innovation perceived by the popular press. *Financial Innovation, 2*(16), 16. Advance online publication. doi:10.118640854-016-0036-7

Zhao, O., Tsai, P., & Wang, J. (2019). Improving financial service innovation strategies for enhancing China's banking industry competitive advantage during the Fintech revolution: A hybrid MCDM model. *Sustainability, 11*, 1–29. doi:10.3390u12010001

Zwinoira, T. (2020). *CBZ clinches digital currency deal*. Retrieved May 15, 2020, from https://www.thestandard.co.zw/2020/03/22/cbz-clinches-digital-currency-deal/

## ADDITIONAL READING

Afuah, A. (2014). *Business Model Innovation: Concept analysis and cases*. Routledge. doi:10.4324/9780203584583

Alt, R., Beck, R., & Smits, M. (2018). FinTech and the transformation of the financial industry. *Electronic Markets, 28*(3), 235–243. doi:10.100712525-018-0310-9

Bofondi, M., & Gobbi, G. (2017). The big promise of fintech. *European Economy, 2*, 107–119.

Frame, W. S., & White, L. J. (2004). Empirical studies of financial innovation: Lots of talk, little action? *Journal of Economic Literature, 42*(1), 116–144. doi:10.1257/002205104773558065

Gandal, N., Hamrick, J. T., Moore, T., & Oberman, T. (2018). Price manipulation in the bitcoin ecosystem. *Journal of Monetary Economics, 95*, 86–96. doi:10.1016/j.jmoneco.2017.12.004

Hernando, I., & Nieto, M. J. (2007). Is the internet delivery channel changing banks' performance? The case of Spanish banks. *Journal of Banking & Finance, 31*(4), 1083–1099. doi:10.1016/j.jbankfin.2006.10.011

Hornuf, L., & Schwienbacher, A. (2017). Should securities regulation promote equity crowdfunding? *Small Business Economics, 49*(3), 579–593. doi:10.100711187-017-9839-9

Moenninghoff, S. C., & Wieandt, A. (2013). The future of peer-to-peer finance. *Schmalenbachs Zeitschrift für betriebswirtschaftliche. Forschung*, *65*(5), 466–487.

## KEY TERMS AND DEFINITIONS

**Banking Sector:** A network or group of financial institutions that provide banking services to corporate and individual customers.

**Business Model:** A company's plan that details how a firm creates value with the aim of making a profit.

**Commercial Bank:** Refers to a financial institution that offers checking account services, accepts deposits, offers basic financial products, and makes various loans to corporates and individuals. For instance, financial products can be Certificates of Deposits (CDs).

**Digital Transformation:** A process whereby a company makes use of smart digital technologies to redefine existing business systems, processes, procedures, culture, and customer experiences in an attempt to meet constantly changing market and business requirements.

**Financial Technology:** It can be defined as a plethora of innovations and technologies adopted by financial institutions so as to facilitate trading, corporate business transactions, and interaction with consumers.

**Information Communication Technology:** Refers to various infrastructures such as wireless networks and cell phones as well as the internet that deal with the dissemination of information. These components play a crucial role in modern computing when it comes to the business world.

**Mobile Banking:** Is a service offered by a bank that allows customers to make financial transactions on mobile devices like tablets or smartphones.

# Chapter 8
# FinTech's Interpretations and Tunisian Ecosystem Analysis

**Fatma Bouaziz**
*Faculty of Economics and Management of Sfax, University of Sfax, Tunisia*

**Amira Sghari**
*Faculty of Economics and Management of Sfax, University of Sfax, Tunisia*

## ABSTRACT

*The evolution of information and communication technology (ICT) affects all areas of activity including the financial industry. Indeed, it leads to rapid development of innovative and modern financial services, namely financial technology (Fintech). The latter is not well defined in the literature. This descriptive chapter aims to propose a comprehension of the Fintech concept based on three interpretations: Fintech as financial services relying on digital technologies, Fintech as startups and IT companies, and Fintech as an industry. An analysis of the components of the Tunisian Fintech ecosystem is then presented. The latter is mainly composed-of Central Bank of Tunisia, fintech startups (financing, payments, loyalty program, blockchain and cryptocurrencies, exchange services and insurance, and technology, IT, and infrastructure), technology developers, traditional financial institutions, and financial customers.*

## INTRODUCTION

The continuous evolution of Information and Communication Technology (ICT) leads to digital transformation. Both, they are radically changing people's habits as well as firms' activities. They are changing the ways in which people produce, buy

DOI: 10.4018/978-1-7998-7110-1.ch008

goods and services, and interact with each other. In the financial services industry, digital technologies disrupt the customers' ways to access products. Moreover, they reshape the value proposition of existing financial services (Swacha-Lech, 2017). They are an accelerator for innovations and changes leading to rapid development of innovative and modern financial services. As a result, a new filed, namely Financial Technology (Fintech), is emerging.

According to Lee and Shin (2018), the emergence of Fintech comes with the development of electronic finance (e-finance) after the internet revolution in the early 1990s. "E-finance refers to all forms of financial services such as banking, insurance, and stock trading performed through electronic means, including the internet and World Wide Web". Lee and Shin (2018) added that advances in e-finance and mobile technologies for financial firms have led to Fintech innovation development, particularly after the worldwide financial crisis in 2008. Fintech innovation combines the e-finance, internet technologies, social networking services, social media, artificial intelligence, and big data analytics.

Interest in Fintech is more and more growing across countries. In 2018, Fintech investments reached 111.8 billion euros worldwide, and the exponential dynamism would be reinforced in the future years (Tnani, 2019). Yazici (2019) highlighted the importance of Fintech by stating that it is reshaping the financial experience of millions of people and businesses on a global scale, and that it has the potential to dramatically change our understanding of financial services tomorrow. The importance of Fintech to economic development, attraction of foreign direct investment as well as the Know-How and the huge investments created by Fintech startups have led the same author to emphasize the importance of creating a dynamic, well-functioning Fintech ecosystem. Ecosystem defines the necessary infrastructure elements for the development of the Fintech area in a country.

However, despite this exponential evolution, at a theoretical level, there is still a lack of consensus on the definition of Fintech among scholars and practitioners (Milian et al., 2019; Iman, 2020; Liudmila et al., 2016). Indeed, in the literature Fintech is not clearly defined, and is still ambiguous for most of the people. One reason for this could be novelty of Fintech field and its rapid evolution (Liudmila et al., 2016; Iman, 2020). Better understanding of the term will help both practitioners to identify the potentials as well as Fintech threats, and researchers to reveal new possibilities for research regarding all its aspects (e.g., technologies behind, ecosystems, organizational matters, etc.) (Liudmila et al., 2016).

In Tunisia, some measures have recently been initiated by the Central Bank to promote the Fintech development. Yet, despite these measures, Fintech remains at an embryonic stage. Tnani (2019) advanced three major reasons to explain Tunisia's lag in Fintech. The first reason is The IT directors' lack of awareness about technological developments and innovative applications offered by Fintech startups. The second reason is the lack of an efficient ecosystem that meets both economic and regulatory challenges and the expectations of the various players in the Fintech sector. The third reason is the need for more synergy between Fintech and the banking and financial sector. To our knowledge, there is no research that has dealt with the Fintech ecosystem in Tunisia. As Fintechs are emerging on the Tunisian market, it is important, at this stage, to describe the Fintech ecosystem in Tunisia in order to give better visibility to researchers and practitioners in this field.

Thus, this descriptive chapter analyzes the Fintech concept and the Tunisian Fintech ecosystem. To achieve this aim, two sections are going to be developed. The first section will focus on Fintech emergence, definitions and the elements of ecosystem. The second section-will propose a description of the Tunisian Fintech ecosystem.

## BACKGROUND

Fintech is part of the process of evolving financial innovation (Thakor, 2020). However, there is conflicting evidence on the origin of the term (Oshodin et al., 2019). Lee and Shin (2018) noted that Fintech innovation emerged after the worldwide financial crisis in 2008 by combining the e-finance, internet technologies, social networking services, social media, artificial intelligence, and big data analytics. By cons, Oshodin et al. (2019) traced the origins of Fintech back to the years 1970s. At this date, Bettinger (1972, cited by Oshodin et al., 2019) referred to "Fintech" as a series of models to analyze and solve problems that were encountered by a bank through a combination of technology and banking expertise. Unlike these authors, Thakor (2020) described three phases of the evolution of Fintech:

- **Phase 1 (1866-1967):** characterized by the laying of the first trans-Atlantic cable and telegraph and Rapid transmission of financial information transactions and payments.
- **Phase 2 (1967-2008):** characterized by the appearance of electronic payments, clearing systems, ATMs and online banking and the use of information technology by traditional financial institutions to enhance products and services.
- **Phase 3 (2008-present):** characterized by the use of technology by new entrants to provide non-intermediated financial services directly to customers and new competitiveness landscape for financial institutions

Since the 2008 global economic crisis, Fintech start-ups and large IT companies enter into the domain of financial industry, gain ground and conquer customers, traditionally served by established providers (Milian et al., 2019).This evolution is at the origin of the multitude of definitions proposed to the concept "fintech".

## Definition of Fintech

Fintech is also labelled as FinTech, Fin-tech, or Fintech (Gomber et al., 2017; Acar and Çıtak, 2019; Milian et al., 2019). It is the abbreviation of "financial technology". Several authors view Fintech as a neologism originating from the words ''financial'' and ''technology'' (Gomber et al., 2017; Liudmila et al., 2016; Milian et al., 2019) or "a portmanteau combining the words "financial" and "technology"" (Ryu, 2017).

Although widely used as a term, Fintech is not clearly defined, and the proposed definitions do not converge to one meaning. Liudmila et al. (2016) assure that the meaning of Fintech remains ambiguous for most people, while Dorfleitner et al. (2017) note the absence of a universally accepted definition for this term. The lack of consensus on Fintech definition has also recently been reported (Acar and Çıtak, 2019; Iman, 2020; Thakor, 2020; Milian et al., 2019).

Thus, to suggest a comprehensive understanding of the term Fintech, a set of definitions from the literature is proposed in tables 1, 2 and 3. It follows that Fintech is used as an umbrella term to refer to several things. Despite this diversity, the existence of three interpretations of Fintech is hereby noted and it is then concluded that Fintech is simultaneously used to refer to:

- financial services relying on digital technologies (Table 1);
- startups and IT companies (Table 2);
- industry (Table 3).

### Fintech as Financial Services Relying on Digital Technologies

Table 1 reports the Fintech definitions as financial services relying on digital technologies. As such, Fintech is generally referred to as innovative financial services and products. All sources agree that Fintech relies on the use of digital technologies to deliver financial services and products. Digital technologies, individually or collectively, facilitate Fintech innovations. They include the technologies that underlie financial services. These technologies include several examples. Liudmila et al. (2016) cite as examples mobile payments, data analytics, crowd-based platforms or crypto currencies. Gomber et al. (2017) present a list of digital finance technologies comprising Blockchains, social networks, NFC, P2P Technology, Big Data Analytics, and Further enablers. The list of Fintech underlying technologies by Iman (2020) encompasses Artificial intelligence,

Bio-recognition, Big data, Blockchain, Cloud-based services, Internet, Machine learning and Mobile communication. Swacha-Lech (2017) mentions a more developed list of technologies important for banks and related to digitalization. These are:

- IoT (basically means wearables, smart TV or smart home appliances),
- Public cloud infrastructure;
- Big data analytics;
- Artificial Intelligence (AI): cognitive computing and machine learning (virtual assistants, Robo-Advisory, e.g. in wealth management);
- Distributed ledger technology (DLT) – e.g. blockchain;
- Biometrics and identity management systems (e.g. finger vein or selfie pay)
- APIs; – software-as-a-service solutions (SaaS)

However, Fintech is more than digital technologies. These technologies rather enable changes-besides the emergence of new and innovative financial services and products (e.g., smart contracts instead of traditional contracts), processes (e.g., C2C instead of B2C), organizational forms (e.g., decentralized instead of centralized organization), and business models (e.g., customer driven data models instead of company-driven data models). Lukanova and Vasiljeva (2016) described Fintech as a technologically driven process in the financial industry that introduces new working methods and approaches to standard processes. In fact, digital technologies in Fintech are not a simple facilitator or enabler to effectively deliver financial services, but they are rather an innovator and a disruptor of the existing value chain by bypassing the existing channels (Ryu, 2017). This way, Fintech might improve the performance of financial services; expand them to mobile environments then customers can benefit from standardized or customized financial services (Ryu, 2017).

## Fintech as Startups and IT Companies

Table 2 exhibits a set of definitions considering Fintech as startups and IT companies that provide or facilitate financial services by using digital technologies. Acar and Çitak (2019) talk about technology companies that disintermediate formal financial institutions and provide consumers with products and services via online and mobile channels. Gimpel et al. (2018)-argued that Fintech is a development within startups and established companies nurtured by substantial monetary investments. As examples, the authors cited the startup iZettle, the established technology company Google, and the established service provider Commerzbank. However, there is no unanimity about banks as examples of Fintech. In fact, banks are excluded from the definition of Fintech companies (Thakor, 2020) which have their origins in the IT industry instead of the traditional banking sector (Gomber et al., 2017; Iman, 2020).

*Table 1. Definitions of Fintech as financial innovations / services*

| Authors | Definitions |
|---|---|
| Kim et al. (2016) | In terms of financial services, it is an innovative service, which provides differentiated financial services using new technologies, such as mobile, social media, and IOT. |
| Liudmila et al. (2016) | FinTech could be understood as a financial service, which is intervened by innovative technologies in order to satisfy the major requirements of "tomorrow": high efficiency, cost reduction, business processes improvement, rapidity, flexibility, innovation. |
| Lukanova and Vasiljeva (2016) | One definition is given by David Lee Kuo Chen (Chen, 2015). He states that "Fintech refers to innovative financial services or products delivered via technology".<br>In this report (PwC, 2015) FinTech is defined as a combination of innovative financial services and the availability of capital through the use of new (digital) technologies, such as crowdfunding. |
| Navaretti et al. (2017) | Fintech refers to the novel processes and products that have become available for financial services thanks to digital technological advancements. More precisely, the Financial Stability Board defines Fintech as "technologically enabled financial innovation that could result in new business models, applications, processes or products with an associated material effect on financial markets and institutions and the provision of financial services". |
| Gomber et al. (2017) | The term ''FinTech'' [...] describes in general the connection of modern and, mainly, Internet-related technologies (e.g., cloud computing, mobile Internet) with established business activities of the financial services industry (e.g., money lending, transaction banking). |
| Ryu (2017) | In this study, Fintech was defined as "innovative and disruptive financial services by non-financial companies, where IT is the key factor." With Fintech, users may engage in a variety of mobile services: making payments, transferring money, making loan requests, purchasing insurance, managing assets, and making investments (Barberis, 2014). In this study, Fintech includes mobile payment, mobile remittance, P2P lending and crowdfunding. |
| Swacha-Lech (2017) | FinTechs offer solutions that can better address customer needs by offering enhanced accessibility, convenience and tailored products. |
| Panetta (2018) | What do we mean exactly by Fintech? The Financial Stability Board defines it as "technologically enabled financial innovation that could result in new business models, applications, processes or products with an associated material effect on financial markets and institutions and the provision of financial services." According to this definition, fintech encompasses a wide range of services and activities. An example may help clarify this. In addition to using banknotes, cheques, or Internet banking, today I can use my mobile phone to transfer money to a friend. All I have to do is to download the appropriate app, type a simple text message and select my friend's name from my contacts list. My friend would receive the money in a few seconds, and could even reuse it immediately for his own payments. |
| Acar and Çıtak (2019) | Fintech integrates finance and technology together, traditional financial structures combined with today's technology-based processes and simple one fintech refers to the application of technology in financial service. |
| Milian et al. (2019) | Fintech: "an acronym which stands for financial technology, combining bank expertise with modern management science techniques and the computer" (Bettinger, 1972, p. 62). |

*continues on following page*

*Table 1. Continued*

| Authors | Definitions |
|---|---|
| Thakor (2020) | At its core, Fintech is the use of technology to provide new and improved financial services.<br>The Financial Stability Board (FSB) defines Fintech as "technologically enabled financial innovation that could result in new business models, applications, processes, or products with an associated material effect on financial markets and institutions, and the provision of financial services." |
| Iman (2020) | Gomber et al. (2017) define Fintech as a neologism coming from "financial" and "technology" and referring to the connection between modern Internet technologies and established business activities of the banking sector.<br>For example, Puschmann (2017) forcefully argues that fintech is "[...] incremental or disruptive innovations in the context of the financial services industry induced by IT developments and resulting in new intra- or inter-organizational business models, products and services, organizations, processes and systems" (p74). Meanwhile, Gomber et al. (2017) describe Fintech as initiatives in the financial sector that are challenging established roles, business models, and service offerings by introducing technology-based innovations. |

*Table 2. Definitions of Fintech as startups and companies*

| Authors | Definitions |
|---|---|
| Liudmila et al. (2016). | The term "FinTech" is also used to refer to companies – and, what is even more common, to start-ups – which serve as enablers of such kinds of services. |
| Lukanova and Vasiljeva (2016) | A definition preferred by Accenture considers FinTech companies as "the ones offering technologies for banking and corporate finance, capital markets, financial data analytics, payments and personal financial management". |
| Dorfleitner et al. (2017) | The term "FinTech," which is the short form of the phrase financial technology, denotes companies or representatives of companies that combine financial services with modern, innovative technologies |
| Gomber et al. (2017) | Typically, FinTech refers to innovators and disruptors in the financial sector that make use of the availability of ubiquitous communication, specifically via the Internet and automated information processing. Such companies have new business models that promise more flexibility, security, efficiency, and opportunities than established financial services. The innovator can be either a start-up (like iZettle), an established technology company (like Google), or an established service provider (like Commerzbank).<br>The term ''FinTech'' puts more emphasis on technological innovations and technological development. This becomes apparent in the fact that most FinTech companies have their origins not in the financial sector but are IT companies that create new solutions for challenges and tasks of the financial industry. |
| Ryu (2017) | Fintech companies are currently expanding their business scope beyond the online platform into the mobile platform (e.g., mobile payment, mobile remittance). The traditional online banking system, provided by traditional financial institutions, is also changing into innovative and differentiated financial services offered by non-financial providers. |

*continues on following page*

*Table 2. Continued*

| Authors | Definitions |
|---|---|
| Romānova and Kudinska (2017) | Nowadays "FinTech" is a noun related to companies that use modern innovative technologies (e.g., software) to enable provision of financial services.<br>Report of Accenture and CB Insights defines FinTech as companies that "offer technologies for banking and corporate finance, capital markets, financial data analytics, payments and personal financial management". |
| Saksonova and Kuzmina-Merlino (2017) | Fintech or financial technology is a term used to denote firms that offer modern technology in the financial sector. |
| Gimpel et al. (2018) | Zavolokina et al. (2016) argue that, besides technology, FinTech is a development within start-ups and established companies nurtured by substantial monetary investments. Distilling the essence of the definitions above, we define FinTech and FinTech start-ups as follows:<br>- FinTech characterizes the usage of digital technologies such as the Internet, mobile computing, and data analytics to enable, innovate, or disrupt financial services.<br>- FinTech start-ups are newly established businesses that offer financial services based on FinTech. |
| Acar and Çıtak (2019) | Officially, World Economic Forum defines Fintechs as "companies that provide or facilitate financial services by using technology. In its current form, Fintech is marked by technology companies that disintermediate formal financial institutions and provide direct products and services to end users, often through online and mobile channels".<br>Gartner defines as "fintechs are startup technology providers that deliver emerging digital technologies that approach financial services in innovative ways or can fundamentally change the way bank products and services are created and distributed, and generate revenue. The term may also refer to the technologies these providers offer". |
| Milian et al. (2019) | Formed by a contraction of the words finance and technology, the term fintech refers to companies that are using technology to operate outside traditional business models for financial services, seeking to change the way these services are offered, using communication, the internet and the automated processing of information. |
| Oshodin et al. (2019) | FinTech start-ups, which refer to organizations that offer novel "financial services or products that are delivered via technologies",<br>Recently though, FinTech refers to firms (typically start-ups) that take advantage of advancements in regulations and technologies to enter into the financial industry to disrupt, improve or enhance service types and delivery by offering novel "financial services or products that are delivered via technologies. |

Swacha-Lech (2017) and Oshodin et al. (2019) identify two key characteristics of Fintech startups and companies. The first characteristic is related to the use of digital technologies to transform traditional financial service practices. These organizations are seen as innovators and disruptors in the financial sector that builds on the potential of digital technologies. The second characteristic is that these companies are customer-centric. As such, they have the ability to meet changing customer needs with new offerings and delivering tailored products. As such,

Fintech organizations need to have new business models as well as a culture that promise more agility, flexibility, security, and efficiency than established financial institutions. Moreover, Fintech firms are mostly micro, small or medium sized firms that do not have a lot of equity, but do have a clear idea of how to introduce new services or how to improve existing ones in the financial service market (Saksonova and Kuzmina-Merlino, 2017). This allows them to challenge established providers by offering new products and services.

Fintech startups, newly established businesses based on Fintech financial services and products (Gimpel et al., 2018), are entrepreneurial and drive major innovations in several areas: payment, weal management, lending, crowdfunding, capital market, and insurances. They incur lower operating costs, target more niche markets, and provide more personalized services than traditional financial firms (Lee and Shin, 2018). According to Panetta (2018), their field of intervention is rapidly expanding from certain segments of the financial sector (such as retail payments, asset management and small loans) into sectors such as lending-based, crowdfunding and chatbox customer- relation services. Panetta (2018) cited the following examples as the leading Fintech players, in China:

- Apple and Google have developed solutions that allow payment instruments to be used in cooperation with banks.
- Amazon grants loans to small businesses.
- Facebook allows users in the U.S. to make payments to others in their contact lists and begins to lend to small businesses.
- Alibaba makes payment services available through its affiliate company Ant Financial.
- Tencent offers a broad range of financial services through its social media app, Wechat.

According to Romanova and Kudinska (2017), Fintech can be classified into two groups:

- Fintech companies providing services complimentary to bank services (e.g., providing technologies used by banks to provide financial services),
- Fintech companies providing services traditionally covered by banks (e.g., payments).

By doing so, Fintech creates competition among the startups working on the service, and forces banks to compete (Liudmila et al., 2016). Lukanova and Vasiljeva (2016) found that Fintech companies are focusing on four main areas: payment-related services, wealth management, peer-to-peer lending (P2P lending), and crowd funding. Moreover, having the objective of Fintech categorization, Iman (2020), Haddad and Hornuf (2019) and Milian et al. (2019) propose similar categories of these organizations. According to their offered services, they include nine different types of startups: those that engage in financing, payment, asset management, insurance (insurtechs), loyalty programs, risk management, exchanges, regulatory technology (regtech), and other business activities. Table 3 provides a definition for each Fintech category as investigated by Haddad and Hornuf (2019).

*Table 3. Definitions of Fintech as an industry*

| Authors | Definitions |
|---|---|
| Kim et al. (2016) | Fintech is an industry, which uses mobile-centered IT technology to enhance the efficiency of the financial system. "Fintech" as a term is a compound of "finance" and "technology", and collectively refers to industrial changes forged from the convergence of financial services and IT. [...] In terms of industry, it refers to the phenomenon where a non-financial business uses innovative technology to provide services, such as remittance, payment and settlement, and investment, without working with a financial company. |
| Lukanova and Vasiljeva (2016) | FinTech is an industry oriented toward arranging financial services for private individuals and industries with the aim of providing customer-oriented solutions in the most efficient way and at the lowest cost possible, ensuring this via innovation and technology. |
| Romānova and Kudinska (2017) | In a broader sense, FinTech is seen as a new market that integrates finance and technology, and replaces traditional financial structures with new technology-based processes. As the FinTech sector borders are difficult to define, available data on FinTech is somewhat controversial, depending on companies included in the report. |
| Swacha-Lech (2017) | FinTech is perceived as "a dynamic segment at the intersection of the financial services and technology sectors where technology-focused start-ups and new market entrants innovate the products and services currently provided by the traditional financial services industry" [PwC 2016, p. 3]. |
| Gimpel et al. (2018) | From an industry perspective, FinTech start-ups are typically non-financial businesses such as technology-driven companies and online businesses. |
| Acar and Çıtak (2019) | Another definition for Fintech by PwC (2016a) is "a dynamic segment at the intersection of the financial services and technology sectors where technology-focused start-ups and new market entrants innovate the products and services currently provided by the traditional financial services industry. |

## Fintech as an Industry

At this level, authors (Table 4) use the terms of industry, sector, market, and segment. As an industry, Fintech results from leveraging IT sector innovations and the latest digital technologies in the field of financial services by non-financial business. IT focused start-ups and companies create innovative financial products and services via technology to offer individuals and firms customer-oriented services. Innovation

*Table 4. Classification of the Fintech landscape (Haddad and Hornuf, 2019)*

| Category | Definition |
|---|---|
| Asset management | We classify Fintech startups as asset management companies if they offer services such as robo-advice, social trading, wealth management, personal financial management apps, or software. |
| Exchange services | We categorize startups as exchanges if they provide financial or stock exchange services, such as securities, derivatives, and other financial instrument trading. |
| Financing | The financing category entails, for example, startups that provide crowdfunding, crowd lending, microcredit, and factoring solutions. |
| Insurance | The insurance category entails, for example, startups that broker peer-to-peer insurance, spot insurance, usage-driven insurance, insurance contract management, and brokerage services as well as claims and risk management services. |
| Loyalty program | We also consider startups that provide loyalty program services to customers, because they often use big data analytics and are closely linked to payment transactions. The loyalty program category involves, for example, startups providing rewards for brand loyalty or giving customers advanced access to new products, special sales coupons, or free merchandise |
| Others | A bulk of Fintech startups offer investor education and training, innovative background services (e.g., near-field communication systems, authorization services), white-label solutions for various business models, or other technical advancements classified under other business activities of Fintech startups. |
| Payment | The payment category entails business models that provide new and innovative payment solutions, such as mobile payment systems, e-wallets, or crypto currencies |
| Regulatory technology | We classify Fintech startups as regulatory technology companies if they offer services based on technology in the context of regulatory monitoring, reporting, and compliance benefiting the finance industry |
| Risk management | The category risk management contains startups that provide services that help companies better assess the financial reliability of their counterparties or better manage their own risk. |

and technology are combined to provide products and services with more efficiency and at lower costs than the traditional financial services industry.

Navaretti et al. (2017) highlight the existence of three areas of actual and potential expansion of Fintech industry. These are transaction execution (payments, clearing and settlement), funds management (deposit, lending, capital raising and investment management) and insurance. Lukanova and Vasiljeva (2016) suggest the following division of activities in the Fintech area:

- Service-oriented: development of technology-related services which are traditionally provided by financial institutions, such as funds transfer or card payments, lending and investment, P2P lending, crowdfunding, or foreign exchange.
- Data-oriented: solutions and technologies devoted to collecting, processing and analyzing information. Although banks do not pay much attention to the

big data phenomenon, recently there have been signs that this tendency is changing.

- Process-oriented: after the financial crisis of 2008, banks all over the world re-defined their operating models. Nowadays, banks are introducing the so-called cost caps and have started working on increasing efficiency and process automation.

Romanova and Kudinska (2017) stated that Fintech industry comprises five major areas: finance and investment, operations and risk management, payments and infrastructure, data security and monetization, and customer interface. Among these services, they highlighted that the most attractive services to investment are finance as well as payments and infrastructure, notably, peer-to-peer lending/ online lending/ scoring, online acquiring and mobile wallets and personal financial management and planning. Iman (2020) enumerated 16 subsectors of Fintech industry, which are Back-end and infrastructure, Banking infrastructure, Business lending, Consumer and commercial banking, Consumer lending, Consumer payments, Crowdfunding, Data and market research, Equity financing, Institutional investing, International remittance, Personal finance, Point of sale, Retail investing, Security, Small and medium enterprise (SME) tools.

All of the above-mentioned areas of Fintech industry are also indicated by Dorfleitner et al. (2017). These authors summarized those areas under four segments of the Fintech industry, which are Financing, Asset Management, Payments and Other Fintechs as indicated in figure 1.

*Figure 1. Segments of the Fintech industry (Dorfleitner et al., 2017)*

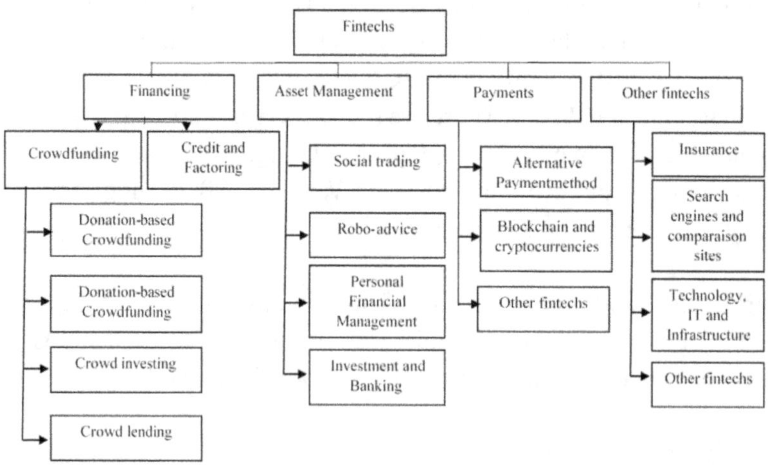

## The Fintech Ecosystem

According to Lee and Shin (2018), understanding the competitive and collaborative dynamics in Fintech innovation requires analyzing the ecosystem. They added that a stable symbiotic Fintech ecosystem is instrumental in the growth of the Fintech industry. In fact, the ecosystem defines the necessary infrastructure elements for the development of the Fintech area in a country (Yazici, 2019). Understanding the Fintech ecosystem is important for the development of mechanisms to ensure the survival and growth of the ecosystem. Diemers et al. (2015, cited by Lee and Shin, 2018) suggested that entrepreneurs, government, and financial institutions are participants in a Fintech ecosystem. In addition to these participants, Lee and Shin (2018) mentioned technology developers and financial customers. Yazici (2019) extended the Fintech ecosystem to the following main components:

- New technologies and tools that enable innovations;
- Telecom and technology companies that create infrastructure for distribution;
- Startups that create innovative business models;
- Government and regulators that define the rules of the game;
- Financial institutions that cooperate with startups;
- Customers and users who benefit from innovations;
- Investors, incubation centers and accelerators that enable both financial aid and space for innovators.

The same author concluded that to create a wealthy Fintech ecosystem, all players and stakeholders must work together and try to create synergy in order to sustain competitive advantages. Accordingly, without interaction, the ecosystem loses its power and competitiveness falls (Yazici, 2019).

Lee and Shin (2018) identify five components of the Fintech ecosystem:

- **Fintech startups** are discussed in the previous sections. They are at the core of the ecosystem. Fintech startups are the new technology-based companies that offer innovative solutions in the financial industry. They are characterized by innovation and flexibility, and they are customer-centric. Hence, on the one hand, they affect the consumer by offering digital and customized services. On the other hand, they have a disruptive influence on banks and create a real threat for the future of these institutions (Swacha-Lech, 2017).
- **Technology developers** deliver digital technologies, such as big data, cloud computing, cryptocurrency, social media, and artificial intelligence (AI), etc., which are underlying the Fintech startup activities. These technologies enable startup businesses to automatize their business processes and offer services

and products within the financial sector. In parallel, Fintech startups generate revenue in favor of technology developers.

- **Government** (e.g., financial regulators and legislature): According to Iman (2020), government regulations could play a pivotal role in the emergence of Fintech start-ups and shape the way industry develops. Governments and regulatory agencies can positively influence different dimensions of the Fintech ecosystem. For example, they can develop initiatives that promote the emergence of Fintech startups by simplifying some procedures, and creating special regulative sandboxes for innovative financial technologies and services approbation. However, they can also have a negative impact, by creating rigid and bureaucratic regulations.
- **Financial customers** (e.g., individuals and organizations): these are the source of revenue generation for Fintech companies. According to Ryu (2017), customers will use the Fintech product or service if its benefits are greater than its risks. Thus, Fintech companies are challenged to increase the potential benefits of Fintech usage while limiting its potential risks. Swacha-Lech (2017) found that, from the customers' perspective, Fintech companies have value in being easy to use (81.9%), offering faster service (81.4%) and providing a good experience (79.6%). Fintech are more focused on individuals and small as well as medium-sized enterprises (SME) than on large organizations (Lee and Shin, 2018). Several authors (Swacha-lech, 2017; Lee and Shin, 2018) found that Fintech clients are majorly among tech-savvy, young, urban, and high-income individuals. Millennials (people between the age of 18 and 34) are more likely than other generation to purchase non-bank services and products. This is favorable for Fintech since the tech-savvy millennials will account for the largest part of the population and drive the growth of Fintech services.
- **Traditional financial institutions** (e.g., traditional banks, insurance companies, stock brokerage firms, and venture capitalists) are the major actors of financial system (Yazici, 2019). Fintech startups may be a source of threats as well as opportunities for traditional financial institutions (Zveryakov et al., 2019). While traditional financial institutions initially treated Fintech companies as threats, they shifted their focus to collaborating with Fintech startups with various funding provisions (Lee and Shin, 2018; Yazici, 2019).

After defining Fintech and presenting the components of its ecosystem, we are going to present in the following section, the Fintech ecosystem in the Tunisian context.

## DESCRIPTION OF THE TUNISIAN FINTECH ECOSYSTEM

Tunisia is lagging behind in Fintech, which is mainly explained by the rigidity of the regulations. Indeed, until today, the Tunisian legislator does not give a definition to the term "Fintech" and does not legislate specific regulations for it.

March 22, 2018[1], the Tunisian Professional Association of Banks and Financial Institutions (TPABFI) organized a seminar on Fintech. The objective was to start discussing the upheaval caused by the development of financial technologies. In this seminar, international experts stressed the importance of creating an efficient ecosystem that meets both economic and regulatory challenges as well as the expectations of the various players-and that of creating synergies between Fintech and the banking sector.

In order to catch up, the BCT has launched several actions, which will be presented in the following section.

### Central Bank of Tunisia

December 2019[2], **Central Bank of Tunisia (CBT)** announced:

- The creation of a Fintech committee, which is going to be the relay between the CBT and the innovation ecosystem in Tunisia and the launch of a website[3] dedicated to this function. Thus, this committee collaborates with research centers and universities on joint innovation initiatives and facilitates Fintech's interaction with the CBT departments.
- The launch of a "CBT-LAB": this is a platform enabling the CBT to digitize certain internal processes and to keep watching over financial technological innovations.
- The launch of a "regulatory Sandbox": this is to authorize Fintech to test innovative solutions with voluntary customers for a limited period of time and under the supervision of the CBT. This initiative will allow the regulator to understand the complexity of the technology used in financial innovation. Adjustment when necessary of the regulatory framework inevitably requires this better understanding. Meanwhile, Fintech will align with regulatory requirements.

The CBT remains very active in innovation exchange of regional and international experiences-by participating in the work of Maghreb Fintech Committee and Regional Fintech Working Group.

## Fintech Startups

Fintech Companies operate in many fields (crowdfunding, mobile payment, savings management, financial advice or decision support) as shown in figure 2. They provide end-user services (within the B2C or B2B market) as well as platform or infrastructure services. DisrupTunisia[4], directory and aggregation of Tunisia startups news, gathers in an online platform, a database of Tunisian startups.

*Financing*

- **Crowdfunding**
    - **Donation-based Crowdfunding**
- **EffectusCoFundy,** created in 2013, offers a crowdfunding platform to boost projects that have a social, environmental and cultural impact on society in Africa. Only Tunisians living abroad can finance online projects with their donations. Tunisians residing in Tunisia are prevented by the regulations in force.
    - **Reward- based Crowdfunding**
- **Coinsence Tunisia (2020)** offers a platform that provides a range of tools to empower people, organizations and communities to collaborate on initiatives that benefit society powered by blockchain. Coinsence Tunisia enables community to fund projects, exchange value in open marketplaces, realize projects, and create impact.
- **Crowd investing**
    - **Aston Technologies**(September 2019) offers a payment platform backed by merchant marketplaces.
    - **Effectus Afrikwity,** launched in 2013, offers an equity crowdfunding platform dedicated to the launch of entrepreneurial projects in Africa.
- **Credit and factoring**
    - **K2lis** (December 2019) is a digital microfinance platform accompanied by a web and mobile Wallet intended for microfinance institutions and their beneficiaries.

*Payments*

- **M AND EL SOLUTION** (January 2020) offers the Pay Grant platform for targeting compensation through mobile payment.
- **Paymee** (April 2019) allows payment as a mobile application. The features are sending money, payment of merchants purchases and receipt of customer payments.
- **TanitCash** allows money transfer from France to Tunisia instantly and 60% cheaper.

- **Sobflous** (June 2019) is an electronic wallet (web and mobile) that offers users phone recharge, money transfer, merchant payment and invoice payment services.
- **Link & Pay** (2015) offers a payment platform for foreign purchases and invoices in Africa. Link & Pay offers Africans abroad to pay online and on mobile for their relatives purchases and invoices in Africa; which saves the cost of transferring money.

***Loyalty program***

- **MintIT** (December 2019), via the platform Grabingo, provides loyal customers with the opportunity to collect points from their favorite stores. It allows a multiplicity of functions to their partners including a progress-tracking feature and helps them attract customers by providing them with stores localization and a genius notification system about the trendy offers.

***Blockchain and cryptocurrencies***

- **SQOIN** (January 2020) consists in setting up a new crypto currency called BASTOJI intended mainly for the African continent. This crypto currency is free, open source and easy to use. It is blockchain that provides a secure, free, fast and fluid exchange system.
- **Medcretech** (April 2019) offers a Blockchain application to trace and fluidize the life cycle of real estate.
- **Universa** (July 2019) is a new generation of blockchain. It is a cooperative state change registry, performed by licensed and trusted nodes, and is capable of handling thousands or tens of thousands of transactions per second.
- **Lightency** (October 2019) develops an electricity exchange platform among individuals, and brings together all the sector's stakeholders on the same platform in order to reduce costs.
- **Tledger** (October 2019) is a Blockchain, Web and Mobile development company, offering network access to financial and non-financial institutions and allowing them to carry out financial transactions in real time through Application Programming Interface (API) and mobiles wallets.
- **Universal Technology Of Infinite Keys (UTIK)** (January 2020) provides personalized services to build digital trust through risk identification and preaching, cryptography and an infrastructure for decentralized applications.
- **Yanalyst** (2016) is an independent research bureau specialized in crypto Assets. It offers a wide range of specialized services in crypto assets and blockchain industry. It drives Blockchain Adoption across all

industries and helps clients to better understand the opportunities and the challenges for their markets.

*Insurance*

- ◦ **Digiconstat** (March 2020) digitizes automobile claims in the Sultanate of Oman. It is a mobile application that allows geo-locating the accident in a few minutes, taking photos and describing the circumstances by voice message. Digiconstat exports its Tunisian product to help insurance companies maintain their claims service during the Covid-19 period.
- ◦ **Dqlick** (April 2019) specializes in digitalization in the insurance sector.
- ◦ **SmartIN** (July 2019) is an InsurTech, which offers innovative solutions for enriching and improving services in the insurance sector.
- ◦ **Insurise** (April 2020) is a data-enabled digital insurance platform for carrying out digital paths such as self-care for better customer relations and operational efficiency.
- ◦ **Neopolis** (April 2019) develops, in offshore and Editing, digitalization and robotization solutions intended for the insurance sector and banks.

*Technology, IT and Infrastructure*

- ◦ **Kaoun** (April 2019) offers new infrastructure for better financial inclusion. It offers identification that allows strong remote authentication of the client when opening an account or before making online payments. Kaoun proposes:
  - ▪ FlouciFlouci, which is the first wallet designed to innovate mobile payment in Tunisia. It's a quick, easy, and convenient way to open a bank account, send and receive money, and pay different merchants online from the app.
  - ▪ Flouci Business is dedicated to companies wishing to monitor their daily transactions and income. The app provides different information about the customers and the store finances via a complete dashboard and summary reports.
  - ▪ Botkeji is designed to automate processes within the bank and provide real-time access to various banking services.

- **Paypos** (March 2019) is a leader in the development of innovative electronic payment solutions and the digitalization of banking and financial distribution channels in Tunisia and Africa.
  - ◦ **Catrim Tech** (July 2019) develops innovative solutions for the trading rooms of investment banks.
  - ◦ **Peak Technologies** (April 2019) specializes in the development of management and controls solutions for transactional operations based on Blockchain technologies.

- **Deepera.Ai** (June 2019) provides smart and AI based solutions for the financial sector.
- **Sookbank** is a 100% digital Tunisian platform for promoting banking culture launched in the late 2018. A virtual advisor supports internet users in their search for information related to the banking sector. Thus, the platform brings together all the latest industry news and practical information on the offers and services of all Tunisian banks. According to the head of digital marketing, in an article[5] published in Magazine Entreprises, Sookbank offers banks a range of digital services.
- **UniQ Soft Technology** (April 2019) is a FinTech firm that provides UniQ Financial Solutions, a next generation Accounting Information System, built based on Event Accounting Approach.
- **Facturation.Tn** (2017) offers an online billing application that complies with Tunisian regulations and which is accessible to several users working on a single interface.
- **SWIVER** (April 2019) Swiver is an ERP in SAS mode intended for Very Small Businesses and Small and Medium Enterprises to digitize their financial management process.
- **Expensya** (April 2019) offers an expense management solution for professionals focused on mobile devices that are based on next generation character recognition technology and machine learning. It offers automation of expense report management.
- **Tools4com OIS** (2008) offers an online, interactive and collaborative solution that allows its user to manage and control the billing process.

***Exchange services***

- **Yanvestee**, created in 2019, offers a management and distribution platform for regulated investment and financing products. It connects investors looking for investment opportunities with financial institutions looking for deposits and financing.
- **Ilboursa** (April 2019) is the first new generation stock exchange portal in Tunisia which allows the development of the stock market and the economic culture and the contribution to the strengthening of Tunisia Stock Exchange visibility to attract new investors.
- **Trading Systems Company (TSC)** offers the Financia application for the stock market. This application includes all the functionalities which stock market professionals (stock market intermediaries, bank account keepers & management companies) use.
- **Insight+** develops highly added value technological products for the Forex market.

*Technology Developers*

- **Monetics Services Solutions** is a specialist in monetics present on the entire value chain of payment systems in Tunisia and abroad. It offers products and solutions for electronic payment, transaction security, and monetic data management.
- **Bitaka Group** is a group of companies that are amongst the major field players in the electronic charging and solution development of IT intergration, for both, telecommunications, and electronic banking.
- **Viamobile** is a software development and operation company that aims to use telecommunication technologies to bring businesses closer to their customers and help them develop new business solutions by deploying innovative mobile applications.
- Other editor and integrator of software for financial sector such as Group International Finance Bank (IFB).

## Traditional Financial Institutions

In recent years, The Tunisian banking system has suffered a certain disengagement from the state, the entry of foreign investors into the shareholding of banks as well as from the access of foreign banks to the local market. Hence, three categories of banks are identified[6]:

- Banks with high state ownership (mainly BNA, STB, and BH).
- Banks with private Tunisian capital (BIAT, BT and Amen Bank).
- Banks with the foreign majority (UIB-SG, UBCI-BNP Paribas, Attijari Bank and ATB).

Currently, there are 25 universal banks, 2 merchant banks, 8 leasing companies and 3 factoring companies.

## Financial Customers

There are mainly two types of financial customers:

- **Individuals:** Mobile access[7] (Smartphones and tablets) increased from 16% in 2013 to 39% in 2015 and traffic from mobile increased from 21% in 2014 to 30% in 2015 (24% Smartphone and 6% tablet).
- **Organizations** (banks, other financial institutions, insurance, companies, ...)

*Figure 2. Components of the Tunisian Fintech Ecosystem*

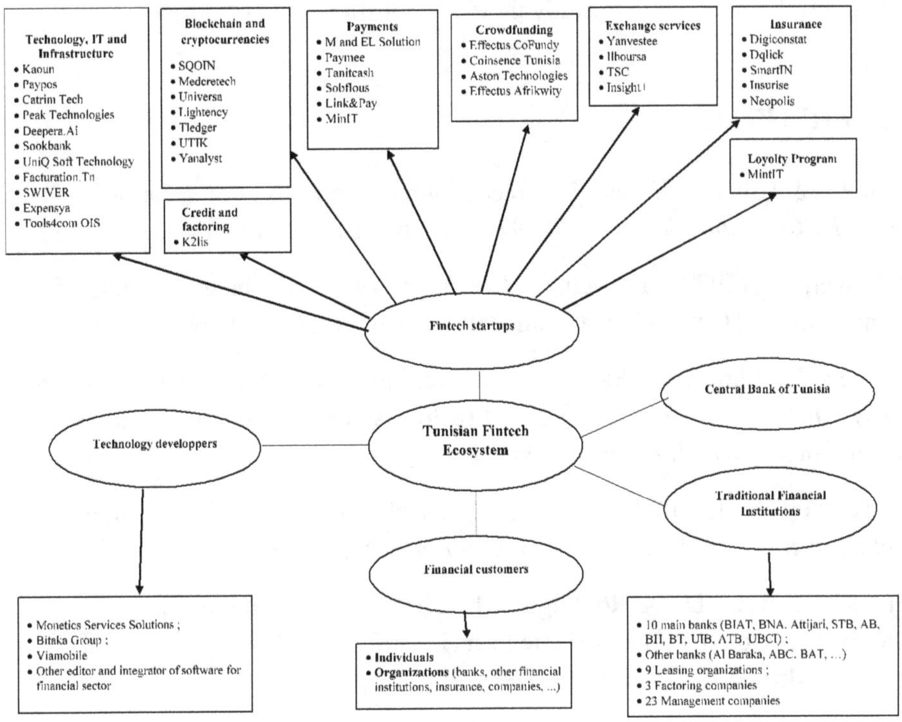


## CONCLUSION

This descriptive chapter attempts to define the Fintech concept and present the components of its ecosystem. Based on this description, we have determined the Tunisian Fintech ecosystem. The latter is composed of Central Bank of Tunisia, Fintech Startups (financing, crowdfunding, credit and factoring), payments, blockchain and cryptocurrencies, insurance, technology, IT and infrastructure, loyalty program and exchange services), technology developers, traditional financial institutions and financial customers.

This paper presents theoretical contributions. It suggests a comprehensive understanding of the term Fintech, through the discussion of this term under three interpretations: Fintech as financial services relying on digital technologies, Fintech as startups and IT companies, and Fintech as industry. Moreover, it will allow researchers, who wish to conduct research on the Tunisian context, as well as practitioners to understand the Tunisian Fintech ecosystem. Despite the contributions cited, this study remains at a descriptive level. It would be interesting to deal in future research with the impact of Fintech on business management as well as on consumer behavior. It would also be interesting to study their relationships with banks.

## REFERENCES

Acar, O., & Çıtak, Y. E. (2019). Fintech Integration Process Suggestion for Banks. *Procedia Computer Science, 158*, 971–978. doi:10.1016/j.procs.2019.09.138

Bettinger, A. (1972). Fintech: A Series of 40 Time Shared Models Used at Manufacturers Hanover Trust Company. *Interfaces, 2*(4), 62–63.

Diemers, D., Lamaa, A., Salamat, J., & Steffens, T. (2015). *Developing a FinTech ecosystem in the GCC*. Strategy. https://www.strategyand.pwc.com/media/file/Developing-aFinTech-ecosystem-in-the-GCC.pdf

Dorfleitner, G., Hornuf, L., Schmitt, M., & Weber, M. (2017). *Definition of FinTech and Description of the FinTech Industry FinTech in Germany*. Springer.

Gimpel, H., Rau, D., & Röglinger, M. (2018). Understanding FinTech start-ups – a taxonomy of consumer-oriented service offerings. *Electronic Markets, 28*(3), 245–264. doi:10.100712525-017-0275-0

Gomber, P., Koch, J. A., & Siering, M. (2017). Digital Finance and FinTech: Current research and future research directions. *J Bus Econ, 87*(5), 537–580. doi:10.100711573-017-0852-x

Haddad, C., & Hornuf, L. (2019). The emergence of the global fintech market: Economic and technological determinants. *Small Business Economics, 53*(1), 81–105. doi:10.100711187-018-9991-x

Iman, N. (2020). The rise and rise of financial technology: The good, the bad, and the verdict. *Cogent Business & Management, 7*(1), 1. doi:10.1080/23311975.2020.1725309

Kim, Y., Park, Y.-J., Choi, J., & Yeon, J. (2016). An Empirical Study on the Adoption of "Fintech" Service: Focused on Mobile Payment Services. *Advanced Science and Technology Letters, 114*, 136–140. doi:10.14257/astl.2015.114.26

Lee, L., & Shin, Y. J. (2018). Fintech: Ecosystem, business models, investment decisions, and challenges. *Business Horizons, 61*(1), 35–46. doi:.bushor.2017.09.003 doi:10.1016/j

Liudmila, Z., Mateusz, D., & Gerhard, S. (2016). FinTech – What's in a Name? *Thirty Seventh International Conference on Information Systems*.

Lukanova, K., & Vasiljeva, T. (2016). Commercial banks and Fintech companies in the digital transformation: Challenges for the future. *Journal of Business and Management, 11*, 25–34.

Milian, E. Z., Spinola, M. M., & de Carvalho, M. M. (2019). Fintechs: A literature review and research agenda. *Electronic Commerce Research and Applications, 34*, 34. doi:10.1016/j.elerap.2019.100833

Navaretti, G. B., Calzolari, G., & Pozzolo, A. F. (2017). Fintech and banks: Friends or foes? Oshodin, O., Karanasios, S., Molla, A., & Ong, C.E. (2019). How do FinTech Start-ups Develop Capabilities? Towards a FinTech Capability Model. *Twenty-Third Pacific Asia Conference on Information Systems.*

Panetta, F. (2018). *Fintech and banking: today and tomorrow Speech by the Deputy Governor of the Bank of Italy.* Harvard Law School Bicentennial Annual Reunion of the Harvard Law School Association of Europe. https://www.bancaditalia.it/pubblicazioni/interventi-direttorio/int-dir-2018/panetta-120518.pdf

Romānova, I., & Kudinska, M. (2017). Banking and fintech: A challenge or opportunity? *Contemporary Issues in Finance: Current Challenges from Across Europe Contemporary Studies in Economic and Financial Analysis, 98*, 21–35. doi:10.1108/S1569-375920160000098002

Ryu, H. S. (2017). What makes users willing or hesitant to use Fintech?: The moderating effect of user type. *Industrial Management & Data Systems.* Advance online publication. doi:10.1108/IMDS-07-2017-0325

Saksonova, S., & Kuzmina-Merlino, I. (2017). Fintech as Financial Innovation – The Possibilities and Problems of Implementation. *European Research Studies Journal, 10*(3A).

Swacha-Lech, M. (2017). The main challenges facing the retail banking industry in the era of digitalization. *Journal of Insurance. Financial Markets and Consumer Protection, 26*(4), 94–116.

Thakor, A. V. (2020). Fintech and banking: What do we know? *Journal of Financial Intermediation*, 41.

Tnani, F. (2019). *Pourquoi la Tunisie est-elle en retard en matière de fintech? L'économiste Maghrébin.* Available at: https://www.leconomistemaghrebin.com/2019/02/27/la-tunisie-en-retard-en-matiere-de-fintech/

Yazici, S. (2019). The analysis of fintech ecosystem in Turkey. *Journal of Business. Economics and Finance, 8*(4), 188–197. doi:10.17261/Pressacademia.2019.1162

Zveryakov, M., Kovalenko, V., Sheludko, S., & Sharah, E. (2019). FinTech sector and banking business: Competition or symbiosis? *Economic Annals-XXI, 175*(1-2), 53–57. doi:10.21003/ea.V175-09

## KEY TERMS AND DEFINITIONS

**Digital Technologies:** Internet technologies, internet of things, social media, artificial intelligence, big data analytics.

**E-Finance:** All forms of financial services such as banking, insurance, and stock trading performed through electronic means, including the internet and world wide web.

**Ecosystem:** Defines the necessary infrastructure elements for the development of the Fintech area in a country

**Fintech:** Financial technology.

**Fintech Innovation:** Combines the e-finance, internet technologies, social networking services, social media, artificial intelligence, and big data analytics.

## ENDNOTES

1 https://www.tustex.com/economie-actualites-economiques/la-fintech-et-les-banques-tunisiennes-en-debat-a-l-initiative-de-l-aptbef-et-kpmg

2 https://www.tunisienumerique.com/

3 https://fintech.bct.gov.tn/fr/BCT-FINTECH

4 https://www.disruptunisia.com/

5 https://www.entreprises-magazine.com/sookbank-la-premiere-plateforme-100-digitale-de-conseil-et-de-culture-bancaire-en-tunisie/

6 Amen Invest (intermediate in stock Exchange) report (March 2011), http://www.businessnews.com.tn/pdf/Secteur-bancaire0311.pdf

7 WMC Portail (webmanagercenter (FR) – Directinfo (FR) – Almasdar (AR))-Online Magazines.

# Chapter 9
# Competition Between Neobanks and Online Banks in the French Retail Banking Market and Reactions From Universal Banks

**Jean Michel Rocchi**
*Sciences Po Aix, France*

## ABSTRACT

*This chapter will provide an analysis of market moves, and innovation sources, from newcomers and incumbent players, based on core and periphery networks theory; and additional survival analysis and VSR model, based on organizational population ecology. The French market neobanks, which are a subpart of fintech, are dominantly set up by entrepreneurs. On the contrary, online banks usually have universal banks as shareholders. Does this difference matter regarding market strategies? Is innovation coming only from peripheral actors like online banks and moreover neobanks, or do large retail banks at the heart of the banking system try to integrate or promote it? The author will discuss these topics to conclude with mixed evidence. Hence, if neobanks, on one hand, tend to converge towards the core; universal banks, on the other hand, are growingly accepting peripheral actors.*

DOI: 10.4018/978-1-7998-7110-1.ch009

Whereas between 1860 and 1990 the French banking industry was marked by steady growth and incremental technological improvements, since the mid-1990s breakthrough innovations (internet, smartphone) profoundly changed the competitive landscape in France and more broadly in the European economic area. In this chapter, we will look at the organizational level, the origin of innovation in the banking and para-banking industry. Our first research question will be: does innovation originate exclusively from the peripheral players (online banks, neobanks), or does it also find its source in the traditional banks that are at the heart of the financial industry? Then, at a second level of analysis, we will ask a new question: why is it that the population of online banks, which benefit from a solid banking shareholding, experience a higher organizational mortality rate than neobanks, even though they were created on the initiative of simple entrepreneurs?

This chapter will be divided into six sections: the literature review, an attempt to define fintechs, a brief review of the history of fintechs and the emergence of digital banks in France, a description of the interactions between core and periphery in France (answering to research question 1), a presentation from the point of view of the organizational population ecology (answering to research question 2), and lastly a discussion and areas for future research.

## LITERATURE REVIEW ON ENTREPRENEURSHIP, INNOVATION, AND ORGANIZATIONAL POPULATION ECOLOGY.

The French word ''entrepreneur'' dates back, to Cantillon (1755/2015) to describe all types of creators exposed to a risk of failure. Say (1803/2018) mentions the qualities that an entrepreneur must possess ''judgment, consistency, knowledge of men and things.'' Knight (1921) pointed out that an entrepreneur operates in an environment dominated by uncertainty and'' the ''specialization" of uncertainty-bearing in the hands of entrepreneurs'' (p.245). Keynes (1973) describes the *''animal spirits''* of the decision-making of entrepreneurs as *''a spontaneous urge to action rather than inaction, and not as the outcome of quantitative benefits multiplied by quantitative probabilities''* (p.161).

The more recent literature is devoted to the concept of opportunity which overlaps two aspects: the discovery of it on the one hand, and the exploitation of it on the other hand. For Kirzner (1973) entrepreneurs specifics, unlike other market participants, consist *"… in their alertness to previously unnoticed changes in circumstances which may make it possible to get far more in exchange for whatever they have to offer than was hitherto possible*" (p.15-16). Kirzner (1997) considers that an opportunity covers two aspects: on the one hand an "*imprecisely defined market need*" and on the other hand, *''an un or under employed resources or capabilities*''. Hence, the entrepreneur is a decision-maker coping with opportunities poorly noticed before his action. For Casson (1982) an entrepreneur is someone taking superior decisions ''*about the coordination of scarce resources*''. Entrepreneurs are a threat to inefficient organizations. Their ability to exploit opportunities is the consequence of the lack of efforts of other individuals.

Superior entrepreneurs are supporting new ideas and pushing for innovation; they are at the periphery while the existing dominant business is on the core. Cattani and Ferriani (2008) within the context of the Hollywood motion picture industry ''*argue that individuals who occupy an intermediate position between the core and the periphery of their social system are in a favorable position to achieve creative results. In addition, the benefits accrued through an individual's intermediate core/periphery position can also be observed at the team level, when the same individual works in a team whose members come from both ends of the core/periphery continuum*'' (p.824). Moreover, Sgourev (2013) in the context of cubism acceptance argue that modern art is a model where: ''*…not only the periphery moves toward the core through collective action, as typically asserted, but the core also moves toward the periphery, becoming more receptive to radical ideas* '' (p.1). But the paradox is that if outsiders seem more efficient in providing innovation, they are less likely to carry them out (Sgourev, 2013; Cattani et al., 2017).

Regarding the market evolution, what does ''*new*'' mean? Davidsson (2016) provides an answer in saying that ''*new*'' is dual as it means*"that either the new activity is an independent start-up, implying that a new firm emerges as a result, or an internal new venture, which means that the firm has previously not been making this particular market offering*'' (p.8). In other words, "new'' covers both entrepreneurship stricto sensu, as well as ''intrapreneuring'' (Pinchot, 1985; Pinchot & Pellman, 1999). Notwithstanding that technological innovation could emerge as the result of both ''*breakthrough*'' or ''*bricolage*'' (Garud & Karnøe, 2003). Now, ''disruptive innovation'' (Christensen et al., 2018) needs to be explained as in one hand ''it gained considerable currency among practitioners'' but on the other hand is characterized by ''widespread misunderstanding of its core principles'' (p.1043). Hence, for Christensen et al., (2018), ''A related issue is overuse of *disruptive innovation/disruption* as a synonym for any new threat (or substantial ongoing change) and underuse of disruptive innovation as a theoretical concept" (p.1044). The original theory of disruptive innovation emerged from empirical observations illustrating that incumbents outperform new entrants at the time of incremental moves but they underperform at disruptive innovations ones (Christensen, 1997). What characterizes disruptive innovations is that they are rare and those new entrants are offering products inferior to the incumbents but have other attributes such as being cheaper, more convenient etc… Over time new entrants move from the low-end of the market to the high-end market (Christensen, 1997).

Lastly, Jourdan et al., (2017) in the context of the French movie industry financing argue that ''*deference is the price outsider organizations pay to pass categorical and symbolic boundaries and gain acceptance in contexts where insiders regard them as impure*'' (p.232).

The author has chosen a dual level of analysis and beyond individual firms trajectories, the population level analysis will also be considered in the light of organizational population ecology (Hannan & Freeman, 1977) and especially variation, selection, retention (VSR) Model (Campbell, 1960, 1969).

In this chapter, the three-level of analysis will be: first, individual (a neobank, or an online bank). At this level, we will investigate the source of innovation and will discuss if the core and periphery networks theory is helping to explain empirical observations. Second, at the population level, we will compare results of neobanks and online banks notably in terms of emergence, mutation, and survival. Third, at the community level of digital banking (including the two populations), we will study their mutual impact and interferences, as well as with traditional banks (universal banks). By doing that, our approach is close to a bioecologist, as explain (Hannan & Freeman, 1977) in organization analysis 5 levels of analysis are sometimes possible: ''*The situation faced by organizations analyst is more complex. Instead of three levels of analysis, he faces at least five: (1) members, (2) subunits, (3) individual organizations, (4) populations of organizations and (5) communities of (populations of) organizations. Levels 3-5 can be seen as corresponding to the three levels discussed for general ecology, with the individual organization taking the place of the individual organism. The added complexity arises because organizations are more nearly decomposable into constituent parts than are organisms. Individual members and subunits may move from organization to organization in a manner which has no parallel in nonhuman organization*'' (p.933-934). In other words, we will not study for instance managers trajectories and their impact on the success of the firm they are leading. For example, successful manager André Coisne launched as General Manager ING Direct (now ING) in France, before joining BforBank, the online bank of Crédit Agricole at the same responsibility level, and then moved as Orange Bank's CEO, the online bank of the Telecom Group Orange. This managerial level of analysis will not be discussed. Nevertheless, as neobanks are mostly entrepreneurial firms, we will discuss the profile of founders using the Nickel case, in the light of the core and periphery networks theory and will conclude to similarities with some observations made in the Hollywood motion picture industry (Cattani & Ferriani, 2008). At the firm level, we will discuss business model and we are using Demil & Lecocq (2010) definition: ''The business model concept generally refers to the articulation between different areas of a firm's activity designed to produce a proposition of value to customers. Two different uses of the term can be noted. The first is a static approach – as a blueprint for the coherence between core business model components. The second refers to a more transformational approach, using the concept as a tool to address change and innovation in the organization, or in the model itself'' (p.227).The author focuses on the second aspect of this definition, innovation in the business model, and its transformation if any.

## DEFINING FINTECH: THE QUEST FOR THE HOLY GRAIL?

As Nicoletti (2017) underlines, *''Financial technology, commonly called ''fintech'', is now a highly used buzzword''* (p.1). Beyond buzzword, fintech is disintermediating the financial services industry. The speed of growth of fintech in the world as well as in France has been outstanding due to some key drivers: a changing economic environment (post-2007-2008 financial crisis), a new regulatory landscape (EU directives on payments systems and electronic banking notably), bright entrepreneurs determined to better serve customers expectations and, growing sums raised through venture capitalists resulting for the most successful ones in notable IPOs. Payments are the heart of the banking industry, Arstanian and Fisher (2019) explain: *''But payments aren't only important to incumbent financial institutions because of the fees that they generate. Payments are the starting point of a typical client's banking journey and an individual's most frequent and visceral connection with their financial institutions. Consequently, they are viewed as the cornerstone of a 'sticky' relationship between banks and their customer''* (p.32). Having said that, the same authors temper their statement by emphasizing four challenges: recruiting talents, regulatory compliance, sufficient access to fundraising, and lastly scaling customer basis.

Proposing a widely accepted definition seems out of reach due to ''blurred lines" (PwC, 2016), and could be compared to ''taming the beast'' (Scheffel, 2016). Evidence, hereafter on Table 1., shows that there are two main possibilities: considering that it is simply a new way to tackle old financial needs (Arner et al., 2016 ; Philippon 2016 ; Schueffel 2016) or trying to describe the scope of products and (or) services provided by fintech (PwC, 2016 ; ACPR, 2017 ; IMF, 2017 ; Navaretti et al., 2017). Proposing a description of the fintech concept is a challenge, as shown in table 1 hereafter.

## FROM WORLD HISTORY OF FINTECH TO THE APPEARANCE OF ONLINE BANKS AND NEOBANKS IN FRANCE

The emergence of fintech can be dated back to the nineteenth century (Arner et al., 2016) with the invention of firstly the telegraph (1838) and secondly the installation of

*Table 1. Some definitions and scope of fintech concept.*

| Source | Date | Scope of the fintech definition. |
|---|---|---|
| Arner et al. | 2016 | ''New Term for an Old Sector '' which'' covers the entire scope of services and products traditionally provided by the financial services industry'' (p.1275-1276). |
| PwC/GFR. | 2016 | ''Areas of disruption'' will be: ''consumer banking, fund transfer & payments, investment & wealth management, SME banking, brokerage services, property & casualty insurance/life insurance, commercial banking, insurance intermediairy, market operators & exchanges, fund operators, investment banking, reinsurance.'' (p.6) |
| Philippon /NBER. | 2016 | '' FinTech covers digital innovation and technology-enabled business model innovations in the financial sector '' (p.2) |
| Schueffel. | 2016 | '' Fintech is a new financial industry that applies technology to improve financial activities.'' (p.45) |
| ACPR. | 2017 | Blockchain/tech, payment/neobank, crowdfunding, insurance, KYC, Financing/lending, financial advisory, other (advisory ...). |
| IMF. | 2017 | Regulation, back-office operations, currency and payments, lending, insurance, savings, advice. |
| Barba Navaretti et al. | 2017 | a) Transactions execution (payments, clearing and settlement) ; b) funds management (deposit, lending, capital raising and investment management) and c) insurance. (p.12). |
| Lee & Shin. | 2018 | '' The technological developments in infrastructure, big data, data analytics, and mobile devices allow fintech startups to disintermediate traditional financial firms with unique, niche, personalized services'' (p.35). |
| Lagarde. | 2018 | ''[...] how will fintech change central banking over the next generation ? [...] I would like to consider the possible impact of three innovations – virtual currencies, new models of financial intermediation, and artificial intelligence '' (p.4). |
| Magnuson | 2019 | Asset management, crowdfunding, virtual currency |
| Arslanian & Fisher. | 2019 | ''Agile, technology-focused 'fintech' firms have sought to upend the established order of financial services, changing the dominant operating models and competitive dynamics of an industry that, in the 50 years prior, had seen remarkably little change in market structure'' (p.25). |
| Haddad & Hornuf. | 2019 | Asset management, exchange services, financing, insurance, loyalty program, others, payment, regulatory technology, risk management. |
| Tardieu et al. | 2020 | Very limited use of the word ''FinTech'' in favour of the expression ''digital service providers'' e.g. neobanks, new digital payment providers, new digital lending platforms. (p.283-284). |

the first transatlantic cable (1868). Hence, fintech is directly related to globalization, moreover, changes in the intensity of globalization could be considered as a variation factor of the environment of fintech, in the sense of the standard Darwinian theory. Arner et al., (2016), are proposing three periods. ''FinTech 1.0 (1866-1987)'', is a technological journey dominated by infrastructure development ''from analogue to digital''. ''FinTech 2.0 (1987-2008) '', is a period of ''development of traditional digital financial services", where the source of innovation is dominantly coming from incumbents (large banks). And lastly, ''FinTech 3.0 (2009-present)'' in developed world relies on ''democratizing digital financial services'', in which newcomers (startups) are playing a major role in the context of the post-2008 financial crisis. For ''developing world'' authors refer to ''FinTech 3.5'', in this environment, the catalyst is market reform.

Banque Directe, the first French online bank (a bank) was launched in 1994 by la Compagnie Bancaire a subsidiary of banking group Paribas. Banque Directe, was then sold to the insurer Axa Group in 2002 and became Axa Banque. In 2020, the organizational population of online banks operating on the French market is numerous as shown in the following census: Boursorama Banque, Revolut, ING, N26, Axa Banque, Hello Bank!, Orange Bank, Fortuneo Banque, Monabanq, BforBanq, Allianz Banque, Ma French Bank, La Nef, Bunq, Manager.one, Apy Bank. It must be added the neobank Qonto waiting for its banking license to become an online bank. Memo Bank (formerly Margo Bank), an entrepreneurial project launched by Jean-Daniel Guyot in April 2017, obtained a licence in June 2020 from the ACPR and the ECB to establish a credit institution, thus becoming an online bank independent of any banking group. Lastly, two UK Challenger Banks (Monzo and Starling Bank) have announced interest for the French market.

The leader Boursorama Banque (a 100% subsidiary of Société Générale) has currently more than 2 million clients, while challengers (Revolut, N26, ING) have more than 1 million clients. N26, is a neobank founded in 2013 in Berlin by entrepreneurs Valentin Stalf and Maximilian Tayenthal. The company was known as Number 26, inspired by the 26-sided Rubik's Cube, until July 2016 when founders received their own banking license from the German regulator BaFin, and decided to rename it N26 Bank, while becoming an online bank. Revolut was a neobank founded in London in 2015 by entrepreneurs Nicolay Storonsky and Vladyslav Yatsenko. In December 2018, Revolut received a specialized banking license from both the European Central Bank and Lithuanian regulator, hence protecting its continental Europe business post-Brexit. Both banking licenses either full for N26, or limited (not authorizing investment services) in the case of Revolut is, providing European passport. European passport authorized local players to have access to all countries of the European Economic Area (EEA): Austria, Belgium, Bulgaria, Croatia, Cyprus, Czech Republic, Denmark, Estonia, Finland, France, Germany, Greece, Hungary, Iceland, Ireland, Italy, Latvia, Liechtenstein, Lithuania, Luxembourg, Malta, Netherlands, Norway, Poland, Portugal, Romania, Slovakia, Slovenia, Sweden. The United Kingdom left both the EU, and de facto the EEA, on 31 January 2020. Because the French market is a compartment of the EEA, it is largely dominated by European players, and more precisely having their head offices in EEA countries. From a banking law perspective there's no difference between network banks and online banks, especially because in EU,the principle in place is the "Single Rulebook" of the European Banking Association (EBA), in other words, whatever their respective size, banks must be compliant with the banking regulation. For the time being, as shown in Rocchi (2018a), the winners on the French digital banking market are online banks and not neobanks. Nevertheless, this temporary victory is not a triumph, and by far. Firstly, online banks have a better position in the value chain as they can provide a full range of products and services (greater economies of scope), and they are not depending on the will of third party like neobanks willing to accept deposits and compelled by the French regulator to find a bank depositor of the "cantonment account" (escrow account). Secondly, there is a clear rationale to the mutation process relating to the ability to generate revenues. A quick look at banking accounting in France provides some very relevant insights, hence the "Produit Net Bancaire or PNB" (banking revenues) of large banks could be split as follows: intermediation revenues (buying cheap deposits and selling with high spread credits) represents 60 to 65% of the total, while payment services provide 20 to 25% and lastly treasury management and proprietary trading could generate 8 to 10%. To oversimplify, in small banks like online banks, the breakdown becomes this time: ¾ of revenues intermediation and ¼ for payment services. In other words, if we were to compare, an online bank and a neobank, all things being equal (especially the number of clients), the online bank will generate revenues four times bigger than the neobank. Having said that, why does being a neobank make sense? Simply, because there is no free lunch. Online banks can provide a full range of products and services because they have greater infrastructures than neobanks (Rocchi, 2018b), or in financial terms a higher beak-even point. The digital banking landscape in France looks like a trade-off for actors in: choosing between low-revenues and low break-even point while being a neobank; or high break-even point and high revenues as being an online bank. The second choice is implying success and the ability to attract sufficient resources, this being the reason why online banks from their creation were funded by banks. Memo Bank (formerly Margo Bank) is the first French online bank created by venture-backed entrepreneurs.

Nevertheless, for the time being, entrepreneurs mostly begin in launching a neobank, afterward transforming it into an online bank (N26, Revolut), and Qonto a French neobank waiting its banking license. For the time being, "neobanking" and online banking are targeting only the retail banking sector as most of the players are mostly opening personal accounts (Boursorama Banque, ING, Axa Banque, Revolut, N26, Nickel), while some others are targeting SMEs accounts (Qonto, Manager. one, Holvi, Shine, Anyway, Paykrom, Blank).

Another Swiss example is also questioning the status of neobanking. Alpian is a Swiss fintech incubated by the Geneva group of private banking Reyl. After an initial Serie A round of 12.2 million Swiss francs, the neobank is now planning second-round financing to acquire sufficient capital to obtain from the Swiss regulator Eidgenössische Finanzmarktaufschit (Finma) a banking license and become an online bank. Alpian is targeting ''mass affluents'', or individuals with savings between 100,000 and 1,000,000 Swiss francs, which is representing a market segment in Switzerland of 2.6 million potential customers. These empirical observations suggest a possible future research question: is neobanking a temporary status? It seems to be so, as the more successful neobanks tend to become online banks. This question can be expanded to Europeans fintech asking for a banking license. Zopa is a UK based peer-to-peer lending platform. This fintech was launched in 2005 and received its banking license in 2016, then became a Challenger Bank (the UK equivalent of the French ''banque en ligne'' or ''online bank''). The Swedish fintech Klarna founded in 2005 is providing payment solutions for online storefronts, having a BtoB business model when Neobank is BtoC oriented. In 2017 Klarna received its banking license from Finansinspektionen the Swedish regulator and was renamed Klarna Bank AB. Last example, Adyen whose name means ''starting from scratch'' in Surinamese is a Dutch BtoB payment platform fintech created in 2006 which obtained a banking license in 2017.

Finally, it is also interesting to notice that the mutation phenomenon is a one-way relationship, hence if some neobanks are mutating into online banks, we didn't observe any online bank mutating into neobank. Such a mutation is not an absurd choice, especially as a mean to avoid a cumbersome level of regulation in favor of a softer one. Nevertheless, apparently such an advantage doesn't counterbalance the huge loss of revenues implied by this strategic choice. It is also interesting to notice that alike in biology where simple organisms mutate into more complex ones, in organizational population ecology the same rule is observed.

*Box 1. A brief history of Boursorama Banque*

The story of the company began as an online stockbroker and an information website on capital markets changing its name to Boursorama Banque in December 2005 and becoming the online bank of Société Générale (SocGen) Group. In 2006, the company acquired CaixaBank France a commercial bank with 45 branch offices, CaixaBank receiving 20% of the shares of Boursorama. Boursorama Banque decided to close-down its banking network to come back to its initial model of a pure online bank. In June 2014, SocGen launched a Tender Offer on minority interests (free float on Euronext). After the results of the Tender Offer, SocGen was holding 79,5% of company shares. In June 2015, SocGen bought the stake of CaixaBank for 218 million euros, which was representing a business valuation of Boursorama Banque close to 1 billion euros. The company was delisted, and since then, Boursorama Banque is a 100% subsidiary of SocGen and the online bank of the Group. The company is offering to open personal accounts and accounts for self-employed persons. At the end of 2014, the number of clients was 600,000, it increased to 1 million at the beginning of 2017, in September 2019 it was announced that the number of 2 million customers had been exceeded. Boursorama Banque is now targeting 3 million clients for 2021. In recent years in France, Boursorama Banque has emerged as the clear leader of online banking. Nevertheless, it is challenged by newcomers like Hello Bank! (BNP Paribas) launched in 2013 and moreover by N26 which arrived in France in 2016, while Revolut was joining them in 2017.

While in France, the first neobank (a fintech), Sogexia was set up in 2011 by French entrepreneurs, the Füg family, based in Lyon France, the firm moved its activity to Luxembourg after obtaining a license of payment services institution. The census of neobanks as of September 2020 underlines the importance of this organizational population: Nickel, Monese, Sogexia, AuMax, Anytime, Shine, Kard, Xaalys, Curve, Olkypay, Lydia, Pixpay, Holvi, Soshop.club, Compte CO2, Paykrom, Moneway, CDC-Net, Ethiko, Blank and Onlyone. Some projects have been announced: Linxo, Vybe, Prismea. Nickel (formerly Compte-Nickel) is by far the leading neobank in France claiming more than 1.5 million clients as of May 2020. On the same date Sogexia is close to 200,000 clients and only a few players (Anytime, Monese, AuMax) announce more than 100,000 clients. A very important specificity on neobanks rely on the multiplicity of their legal status while online banks have only one, the credit institution status, more commonly known by clients as banks. The two most used status used by local players are payment services institution (example Nickel) and electronic money institution or agent of one of them (example Monese). These status are European, and defined by EU directives, while some actors are depending on French status. For instance, Soshop.club is a IOBSP (''intermédiaireen operation de banque et de service de payments'') meaning intermediary in banking and payment services, Lydia is a APSP (''agent prestataire de services de paiements'') agent proposing payment services, Kard is a DME (''Distributeur de monnaie électronique'') or electronic money distributor. CDC-Net is an online banking service provided by the Caisse des Dépôts et Consignations (CDC) which is a public administrative establishment with special-purpose founded in 1816. CDC-Net accepts deposit and grants loans alike online banks, but from a legal point of view, it is not a bank as CDC is not a bank. CDC is a fully owned by the French state. CDC-Net could be described as *sui generis* in legal terminology, in organization theory it is a one-of-a kind organization. Another specific, CDC-Net could only provide services to a niche of clients strictly defined by law: notary, lawyer and adults protected under guardianship and curatorship. Having said that, CDC-Net, it is obvious that if it is part of the competitive landscape, it doesn't contribute to the cut-throat competition on the French retail banking market.

The huge advantage of using a European status (electronic money institution or payment services institution) is that it implies a European passport and hence provides access to EEA.

If we come back to Arner et al. (2016) periodization, the author underlines that French online banks are related to ''FinTech 2.0'' type of innovation, while neobanks appeared in France during the current ''FinTech 3.0'' era. The recent years in the banking industry are characterized by converging disruptive technologies (Walker, 2014).

*Box 2. A brief history of Nickel (at inception Compte-Nickel)*

| The firm, "la Financière des Placements Electroniques (FPE)", was set up in 2014 by Ryad Boulanouar an electronic engineer and Hugues Le Bret a former senior executive banker at Société Générale, they choose Compte-Nickel as a brand name. It is important to underline the great complementarity of founders. Ryad Boulanouar was considering himself as he explained in an interview to the newspaper *Le Monde* located at the fringe of the French society because his family was poor and had an Algerian origin. His perception was reinforced when he was hit by a banking ban and that his checkbook was confiscated. When this took place, he had the idea to create a new company which corporate name which would have been called''no bank'', finally not retained as too negative. It took years, for the project to become a reality. The other founder, Hugues Le Bret (2011, 2016) was in the French banking establishment as formerly CEO of Boursorama Banque and previously heading the communication at Société Générale. In other words, Mr Boulanouar was at the periphery, while Mr Le Bret (2013) was at the core. The acquisition of Compte-Nickel which took place in April 2017 by BNP Paribas was carried out without immediate integration, preserving the decisions' operational autonomy. The management remained in place as well as all employees, while at the same time the strategy was confirmed. Nevertheless, soon after the motto ''le compte sans banque'' (the bankless account) became ''le compte pour tous'' (an account for everybody). One year after the acquisition the corporate name Compte-Nickel was shortened to Nickel. More recently, the neobank which had a pure low-cost strategy targeting the unbanked and the poor segment of the population, launched an additional offer to serve the mainstream market. The acquisition was a clear success as the number of clients moved from 0.5 million in April 2017, to more than 1.5 million in March 2020, figure that had to be put in perspective with a population of 67 million inhabitants. The last incremental change of identity is a European expansion decided by BNP Paribas, but already imagined by founders. |
|---|
| The question of the discovery of the opportunity deserves to be analyzed. In France, using a new distribution channel, the network of tobacco shops in France while partnering with the "Confédération des buralistes" (French professional organization of tobacconists) was a new idea and moreover some observers at the beginning were very skeptical about it. The ''Confédération des buralistes" was committed to success for two reasons. Firstly, it was offering a new source of revenue for its members suffering from a decline of turnover (a declining number of smokers, a growing smuggling activity to avoid French high taxes). Secondly, the "Confédération des buralistes" obtained 5% of the shares of "la Financière des Placements Electroniques". Nevertheless, the idea was not new in Europe: in Italy, in 2008 some entrepreneurs and "Federazione Italiana Tabaccai" founded Itb bank (nicknamed ''banca dei tabaccai'' or bank of tobacconists). In 2016, Intesa Sanpaolo acquired 100% of banca Itb's shares for € 153 million and rename it Banca 5. In France, Nickel's exploitation of the idea is more original, as they provide to the tobacconists an electronic terminal that could be used by clients to open an account in a few minutes. Still, it was more ''bricolage'' than a ''disruptive technology''. Precisely, the huge success seems to be attributable to a new business model based on the combination of a new channel and a useful and well-accepted technology (Davis, 1989). The electronic terminal was soon very well accepted by candidates for a bank account opening, even if a very small number of future clients (illiterate people, which are representing 1 to 2% of the French population) were requesting the help of the tobacco reseller to successfully complete the registration. |

## CRITERIA FOR DISTINGUISHING BETWEEN ONLINE BANKS AND NEOBANKS

Neobanks and online banks differ in their legal status and usually also in the nature of their shareholders.

### *Neobanks are a subpart of the universe of fintechs*

According to a study by the French regulator, Autorité de Contrôle Prudentiel - ACPR (2017), the first segment in number within the French fintech landscape was the payment instruments sector: neobanks with 26 players, followed by blockchain/tech (17), insurtech (12), financial advice (11), crowdfunding (10), other advice (9), know your customer (8), financing/credit (7). Among the French neobanks the most frequently chosen organizational choices are ''payment services institutions'' and ''electronic money institutions''. Generally, shareholders of neobanks are entrepreneurs and successful ones are backed by VCs. According to Tardieu et al., (2020) neobanks are one of the kinds of ''digital service providers".

*While online banks are banks (credit institutions or in French "établissement de crédit')*

Online banks like traditional banks can accept deposits, grant credits, and offers means of payment. Generally, shareholders of online banks are universal banks.

*Table 2. Financial barriers to entry: capital requirement by statutes.*

| Status. | Capital adequacy (at minimum). |
|---|---|
| Banks (including online banks). | € 5,000,000. |
| Electronic payments institutions (Fintech). | € 350,000 plus 2% of the issued electronic money supply. |
| Payment services institutions (Fintech). | € 20,000, or 50,000 or 125,000 depending on the width of the offering. |

## THE CORE AND PERIPHERY INTERACTIONS ON THE FRENCH MARKET: ANSWERING TO RESEARCH QUESTION 1.

Regarding shareholding and scope of the offering online banks are close to the core of the retail banking industry while neobanks are more on the periphery.

*The core moving towards the periphery: banks creating neobanks and banks acquiring neobanks without immediately integrating them.*

The universal banks who choose the model of intrapreneurship and who create a neobank without being forced to resort to this choice testify on the contrary that there would well be a specific advantage to the fintech industry. We will now discuss two emblematic examples of fintech AuMax and Prismea created by major French banks. The neobank AuMax was founded in 2016 by Crédit Mutuel Arkéa. This creation was carried out implicitly in an intrapreneurial model, in order to avoid the bureaucratic drifts of a large group, to give free rein to the creative spirit of managers and remain responsive to market developments. Prismea is a pure product of the intrapreneurship model since it won an internal competition within the Société Générale (SocGen) which was entitled ''*Internal Startup Call*''. Within SocGen Group, Prismea neobank for professionals and SMBs has been housed within Crédit du Nord, a Group subsidiary very well established within this customer base.

*The move from the core to the periphery: emergence of coopetition and platforms (trend 2)*

For instance, SocGen has bought the French payment services fintech Treezor which is offering neobanking services in white brand serving external clients of the group and notably three neobanks (Qonto, Lydia and Compte CO2) and is also developing the technological infrastructure of the new group neobank Prismea.

*The move from the periphery to the core: neobank mutating into online bank (trend 1)*

The two European leaders in the retail market, Revolut, which claims 12 million customers (May 2020), and N26, which claims 5 million (January 2020), initially set up as neobanks, have both obtained a banking license and are now attacking traditional retail banking players head-on. French Qonto, which claims in mid-2020 to have more than 100,000 corporate clients, is awaiting a banking license. These actors, now active in the world of online banking, have also in common to have raised, as per Crunchbase figures on September 24, 2020, considerable sums to develop: Revolut $ 917 million, N26 $ 782 million, Qonto $ 151 million.

*Deference matters, another move from core to the periphery: neobanks accepting deposits (trend 2)*

The French regulator ACPR requires neobanks to open a cantonment account (''comptes de cantonnement'') in a banking institution if they want to accept client deposits. This escrow account will take place to separate client money and to keep it out of reach from company cash use. The first neobank set up in France in 2011, Sogexia, has chosen BNP Paribas for his cantonment account (escrow account), Compte-Nickel choose Crédit Mutual Arkéa and our last example Qonto is using BNP Paribas until he receives its own banking license from both the French supervisor the Autorité de Controle Prudentiel et de Régulation (ACPR) and from the Eurozone regulator the European Central Bank (ECB), and hence mutating to an online bank. That proves that deference tends to legitimize newcomers and helps them to move from the periphery to the core. Neobanks choosing to accept deposits must engage into a deference relationship with a universal bank to adopt such a business, in return empirical observation shows that this relation seems favorable for both parties.

*Between deference and partnership: the question of ''phigital'' banking and neobanking (trend 3)*

In France, a new word has been coined ''phygitale'' which is composed of ''physique'' (physical or tangible) and ''digitale'' (digital or virtual). What does digital banking or digital neobanking means? In fact, empirical observations are showing that some online players (banks or neobanks) are also using an alternative physical channel that is not bank offices. This trend is not new, but it tends to be more diversified in recent years: in the 2000' it was only insurance offices, since 2010' miscellaneous non-financial sectors are involved, as shown in table 3 below.

*Table 3. the ''phygital'' banking and neobanking phenomenon in France.*

| Name & country. | Population. | Nature of the alternative network. |
|---|---|---|
| *Axa Banque* (France). | Online Bank | Insurance branches of the Parent Company *Axa*. |
| *Allianz Banque* (Germany). | Online Bank. | Insurance branches of the Parent Company *Allianz*. |
| *C-zam* (Carrefour Banque) (France). | Online Bank. | The C-zam box (creditcard + IBAN) was available in self-service in the 3,000 hypermarkets and supermarkets of *Carrefour*. In June 2020 the closure of C-zam was announced despite the existence of more than 100,000 customers. |
| *Orange Bank* (France). | Online Bank. | Minority shareholder: insurer *Groupama* (35%)<br>Majority shareholder: *Orange* (65%).<br>Available in telco shops of *Orange* and in the insurance branches of *Groupama* and *Gan*. |
| *Nickel (France).* | Neobank. | Network of 5,500 French tobacconists resellers as of April 2020. Plans to expand in Europe. |
| *Anytime* (Belgium) | Neobank. | Partnership: *Photomaton* (Photo-me International).<br>New photograph cabins also permitting to open a banking account (10 currently tested in Paris). Existing network: 8,000 cabins in France, and 28,500 cabins in 18 foreign countries. |
| *Ma French Bank* (France). | Online Bank. | 16,000 local post-offices of the parent company *La Banque Postale* (the French Postbank). |

In a certain way, ''phigital'' banking and neobanking tends to demonstrate that the client's perception of a pure intangible business relation, through the web or an app of a smartphone, is not as true as it seems at first glance. ''Phigital'' banking is not necessarily a phenomenon specific to France, there are also some similarities with the United Kingdom market. In the UK, it is more common for Challenger Banks and neobanks to accept cash payments and withdrawals from clients. Two Challenger Banks (Monzo and Starling Bank) and two neobanks (Tide and Monese) are using the Paypoint network which comprises 28,200 local shops in the UK, 500 in Ireland and 6,000 in Romania. Starling Bank, in addition to the Paypoint agreement, is also partnering with the Post Office and is using its 11,500 local post offices for cash operations without limitation of amount. In France, ''Phygital'' banking and neobanking is not a way to cash deposits and withdrawals, excepting for Nickel, with tobacconist accepting small amounts strictly limited by law. These alternative networks are mainly used as another way to open an account. In 2019, Orange Bank's CEO explained that since the launching, 2/3 of bank accounts openings took place in Orange telco shops while the 1/3 remaining was attracted online. Moreover, the online client was generally young with low incomes, while physical clients were older and having a national average income.

*The move from core to the periphery: the question of the existence of disruptive innovation (trend 4)*

Disruptive innovation plays a relatively small role in the emergence of online banking and neobanking in France because only three trajectories can be linked to it, but the important success of two of them means that this role is not marginal. Disruptive innovation is rare in the world of French digital banking which tends to support the theory (Christensen, 1997). The online bank ING Direct (now ING bank), when established in France, offered a unique product consisting of savings account remunerated at a higher rate than the observed market rate, targeting the entire market and only offering the opening of a secondary account. Only afterward, when it had a large customer base, it offered a complete range of products and services, also targeting high-end customers and offering to be the main or even sole bank for its customers. The online bank Egg France at its launch was based on a disruptive innovation: the cashback credit card, targeting rather the low-end clientele - a strategy that made the success of its parent company in the United Kingdom. But the principle of cash back was unknown in France, and if we add a bad communication campaign, this experience led to the closure of Egg France. In 2013, The neobank Compte-Nickel (now Nickel) launched a bank account associated with a withdrawal card that was accessible to everybody without means testing, including banned customers. After the great success of this initial strategy, it was decided by the new majority shareholder BNP Paribas to also target medium and high-end customers by offering new products and services.

## AN ORGANIZATIONAL POPULATION ECOLOGY VIEW: ANSWERING TO RESEARCH QUESTION 2.

According to Darwinian view without variations of the environment there is no possible selection, and its outcome the retention rate or in Charles Darwin words "survival of the fittest". There are four major variation factors affecting the environment of fintech: financial innovation, digital innovation, globalization, and financial laws. Financial innovation is defined by Lerner and Tufano (2011) as ''the art of creating and then popularizing new financial instruments, as well as new financial technologies, institutions and markets'' (p. 525). Fishman et al. (2014) described digital innovation as '' a product, process, or business model that is perceived as new, requires some significant change on the part of adopters, and is embodied in or enabled by IT'' (p.330). Globalization dates back to the second part of the 19th Century (Arner et al., 2016), commonly considered as self-reinforcing over time, it could also be seriously temporarily affected by the major crisis as world war I and II, or by a major pandemic like Covid 19 and it's Great Lockdown. The evolution of financial laws is key to understand the emergence of fintech especially in the European Union environment (de Vauplane, 2015) with the enactment of electronic money directives and payment services directives, but it is also relevant in other countries (Magnuson, 2019). Moreover, these variation factors are interfering with each other, for instance, globalization is impacting financial laws. French regulation on fintech operating on crowdfunding was inspired by US laws.

The fintech population (of which neobanks) is strongly dependent on its environment and hence survival depends mainly on the continuing ability to attracts clients or to be acquired, and successful neobanks could also consider becoming an online bank. Among neobank population operating in France the mortality rate is relatively moderated, hence only UK based Ipagoo suspended its activity in both countries in August 2019, the same month the French neobank Monaize was placed in judicial liquidation, the French neobank Morning closed-down operations in 2020. Finally, Boon, the neobank subsidiary of the bankrupt German fintech Wirecard, announced that it will cease operations in October 2020. Conversely, online bank mortality rate is significantly higher in light of numerous closures: ebanking (2001), Egg France (2004), Banque Bipop (2005), VTB Direct France (2017), Fidor Bank France (2019), C-zam, Ditto Bank and Ferratum Bank (2020).

Will the year 2020 be an *annus horribilis* for digital banking? Also in the UK, Bo, the digital subsidiary of RBS, closed its doors in April 2020 after only 5 months of activity.

What could explain this conundrum? Hence, neobanks have often only entrepreneurs and VCs as shareholders, while online banks have most of the time universal banks as parent companies. In other words, the Darwinian view of survival

*Box 3. A brief history of Morning, Hush and Eric Charpentier*

| **Morning: Birth as a fintech, mutation to neobank and organizational death.** |
|---|
| ''Morning" formerly called "Payname" was an entrepreneurial fintech created by Eric Charpentier and located in Saint-Elix le Château 50 km from Toulouse in the south of France. "Morning"originally offers "cagnotte en ligne" (online funding pot) services for young people but by 2016 the cash position was very tight due to losses. Founder Eric Charpentier made a strategic change and decides to turn it into a neobank, offering its many users free services to open a low-cost bank account. Short of treasury to do this, he withdraws money from the cantonment account of his clients, which is strictly forbidden by law. Once the facts are discovered by the ACPR regulator, customer accounts are immediately frozen, and the payment institution license is suspended. At the beginning of 2017, just after Eric Charpentier was excluded from the company, the Bank Edel, a subsidiary of the Edouard Leclerc group, injects the necessary funds to save the neobank by taking majority control and recovers the license of payment institution. The transformation into a neobank continues and in 2019 the figure of 100,000 customers with bank accounts is exceeded. But losses continue to accumulate and at the beginning of 2020, the closure of Morning operations is announced. |
| Having left "Morning", Eric Charpentier decide in 2017 to embark on a new entrepreneurial project by creating the neobank Hush, which aims to be at the forefront of payment services and investments in cryptocurrency made on behalf of its clients. At the end of 2017, an initial coin offering (ICO) is launched, which was supposed to bring 20 million euros (or cryptocurrency equivalent) to finance the project. In April 2018, the result of the sums raised during the ICO is disclosed, it is only 540,000 euros and 245 ethers or in total about 600,000 euros, notoriously insufficient amount to launch the Hush neobank. According to various press sources in the summer of 2018, Eric Charpentier disappeared, as did Hush. The investors who participated in the ICO had received Hush token as compensation, which is now worthless. The Hush case is an illustration of pre-entry mortality that should not be underestimated (Carroll & Khessina, 2004). |

of the fittest, does not match with survival of the richest. As previously presented neobanks have a much smaller capital than online banks, but at the same time, their break-even point is much lower as they provide only payment services versus full banking services for online banks. Moreover, monthly cash burn is much higher, all things being equal, for online banks than for neobanks. The organizational death of online banks is a simple story: their shareholders decided to stop financing losses. Most of these shareholders were foreign and more precisely European: The United Kingdom-based for Egg France and Ditto Banque, Belgian for eBanking, Italian for Bipop Banque, Russian for VTB Direct France. This over-representation of firms with foreign shareholders seems rather supportive of the theory of the liability of foreignness (Zaheer, 1995; Zaheer & Mosakowski, 1997); as well as the cost of doing business abroad (CDBA) theory (Hymer, 1976). Such empirical observation is not relevant for neobanks as previously mentioned the failures of the French firm Monaize and Morning is not counterbalanced by the UK based Ipagoo in serious trouble.

At first glance, the high failure rate to the emergence of online banking seems challenging the organizational population ecology fundamental (Hannan et al., 2007): ''This well-established theory of long term organizational population evolution holds that growth in density initially enhances a population's (constitutive) legitimation, thereby raising its founding rate and lowering its mortality rate. These effects initially induce further growth in density. However, persistent growth in density eventually generates intense competition, which depresses founding rates and elevates mortality rates'' (p.79). Nevertheless, carrying capacity also matters and explain such empirical results. The first wave of online bank failures (2001-2005) occurred during a period characterized by low internet penetration in the French households, in other words by a very low biotic capacity. The second wave of closures (2017-2020) is mainly the consequence of a significant increase of the competition due to the higher density. If we now consider the population of neobanks, we can see that the founding rate is increasing, a significant number of foreign firms are entering the French market while the mortality rate remains low. In this case also, the carrying capacity is the key to understand such results. Neobanks are depending on the smartphone penetration in French population which is very high and still in steady growth. In other words, the environment is more favorable. To summarize, at the end of the selection process the retention (on the market) will be the sum of surviving firms able to attract a significant number of clients, those mutating into online banks (move from one population to another) and lastly acquired firms. Indeed, we support the definition that the organizational death is characterized by a complete loss of identity (Sutton, 1987) hence M&As are not organizational deaths.

Hence, if mutating means surviving, it also implies a change of population, moving from the neobank population to the online bank one. Mutating firms are successful firms, which have two main characteristics: firstly, an ability to attract a high number of clients, secondly, having a raised a huge amount of money. Since January 2020, the french neobank Qonto submit to ACPR and ECB an application for a banking license to become an online bank. Notwithstanding, in case of an acquisition a partial loss of identity is often gradually noted as it was previously explained on the Nickel case. Hereafter, on figure 1., the representation of VSR model applied to the population of neobanks operating in France.

*Figure 1. Neobank's VSR Model*

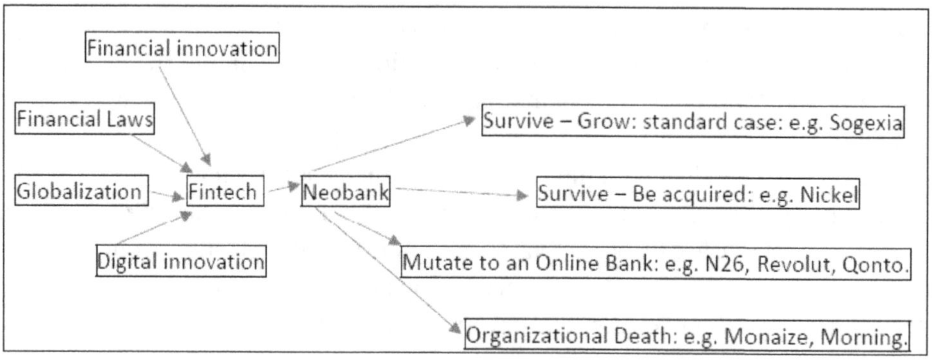

## DISCUSSION AND AREAS FOR FUTURE RESEARCH

There are many organizational population ecology works on traditional banks, so without claiming to be exhaustive we can cite for example the studies on banks in the United States (Barron et al., 1994 ; Barron, 1998), in Italy (Lomi, 1995a, 1995b), Denmark (Lomi, 2000), in China (Kuilman and Li, 2006, 2009) or Japan (Greve, 2000, 2002). Everything remains to be written, however, in regard to digital banks, which in particular leads us to rethink the geographical dimension as well as the reality of the material presence in a given country. For example, Revolut, which has more than a million French customers, has only a handful of French employees in a coworking center, and Bunq limits itself to offering a website in French operated by French-speaking employees located in the Netherlands.

Organizational population ecology postulates density dependence, in other words the impact of the growth of population on the probability of surviving. As a matter of fact, in order to survive an actor operates on a niche that can be defined as a set of resources (Hutchinson, 1957), and two distinct populations begin to compete as soon as their niche intersects (Hannan & Carroll, 1992), the more significant the overlap between the niches, the greater the increase in competition for resources will be (Barron et al., 1994). Having said that, how do you measure population density ? There are three main ways. Firstly, the increase in *density* is measured by the observation of a growing number of actors (Hannan & Freeman, 1977), which was our choice in this chapter. Secondly, *fuzzy-density* moves away from simple actor counting by taking into account a qualitative dimension linked to their own characteristics such as the grade of membership or audience within the population studied (Kuilman and Li, 2006, 2009). While it allows for greater sophistication of the study, the subjectivity involved in the calibration of actors has led us to discard this method. Thirdly, the ''mass dependence model'' (Barnett & Amburgey, 1990) postulates that larger organizations generate greater competition. Thus, for our case study, the market should be analysed as the sum of the aggregated accounts of digital banks (online banks and neobanks) and the impact of a player on density will depend on the number of accounts held. We would have chosen this simple and yet attractive approach, as it is intuitively easy to perceive that the arrival of major players (Revolut, N26) on the French market will have a greater impact on competitive intensity than the launch of two new neobanks by entrepreneurs with limited resources. In the short term, such an assumption seems highly plausible.

We also didn't investigate pre-entry organizational population ecology (Carroll & Khessina, 2004), which postulates that the emergence of organization is affected on the one hand by ''success in founding attempts'' and on the other hand by ''mortality on new organization''. In addition, the number of organizations in a population is directly affected by the mortality rate of the founding attempts and the founding rate itself (Delacroix & Carroll, 2003). Because of the different nature of the shareholding already mentioned, it seems that, all things being equal, the ability to create a neobanking project is more uncertain than an online banking one because of the question of access to resources – of course, this argument is not valid for neobanks created by large banks such as AuMax or Prismea. Hence, a global death rate including pre-entry mortality rate (or ecology of neobanking entrepreneurship) could be an agenda for future research. Intuition suggests that there are more projects of neobanks failing that online banks due to the different nature of shareholders.

A last word about the size of the populations studied, seeing as they are micro-populations and even at the community level of digital banks, we are far below the threshold of one hundred organizations to carry out quantitative research. Precisely, we are in the small N zone (5 to 100) for which the qualitative comparative analysis or QCA (Ragin, 1987) is very suitable. For instance, Rocchi (2019) carry out two binary studies in using Boolean algebra of crisp-set QCA (Ragin, 1987), the first study was on survival (or not) and the second on acquisition (or not) of digital players operating on the French market. We could also imagine studies on digital banks more focused on grades of membership, for such studies the relevant method would be fuzzy-set QCA (Ragin, 2000).

## CONCLUSION

To conclude, the French market provides evidence that if neobanks are disrupting the market, they are also offering an opportunity to universal banks to regenerate themselves. Even more, the covid 19 crisis has heightened customer awareness of the benefits of digitalisation, exerting strong pressure on all players, since more than ever before innovation comes from both sides of the market: the periphery but also the core.

There is a paradox on the French market, if the public opinion tends to consider online banks as less risky than neobanks, empirical observation from organizational mortality in both populations suggest the opposite.

The digital banking industry regarding the optimal size of populations (the small N zone) notably in the EEA could become an attractive sector for QCA researchers having the choice to study either at a community level (digital banking), or at a population level (online banks or neobanks). Moreover, as Aldrich (2001) points out, evolutionary studies tend to be too narrowly confined to large listed companies, and should give more emphasis to SMEs and emerging firms. Digital banks can therefore be an excellent topic for academic work from both evolutionary and QCA perspectives, which are not mutually exclusive.

## REFERENCES

ACPR. – Banque de France. (2017, July-August). Les enjeux de régulation et de supervision liés aux fintechs et à la rupture digitale [Regulation and supervision issues related to fintechs and digital disruption]. *Bulletin*, (212), 39–46.

Aldrich, H. E. (2001). Who Wants to Be an Evolutionnary Theorist? Remarks On the Occasion of the Year 2000 OMT Distinguished Scholarly Career Award Presentation. *Journal of Management Inquiry*, *10*(2), 115–127. doi:10.1177/1056492601102004

Arner, D. W., Barberis, J., & Buckley, R. P. (2016). The evolution of FinTech: A new post-crisis paradigm? *Georgetown Journal of International Law*, *47*(4), 1272–1319.

Arslanian, H., & Fisher, F. (2019). *The Future of Finance, The Impact of Fintech, AI, and Crypto on Financial Services*. Palgrave Mac Millan. doi:10.1007/978-3-030-14533-0

Barba Navaretti, G., Calzolari, G., & Pozzolo, A. F. (2017). FinTech and Banks: Friends or Foes? *European Economy*, *2*, 9–30.

Barnett, W. P., & Amburgey, T. L. (1990). Do Larger Organizations Generate Stronger Competition? In J. V. Singh (Ed.), *Organizational Evolution: New Directions* (pp. 78–102). Sage.

Barron, D. N. (1998). Pathways to Legitimacy among Consumer Loan Providers in New York City, 1914-34. *Organization Studies*, *19*(2), 207–233. doi:10.1177/017084069801900203

Barron, D. N., West, E., & Hannan, M. T. (1994). A Time to Grow and a Time to Die: Growth and Mortality of Credit Unions in New York City, 1914-1990. *American Journal of Sociology*, *100*(2), 381–421. doi:10.1086/230541

Campbell, D. T. (1960). Variation and selective retention in creative thought as in other knowledge process. *Psychological Review*, *67*(6), 380–400. doi:10.1037/h0040373 PMID:13690223

Campbell, D. T. (1969). Variation and selective retention in sociocultural evolution. *General Systems*, *14*, 69–85.

Cantillon, R. (2015). *Essay on the Nature of Trade in General* (A. E. Murphy, Trans.). Liberty Fund Inc. (Original work published 1755)

Carroll, G. R., & Khessina, O. M. (2005). The ecology of entrepreneurship. In Handbook of Entrepreneurship Research (pp. 167-200). Berlin: Springer.

Casson, M. (1982). *The entrepreneur: An economic theory*. Barnes & Nobles.

Cattani, G., & Ferriani, S. (2008, November-December). A Core/Periphery Perspective on Individual Creative Performance: Social Networks and Cinematic Achievements in the Hollywood Film Industry. *Organization Science*, *19*(6), 824–844. doi:10.1287/orsc.1070.0350

Cattani, G., Ferriani, S., & Lanza, A. (2017, November-December). Deconstructing the Outsider Puzzle: The Legitimation Journey of Novelty. *Organization Science*, *28*(6), 965–992. doi:10.1287/orsc.2017.1161

Christensen, C. (1997). *The Innovator's Dilemma: When New Technologies Cause Great Firms to Fail*. Harvard Business Review Press.

Christensen, C., McDonald, R., Altman, E. J., & Palmer, J. E. (2018). Disruptive Innovation: An Intellectual History and Directions for Future Research. *Journal of Management Studies*, *55*(7), 1043–1048. doi:10.1111/joms.12349

Christensen, C., & Raynor, M. E. (2003). *The Innovator's Solution: Creating and Sustaining Successful Growth*. Harvard Business School Press.

Davidsson, P. (2016). *Researching Entrepreneurship, Conceptualization and Design*. Springer. doi:10.1007/978-3-319-26692-3

Davis, F. D. (1989). Perceived Usefulness, Perceived Ease of Use, and User acceptance of Information Technology. *Management Information Systems Quarterly*, *13*(3), 319–340. doi:10.2307/249008

Delacroix. J. & Carroll. G.R. (1983). Organizational Foundings: An Ecological Study of the Newspaper Industries of Argentina and Ireland. *Administrative Science Quarterly*, *28*(2), 274–291.

Demil, B., & Lecocq, X. (2010). Business Model Evolution: In Search of Dynamic Consistency. *Long Range Planning*, *43*(2-3), 227–246. doi:10.1016/j.lrp.2010.02.004

Fishman, R. G., Dos Santos, B. L., & Zheng, Z. E. (2014). Digital innovation as a fundamental and powerful concept in the information systems curriculum. *Management Information Systems Quarterly*, *38*(2), 329–343. doi:10.25300/MISQ/2014/38.2.01

Garud, R., & Karnøe, P. (2003). Bricolage versus breakthrough: Distributed and embedded agency in technology entrepreneurship. *Research Policy*, *32*(2), 277–300. doi:10.1016/S0048-7333(02)00100-2

Greve, H. (2000, October). Market Niche Entry Decisions: Competition, Learning, and Strategy in Tokyo Banking, 1894-1936. *Academy of Management Journal*, *43*(5), 816–836.

Greve. H. (2002). An Ecological Theory of Spatial Evolution: Local Density Dependence in Tokyo Banking, 1894–1936. *Social Forces*, *80*(3), 847–880.

Haddad, C., & Hornuf, L. (2019). The emergence of the global fintech market: Economic and technological determinants. *Small Business Economics*, *53*(1), 81–105. doi:10.100711187-018-9991-x

Hannan, M. T., & Carroll, G. R. (1992). Dynamics of Organizational Populations. Oxford University Press.

Hannan, M. T., & Freeman, J. (1977, March). The Population Ecology of Organizations. *American Journal of Sociology*, *82*(5), 929–964. doi:10.1086/226424

Hannan, M. T., Pólos, L., & Carroll, G. (2007). *Logics of Organization Theory. Audiences, Codes, and Ecologies*. Princeton Press.

Hutchinson, G. E. (1957). Concluding Remarks. *Cold Spring Harbor Symposia on Quantitative Biology*, *22*(2), 415–427. doi:10.1101/SQB.1957.022.01.039

Hymer, S. H. (1976). *The International Operations of National Firms: A Study of Direct Investment*. MIT Press.

Jourdan, J., Durand, R., & Thornton, P. (2017, July). The Price of Admission: Organizational Deference as Strategic Behavior. *American Journal of Sociology*, *123*(1), 232–275. doi:10.1086/692248

Keynes, J. M. (1973). The Collected Writings of John Maynard Keynes, vol. VII, The General Theory of Employment, Interest and Money (D. Moggridge, Ed.). London: Macmillan for the Royal Economic Society.

Kirzner, I. (1973). *Competition and Entrepreneurship*. University of Chicago Press.

Kirzner, I. (1979). *Perception, Opportunity, and Profit: Studies in the Theory of Entrepreneurship*. University of Chicago Press.

Knight, F. (1921). *Risk, Uncertainty and Profit*. Houghton Mifflin.

Kuilman, J. G., & Li, J. T. (2006). The organizers' ecology: An empirical study of foreign banks in Shanghai. *Organization Science*, *17*(3), 385–401. doi:10.1287/orsc.1060.0182

Kuilman, J. G., & Li, J. T. (2009). Grades of membership and legitimacy spillovers: Foreign banks in Shanghai, 1847–1935. *Academy of Management Journal*, *32*(2), 229–245. doi:10.5465/amj.2009.37308018

Lagarde, C. (2018). Central Banking and Fintech. A Brave New World. *Innovations, 12*(1), 4–8. doi:10.1162/inov_a_00262

Le Bret H. (2011). *La semaine ou Jérome Kerviel a failli faire sauter le système financier mondial, Journal intime d'un banquier* [The week when Jérome Kerviel nearly blew up the global financial system, Diary of a banker]. Paris: Les arènes.

Le Bret H. (2013). *No Bank, l'incroyable histoire d'un entrepreneur de banlieue qui veut révolutionner la banque* [No Bank, the incredible story of a suburban entrepreneur who wants to revolutionize banking]. Paris: Les arènes.

Le Bret H. (2016). Le Compte-Nickel: un compte pour tous, sans banque [The Nickel Account: an account for all, without a bank]. *Le journal de l'école de Paris du management, 2016*(6), 24-30.

Lee, I., & Shin, Y. J. (2018). Fintech: Ecosystem, business models, investment decisions, and challenges. *Business Horizons, 61*(1), 35–46. doi:10.1016/j.bushor.2017.09.003

Lerner, J., & Tufano, P. (2012). The Consequences of Financial Innovation. A Counterfactual Research Agenda. In J. Lerner & S. Stern (Eds.), *The Rate and Direction of Inventive Activity Revisited* (pp. 523–575). University of Chicago Press. doi:10.7208/chicago/9780226473062.003.0017

Lomi, A. (1995a). The Population Ecology of Organizational Founding: Location Dependence and Unobserved Heterogenity. *Administrative Science Quarterly, 40*(1), 111–144. doi:10.2307/2393702

Lomi, A. (1995b). The population and community ecology of organizational founding; Italian cooperative banks, 1936-1989. *European Sociological Review, 11*(1), 75–98. doi:10.1093/oxfordjournals.esr.a036350

Lomi, A. (2000). Density Dependence and Spacial Duality in Organizational Founding Rates: Danish Commercial Banks, 1846-1989. *Organization Studies, 21*(2), 433–461. doi:10.1177/0170840600212006

Magnuson. W. (2019). Regulating Fintech, *Vanderbilt Law Review, 71*(4), 1167-1226.

Nicoletti, B. (2017). *The Future of Fintech. Integrating Finance and Technology in Financial Services*. Palgrave Macmillan.

Philippon, T. (2016). *The Fintech Opportunity*. NBER, Working Paper 22476.

Pinchot, G. (1985). *Intrapreneuring: Why You Don't Have to Leave the Corporation to Become an Entrepreneur*. Harper and Row.

Pinchot, G., & Pellman, R. (1999). *Intrapreneuring in action: A Handbook for Business Innovation*. Berrett-Koehler Publishers.

PwC. (2016). *Blurred lines: How FinTech is shaping Financial Services,* Global FinTech Report.

Ragin, C. C. (1987). *The Comparative Method, Moving Beyond qualitative and quantitative strategies*. University of California Press.

Ragin, C. C. (2000). *Fuzzy-Set Social Science*. University of Chicago Press.

Rocchi, J.-M. (2019). Les banques en ligne et les néobanques en France (1994-2019): émergence, mutation, et survie. Une étude mixte par la méthode des cas multiples et l'AQQC simple (csQCA) [Online banks and neobanks in France (1994-2019): emergence, mutation, and survival. A mixed study using the multiple case study method and crisp-set QCA (csQCA)] (Unpublished EBDA doctoral dissetation). Paris Dauphine – PSL University, Paris.

Rocchi, J-M. (2018a). La victoire annonçée des banques en ligne [The announced victory of online banks]. *Revue Banque*, *818*, 66-71.

Rocchi, J-M. (2018b). Radiographie des néobanques [Radiography of neobanks]. *Revue Banque*, *820*, 65-68.

Say, J. B. (2018). *A Treatise on Political Economy*. HardPress. (Original work published 1803)

Schueffel, P. (2016). Taming the Beast: A Scientific Definition of Fintech. *Journal of Innovation Management*, *4*(4), 32–44. doi:10.24840/2183-0606_004.004_0004

Sgourev, S. (2013). How Paris Gave Rise to Cubism (and Picasso): Ambiguity and Fragmentation in Radical Innovation. *Organization Science*, *24*(6), 1–17. doi:10.1287/orsc.1120.0819

Staff Discussion Note, I. M. F. (2017, June). Fintech and Financial Services. *Initial Considerations, SDN*, *17*(05), 2–49.

Sutton, R. I. (1987). The Process of Organizational Death: Disbanding and Reconnecting. *Administrative Science Quarterly*, *32*(4), 542–569. doi:10.2307/2392883

Tardieu, H., Daly, D., Esteban-Lauzán, J., Hall, J., & Miller, G. (2020). *Deliberately Digital. Rewriting Enterprise DNA for Enduring Success*. Springer. doi:10.1007/978-3-030-37955-1

Vauplane, H. de. (2015). Les FinTech et la réglementation bancaire et financière [FinTech and banking and financial regulations]. *Banque & Stratégie*, *339*, 32-36.

Walker, A. (2014). Banking without banks: Exploring the disruptive effects of converging technologies that will shape the future of banking. *Journal of Securities Operations & Custody*, *7*(1), 69–80.

Zaheer, S. (1995). Overcoming the liability of foreignness. *Academy of Management Journal*, *38*(2), 341–363.

Zaheer, S., & Mosakovski, E. (1997). The dynamics of the liability of foreignness: A global study of survival in financial services. *Strategic Management Journal*, *18*(6), 439–464. doi:10.1002/(SICI)1097-0266(199706)18:6<439::AID-SMJ884>3.0.CO;2-Y

# Chapter 10
# Quality and Online Banking Case Study:
## "We Bank" Attijari Bank in Tunisia

**Aida Allaya**
*University of Tunis, Carthage, Tunisia*

**Bouthaina Allal**
*University of Tunis, Carthage, Tunisia*

## ABSTRACT

*The aim of this chapter is to study the online banking quality and its impact on the satisfaction and loyalty of the consumers. To reveal the quality's importance, the authors studied the Attijari Bank online services, namely Webank. The results of this chapter demonstrate that this bank respects all the quality norms and criteria: reliability, responsiveness, competence, courtesy, credibility, access, communication, understanding the customer, collaboration, continuous enrollment, content, accuracy, ease of use, timeliness, aesthetics, security, and diverse features that led to its success.*

## INTRODUCTION

Internet and the digital expansion have instigated the soaring of online banks. These banks offer free or cheap online services because as its name states it, it functions only online. These banks and especially the apps are particularly attractive to young consumers who are usually tech savvy users, in order to carry out transfers and various other operations. Only a small number of them resort to going to the agency. Online banks also target all those who wish to have a complete autonomy

DOI: 10.4018/978-1-7998-7110-1.ch010

and are well satisfied with virtual relationships, knowing that online banks offer a great variety of contact ways. This is the outcome of technological competitiveness (Mujinga, 2020).

To satisfy and retain its consumers, online banks have to provide a high standard of services, updates and information owing to the fact that, it impacts the consumers' experience. As a consequence, if the consumers consider that the payment system is weak and the answers are slow or tardy, online bank usage would diminish drastically. Hence the necessity of a customer service meant to listen and understand the users' issues; thus the service quality would inevitably improve. This initiative would certainly lead to the consumers' satisfaction because the interaction with the employees of the customer service influences positively this service usage intention. The customer service should cope with the complaints received from the customers' calls. As a result, the online bank system can increase the consumers' satisfaction and improve their experience as a whole.

Indeed, as defined by Nunkoo and Dwivedi (2018), the online bank service and information quality represents the support received by the user. The best representatives and responsible for this type of quality are the Integration Technology (IT) services and the support system (Delone & McLean, 2003; Seddiki & Rastogi, 2017). For this reason, Pitt et al. (1995) insisted on the inclusion of the service quality as an important measurement in order to insure the IT system efficiency. In addition, Gefen (2002) noted that the online bank gateway presents numerous problems such as, the technical constraints of a mobile device for instance (Kuo & Deng, 2009).

These researches have shown that the online bank's service and information quality were at the heart of research studies led during these last decades. Consequently, various models have been developed to explain what quality stands for. They proved that there were mainly two different approaches or strategies. The first approach is based on the confirmation of the measuring scales concerning the customer's perception and expectations in terms of quality. The second approach simply consists in confirming the measuring scales of online banks performances. In fact, these two approaches are divergent but complementary to evaluate the online bank's quality. These research models dimensions showed their importance to gauge the quality of the online banks in order to satisfy and retain the various clients.

The results of the survey conducted from June 17 to June 24 2020 on behalf 3,285 individuals showed that 41.5% tend to trust the online bank services. Only 23% of the people interviewed prefer going to the agency. The study reveals that the online bank is gaining more and more market shares and that the bank's digitalization is more and more regarded as a must. Concerning the detailed reasons leading to the choice of the main bank as well as the means used; interviews revealed that 1/5 of the interviewed is dissatisfied with its bank. For these dissatisfied consumers, 38.9% of them consider that the service quality and the communication quality are despicable.

Moreover, according to US data Lightico, March 2020 the banking use exploded because of Covid-19 pandemic and the containment that followed.

Thanks to these findings, the research question that motivated this study therefore concerns how the quality of online banking is determinant for the customer's satisfaction and the bank's ranking within the market. Consequently, our research question would be dedicated to the identification of the criteria that allowed we bank to be acknowledged as a quality bank.

Thus, in order to familiarize with the Tunisian online banks quality, in this chapter we focused on the Attijari online bank « Webank ». This bank enables the customers to live a new experience which starts with the opening of a remote account and continues with the follow-up of these operations, the management of the card, the loan application etc. Thanks to « Webank », the customer would benefit from the online bank services daily while enjoying a high level of security and up to date information in real time.

By dint of its service and information quality, « Webank » was elected best online bank in 2017 by "The Banker" magazine of the Financial Times group. Webank put in place a call center and developed its presence on the web in order to provide a greater proximity with its Webank customers via a Mobile and Web platform meant to satisfy the needs of the connected Client.

In this chapter, we would introduce the literature review which comprises the service quality, the information quality and the different dimensions of quality service and information Then, we would present our methodology and provide a case study presentation. Finally, we would analyse the case study analysis.

## LITERATURE REVIEW

In this section, we would present the various research elaborated concerning service quality, information quality and the dimension measuring these aspects.

### The Service Quality

The service quality affects the users. So, if the user realizes that the system is weak and that the answers are slow, the online banking service usage is regarded as negative. However, if there is a customer service available and trained to listen and understand the users' issues, then the service quality improves. This initiative would certainly lead to the customer's satisfaction because the interaction with the offered service and the employees would positively influence the service usage intention. This means that the customer service has to cope with the complaints received from the customers 'calls. So, the quality of the online banking system can increase the users satisfaction and improve the overall experience.

From a marketing perspective, a performing service quality strengthens the supplier service's loyalty (Nunkoo, Teeroovengadum, Thomas, & Leonard, 2017). Consequently the research of Abou-Shouk and Khalifa (2017), Ahmad et al. (2017), Pee et al.(2018) and Toufaily and Pons (2017) has demonstrated that the electronic service quality is positively correlated to the customer's loyalty. This loyalty to the system reflects the individual's intention to continue to use the system. As a result, Kim et al. (2011) noticed in their research works that intention to continue is an indirect indicator of the customer's loyalty.

Moreover, the ease of use perceived by the online bank's customers amplifies their satisfaction. The perceived ease of use presents the degree with which an individual thinks that a given system usage is effortless (Davis, 1989). In fact, perceived ease of use represents the degree with which an innovation is regarded as easy to comprehend, learn and exploit. This author adds that the ease of use measures the consumer's perception that the new service or product is better than its substitutes. Zeithaml et al. (2002) have declared that the understanding and usage fluency of an innovation could be regarded as an ease of usage perception.

Concerning the online bank transactions, Mathieson (1991) affirms that a users' perceived utility plays an important role to judge the online bank service quality. This perceived ease of use could refer to the consumers' capacity to experiment an innovation and to easily evaluate its advantages (Conslut,2002). This author also affirmed that online bank services growth engines are determined by the perceived ease of use that associates the convenience offered to the people that enjoy an easy access to internet and the availability of the functionalities of highly secured electronic banking.

## Information Quality

To judge the online bank services quality, the information quality plays a key role in the online bank's level of satisfaction. Thereby, the customer is imperatively affected by the content quality (Jung, Perez & Wiley, 2009). Zhou (2013) highlighted the fact that, in the absence of a good information quality, lots of efforts are required from the users to dissect the information that would increase their operational difficulties.

The service quality then represents the systems' characteristics such as pertinence, sufficiency, accuracy and opportunity. Akter et al.(2013) have observed that the information quality is one of the key factors that influences the users attitude towards the technology they use. As a consequence, the information quality could be regarded as the major construction bringing satisfaction because it impacts some behavioral beliefs that can influence the online banks usage intention (Urbach, Smolnik, &Riempp, 2010).

## The Dimensions Measuring the Service and the Information Quality of Online Banks

Jun and Cai (2001) led surveys to find the major determinants of the online banking services quality. These searchers could identify seventeen dimensions of the online banking services quality. These dimensions are the following: reliability, responsiveness, competence, courtesy, credibility, access, communication, understanding the customer, collaboration, continuous enrollment, content, accuracy, ease of use, timeliness, aesthetics, security and diverse features. For these authors, the most important dimensions to take into consideration in order to have a high service of online banking are the responsiveness, the reliability, the access' ease and the accuracy

Broderick and Vachirapornpuk (2002) led qualitative research in the UK on the online banks service quality. This study used the participant's observation and the analyses of the banks' websites to determine how the customers interpret the online banks service quality. The results of this study showed that the most important criteria that determine the online banks service quality are the reliability, the efficiency, the responsiveness, the ease of use and the information quality.

Han and Baek (2004) used the SERVQUAI model to measure online banks service quality. The factor and confirmatory analysis results showed that the most pertinent dimensions to evaluate quality are the following: tangibility, reliability, responsiveness, and empathy. Thanks to this survey, the commercial banks in South Korea demonstrated via their website that there is a relationship between the quality, the satisfaction and the loyalty of the consumer.

Liao and Cheung (2005) presented a basic framework by surveying the users of the online bank service. This survey has been distributed to 500 peoples that were invited to provide their evaluation while following the seven points Linkert scale going from "strongly disagree" to "highly agree". The empirical results showed that the most important dimensions are usefulness, ease of use, reliability, responsiveness, security, privacy, and continuous improvement of e-banking services, which significantly influence customer attitudes towards online banking.

To evaluate the online banks service quality, Wu et al. (2008) used the ZPM electronic service quality model. These searchers surveyed employees, users and administrators of online banks. Using the results, a quality table was elaborated proving that these dimensions influence the online bank quality: "efficiency", "reliability", "privacy", "compensation", "responsiveness", "contact", "sense of beauty" and "individualization".

Through a qualitative study, Loonam and O'Loughlin (2008) studied the perception of the free-service online bank clients in the Irish financial service sector. This study explored the interactions and the consumers' experiences in terms of electronic online banks services. The ultimate goal was to evaluate the quality of the Dutch online banks processes .The outcomes of this research are the following: webusability, security, information quality, accessibility, trust, reliability, flexibility, responsiveness, service recovery, and customization. Moreover, the results proved that the processes quality is among the key factors of the online banks services quality.

Khan et al. (2009) evaluated the online banks services in India through a survey comprises 44 items that measure the quality. Via the analysis of the major components, seven bank services quality measures were detected, reliability, accessibility, user friendliness, privacy/security, efficiency, responsiveness and fulfillment. These authors later proposed a mathematical model to evaluate the online banks global quality. They tested this model through regression and found that fours dimensions determined the quality: reliability, accessibility, privacy, security, responsiveness and fulfillment.

## CONCEPTUAL FRAMEWORK

This chapter's objective is to provide a conceptual framework after the examination of the various recent literatures concerning the online bank.

### Methodology and Presentation of the Case Study

Qualitative, interpretative case study was chosen for this study in order to gather rich data not only on the research phenomenon but also on the qualitative criteria in which it is embedded. Qualitative methodology is regarded as optimal for obtaining context sensitive and deep insight about the Webank's success in Tunisia.

This study is based on the interpretative paradigm. Interpretative paradigm tries to comprehend a research issue from subjective and contextual perspective. As a matter of fact, this paradigm follows subjective rather than objective methodology. The epistemological perspective of interpretative research is the most appropriate perspective owing to the fact that this study's purpose is to focus and study in depth the Webank and the key elements leading to its outstanding success in Tunisia. This perspective was regarded as the most appropriate and efficient because our goal was to demonstrate the reasons behind this success story rather than a willingness to generalizing our findings.

## Collecting Data

This research oriented our observations on the online bank's quality "We Bank". The exploratory research was based on interviewing agencies managers, marketing and IT managers and most importantly WeBank customers to cope with the information and service quality of WeBank.

This exploratory phase via open interviews helped us highlight a crucial phenomenon that is the perception of the online bank by the managers and the customers of the bank.

The sampling was conducted following two well identified criteria:

- Those who were surveyed had to be managers or agency managers.
- The customers surveyed have to be WeBank customers aging below 35 owing to the fact that through the interviews conducted with the various managers of the bank, it has been revealed to us that the Bank's objective was to entice the young adults mostly tech savvy and connected.

For this study, 20 interviews with agency managers and 40 Webank clients; including 22 male individuals and 18 female individuals were led. The interviews lasted approximately 45 minutes.

The open interview was used as an instrument for exploratory investigation and asked what were the criteria that attracted them in the Webank and the quality criteria that instigated customer loyalty.

To answer the questions raised concerning the online bank's quality of the Webank, a documentary analysis seems necessary to understand the phenomenon in depth.

This documentary analysis is a method that allows a high quality of data analysis hence a high quality of information (Waller & Masse, 1999). We used internal documentation of the online bank, published articles from 2014 to 2020 and consulted the Attijari Bank website and Real Time platform.

## Description of the Webank and Its Environment

The online bank environment in Africa is immature as opposed to Europe because of the low level of banking coverage. However, the development of the 3G and now the 4G and the explosion of mobile phone users (according to GSMA-smartphone use is expected to reach 463 million by 2020 which implies a rise of 167 million compared to 2016) paved the way for the democratization access to banking services. The disruptive innovation of the system is regarded as a major impediment for the development of the online banking system.

In Tunisia, the online banking system is underdeveloped hence the competitiveness between only two online banks namely the Amen First Bank launched in 2015 and the Attijari Webank in 2014, while the other banks provide solely e-banking services. Attijari bank was chosen because of its prominence on the Tunisian market and also because it was elected best online bank four years in row.

Attijari Bank is a Tunisian and international bank that enjoys the most extended network made out of 207 agencies and business centers. In 2017, it was elected for the fourth and consecutive time, "Bank of the year" in Tunisia, by the prestigious "The Banker" Magazine.

Because of this prowess and its remarkable and pioneer situation in the launching of the online bank in Tunisia, this bank seemed to meet the standards we wanted to study in the Tunisian market. The Attijari online bank, the "Webank", is the first online bank on the Tunisian market. It enables its clients to open of a remote account in less than eight minutes and proceed to numerous bank operations.

Indeed, on account of this Webank project, the Attijari Bank was able to raise the standards and meet the challenge of digitalization within the difficult context of the emerging countries' digital analphabetisation. Although Tunisia enjoys an advantageous position in Africa, it was nonetheless a risky bet to launch it within a country which did not fulfill its digital transition yet.

The Webank was a prominent project because it finally met the young generation's need for digitilisation and self reliance. Its undeniable quality led to the loyalty and satisfaction of its customers.

## Description of the Webank Offers

Via these various data collection we found out that the bank provides two major offers the WeStart and the WeTrust .

The **Westart** is a call offer which provides free services. Those services comprise transfers, (the issued transfers to beneficiaries), the credit card tracking (credit card activation and disactivation, the checking of the credit card limit), the bank account follow up/ tracking (consultation of the bank balance, bank statement etc), notifications (bank customer interaction).

This offer also guaranties the following advantages: a welcome offer (with loyalty points), a **S**ight **D**eposit **A**ccount, a national Mastercard, a visual personalization, a checker, remote account management, reduction of transfers emitted online, free transfers received.

The **WeTrust**,on the other hand,is a more developed product aiming at anticipating the client's growing needs and expectations. Indeed, this product is not free and offers a greater variety of services than the former one. On top of the services provided by the Westart, this offer permits the online bank credit request, the consumer loans, the overdrafts requests as well as the checkbook requests.

This offer assures the following benefits to the clients: a welcome offer (with loyalty points), a **S**ight **D**eposit **A**ccount, a national Mastercard, a visual personalization, a checker, remote account management, reduction of transfers emitted online, free transfers received, request for an overdraft authorization, online consumer credit application, an overdraft insurance, means of payment insurance (secure+), guaranteed purchase insurance. This card covers the opposition fees for stolen or lost cards, the card renewal fees, the replacement of keys and official identity papers. It also guaranties, the accidental damage to the guaranteed property one week after the purchase and the characterized theft of guaranteed property 48 hours after the purchase. Home telephone assistance for medical guidance is also provided and allowing the following services: contact information of professionals and health centers, putting a client through a physician for telephone medical assistance, and insure a medical appointment.

One of the core values of Webank is the high level of security ensured to all customers. Indeed, they have access to a secure platform insuring the customer's identification as well as the operations tracking.

To insure a high standard and quality service for its clients, Webank relies on a dedicated team of trained employees at a call center specialized in the treatment of issues related to the online bank management. This platform is so crucial to the well functioning of the whole system that these online advisors deal with the customers before they get in contact with an agency.

To further magnet its clients, Webank offers its We card clients the ability to personalize their card according to their style for 1dt only. Aware of the younger generation's sensitivity towards marketing and personalization wants, Webank thought of empowering its clients by giving them the choice to personalize their card within a plethora of choices available.

In addition, Attijari Bank deviced the Attijari Real time which is a service that provides the customers a supple and practical solution to manage their remote accounts via an internet connexion as well as an edition tool and document consultation, namely Attijari Doc. This service targets the personal, professionals and businesses.

The Real Time service offers the following options:

**The accounts management**: the accounts list, the real time account balance, the real time, account transactions, the transactions' history over four months, the downloading of account statement (ETBAC, ETBAC 3, AFB 120, EXCEL, Money, Quicken),Edition of Bank details, balance evolution curve

**Checks:** edition of check remittance slip, checks consultation, checker's request, outstanding credit, a term deposit, coupons

**Other services** encompass the following products: the currency rate, receiving account status alerts (debit balance, credit balance etc),receiving messages from the web administrator and manager, personalization of the access parameters: change of account name, password change, etc

Moreover, the Attijari Real Time provides the following services via the Attijari Doc platform: the downloading of transaction notices, the checking of check images, the downloading of the interests' scales, and the viewing of Swift messages.

All this is meant to enable instantaneous information avoiding then unnecessary client's displacement. Indeed, the service is available 24/7, allows a better reactivity, a rapid decision making and a better tracking of the transactions.

However, few drawbacks have been noticed while comparing the services provided by the online banks on the international scale. Webank still lacks services compared to an online bank, some updates are necessary. The application did not receive any update since June 21, 2019. Some other services should be included such as the NFC Mobile payment.

## CASE STUDY ANALYSIS

We Bank is an online quality bank that enjoys several key elements of success. According to some empirical researches, online banks' criteria of success are the following: reliability, responsiveness, competence, courtesy, credibility, access, communication, understanding the customer, collaboration, continuous enrollment, content, accuracy, ease of use, timeliness, aesthetics, security and diverse features. In this analysis we would display the online bank's qualities through these dimensions.

### Reliability and Security

To begin with, in terms of reliability and security We Bank enjoys a high level of security. This Bank is recognized for the safety and high security of its transactions. It provides a secured access to the platform ensuring the customer's identification as well as the control and tracking of the operations. In 2020, the bank reinforced the online payments security by adopting the "3D-secure" protocol. As a result, for every online payment with an Attijari Bank card, the client receives a confirmation code to be typed during the payment. In case the client does not introduce the given code, the transaction is automatically rejected. This service has been activated as a default service to all the Attijari customers and the information has been communicated on social networks as well as Attijari's web site. Consequently, the client whose mobile number is not well informed on MXP won't be able to proceed to online payments. "*Webank answers and meets the expectations of a population who's more and more connected and seeks ease of use, efficiency and banking system's speed. This offer is essentially based on bank transactions. It is an interactive starter offer on the technological platform that enjoys great reliability as well as the all advising provided by the bank's call center.* " "*The online accounts are always tracked even in the absence of transactions."(Customer's interview extract, 16/12/2019).*

## Accessibility

The access to the website itself requires a username and a password chosen by the client, who's then responsible for the confidentiality his/her username and password. The site enjoys an automatic system of data treatment: "*A very good digital experience, a free account, a free card with a franco access to the application 24/7. I opened with account with a couple clicks and until now I did not pay any fee or any irregular billing" (Customer's interview extract 20/02/2020).* All fraudulent accesses including personal spaces is forbidden and legally sanctioned. The bank provides its best effort to secure the site and the user is invited to take all necessary measures to protect his/her personal information from possible online virus attacks. The Webank is engaged within the framework of its activities and in accordance with current regulations to insure the protection, the confidentiality and the personal data security, as well as the respect of privacy in accordance with the organic law n°2004-63 of July 27, 2004, concerning the protection of personal and private data. This demonstrates the bank's seriousness in terms of privacy and security of its transactions but also the swiftness and the overall instantaneous communication strategy applied by the bank.

## Communication

Other than security of transactions, this online bank is recognized for the pertinence and accuracy of its communication. Indeed, communication is crucial to the well functioning of the system. Attijari webank's website is very up to date concerning the transmission of valuable information to its users and extremely informative because it displays the offered services in detail and facilitates the immediate registration to the service. It also provides access to their team of advisors (the webank call center) by registering for an appointment with an advisor according to the client's convenience. Moreover, the website's content is very well thought of, organized, detailed and structured. It is designed in a way that facilitates its use and makes it accessible to all customers no matter their age group or their level of education. In fact, the webpage is very bright, clear, attractive, decluttered, simple and neat, all this to say that the webpage is reassuring, very accessible and easy to manipulate. The site is devised around the added value services for the user without any form of limitations which implies: the request to open an online bank account, the practical information of the bank's products and services, the account's follow up, the communication with the bank via the call center, the online information forms and the request for a consumer loan: "*The launching of this new bank is part of the ambition to contribute to the efforts to attract the young generation. This new project of digitalisation is an innovation to answer the changes and contribute to the process of digital transformation. We would have to align with the international innovation which becomes a compulsory task and not choice." (Manager's interview extract, 06/01/2020)*

## Aesthetics

Aesthetically speaking, the website as well as all the online products are considered as highly attractive owing to the fact that, the website uses its official logo's colours, red, orange/yellow and black: *"One of the best apps in Tunisia in terms of Design, but requires some improvements*" (customer interview extract,18/02/2020). These colours were not chosen out of the blue on the contrary, knowing the colours' impact on the viewer and especially the customer, these colours were meant heighten the viewers' alertness and attention, thus, the psychology of colours is meant to arouse emotional reactions and are constantly used in advertising and marketing, owing to the fact that it can deeply impact people's behavior and decision making and that people make subconscious judgements within a few seconds or minutes. Via their choice of colour in logos, signage and advertising, brands can sway clients to buy on impulse, or select their product or service over challengers. Let's now delve into Webank's choice of colours and its impact on the consumer. As stated above, the Webank's logo is shaped like a rainbow of colours including the original Attijari colours which are various shades of red, orange and yellow while the brand is written in black. In psychology, the colour red is associated with strong emotions and arouses a sense of urgency. It is regarded as the best colour to use in marketing as it increases sales and is associated with power. The red colour stimulates the body by increasing the blood pressure and the heart pace. It is often equated with movement, excitement and passion. It urges viewers to act and is crucial for call-to-action buttons on websites for instance. On the other hand, orange and yellow are regarded as jovial and beget optimism. It is also worth noting that it has been scientifically proven that both red and yellow are the most eye catching colors, hence their omnipresence in several brands logos and in the field of advertisement. The black colour (as there is a black zigzag in the middle of the logo) is associated with authority, power, stability, confidence and strength. Besides, it is often used as a symbol of intelligence. All this to say that, Attijari's logo and website are key elements in the online bank's success with the customer. Webank's level of attractiveness is very high according to this psychological analysis of the colours attractiveness for the customer.

## Responsiveness, Reliability and Timeliness

In terms of reliability, the bank enjoys several elements that allow its efficiency. In fact, other than the websites' effectiveness and proficiency, the bank relies on a well trained team of advisors in their call centers answering through calls, mails and chat from local and foreign customers from 8:00 am to 8:00 pm from Monday to Saturday, which insures the timeliness of the response to the client's needs: *"The transfer fees from a Webank customer to a classical Attijari account costs 1,785 dt while these fees reach 2,916 dt in the other banks." "A students whose pocket money derives from a monthly transfer from his parents bank account and some part time jobs he does, was directed towards the We Start offer in order to have access to free transfers and reduced fees for the emitted transfers (1.131 instead of 1.785)."* (Customer's interview extract, 07/01/2020).Besides, a dedicated team of professionals in the agencies are now muting their task from random bankers to advisors and counselors. The Attijari online bank; other than the necessity to meet the customer's needs, was also meant to raise the bank's accessibility to the customer and improve the bank's (mostly the team of professionals in direct contact with the clients) understanding of the customer and anticipating their needs while keeping them satisfied via the teams' training for courtesy to maintain the customer's level of satisfaction at its peak. Besides, the bank's website enjoys a good hosting and referencing that allows a 24/7 access and the hypertext links are meant to optimize the visibility of every webpage, via these internal hypertext links, users can browse though the whole online bank catalogue of products.

## Ease of Use

Concerning the perceived ease of use, several strategies are used to facilitate the user's comprehension of the offers as well as his/her management of the account. For instance, the introductory video which is meant to explain the webank's advantage for the customer is designed in Tunisian vernacular and is within one's grasp in order to maximize the chances of understanding the service: *"The registration phase took place without any difficulty. After the subscription confirmation, I have been contacted by the Webank customer service to schedule the day and time in which I would go to the chosen Attijari agency to finalize the account opening with a contract signature and receive my credit card."* (Customer's interview extract, 08/01/2020).

Besides, the bank's digitilisation is a win win experience. The client experiences a simplification of the customer's journey through the self-management of the regular operations and transactions at a very low cost. This is a very empowering experience for most Tunisians who (because of the non digitalization of most sectors and the troubles met to get any legal paper) abhor paper works. On the other hand, the bank is able to handle the new threats such as GAFA, Telcos and to save time in order to invest it in the client's relationship and develop a better understanding of the customer. Indeed, the banker is expected to understand and anticipate better the customer's wants through the exploration of the various data provided, hence, the banker's role evolution from banker to advisor.

## CONCLUSION

This chapter studied the quality of the Attijari's online bank, the "Webank". This bank is the first Tunisian online bank whose main objective is to meet the young generation of customers' expectations; who've been neglected by the most other banks to this day. Our findings show that this bank offers a high level of service and information quality thanks to its responsiveness, reliability etc.

This platform is available both in mobile and web format to instigate an online payment culture. The bank seeks to enable its clients an enjoyable, simple, flexible and safe experience. By virtue of its outstanding quality, Webank is an innovation meant to answer the changes and contribute to the process of digital transformation in Tunisia.

In terms of contribution, the originality of this paper stems from the focus on the Tunisian experience of the online bank. The Webank took the initiative to launch its digital bank while the country was initiating its digitalization which is still in process to this day. It was a daring bet but the quality of the product made its undeniable success. Indeed, Webank meets the 17 quality criteria as proven through this case study leading to the consumer's satisfaction and loyalty.

The limitation of this paper is its use of a single case study. These findings are not expected to be generalized geographically to all developing countries. In terms of future research directions, other research can focus on the Tunisian cultural context or the socio-economic context.

## REFERENCES

Akter, S., D'Ambrab, J., & Rayb, P. (2013). Development and validation of an instrument to measure user perceived service quality of m-Health. *Information & Management*, *50*(4), 181–195. doi:10.1016/j.im.2013.03.001

Broderick, J. A., & Vachirapornpuk, S. (2002). Service Quality of Internet banking: The Importance of Customer Role. *Marketing Intelligence & Planning*, *20*(6), 327–335. doi:10.1108/02634500210445383

Delone, W. H., & McLean, E. R. (2003). The Delone and McLean Model of Information System Success: A Ten Year Update. *Journal of Management Information Systems*, *19*(4), 9–30. doi:10.1080/07421222.2003.11045748

Fred, D., & Davis, D. (1989). Perceived Usefulness, Perceived Ease of Use, and User Acceptance of Information Technology. *Management Information Systems Research Center*, *13*, 319–340.

Gefen, D. (2002). Customer Loyalty in E-Commerce. *Journal of the Association for Information Systems*, *3*(1), 27–51. doi:10.17705/1jais.00022

Han, S., & Baek, S. (2004). Antecedents and Consequences of Service Quality in Online Banking: An Application of the SERVQUAL Instrument. *Advances in Consumer Research. Association for Consumer Research (U. S.)*, *31*, 208–214.

Khan, M. S., Mahapatra, S. S., & Sreekumar, A. (2009). Service quality evaluation in internet banking: An empirical study in India. *Indian Culture and Business Management*, *2*(1), 30–46. doi:10.1504/IJICBM.2009.021596

Kieran, M. (1991). Predicting User Intentions: Comparing the Technology Acceptance Model with the Theory of Planned Behavior information system research. *Information Systems Research*, *2*, 73–191.

Kim, H., & Min, L. (2011). Antecedents of application service continuance: A synthesis of satisfaction and trust. *Expert Systems with Application*, *38*, 9530-9542.

Kuo, Y. F., Wu, C. M., & Deng, W. J. (2009). The relationships among service quality, perceived value, customer satisfaction and post purchase intention in mobile value added services. *Computers in Human Behavior*, *25*(4), 887–896. doi:10.1016/j.chb.2009.03.003

Liao, Z., & Cheung, M.T. (2005) .Service Quality in Internet e-Banking: A User-based Core Framework. *Proceedings IEEE international Conference e-Technology, e-Commerce and e-Service*.

Loonam, M. O., & Loughlin, D. (2008). Exploring e-service quality: A study of Irish online banking. *Marketing Intelligence & Planning*, *26*(7), 759–780. doi:10.1108/02634500810916708

Minjoon, J., & Shaohan, C. (2011). The key determinants of Internet banking service quality: A content analysis. *International Journal of Bank Marketing*, *19*, 276–291.

Nils, U., Stefan, S., & Gerold, R. (2013). An empirical investigation of employee portal success. *The Journal of Strategic Information Systems*, *19*, 184–206.

Nunkoo, R., Ramkissoon, H., & Gursoy, D. (2013). use of structural equation modeling in tourism reaserch past, present and future. *Journal of Travel Research*, *52*, 759–771. doi:10.1177/0047287513478503

Pee, J., & Klein, T. P. (2017). E-store loyalty: Longitudinal comparison of website usefulness and satisfaction. *International Journal of Market Research*, *60*, 1–17.

Pitt, L. F., Watson, R. T., & Kavan, C. B. (1995). Service quality: A measure of information systems effectiveness. *Management Information Systems Quarterly*, *19*(2), 73–187. doi:10.2307/249687

Valarie, A., Zeithaml, A., Parsu, P., & Arvind, M. (2002). Service Quality Delivery Through Web Sites: A Critical Review of Extant. *Journal of the Academy of Marketing Science*, *30*(4), 362–375. doi:10.1177/009207002236911

Veeramotoo, M., Nunkoo, R., & Dwivedi, A. (2018). What determine sucess of an e-government service validation of an aintegartive mode of E filing continuance usage. *Government Information Quarterly*, *35*(2), 161–174. doi:10.1016/j.giq.2018.03.004

Waller, S., & Masse, C. (1999). *L'analyse documentaire: une approche méthodologique* [Thedocumentary analysis: a methodological approach]. ADBS Edition.

Ying, F. K., Chi-Ming, W., Wei-Jaw, A., & Deng, W. J. (2009). The relationships among service quality, perceived value,customer satisfaction, and post-purchase intention in mobile value-added services. *Computers in Human Behavior*, *25*(4), 887–896. doi:10.1016/j.chb.2009.03.003

Zhou, T. (2013). An empirical examination of continuance intention of mobile payment services. *Decision Support Systems*, *54*(2), 1085–1091. doi:10.1016/j.dss.2012.10.034

## KEY TERMS AND DEFINITIONS

**Accessibility:** Accessibility is the provision of a website to the greatest number of consumers.

**Aesthetics:** The bank's web site is regarded as highly attractive to consumers.

**Consumer Satisfaction:** Satisfaction is a prior expectation of the consumer. It reflects the discrepancy between the expectations and the performance of a service.

**Information Quality:** Reflects the performance of the banking information system.

**Online Banking:** Is a credit institution that does not have a physical bank branch. Customers open and manage their account by logging into the bank's website or mobile application.

**Quality Service:** The quality and ability to meet the explicit and implicit customer expectations.

**Reliability:** The bank enjoys several elements that allow its efficiency.

**Responsiveness:** Is the ability to act in the face of a changing banking information.

# Compilation of References


Abell, D. F. (1980). *Defining the business: The starting point of strategic planning*. Prentice Hall.

Acar, O., & Çıtak, Y. E. (2019). Fintech Integration Process Suggestion for Banks. *Procedia Computer Science*, *158*, 971–978. doi:10.1016/j.procs.2019.09.138

Accenture. (2013). *Corporate Innovation Is Within Reach: Nurturing and Enabling an Entrepreneurial Culture*. https://www.accenture.com/t20150523T052044__w__/us-en/_acnmedia/Accenture/Conversion-Assets/DotCom/Documents/Global/PDF/Strategy_2/Accenture-Survey-Enabling-Culture-Innovation-Entrepreneurialism.pdf

Accenture. (2016a). *Beyond the everyday bank: How a GAFA approach to digital banking transformation will increase revenues, improve customer engagement, while reducing the cost base*. https://www.accenture.com/t20160502T051308Z__w__/us-en/_acnmedia/PDF-10/Accenture-Banking-Beyond-Everyday-Bank-pdf.pdf#zoom=50

Accenture. (2016b). *FinTech and the evolving landscape: landing points for the industry*. https://www.accenture.com/t20161011T031409Z__w__/pl-en/_acnmedia/PDF-15/Accenture-FinTech-Evolving-Landscape.pdf

ACPR. – Banque de France. (2017, July-August). Les enjeux de régulation et de supervision liés aux fintechs et à la rupture digitale [Regulation and supervision issues related to fintechs and digital disruption]. *Bulletin*, (212), 39–46.

Adil Shafi, P., & Kajal Patel, A. (2018). *Blockchain technology and cryptocurrencies: regulatory framework in the UAE*. Retrieved from https://ach-legal.com/blog/Blockchain-technology-cryptocurrencies-regulatory-framework-UAE

Admati, A. R., & Hellwig, M. (2013). *The bankers' new clothes*. Princeton University Press.

Aghion, P., Bloom, N., Blundell, R., Griffith, R., & Howitt, P. (2005). Competition and innovation: An inverted-U relationship. *The Quarterly Journal of Economics*, *120*(2), 701–728.

Ahamed, M. M., & Mallick, S. K. (2019). Is financial inclusion good for bank stability? International evidence. *Journal of Economic Behavior & Organization*, *157*, 403–427. doi:10.1016/j.jebo.2017.07.027

Ahl, A., Goto, M., Yarime, M., Tanaka, K., & Sagawa, D. (2019). Practical Challenges and Opportunities of Blockchain in the Energy Sector: Expert Perspectives in Germany. *International Conference on Applied Energy.*

Ainsworth, R. T., & Viitasaari, V. (2017). Payroll Tax & the Blockchain. *Tax Notes International, 13*, 1007-1024.

Akter, S., D'Ambrab, J., & Rayb, P. (2013). Development and validation of an instrument to measure user perceived service quality of m-Health. *Information & Management, 50*(4), 181–195. doi:10.1016/j.im.2013.03.001

Alabi, K. (2020). A 2020 perspective on "Digital blockchain networks appear to be following Metcalfe's Law.". *Electronic Commerce Research and Applications, 40*, 40. doi:10.1016/j.elerap.2020.100939

Al-Ajlouni, A. T., & Al-Hakim, M. (2018). *Financial technology in banking industry: Challenges and opportunities*. Paper presented at International Conference on Economics and Administrative Sciences. Applied Sciences University, Jordan. 10.2139srn.3340363

Aldrich, H. E. (2001). Who Wants to Be an Evolutionnary Theorist? Remarks On the Occasion of the Year 2000 OMT Distinguished Scholarly Career Award Presentation. *Journal of Management Inquiry, 10*(2), 115–127. doi:10.1177/1056492601102004

Alharthi, A., Krotov, V., & Bowman, M. (2017). Addressing barriers to big data. *Business Horizons, 60*(3), 285–292. doi:10.1016/j.bushor.2017.01.002

Allaire, Y., & Firsirotu, M. E. (1993). Strategy and Performance Drivers (French) Theories of organizational culture. *Organization Studies, 5*(3), 193–226. doi:10.1177/017084068400500301

Almeida, F. L. (2017). Benefits, challenges and tools of big data management. *Journal of Systems Integration, 8*(4), 12–20.

Aloulou, W. J. (in press). Mapping incubation mechanisms in Saudi Arabia: State-of-the-art and challenges for the future. In International Handbook of Research on Business and Technology Incubation. Edward Elgar Publishing.

Aloulou, W.J., (2019). Entrepreneurship and innovation in the era of digitalization: Exploring uncharted territories. In *Business Transformations in the Era of Digitalization*. IGI Global.

Alt, R., Beck, R., & Smits, M. T. (2018). Fintech and the transformation of the financial industry. *Electronic Markets, 2018*(28), 235–243. doi:10.100712525-018-0310-9

Alt, R., & Zimmermann, H. D. (2001). Preface: Introduction to special section–business models. *Electronic Markets, 11*(1), 3–9.

Anagnostopoulos, I. (2018). FinTech and Regtech: Impact on Regulators and Banks. *Journal of Economics and Business, 100*, 7–25. doi:10.1016/j.jeconbus.2018.07.003

Anand, D., & Mantrala, M. (2019). Responding to disruptive business model innovations: The case of traditional banks facing FinTech entrants. *Journal of Banking and Financial Technology, 3*(1), 19–31. doi:10.100742786-018-00004-4

Anonymous. (2015). The Fintech revolution: A wave of startups is changing finance—For the better. *The Economist.*

Arner, D. W., Barberis, J. N., & Buckley, R. P. (2015). *The evolution of fintech: A new post-crisis paradigm?* Retrieved May 10, 2020, from https://core.ac.uk/download/pdf/38088713.pdf

Arner, D. W., Buckley, R. P., & Zetzsche, D. A. (2018). *Fintech for financial inclusion: A framework for digital financial transformation. AFI special report.* https://www.cnbs.gob.hn/wp-content/uploads/2020/01/AFI_FinTech_Special-Report_AW_digital.pdf

Arner, D. W., Barberis, J., & Buckley, R. P. (2015). The evolution of FinTech: A new post-crisis paradigm. *Geo. J. Int'l L., 47*, 1271. doi:10.2139srn.2676553

Arner, D. W., Barberis, J., & Buckley, R. P. (2016). The evolution of FinTech: A new post-crisis paradigm? *Georgetown Journal of International Law, 47*(4), 1272–1319.

Arslanian, H., & Fischer, F. (2019). *The Future of Finance: The Impact of FinTech, AI, and Crypto on Financial Services*. Springer. doi:10.1007/978-3-030-14533-0

Ashta, A., & Biot-Paquerot, G. (2018). FinTech evolution: Strategic value management issues in a fast changing industry. *Strategic Change, 27*(4), 301–311. doi:10.1002/jsc.2203

Auta, E. M. (2010). E-banking in developing economy: Empirical evidence from Nigeria. *Journal of Applied Quantitative Methods, 5*(2), 212–222.

Autio, E., Nambisan, S., Thomas, L. D., & Wright, M. (2018). Digital affordances, spatial affordances, and the genesis of entrepreneurial ecosystems. *Strategic Entrepreneurship Journal, 12*(1), 72–95. doi:10.1002ej.1266

Averch, H., & Johnson, L. L. (1962). Behaviour of the firm under regulatory constraint. *The American Economic Review, 52*(5), 1052–1069.

Ávila, L., & Teixeira, L. (2019). The Main Concepts Behind the Dematerialization of Business Processes. In M. Khosrow-Pour (Ed.), *Advanced Methodologies and Technologies in Business Operations and Management* (pp. 508–519). IGI Global. doi:10.4018/978-1-5225-7362-3.ch037

Baines, T., Bigdeli, A. Z., Bustinza, O. F., Shi, V. G., Baldwin, J., & Ridgway, K. (2017). Servitization: Revisiting the state-of-the-art and research priorities. *International Journal of Operations & Production Management, 37*(2), 256–278. doi:10.1108/IJOPM-06-2015-0312

Bank, E. C. (2018). *Annual Report of the Euro Retail Payments Board 2017 /2018.* Retrieved October 13, 2001, from https://eur-lex.europa.eu/legal-content/EN/TXT/PDF/?uri=CELEX:32015L2366&from=EN

Bara, A., & Mudzingiri, C. (2016). Financial innovation and economic growth: Evidence from Zimbabwe. *Investment Management and Financial Innovations, 13*(2), 65–75. doi:10.21511/imfi.13(2).2016.07

Barba Navaretti, G., Calzolari, G., & Pozzolo, A. F. (2017). FinTech and Banks: Friends or Foes? *European Economy, 2*, 9–30.

Bardawil, N. (2018). FinTech and the Accelerator Culture. *Int'l Fin. L. Rev., 37*, 101.

Barnett, W. P., & Amburgey, T. L. (1990). Do Larger Organizations Generate Stronger Competition? In J. V. Singh (Ed.), *Organizational Evolution: New Directions* (pp. 78–102). Sage.

Barrett, M., Davidson, E., Prabhu, J., & Vargo, S. L. (2015). Service innovation in the digital age: Key contributions and future directions. *Management Information Systems Quarterly, 39*(1), 135–154. doi:10.25300/MISQ/2015/39:1.03

Barron, D. N. (1998). Pathways to Legitimacy among Consumer Loan Providers in New York City, 1914-34. *Organization Studies, 19*(2), 207–233. doi:10.1177/017084069801900203

Barron, D. N., West, E., & Hannan, M. T. (1994). A Time to Grow and a Time to Die: Growth and Mortality of Credit Unions in New York City, 1914-1990. *American Journal of Sociology, 100*(2), 381–421. doi:10.1086/230541

Barsan, I. M. (2017). Legal challenges of initial coin offerings (ICO). *Revue Trimestrielle de Droit Financier,* (3), 54-65.

Baru, S. (2018). Blockchain: The next innovation to make our cities smarter. Academic Press.

Baydakova, A. (2020). *Russian Prime Minister Introduces Bill to Allow Fintech Sandboxes, Blockchain Included.* Retrieved from https://www.coindesk.com/russian-prime-minister-introduces-bill-to-allow-fintech-sandboxes-blockchain-included

BCBS (Basel Committee on Banking Supervision). (2018). *Sound Practices-Implications ofFintech Developments for Banks and Bank Supervisors.* Bank for International Settlements.

Beck, T., Chen, T., Lin, C., & Song, F. M. (2016). Financial innovation: The bright and the dark sides. *Journal of Banking & Finance, 72*, 28–51. doi:10.1016/j.jbankfin.2016.06.012

Belt, A., & Kok, S. (2018). A Reality Check for Blockchain in Commodity Trading. *Bonston Consulting Group.* https://www.bcg.com/publications/2018/reality-check-blockchain-commodity-trading.aspx

Benchoufi, M., & Ravaud, P. (2017). Blockchain technology for improving clinical research quality. *Trials, 18*(1), 1–5. doi:10.118613063-017-2035-z PMID:28724395

Berdak, O., Ensor, B., Ng, Z. Y., Giudice, D. L., & Causey, A. (2016). *How to work with FinTech startups. Partner with financial technology startups to boost innovation.* Forrester.

Best, R. d. (2020, April 22). *Total net income of payments company Adyen from 2015 to 2019.* Retrieved August 22, 2020, from Statista: https://www.statista.com/statistics/870088/net-income-of-adyen/

Bettinger, A. (1972). Fintech: A Series of 40 Time Shared Models Used at Manufacturers Hanover Trust Company. *Interfaces*, *2*(4), 62–63.

Bhardwaj, G. N., Sinha, G., & Pal, S. (2019). FinTech and the Younger Generation. *IUP Journal of Information Technology*, *15*(1), 16–33.

Bicknell, T. (2019). *Cryptoasset regulations*. Retrieved from https://www.pinsentmasons.com/out-law/news/uae-outlines-proposed-cryptoasset-regulations

Blind, K. (2012). The influence of regulations on innovation: A quantitative assessment for OECD countries. *Research Policy*, *41*(2), 391–400. doi:10.1016/j.respol.2011.08.008

Bömer, M., & Maxin, H. (2018). Why FinTechs cooperate with banks—evidence from Germany. *Zeitschrift für die gesamte Versicherungswissenschaft*, *107*(4), 359-386.

Boujemi, H. (2017). *Policy and Regulatory Challenges To Deploying Blockchain Technologies*. Faculty of Arts, University of Malta.

Bradshaw, C., Atkinson, S., & Doody, O. (2017). Employing a qualitative description approach in health care research. *Global Qualitative Nursing Research*, *4*, 2333393617742282. doi:10.1177/2333393617742282 PMID:29204457

Brandl, B., & Hornuf, L. (2020). *Where did FinTechs come from, and where do they go? The transformation of the financial industry in Germany after digitalization. In Frontiers in Artificial Intelligence*. Artificial Intelligence in Finance. doi:10.3389/frai.2020.00008

Braun, V., & Clarke, V. (2006). Using thematic analysis in psychology. *Qualitative Research in Psychology*, *3*(2), 77–101. doi:10.1191/1478088706qp063oa

Braun, V., & Clarke, V. (2012). Thematic analysis. In H. Cooper (Ed.), *APA Handbook of research methods in psychology: Research design: Quantitative, Qualitative, Neuropsychological and Biological* (Vol. 2, pp. 57–71). American Psychological Association. doi:10.1037/13620-004

Breidbach, C. F., Keating, B. W., & Lim, C. (2019). FinTech: Research directions to explore the digital transformation of financial service systems. *Journal of Service Theory and Practice*, *30*(1), 79–102. doi:10.1108/JSTP-08-2018-0185

Broderick, J. A., & Vachirapornpuk, S. (2002). Service Quality of Internet banking: The Importance of Customer Role. *Marketing Intelligence & Planning*, *20*(6), 327–335. doi:10.1108/02634500210445383

Bryman, A., & Bell, E. (2011). *Business research methods* (3rd ed.). Cambridge University Press.

Bugrov, D., Dietz, M., & Poppensieker, T. (2017). *A brave new world for global banking. McKinsey Global Banking Annual Review 2016*. McKinsey and Company.

Burton, M. (2017). Blockchain Booster: Singapore Eyes Commodity Fintech Firms. *Reuters*. https://www.reuters.com/article/us-commodities-fintech/blockchain-booster-singapore-eyes-commodity-fintech-firms-idUSKCN1C10ZZ

Businesswire. (2016). *More Financial Institutions Join Ripple's Global Network.* https://www.businesswire.com/news/home/20160622005370/en/Financial-Institutions-Join-Ripple%E2%80%99s-Global-Network

Camarda, B. (2018). *Improving "Know Your Customer" Processes for Trade Finance and Other Purposes*. American Express.

Campbell, D. T. (1960). Variation and selective retention in creative thought as in other knowledge process. *Psychological Review*, *67*(6), 380–400. doi:10.1037/h0040373 PMID:13690223

Campbell, D. T. (1969). Variation and selective retention in sociocultural evolution. *General Systems*, *14*, 69–85.

Campenon, B. (2016). Fintech and the future of securities services. *Journal of Securities Operations and Custody*, *8*(2), 107–112.

Cant, B., Khadikar, A., Ruiter, A., Bronebakk, J. B., Coumaros, J., Buvat, J., & Gupta, A. (2016). Smart contracts in financial services: Getting from hype to reality. *Capgemini Consulting*, 1-24.

Cantillon, R. (2015). *Essay on the Nature of Trade in General* (A. E. Murphy, Trans.). Liberty Fund Inc. (Original work published 1755)

Capgemini Consulting. (2016, October 11). *Smart Contracts in Financial Services: Getting from Hype to Reality*. Author.

Carroll, G. R., & Khessina, O. M. (2005). The ecology of entrepreneurship. In Handbook of Entrepreneurship Research (pp. 167-200). Berlin: Springer.

Casino, F., Dasaklis, T. K., & Patsakis, C. (2019). A systematic literature review of blockchain-based applications: Current status, classification and open issues. *Telematics and Informatics*, *36*, 55–81.

Casson, M. (1982). *The entrepreneur: An economic theory*. Barnes & Nobles.

Cattani, G., & Ferriani, S. (2008, November-December). A Core/Periphery Perspective on Individual Creative Performance: Social Networks and Cinematic Achievements in the Hollywood Film Industry. *Organization Science*, *19*(6), 824–844. doi:10.1287/orsc.1070.0350

Cattani, G., Ferriani, S., & Lanza, A. (2017, November-December). Deconstructing the Outsider Puzzle: The Legitimation Journey of Novelty. *Organization Science*, *28*(6), 965–992. doi:10.1287/orsc.2017.1161

Cenamor, J., Sjödin, D. R., & Parida, V. (2017). Adopting a platform approach in servitization: Leveraging the value of digitalization. *International Journal of Production Economics*, *192*, 54–65. doi:10.1016/j.ijpe.2016.12.033

Cetorelli, N., McAndrews, J., & Traina, J. (2014). Evolution in bank complexity. *Economic Policy Review, 20*(2), 85–106.

Cheah, S., & Wang, S. (2017). Big data-driven business model innovation by traditional industries in the Chinese economy. *Journal of Chinese Economic and Foreign Trade Studies.*

Chen, F. M., Feng, M. C., Chen, T. C., Hsieh, M. H., Kuo, S. H., Chang, H. L., & Chen, Y. H. (2020). (in press). Big data integration and analytics to prevent a potential hospital outbreak of COVID-19 in Taiwan. *Journal of Microbiology, Immunology, and Infection*. Advance online publication. doi:10.1016/j.jmii.2020.04.010 PMID:32327328

Chen, M. A., Wu, Q., & Yang, B. (2019). How valuable is FinTech innovation? *Review of Financial Studies, 32*(5), 2062–2106. doi:10.1093/rfs/hhy130

Chesbrough, H. W. (2010). Business Model Innovation: Opportunities and Barriers. *Long Range Planning, 43*(2-3), 354–363. doi:10.1016/j.lrp.2009.07.010

Chirima, D. T., & Chikochi, K. (2016). The impact of electronic banking on the competitiveness of commercial banks in Zimbabwe (2014–2015). *International Journal of Case Studies, 5*(1). Retrieved May 12, 2020, from https://www.academia.edu/30268731/The_Impact_of_Electronic_Banking_on_the_Competitiveness_of_Commercial_Banks_in_Zimbabwe_2014-2015

Chishti, S., & Barberis, J. (2016). *The FinTech book: The financial technology handbook for investors, entrepreneurs and visionaries*. John Wiley & Sons. doi:10.1002/9781119218906

Chishti, S., & Puschmann, T. (2018). *The Wealthtech book: The FinTech handbook for investors, `entrepreneurs and finance visionaries*. John Wiley & Sons. doi:10.1002/9781119444510

Christensen, C. (1997). *The Innovator's Dilemma: When New Technologies Cause Great Firms to Fail*. Harvard Business Review Press.

Christensen, C., McDonald, R., Altman, E. J., & Palmer, J. E. (2018). Disruptive Innovation: An Intellectual History and Directions for Future Research. *Journal of Management Studies, 55*(7), 1043–1048. doi:10.1111/joms.12349

Christensen, C., & Raynor, M. E. (2003). *The Innovator's Solution: Creating and Sustaining Successful Growth*. Harvard Business School Press.

Cizinska, R., Krabec, T., & Venegas, P. (2016). FieldsRank: The network value of the firm. *International Advances in Economic Research, 22*(4), 461–463. doi:10.100711294-016-9604-x

CNBC. (2018). *Facebook will reportedly use cryptocurrency for transferring money through WhatsApp*. www.cnbc.com/2018/12/21/facebook-reportedly-working-on-a-cryptocurrency-for-transfering-money-through-whatsapp-.html

Commission, E. (2019). *European Commission. Retrieved from Frequently Asked Questions: Making electronic payments and online banking safer and easier for consumers*. https://ec.europa.eu/commission/presscorner/detail/en/QANDA_19_5555

Compliance, P. (2017). *An Overview of Blockchain Legislation and Regulatory Measures*. Retrieved from https://www.planetcompliance.com/2017/07/04/overview-blockchain-regulation-legislation/

ConsenSys. (2020). *komgo: Blockchain Case Study for Commodity Trade Finance*. https://consensys.net/blockchain-use-cases/finance/komgo/

Cortina, J. J., & Schmukler, S. L. (2018). The FinTech Revolution: A Threat to Global Banking? *World Bank Research and Policy Briefs*, (125038).

Courbe, J. (2016). Financial services technology 2020 and beyond: Embracing disruption. PWC.

Creswell, J. W. (2014). *Research design: Qualitative, quantitative, and mixed-method approaches* (4th ed.). Sage Publication.

Crosby, Nachiappan, Pattanayak, Verma, & Kalyanaraman. (2017). *Blockchain Technology: Beyond Bitcoin*. Retrieved from https://j2-capital.com/blockchain-technology-beyond-bitcoin

Cumming, D. J., & Schwienbacher, A. (2018). FinTech venture capital. *Corp. Gov. International Review*, *26*, 374–389. doi:10.1111/corg.12256

Dahlberg, T., Guo, J., & Ondrus, J. (2015). A critical review of mobile payment research. *Electronic Commerce Research and Applications*, *14*(5), 265–284. doi:10.1016/j.elerap.2015.07.006

Dapp, T., Slomka, L., & Hoffmann, R. (2014). Fintech–The digital (r) evolution in the financial sector. Deutsche Bank Research.

Dapp, T. F. (2017). Fintech: the digital transformation in the financial sector. In *Sustainability in a Digital World* (pp. 189–199). Springer. doi:10.1007/978-3-319-54603-2_16

DaSilva, C. M., & Trkman, P. (2016). Business Model: What It Is and What It Is Not. *Long Range Planning*, *47*(6), 379–389. doi:10.1016/j.lrp.2013.08.004

DaSilva, C. M., Trkman, P., Desouza, K., & Lindič, J. (2013). Disruptive technologies: A business model perspective on cloud computing. *Technology Analysis and Strategic Management*, *25*(10), 1161–1173. doi:10.1080/09537325.2013.843661

Davidsson, P. (2016). *Researching Entrepreneurship, Conceptualization and Design*. Springer. doi:10.1007/978-3-319-26692-3

Davis, F. D. (1989). Perceived usefulness, perceived ease of use, and user acceptance of information technology. *Management Information Systems Quarterly*, *13*(3), 319–340. doi:10.2307/249008

de Reuver, M., Verschuur, E., Nikayin, F., Cerpa, N., & Bouwman, H. (2015). Collective action for mobile payment platforms: A case study on collaboration issues between banks and telecom operators. *Electronic Commerce Research and Applications*, *14*(5), 331–344. doi:10.1016/j.elerap.2014.08.004

Delacroix. J. & Carroll. G.R. (1983). Organizational Foundings: An Ecological Study of the Newspaper Industries of Argentina and Ireland. *Administrative Science Quarterly*, *28*(2), 274–291.

Dellermann, D., Fliaster, A., & Kolloch, M. (2017). Innovation risk in digital business models: The German energy sector. *The Journal of Business Strategy*, *38*(5), 35–43. doi:10.1108/JBS-07-2016-0078

Delone, W. H., & McLean, E. R. (2003). The Delone and McLean Model of Information System Success: A Ten Year Update. *Journal of Management Information Systems*, *19*(4), 9–30. doi:10.1080/07421222.2003.11045748

Demil, B., & Lecocq, X. (2010). Business Model Evolution: In Search of Dynamic Consistency. *Long Range Planning*, *43*(2-3), 227–246. doi:10.1016/j.lrp.2010.02.004

Detrixhe, J. (2017). Big tech firms like Amazon are eager to eat the banking industry's lunch. *Quartz*. https://qz.com/1112460/banks-are-under-threat-from-big-tech-firms-like-apple-amazon-and-facebook-according-to-mckinsey/

Diemers, D., Lamaa, A., Salamat, J., & Steffens, T. (2015). *Developing a FinTech ecosystem in the GCC*. Dubai: Strategy. https://www.strategyand.pwc.com/media/file/Developing-a-FinTechecosystem-in-the-GCC.pdf

Diemers, D., Lamaa, A., Salamat, J., & Steffens, T. (2015). *Developing a FinTech ecosystem in the GCC*. Strategy. https://www.strategyand.pwc.com/media/file/Developing-aFinTech-ecosystem-in-the-GCC.pdf

Dijkman, R. M., Sprenkels, B., Peeters, T., & Janssen, A. (2015). Business models for the Internet of Things. *International Journal of Information Management*, *35*(6), 672–678. doi:10.1016/j.ijinfomgt.2015.07.008

Dodgson, M., Gann, D., Waldawsky-Berger, I., Sultan, N., & George, G. (2015). Managing Digital Money. *Academy of Management Journal*, *58*(2), 325–333. doi:10.5465/amj.2015.4002

Domeher, D. J., Frimpong, M., & Appiah, T. (2014). Adoption of financial innovation in Ghanaian banking industry. *African Review of Economics and Finance*, *6*(2), 207–243.

Dorfleitner, G., & Hornuf, L. (2019). Fintech Business Models. In *Fintech and Data Privacy in Germany* (pp. 85–106). Springer. doi:10.1007/978-3-030-31335-7_5

Dorfleitner, G., Hornuf, L., Schmitt, M., & Weber, M. (2017). *Definition of FinTech and Description of the FinTech Industry FinTech in Germany*. Springer.

Dorfleitner, G., Hornuf, L., Schmitt, M., & Weber, M. (2017). Definition of FinTech and Description of the FinTech Industry. In G. Dorfleitner, L. Hornuf, & M. Schmitt (Eds.), *FinTech in Germany* (pp. 5–10). Springer. doi:10.1007/978-3-319-54666-7_2

Dorfleitner, G., Hornuf, L., Schmitt, M., & Weber, M. (2017). *FinTech in Germany*. Springer International Publishing. doi:10.1007/978-3-319-54666-7

Dorfleitner, G., Hornuf, L., Schmitt, M., & Weber, M. (2017). The fintech market in Germany. In *FinTech in Germany* (pp. 13–46). Springer. doi:10.1007/978-3-319-54666-7_4

Dornyei, Z. (2007). Research Methods in Applied Linguistics. Oxford University Press.

Doyle, L., McCabe, C., Keogh, B., Brady, A., & McCann, M. (2019). An overview of the qualitative descriptive design within nursing research. *Journal of Research in Nursing*.

Drasch, B. J., Schweizer, A., & Urbach, N. (2018). Integrating the 'Troublemakers': A taxonomy for cooperation between banks and FinTechs. *Journal of Economics and Business, 100*(March), 26–42. doi:10.1016/j.jeconbus.2018.04.002

Drosatos, G., & Kaldoudi, E. (2019). Blockchain applications in the biomedical domain: A scoping review. *Computational and Structural Biotechnology Journal, 17*, 229–240. doi:10.1016/j.csbj.2019.01.010 PMID:30847041

Drummer, D., Jerenz, A., Siebelt, P., & Thaten, M. (2016). *FinTech: Challenges and Opportunities -How digitization is transforming the financial sector*. McKinsey.

Dubey, R., Luo, Z., Gunasekaran, A., Akter, S., Hazen, B. T., & Douglas, M. A. (2018). Big data and predictive analytics in humanitarian supply chains. *International Journal of Logistics Management, 29*(2), 485–512. doi:10.1108/IJLM-02-2017-0039

Dumont, M. (2020). *Apollo signs MoA with Zimbabwean bank*. Retrieved May 10, 2020, from https://medium.com/@apollocurrency/apollo-signs-mou-with-zimbabwean-bank-d0fde9e61431

ECB, t. E. (2020). *Sweden joins ECB's instant payments settlement platform*. Academic Press.

Economist. (2015). *Blockchain: The Next Big Thing or Is It?* Special Report.

Ehret, M., & Wirtz, J. (2017). Unlocking value from machines: Business models and the industrial internet of things. *Journal of Marketing Management, 33*(1-2), 111–130. doi:10.1080/0267257X.2016.1248041

Eickhoff, M., Muntermann, J., & Weinrich, T. (2017). *What do FinTechs actually do? A taxonomy of FinTech business models*. Academic Press.

Eickhoff, M., Muntermann, J., & Weinrich, T. (2017). What do FinTechs actually do? A taxonomy of FinTech business models. *ICIS 2017 Proceedings*.

El Sawy, O. A., & Pereira, F. (2013). *Business modelling in the dynamic digital space: An ecosystem approach*. Springer. doi:10.1007/978-3-642-31765-1

El-Masri, M., Al-Yafi, K., & Sherif, K. S. (2019). The Digital Transformation of Fintech: Disruptions and Value Paths. *Twenty-Third Pacific Asia Conference on Information Systems*.

Eloranta, V., & Turunen, T. (2016). Platforms in service-driven manufacturing: Leveraging complexity by connecting, sharing, and integrating. *Industrial Marketing Management, 55*, 178–186. doi:10.1016/j.indmarman.2015.10.003

Ernest & Young. (2017). *Overview of Blockchain for Energy and Commodity Trading*.

Ernst & Young. (2016). *UK FinTech On the cutting edge an evaluation of the international FinTech sector*. https://FinTechauscensus.ey.com/2018/Documents/EY-UK-FinTech-On-the-cutting-edge.pdf

Ernst & Young. (2016). *UK fintech on the cutting edge: An evaluation of the intentional fintech sector*, EY. Retrieved May 16, 2020, from https://www.ey.com/Publication/vwLUAssets/EY-UK-FinTech-On-the-cutting-edge/$FILE/EY-UK-FinTech-On-the-cutting-edge.pdf>

Ernst & Young. (2017). *Unleashing the potential of FinTech in banking*. https://www.ey.com/Publication/vwLUAssets/ey-unleashing-the-potential-offin-tech-in-banking/$File/ey-unleashing-the-potential-of-fin-tech-in-banking.pdf

Ernst & Young. (2019). *FinTechs in Sub-Saharan Africa: An overview of market developments and investment opportunities*. Retrieved March 01, 2020, from https://hollandfintech.com/wp-content/uploads/2019/02/ey-fin-tech-market-opportunities-2019.pdf

Ernst & Young. (2019). *Global FinTech Adoption Index 2019*. https://FinTechauscensus.ey.com/2019/Documents/ey-global-FinTech-adoption-index-2019.pdf

Ernst and Young. (2016). *UK Fintech-On the cutting edge*. Ernst and Young Report. Retrieved from https://Fintechauscensus.ey.com/2018/Documents/EY-UK-Fintech-On-the-cutting-edge.pdf

Etikan, I., Musa, S. A., & Alkassim, R. S. (2016). Comparison of convenience sampling and purposive sampling. *American Journal of Theoretical and Applied Statistics*, *5*(1), 1–4. doi:10.11648/j.ajtas.20160501.11

European Commission. (2015). Retrieved October 13, 2001, from https://europa.eu/rapid/press-release_IP-15-5792

Evans, D. S., & Pirchio, A. (2014). An empirical examination of why mobile money schemes ignite in some developing countries but flounder in most. *Review of Network Economics*, *13*(4), 397–451. doi:10.1515/rne-2015-0020

Feki, M. (2019). Big Data Analytics Driven Supply Chain Transformation. In K. Mezghani & W. Aloulou (Eds.), *Business Transformations in the Era of Digitalization* (pp. 106–124). IGI Global. doi:10.4018/978-1-5225-7262-6.ch007

Findexable. (2020). *The global FinTech index 2020. The global FinTech index city ranking report*. https://findexable.com/wp-content/uploads/2019/12/Findexable_Global-FinTech-Rankings-2020exSFA.pdf

FinTech Network. (2018). *Four Blockchain Use Cases for Banks*. https://germanyfintech.org/wp-content/uploads/2018/01/fintech_blockchain_report_fintech_network.pdf

Fintech, T. E. (2019). Retrieved from https://insights.invyo.io/europe/mapping/the-european-top-50-ofthe-most-valuedfintech

Fishman, R. G., Dos Santos, B. L., & Zheng, Z. E. (2014). Digital innovation as a fundamental and powerful concept in the information systems curriculum. *Management Information Systems Quarterly*, *38*(2), 329–343. doi:10.25300/MISQ/2014/38.2.01

Forbes. (2020). *2020 Forbes Blockchain 50 List*. Author.

Foss, N. J., & Saebi, T. (2017). Fifteen years of research on business model innovation: How far have we come, and where should we go? *Journal of Management*, *43*(1), 200–227. doi:10.1177/0149206316675927

Fred, D., & Davis, D. (1989). Perceived Usefulness, Perceived Ease of Use, and User Acceptance of Information Technology. *Management Information Systems Research Center*, *13*, 319–340.

FT Partners FinTech industry Research. (2020). *The rise of Challenger Banks. Are the apps taking over?* https://ftpartners.docsend.com/view/suxcjc4

Fu, J., & Mishra, M. (2020). *The Global Impact of COVID-19 on FinTech Adoption*. Swiss Finance Institute Research Paper No. 20-38. Available at SSRN: https://ssrn.com/abstract=3588453

Fuscaldo, D. (2019). Small Businesses Are The Next Wave Of FinTech Focus. *Forbes*. https://www.forbes.com/sites/donnafuscaldo/2019/02/12/small-businesses-are-the-next-wave-of-FinTech-focus/#53783afb8663

Gai, K., Qiu, M., & Sun, X. (2018). A survey on Fintech. *Journal of Network and Computer Applications*, *103*, 262–273. doi:10.1016/j.jnca.2017.10.011

Galvin, J., Han, F., Hynes, S., Qu, J., Rajgopal, K., & Shek, A. (2018). *Synergy and disruption: Ten trends shaping FinTech*. McKinsey & Company. https://www.mckinsey.com/industries/financial-services/our-insights/synergy-and-disruption-ten-trends-shaping-FinTech

Gandomi, A., & Haider, M. (2015). Beyond the hype: Big data concepts, methods, and analytics. *International Journal of Information Management*, *35*(2), 137–144. doi:10.1016/j.ijinfomgt.2014.10.007

Gannamaneni, A., Ondrus, J., & Lyytinen, K. (2015, January). A post-failure analysis of mobile payment platforms. In *2015 48th Hawaii International Conference on System Sciences* (pp. 1159-1168). IEEE. 10.1109/HICSS.2015.141

Gartner. (2018). *Digitalization will make most heritage financial firms irrelevant*. https://www.gartner.com/en/doc/337197-innovation-insight-for-insurance-cios-analyzing-the-digital-maturity-of-insurtechs

Garud, R., & Karnøe, P. (2003). Bricolage versus breakthrough: Distributed and embedded agency in technology entrepreneurship. *Research Policy*, *32*(2), 277–300. doi:10.1016/S0048-7333(02)00100-2

Gazel, M., & Schwienbacher, A. (2020). Entrepreneurial FinTech clusters. *Small Business Economics*, 1–21.

Gefen, D. (2002). Customer Loyalty in E-Commerce. *Journal of the Association for Information Systems*, *3*(1), 27–51. doi:10.17705/1jais.00022

Geissdoerfer, M., Vladimirova, D., & Evans, S. (2018). Sustainable business model innovation: A review. *Journal of Cleaner Production*, *198*, 401–416. doi:10.1016/j.jclepro.2018.06.240

Ghazali, N. H., & Yasuoka, T. (2018). Awareness and Perception Analysis of Small Medium Enterprise and Start-up Towards FinTech Instruments: Crowd funding and Peer-to-Peer Lending in Malaysia. *International Journal Of Finance and Banking Research*, *4*(1), 13–24. doi:10.11648/j.ijfbr.20180401.12

Gimpel, H., Rau, D., & Röglinger, M. (2018). Understanding FinTech start-ups–a taxonomy of consumer-oriented service offerings. *Electronic Markets*, *28*(3), 245–264. doi:10.100712525-017-0275-0

Goh, T. C. (2020). A Production Crossroads: The Food and Beverage Conundrum. *Omdia Technology*. https://technology.informa.com/625247/a-production-crossroads-the-food-and-beverage-conundrum

Goldman Sachs. (2016). Blockchain: Putting Theory into Practice. *Profiles in Innovation*. https://www.finyear.com/attachment/690548/

Goldman Sachs. (2020). *Blockchain - The New Technology of Trust*. https://www.goldmansachs.com/insights/pages/blockchain/

Gomber, P., Kauffman, R. J., Parker, C., & Weber, B. W. (2018). On the fintech revolution: Interpreting the forces of innovation, disruption, and transformation in financial services. *Journal of Management Information Systems*, *35*(1), 220–265. doi:10.1080/07421222.2018.1440766

Gomber, P., Koch, J.-A., & Siering, M. (2017). Digital Finance and FinTech: Current Research and Future Research Directions. *Journal of Business Economics*, *87*(5), 537–580. doi:10.100711573-017-0852-x

Gozman, D., Liebenau, J., & Mangan, J. (2018). The innovation mechanisms of fintech start-ups: Insights from SWIFT's innotribe competition. *Journal of Management Information Systems*, *35*(1), 145–179. doi:10.1080/07421222.2018.1440768

Greve. H. (2002). An Ecological Theory of Spatial Evolution: Local Density Dependence in Tokyo Banking, 1894–1936. *Social Forces*, *80*(3), 847–880.

Greve, H. (2000, October). Market Niche Entry Decisions: Competition, Learning, and Strategy in Tokyo Banking, 1894-1936. *Academy of Management Journal*, *43*(5), 816–836.

Gulamhuseinwala, I., Bull, T., & Lewis, S. (2015). *FinTech is gaining traction and young, high-income users are the early adopters*. https://www.ey.com/Publication/vwLUAssets/ey-FinTech-is-gaining-traction-and-young-high-income-users-are-the-early-adopters/$FILE/ey-FinTech-is-gaining-traction-and-young-high-income-users-are-the-early-adopters.pdf

Gulamhuseinwala, I., Hatch, M., & Lloyd, J. (2017). *EY Fintech Adoption Index 2017: The rapid emergence of Fintech.* Retrieved from https://www.ey.com/Publication/vwLUAssets/ey-Fintech-adoption-index-2017/$FILE/ey-Fintech-adoption-index-2017.pdf

Gupta, M., & George, J. F. (2016). Toward the development of a big data analytics capability. *Information & Management, 53*(8), 1049–1064. doi:10.1016/j.im.2016.07.004

Gürkaynak, G., & Yilmaz, I. (2015). Regulating payment services and electronic money: A comparative regulatory approach with a specific focus on Turkish legislation. *Computer Law & Security Review, 31*(3), 401–411. doi:10.1016/j.clsr.2015.03.009

Haddad, C., & Hornuf, L. (2016). *The emergence of the global Fintech market: Economic and technological determinants*. Retrieved March 01, 2020, from https://papers.ssrn.com/sol3/papers.cfm?abstract_id=2830124

Haddad, C., & Hornuf, L. (2019). The emergence of the global FinTech market: Economic and technological determinants. *Small Business Economics, 53*(1), 81–105. doi:10.100711187-018-9991-x

Haig, S. (2017). *Saudi Central Bank Says Cryptocurrency Industry is "Not Mature Enough" to Warrant Regulation.* Retrieved from https://news.bitcoin.com/saudi-central-bank-says-cryptocurrency-industry-is-not-mature-enough-to-warrant-regulation/

Han, K., Kauffman, R. J., & Nault, B. R. (2008). Relative importance, specific investment, and ownership in inter-organizational systems. *Information Technology Management, 9*(3), 181–200. doi:10.100710799-008-0039-9

Hannan, M. T., & Carroll, G. R. (1992). Dynamics of Organizational Populations. Oxford University Press.

Hannan, M. T., & Freeman, J. (1977, March). The Population Ecology of Organizations. *American Journal of Sociology, 82*(5), 929–964. doi:10.1086/226424

Hannan, M. T., Pólos, L., & Carroll, G. (2007). *Logics of Organization Theory. Audiences, Codes, and Ecologies*. Princeton Press.

Han, S., & Baek, S. (2004). Antecedents and Consequences of Service Quality in Online Banking: An Application of the SERVQUAL Instrument. *Advances in Consumer Research. Association for Consumer Research (U. S.), 31*, 208–214.

Harris, M. A., Chin, A. G., & Beasley, J. (2019). *Mobile payment adoption: An empirical review and opportunities for future research. Southern Association of Information Systems*. SAIS.

Hatch, E. M., & Lazaraton, A. (1991). *The research manual: Design and statistics for applied linguistics*. New York, NY: Newbury House Publishers.

Hatzakis, E. D., Nair, S. K., & Pinedo, M. (2010). Operations in financial Services—An overview. *Production and Operations Management, 19*(6), 633–664. doi:10.1111/j.1937-5956.2010.01163.x

Hazik, M., & Hassanian, A. (2018). Blockchain and the Digital Economy. In M. Hazik & A. Hassanian (Eds.), *Blockchain, Fintech, and Islamic Finance: Building the Future in the New Islamic Digital Economy* (pp. 111–138). Walter de Gruyter GmbH & Co KG.

HBS Digital Initiative. (2017. December 18). *Why millennials flock to FinTech for personal investing*. Harvard Business School. https://digital.hbs.edu/FinTech-digital-currencies/millennials-flock-FinTech-personal-investing/

Helm, T., Low, A., & Townson, J. (2019). *UK fintech: State of the nation*. Department for International Trade.

Hendrikse, R., van Meeteren, M., & Bassens, D. (2019). Strategic coupling between finance, technology and the state: Cultivating a FinTech ecosystem for incumbent finance. *Environment and Planning A: Economy and Space*.

Hendrikse, R., Bassens, D., & Van Meeteren, M. (2018). The Appleization of finance: Charting incumbent finance's embrace of FinTech. *Finance and Stochastics*, *4*(2), 159–180.

Hennig-Thurau, T., Hofacker, C. F., & Bloching, B. (2013). Marketing the pinball way: Understanding how social media change the generation of value for consumers and companies. *Journal of Interactive Marketing*, *27*(4), 237–24. doi:10.1016/j.intmar.2013.09.005

Henry, G. T. (1990). *Practical sampling* (Vol. 21). Sage. doi:10.4135/9781412985451

Hess, C. M., & Kemerer, C. F. (1994). Computerized loan origination systems: An industry case study of the electronic markets hypothesis. *Management Information Systems Quarterly*, *18*(3), 251–275. doi:10.2307/249618

Hirt, M., & Willmott, P. (2014). *Strategic principles for competing in the digital age*. Retrieved May 15, 2020, from https://www.mckinsey.com/business-functions/strategy-and-corporate-finance/our-insights/strategic-principles-for-competing-in-the-digital-age

Holotiuk, F., Pisani, F., & Moormann, J. (2017). *The impact of blockchain technology on business models in the payments industry*. Academic Press.

Hornuf, L., Klus, M. F., Lohwasser, T. S., & Schwienbacher, A. (2020). How do banks interact with FinTech startups? *Small Business Economics*, 1–22. doi:10.100711187-020-00359-3

Hubspot. (2020). *The Top 7 Search Engines, Ranked by Popularity*. https://blog.hubspot.com/marketing/top-search-engines

Humbani, M., & Wiese, M. (2019). An integrated framework for the adoption and continuance intention to use mobile payment apps. *International Journal of Bank Marketing*, *37*(2), 646–664. doi:10.1108/IJBM-03-2018-0072

Hutchinson, G. E. (1957). Concluding Remarks. *Cold Spring Harbor Symposia on Quantitative Biology*, *22*(2), 415–427. doi:10.1101/SQB.1957.022.01.039

Hymer, S. H. (1976). *The International Operations of National Firms: A Study of Direct Investment*. MIT Press.

IBM Report. (2017). Leading the pack in blockchain banking. IBM. Innovative Analytics (GBE03664-USEN-02).

Idowu, A. A., Ngumi, P., & Muturi, W. (2016). Financial innovation adoption and turnaround time. *Journal of Research in Economics and International Finance*, *5*(2), 14–28.

IFLR. (2016). *Blockchain: Regulating the future of finance*. https://www.iflr.com/article/b1lsps8kgddhbq/blockchain-regulating-the-future-of-finance

Iman, N. (2018). Is mobile payment still relevant in the fintech era? *Electronic Commerce Research and Applications*, *30*, 72–82. doi:10.1016/j.elerap.2018.05.009

Iman, N. (2020). The rise and rise of financial technology: The good, the bad, and the verdict. *Cogent Business & Management*, *7*(1), 1. doi:10.1080/23311975.2020.1725309

Imerman, M. B., & Fabozzi, F. J. (2020). Cashing in on innovation: A taxonomy of FinTech. *Journal of Asset Management*, *21*(3), 167–177. doi:10.105741260-020-00163-4

Insights, C. B. (2019). *FinTech trends to watch in 2019*. https://www.cbinsights.com/research/report/FinTech-trends-2019/

International Finance Corporation. (2020). *IFC Mobile Money Scoping Reports 2020*. Author.

International Monetary Fund. (2019). *FinTech in Sub-Saharan African countries: A game changer?* Retrieved March 01, 2020, from https://www.imf.org/en/Publications/Departmental-Papers-Policy-Papers/Issues/2019/02/13/FinTech-in-Sub-Saharan-African-Countries-A-Game-Changer-46376

Irish Tech News. (2019). *How has FinTech Revolutionised Commodities Trading?* Academic Press.

Isenberg, D. J. (2011). The Entrepreneurship Ecosystem Strategy as a New Paradigm for Economic Policy: Principles for Cultivating Entrepreneurships. *The Babson Entrepreneurship Ecosystem Project*, *1*(781), 1–13. doi:10.1093/rfs/hhr098

Jakšič, M., & Marinč, M. (2015). *The future of banking: The role of information technology*. Bancni vestnik: Banking Sector at the Crossroads: Challenges For The Future. Retrieved May 15, 2020, from https://ssrn.com/abstract=2656388

Jessé, M. B. D. (2018). TARGET Instant Payment Settlement: The Euro system's response to an evolving payments landscape. *Journal of Payments Strategy & Systems*, *12*(4), 322–327.

Jourdan, J., Durand, R., & Thornton, P. (2017, July). The Price of Admission: Organizational Deference as Strategic Behavior. *American Journal of Sociology*, *123*(1), 232–275. doi:10.1086/692248

Juengerkes, B. E. (2016). FinTechs and banks: Collaboration is key. In S. Chishti & J. Barberis (Eds.), *The FinTech book: the financial technology handbook for investors, entrepreneurs and visionaries* (pp. 179–182). Wiley. doi:10.1002/9781119218906.ch47

Kandpal, V., & Mehrotra, R. (2019). Financial inclusion: The role of fintech and digital financial services in India. *Indian Journal of Economics and Business*, *19*(1), 85–93.

Kang, J. (2018). Mobile payment in Fintech environment: Trends, security challenges, and services. *Human-centric Computing and Information Sciences*, *8*(1), 1–16. doi:10.118613673-018-0155-4

Karagiannaki, A., Vergados, G., & Fouskas, K. (2017). The impact of digital transformation in the financial services industry: insights from an open innovation initiative in Fintech in Greece. *Mediterranean Conference on Information Systems (MCIS). Association For Information Systems.*

Kaushal, V., & Balaini, A. (2016). E-banking: Challenges and issues. *Hill Quest*, *3*(3-4), 69–73.

Kaveri, V. S. (2014). Bank frauds in India: Emerging challenges. *Journal Of Commerce and Management Thought*, *5*(1), 14–26. doi:10.5958/j.0976-478X.5.1.002

Kavuri, A. S., & Milne, A. (2019). *FinTech and the future of financial services: What are the research gaps?* CAMA Working Paper No. 18/2019. Available at SSRN: https://ssrn.com/abstract=3333515

Kerényi, Á., & Müller, J. (2019). Brave New Digital World? Financial Technology and the Power of Information. *Financial and Economic Review*, *18*(1), 5–32. doi:10.33893/FER.18.1.532

Keynes, J. M. (1973). The Collected Writings of John Maynard Keynes, vol. VII, The General Theory of Employment, Interest and Money (D. Moggridge, Ed.). London: Macmillan for the Royal Economic Society.

Khan, M. S., Mahapatra, S. S., & Sreekumar, A. (2009). Service quality evaluation in internet banking: An empirical study in India. *Indian Culture and Business Management*, *2*(1), 30–46. doi:10.1504/IJICBM.2009.021596

Kharpal, A. (2017). *Cryptocurrencies 'not mature enough' to assess impact: Saudi Arabia regulator.* Retrieved from https://www.cnbc.com/2017/10/23/cryptocurrencies-not-mature-enough-to-assess-impact-saudi-arabia-regulator.html

Kiel, D., Arnold, C., & Voigt, K. I. (2017). The influence of the Industrial Internet of Things on business models of established manufacturing companies–A business-level perspective. *Technovation*, *68*, 4–19. doi:10.1016/j.technovation.2017.09.003

Kieran, M. (1991). Predicting User Intentions: Comparing the Technology Acceptance Model with the Theory of Planned Behavior information system research. *Information Systems Research*, *2*, 73–191.

Kim, H., & Min, L. (2011). Antecedents of application service continuance: A synthesis of satisfaction and trust. *Expert Systems with Application, 38*, 9530-9542.

Kim, Y., Choi, J., Park, Y. J., & Yeon, J. (2016). The adoption of mobile payment services for "FinTech.". *International Journal of Applied Engineering Research*, *11*(2), 1058–1061.

Kim, Y., Park, Y. J., Choi, J., & Yeon, J. (2015). An empirical study on the adoption of "Fintech" service: Focused on mobile payment services. *Advanced Science and Technology Letters*, *114*(26), 136–140. doi:10.14257/astl.2015.114.26

King, B. (2014). *Breaking Banks*. Wiley. doi:10.1002/9781118958247

Kirzner, I. (1973). *Competition and Entrepreneurship*. University of Chicago Press.

Kirzner, I. (1979). *Perception, Opportunity, and Profit: Studies in the Theory of Entrepreneurship*. University of Chicago Press.

Klarna. (2019). *Annual report.* Retrieved August 20, 2020, from https://www.klarna.com/assets/2020/04/Klarna_Bank_AB_publ_Annual_Report_2019_EN.pdf

Knight, F. (1921). *Risk, Uncertainty and Profit*. Houghton Mifflin.

Konigsheim, C., Lukas, M., & Noth, M. (2017). Financial knowledge, risk preferences, and the demand for digital financial services. *Schmalenbach Business Review*, *18*(4), 343–375. doi:10.100741464-017-0040-0

Kotarba, M. (2016). New factors inducing changes in the retail banking customer relationship management (CRM) and their exploration by the FinTech industry. *Foundations of Management*, *8*(1), 69–78. doi:10.1515/fman-2016-0006

Kothari, M., & Moolani, S. (2015). Reliability of "Google" for obtaining medical information. *Indian Journal of Ophthalmology*, *63*(3), 267. doi:10.4103/0301-4738.156934 PMID:25971176

KPMG. (2018). The pulse of FinTech. Global report on FinTech investment trends. *H1' 2018*.

Kuilman, J. G., & Li, J. T. (2006). The organizers' ecology: An empirical study of foreign banks in Shanghai. *Organization Science*, *17*(3), 385–401. doi:10.1287/orsc.1060.0182

Kuilman, J. G., & Li, J. T. (2009). Grades of membership and legitimacy spillovers: Foreign banks in Shanghai, 1847–1935. *Academy of Management Journal*, *32*(2), 229–245. doi:10.5465/amj.2009.37308018

Kuo, Y. F., Wu, C. M., & Deng, W. J. (2009). The relationships among service quality, perceived value, customer satisfaction and post purchase intention in mobile value added services. *Computers in Human Behavior*, *25*(4), 887–896. doi:10.1016/j.chb.2009.03.003

Labrinidis, A., & Jagadish, H. V. (2012). Challenges and opportunities with big data. *Proceedings of the VLDB Endowment International Conference on Very Large Data Bases*, *5*(12), 2032–2033. doi:10.14778/2367502.2367572

Lagarde, C. (2018). Central Banking and Fintech. A Brave New World. *Innovations*, *12*(1), 4–8. doi:10.1162/inov_a_00262

LaValle, S., Lesser, E., Shockley, R., Hopkins, M. S., & Kruschwitz, N. (2011). Big data, analytics and the path from insights to value. *MIT Sloan Management Review*, *52*(2), 21–32.

Le Bret H. (2011). *La semaine ou Jérome Kerviel a failli faire sauter le systèmefinancier mondial, Journal intime d'un banquier* [The week when Jérome Kerviel nearly blew up the global financial system, Diary of a banker]. Paris: Les arènes.

Le Bret H. (2013). *No Bank, l'incroyable histoire d'un entrepreneur de banlieue qui veut révolutionner la banque* [No Bank, the incredible story of a suburban entrepreneur who wants to revolutionize banking]. Paris: Les arènes.

Le Bret H. (2016). Le Compte-Nickel: un compte pour tous, sans banque [The Nickel Account: an account for all, without a bank]. *Le journal de l'école de Paris du management, 2016*(6), 24-30.

Lee, L., & Shin, Y. J. (2018). Fintech: Ecosystem, business models, investment decisions, and challenges. *Business Horizons, 61*(1), 35–46. doi:.bushor.2017.09.003 doi:10.1016/j

Lee, D. K. C., & Teo, E. G. S. (2015). Emergence of FinTech and the LASIC Principles. *Journal of Financial Perspectives, 3*(3), 1. doi:10.2139srn.2668049

Lee, I., & Shin, Y. J. (2018). FinTech: Ecosystem, business models, investment decisions, and challenges. *Business Horizons, 61*(1), 35–46. doi:10.1016/j.bushor.2017.09.003

Lenka, S., Parida, V., & Wincent, J. (2017). Digitalization capabilities as enablers of value co-creation in service firms. *Psychology and Marketing, 34*(1), 92–100. doi:10.1002/mar.20975

Leong, C., Tan, B., Xiao, X., Tan, F. T. C., & Sun, Y. (2017). Nurturing a FinTech ecosystem: The case of a youth microloan startup in China. *International Journal of Information Management, 37*(2), 92–97. doi:10.1016/j.ijinfomgt.2016.11.006

Lerner, J., & Tufano, P. (2012). The Consequences of Financial Innovation. A Counterfactual Research Agenda. In J. Lerner & S. Stern (Eds.), *The Rate and Direction of Inventive Activity Revisited* (pp. 523–575). University of Chicago Press. doi:10.7208/chicago/9780226473062.003.0017

Liao, Z., & Cheung, M.T. (2005) .Service Quality in Internet e-Banking: A User-based Core Framework. *Proceedings IEEE international Conference e-Technology, e-Commerce and e-Service*.

Liébana-Cabanillas, F., García-Maroto, I., Muñoz-Leiva, F., & Ramos-de-Luna, I. (2020). Mobile Payment Adoption in the Age of Digital Transformation: The Case of Apple Pay. *Sustainability, 12*(13), 5443. doi:10.3390u12135443

Liebenau, J., & Elaluf-Calderwood, S. (2016). *Blockchain innovation beyond bitcoin and banking*. Available at SSRN 2749890

Lin, T. C. (2015). Infinite financial intermediation. *Wake Forest Law Review, 50*, 643.

Litvin, A., Korenev, S., Knyazeva, E., & Litvin, V. (2019). The Possibilities of Blockchain Technology in Medicine. *Современные технологии в медицине, 11*(4).

Liu, C. (2019a). Finance strategies for medium-sized enterprises: FinTech as the game changer. In Strategic Optimization of Medium-Sized Enterprises in the Global Market (pp. 162-184). IGI Global.

Liu, C. (2019b). FinTech and its disruption to financial institutions. In A. Guerra Guerra (Ed.), *Organizational Transformation and Managing Innovation in the Fourth Industrial Revolution* (pp. 104–124). IGI Global. doi:10.4018/978-1-5225-7074-5.ch006

Liudmila, Z., Mateusz, D., & Gerhard, S. (2016). FinTech – What's in a Name? *Thirty Seventh International Conference on Information Systems.*

Li, Y., Spigt, R., & Swinkels, L. (2017). The impact of fintech start-prices. *Financial Innovation, 3*(1), 26. doi:10.118640854-017-0076-7

Llorca, M. (2017). Les banques aux prises avec les Fintech [Banks grappling with FinTech]. *Economics and Politics*, (3), 43–58.

Loderer, C., Stulz, R., & Waelchlig, U. (2017). Firm Rigidities and the Decline in Growth Opportunities. *Management Science, 63*(9), 1–20.

Loebbecke, C., & Picot, A. (2015). Reflections on Societal and Business Model Transformation Arising from Digitization and Big Data Analytics: A Research Agenda. *The Journal of Strategic Information Systems, 24*(3), 149–157. doi:10.1016/j.jsis.2015.08.002

Lomi, A. (1995a). The Population Ecology of Organizational Founding: Location Dependence and Unobserved Heterogenity. *Administrative Science Quarterly, 40*(1), 111–144. doi:10.2307/2393702

Lomi, A. (1995b). The population and community ecology of organizational founding; Italian cooperative banks, 1936-1989. *European Sociological Review, 11*(1), 75–98. doi:10.1093/oxfordjournals.esr.a036350

Lomi, A. (2000). Density Dependence and Spacial Duality in Organizational Founding Rates: Danish Commercial Banks, 1846-1989. *Organization Studies, 21*(2), 433–461. doi:10.1177/0170840600212006

Loonam, M. O., & Loughlin, D. (2008). Exploring e-service quality: A study of Irish online banking. *Marketing Intelligence & Planning, 26*(7), 759–780. doi:10.1108/02634500810916708

Louati, R., & Mekadmi, S. (2019). Toward a Conceptualization of Big Data Value Chain: From Business Problems to Value Creation. In K. Mezghani & W. Aloulou (Eds.), *Business Transformations in the Era of Digitalization* (pp. 76–92). IGI Global. doi:10.4018/978-1-5225-7262-6.ch005

Lu, L. (2018). Decoding Alipay: mobile payments, a cashless society and regulatory challenges. *Butterworths Journal of International Banking and Financial Law*, 40-43.

Lucas, H. Jr, Agarwal, R., Clemons, E. K., El Sawy, O. A., & Weber, B. (2013). Impactful research on transformational information technology: An opportunity to inform new audiences. *Management Information Systems Quarterly, 37*(2), 371–382. doi:10.25300/MISQ/2013/37.2.03

Lukanova, K., & Vasiljeva, T. (2016). Commercial banks and Fintech companies in the digital transformation: Challenges for the future. *Journal of Business and Management, 11*, 25–34.

Mackenzie, A. (2015). The FinTech revolution. *London Business School Review, 26*(3), 50–53. doi:10.1111/2057-1615.12059

Madir,J.(2019).*FinTech:LawandRegulation.*EdwardElgarPublishing.doi:10.4337/9781788979023

Magnuson, W. (2017). The next crisis will start in Silicon Valley. *Bloomberg View, 18.*

Magnuson. W. (2019). Regulating Fintech, *Vanderbilt Law Review, 71*(4), 1167-1226.

Malone, V. (2020). *Fintech culture is here to stay. Horizon Fintex.* https://medium.com/@horizonfintex/fintech-culture-is-here-to-stay-207657a533e0

Malone, T. W., & Crowston, K. (1987). J. Yates, RI Benjamin. 1987. *Electronic markets and electronic hierarchies. Communications of the ACM, 30*(6), 484–497. doi:10.1145/214762.214766

Maswaure, F., & Choga, F. (2016). Electronic banking uptake in Zimbabwe. *Journal of Business and Management, 18*(4), 80–82.

Mavaza, T. (2019). E-Banking adoption by Zimbabwe banks: An exploratory study. *PM World Journal, 8*(11), 1–10.

McAfee, A., Brynjolfsson, E., Davenport, T. H., Patil, D. J., & Barton, D. (2012). Big data: The management revolution. *Harvard Business Review, 90*(10), 60–68. PMID:23074865

Mearian, L. (2019). *What is blockchain? The complete guide*. Retrieved from https://www.computerworld.com/article/3191077/what-is-blockchain-the-complete-guide.html

Mearian, L. (2017). What is blockchain? The most disruptive tech in decades. *Computerworld*, 1–8.

Mei, S., Peiguang, L., & Xiushan, N. (2018). Research on FinTech Industry Development and Talent Training Status. In *2018 13th International Conference on Computer Science & Education (ICCSE)* (pp. 1-4). IEEE. 10.1109/ICCSE.2018.8468796

Mention, A. L. (2019). The future of FinTech. *Research Technology Management, 62*(4), 59–61. doi:10.1080/08956308.2019.1613123

Metzlar, A. (2017). Strategic intent and the strategic position of smallholders: A case study of a smallholders' organization in the Ghanaian cocoa industry. *Review of Social Economy, 75*(3), 371–387. doi:10.1080/00346764.2017.1299202

Mezghani, K., & Aloulou, W. (2019). Business Transformations in the Era of Digitalization. Hershey, PA: IGI Global. doi:10.4018/978-1-5225-7262-6

Mezghani, K. (2019). On the Need for Big Data Analytics in the Era of Digitalization. *Proceedings of the 34th conference of "International Business Information Management Association".*

Micu, I., & Micu, A. (2016). Financial technology (fintech) and its implementation on the Romanian non-banking capital market. *SEA-Practical Application of Science, 11*, 379–384.

Milian, E. Z., Spinola, M. M., & de Carvalho, M. M. (2019). Fintechs: A literature review and research agenda. *Electronic Commerce Research and Applications*, *34*, 34. doi:10.1016/j.elerap.2019.100833

Mills, K., & McCarthy, B. (2017). How banks can compete against an army of FinTech startups. *Harvard Business Review*. https://hbr.org/2017/04/how-banks-can-compete-against-an-army-of-FinTech-startups

Minjoon, J., & Shaohan, C. (2011). The key determinants of Internet banking service quality: A content analysis. *International Journal of Bank Marketing*, *19*, 276–291.

Miskam, S., & Eksan, S. H. R. (2018). Big Data and Fintech In Islamic Finance: Prospects and Challenges. *4thMuzakarah Fiqh & International Fiqh Conference.*

Mobile POS Payments in Europe. (2020). Retrieved August 20, 2020, from Statista: https://www.statista.com/outlook/331/102/mobile-pos-payments/europe#market-revenue

Modgil, S., & Sonwaney, V. (2019). Planning the application of blockchain technology in identification of counterfeit products: Sectorial prioritization. *IFAC-PapersOnLine*, *52*(13), 1–5. doi:10.1016/j.ifacol.2019.11.080

Moktadir, M. A., Ali, S. M., Paul, S. K., & Shukla, N. (2019). Barriers to big data analytics in manufacturing supply chains: A case study from Bangladesh. *Computers & Industrial Engineering*, *128*, 1063–1075. doi:10.1016/j.cie.2018.04.013

Munteanu, B. (2016). Shadow banking – developments in times of financial crisis. *"Ovidiu s" University Annals. Economic Sciences Series*, *16*(2), 43–47.

Muro, M., Liu, S., Whiton, J., & Kulkarni, S. (2017). Digitalization and the American Workforce. Metropolitan Policy Program.

Murphy, S., Burch, D., & Clapp, J. (2012). Ceral Secrets: The World's Largest Grain Traders and Global Agricuture. *Oxfam Research Reports.*

Muthukannan, P., & Gozman, D. (2019). Meeting the Challenge of FinTech Startups: The Development of Dynamic Capabilities at Incumbent Banks. *ICIS 2019 Proceedings.* https://aisel.aisnet.org/icis2019/blockchain_FinTech/blockchain_FinTech/6

Nakaso, H. (2016). *FinTech and the future of money*. Retrieved May 16, 2020, from https://www.bis.org/review/r161214a.htm

Narsalay, R., & Patrao, M. (2016). Thriving with FinTechs: Strategies for Large Indian Banks. *Vinimaya*, *37*(1), 5.

NASDAQ. (2016). *Building on the Blockchain.* https://www.nasdaq.com/articles/building-blockchain-2016-03-23

Nasser, T., & Tariq, R. S. (2015). Big data challenges. *J Comput Eng Inf Technol, 4,* 3. doi: http://dx.doi.org/,9307(2) doi:10.4172/2324

Navaretti, G. B., Calzolari, G., & Pozzolo, A. F. (2017). Fintech and banks: Friends or foes?
Oshodin, O., Karanasios, S., Molla, A., & Ong, C.E. (2019). How do FinTech Start-ups Develop Capabilities? Towards a FinTech Capability Model. *Twenty-Third Pacific Asia Conference on Information Systems.*

NESTA. (2014). *Startup Accelerator Programmes: A Practice Guide*. www.nesta.org.uk

NEXI. (2020). *The Nexi Group*. Retrieved August 20, 2020, from NEXI: https://www.nexi.it/en/about-us/brand/group.html

Nicoletti, B. N., & Weis. (2017). Future of Fintech. Basingstoke, UK: Palgrave Macmillan.

Nicoletti, B. (2017). *The Future of Fintech. Integrating Finance and Technology in Financial Services*. Palgrave Macmillan.

Nicoletti, B. (2017). *The Future of FinTech: Integrating Finance and Technology in Financial Services*. Springer. doi:10.1007/978-3-319-51415-4

Nils, U., Stefan, S., & Gerold, R. (2013). An empirical investigation of employee portal success. *The Journal of Strategic Information Systems, 19*, 184–206.

Nishmitha, N. (2018). *Financial technology implications: Indian context* (Master thesis). National Institute of Technology, Surathkal.

Nofer, M., Gomber, P., Hinz, O., & Schiereck, D. (2017). Blockchain. *Business & Information Systems Engineering, 59*(3), 183–187. doi:10.100712599-017-0467-3

Nordea. (2020). *Mobile payments*. Retrieved June 13, 2020, from https://www.nordea.com/en/our-services/cashmanagement/oursolutions/mobile-payments/

Nowiński, W., & Kozma, M. (2017). How can blockchain technology disrupt existing business models? *Entrepreneurial Business and Economics Review, 5*(3), 173–188. doi:10.15678/EBER.2017.050309

Nunkoo, R., Ramkissoon, H., & Gursoy, D. (2013). use of structural equation modeling in tourism reaserch past, present and future. *Journal of Travel Research, 52*, 759–771. doi:10.1177/0047287513478503

Oakley, M., Hughes, S., Gulati, S., & Miscampbell, G. (2018). *Supporting UK fintech: Accessing a global talent pool*. Innovate Finance.

Obaid, M., Bayram, Z., & Saleh, M. (2019). Instant secure mobile payment scheme. *IEEE Access: Practical Innovations, Open Solutions, 7*, 55669–55678. doi:10.1109/ACCESS.2019.2913430

Omarini, A. (2017). *The digital transformation in banking and the role of Fintechs in the new financial intermediation scenario*. MPRA Paper. Retrieved from https://mpra.ub.uni-muenchen.de/85228/

Omarini, A. E. (2018). Banks and FinTechs: How to develop a digital open banking approach for the bank's future. *International Business Research, 11*(9), 23–36. doi:10.5539/ibr.v11n9p23

Omdia Technology. (2020). *Connecting the Dots: Key Strategic Opportunities in a Post-COVID-19 World.* Author.

Ondrus, J., Lyytinen, K., & Pigneur, Y. (2009). Why mobile payment fail? Towards a dynamic and multi-perspective explanation. In *The 42nd Hawaii International Conference on System Science (HICSS'09).* IEEE.

Oracle. (2018). *Bank and insurance innovators to benefit from European Oracle FinTech innovation program with B-Hive Europe.* Press Release. www.oracle.com/corporate/pressrelease/oracle-FinTech-innovation-program-062818.html

Oshodin, O., Karanasios, S., Molla, A., & Ong, C. E. (2019). How do FinTech Start-ups Develop Capabilities? Towards a FinTech Capability Model. *Twenty-Third Pacific Asia Conference on Information Systems.*

Oshodin, O., Molla, A., Karanasios, S., & Ong, C. E. (2017). Is FinTech a disruption or a new eco-system? An exploratory investigation of Banksr response to FinTech in Australia. In *Proceeding of Australasian Conference on Information Systems* (pp. 1-11). Academic Press.

Osterwalder, A., Pigneur, Y., & Tucci, C. L. (2005). Clarifying business models: Origins, present, and future of the concept. *Communications of the Association for Information Systems, 16*(1), 1. doi:10.17705/1CAIS.01601

Ozelli, S. (2020). *US Takes Regulatory Steps for Blockchain Technology Adoption.* Retrieved from https://cointelegraph.com/news/us-takes-regulatory-steps-for-blockchain-technology-adoption

Palmié, M., Wincent, J., Parida, V., & Caglar, U. (2020). The evolution of the financial technology ecosystem: An introduction and agenda for future research on disruptive innovations in ecosystems. *Technological Forecasting and Social Change, 151*, 119779. doi:10.1016/j.techfore.2019.119779

Pan, D. (2019). *India Plans to Issue a National Blockchain Framework.* Retrieved from https://www.coindesk.com/india-plans-to-issue-a-national-blockchain-framework

Panetta, F. (2018). *Fintech and banking: today and tomorrow Speech by the Deputy Governor of the Bank of Italy.* Harvard Law School Bicentennial Annual Reunion of the Harvard Law School Association of Europe. https://www.bancaditalia.it/pubblicazioni/interventi-direttorio/int-dir-2018/panetta-120518.pdf

Pantielieieva, N., Krynytsia, S., Khutorna, M., & Potapenko, L. (2018, October). FinTech, transformation of financial intermediation and financial stability. In *2018 International Scientific-Practical Conference Problems of info communications. Science and Technology (PIC S&T)* (pp. 553-559). IEEE. 10.1109/INFOCOMMST.2018.8632068

Parida, V., Sjödin, D., & Reim, W. (2019). *Reviewing the literature on digitalization, business model innovation, and sustainable industry: Past achievements and future promises.* Academic Press.

Parida, V., Sjödin, D. R., Wincent, J., & Kohtamäki, M. (2014). Mastering the transition to product-service provision: Insights into business models, learning activities, and capabilities. *Research Technology Management, 57*(3), 44–52.

Patton, M. Q. (2015). *Qualitative research and evaluation methods: Integrating theory and practice* (4th ed.). Sage.

Payne, J. (2018). Blockchain Platform Goes Live for North Sea Crude Oil Trading. *Reuters*. https://www.reuters.com/article/us-blockchain-oil-trading/blockchain-platform-goes-live-for-north-sea-crude-oil-trading-idUSKCN1NY0X6

Paypers, T. (2019). *European payments council*. Retrieved August 20, 2020, from https://www.europeanpaymentscouncil.eu/sites/default/files/inline

Pee, J., & Klein, T. P. (2017). E-store loyalty: Longitudinal comparison of website usefulness and satisfaction. *International Journal of Market Research*, *60*, 1–17.

Philippon, T. (2016). *The Fintech Opportunity*. NBER, Working Paper 22476.

Philippon, T. (2018). *The fintech opportunity*. Retrieved May 15, 2020, from http://pages.stern.nyu.edu/~tphilipp/papers/FinTech.pdf

Pinchot, G. (1985). *Intrapreneuring: Why You Don't Have to Leave the Corporation to Become an Entrepreneur*. Harper and Row.

Pinchot, G., & Pellman, R. (1999). *Intrapreneuring in action: A Handbook for Business Innovation*. Berrett-Koehler Publishers.

Pitt, L. F., Watson, R. T., & Kavan, C. B. (1995). Service quality: A measure of information systems effectiveness. *Management Information Systems Quarterly*, *19*(2), 73–187. doi:10.2307/249687

Plume, K. (2018). ABCD Quartet of Grain Traders Partner to Digitilize Global Trades. *Reuters*. https://www.reuters.com/article/us-global-grains-traders/abcd-quartet-of-grain-traders-partner-to-digitize-global-trades-idUSKCN1MZ2E8

Pollari, I. (2016). The rise of FinTech opportunities and challenges. *Jassa The Finsia Journal of Applied Finance*, (3), 15.

Popper, N. (2015). *Digital gold: Bitcoin and the inside story of the misfits and millionaires trying to reinvent money*. Harper.

Porter, M. E., & Heppelmann, J. E. (2015). How smart, connected products are transforming companies. *Harvard Business Review*, *93*(10), 96–114.

Prahalad, C. K., & Hamel, G. (1989, May). Strategic Intent. Harvard Business Review, 63–76.

Prasanth, S., & Sudhamathi, S. (2018). Challenges faced by banking sector on digital innovation. *Journal of Technologies and Innovative Research*, *5*(10), 964–967.

Proeger, T., & Runst, P. (2019). Digitization and Knowledge Spillover Effectiveness - Evidence from "German MitteIsland.". *Journal of the Knowledge Economy*. Advance online publication. doi:10.100713132-019-00622-3

Puschmann, T. (2017). Fintech. *Business & Information Systems Engineering*, *59*(1), 69–76. doi:10.100712599-017-0464-6

PwC. (2016). *Blurred lines: How FinTech is shaping Financial Services – Global FinTech Report*. New York. https://www.pwc.com.au/pdf/pwc-FinTech-global-report-2016.pdf

PwC. (2016). *Blurred lines: How FinTech is shaping Financial Services,* Global FinTech Report.

PwC. (2016). *Blurred lines: How FinTech is shaping financial services*. PwC.

Rachinger, M., Rauter, R., Müller, C., Vorraber, W., & Schirgi, E. (2019). Digitalization and its influence on business model innovation. *Journal of Manufacturing Technology Management*, *30*(8), 1143–1160. doi:10.1108/JMTM-01-2018-0020

Ragin, C. C. (1987). *The Comparative Method, Moving Beyond qualitative and quantitative strategies*. University of California Press.

Ragin, C. C. (2000). *Fuzzy-Set Social Science*. University of Chicago Press.

Ratecka, P. (2020). FinTech—Definition, taxonomy and historical approach. *Zeszyty Naukowe Małopolskiej Wyższej Szkoły Ekonomicznej w Tarnowie*, *1*(45), 53–67.

Reiff, N. (2020). *Blockchain explained*. Retrieved from https://www.investopedia.com/terms/b/blockchain.asp

Reserve Bank of Zimbabwe. (2019a). *2019 Midterm monetary policy statement: Transition to normalcy*. Retrieved May 10, 2010, from https://www.rbz.co.zw/documents/mps/MPS-September-2019-.pdf

Reserve Bank of Zimbabwe. (2019b). *Financial stability report June 2019*. Retrieved May 15, 2020, from https://www.rbz.co.zw/documents/BLSS/2020/Zimbabwe-Financial-Stability-Report-as-at-30-June-2019.pdf

Reserve Bank of Zimbabwe. (2020). *Monetary policy statement 2020: Focusing on price and exchange rate stability*. Retrieved May 16, 2020, from https://www.rbz.co.zw/documents/mps/Monetary-Policy-Statement-17-February-2020.pdf

Riasanow, T., Flötgen, R. J., Setzke, D. S., Böhm, M., & Krcmar, H. (2018). The Generic Ecosystem and Innovation Patterns of the Digital Transformation in the Financial Industry. *22nd Pacific Asia Conference on Information Systems (PACIS)*.

Riemer, K., Hafermalz, E., Roosen, A., Boussand, N., El Aoufi, H., Mo, D., & Kosheliev, A. (2017). *The FinTech Advantage: Harnessing digital technology, keeping the customer in focus*. University of Sydney, Business School and Capgemini.

Ritter, T., & Lettl, C. (2018). The broader implications of business-model research. *Long Range Planning*, *51*(1), 1–8. doi:10.1016/j.lrp.2017.07.005

Roberts, D. (2016). *Walmart to team with IBM (IBM) and Tsinghua University to track the pork supply chain in China using blockchain*. Academic Press.

Rocchi, J.-M. (2019). Les banques en ligne et les néobanques en France (1994-2019): émergence, mutation, et survie. Une étude mixte par la méthode des cas multiples et l'AQQC simple (csQCA) [Online banks and neobanks in France (1994-2019): emergence, mutation, and survival. A mixed study using the multiple case study method and crisp-set QCA (csQCA)] (Unpublished EBDA doctoral dissetation). Paris Dauphine – PSL University, Paris.

Rocchi, J-M. (2018a). La victoire annonçée des banques en ligne [The announced victory of online banks]. *Revue Banque*, *818*, 66-71.

Rocchi, J-M. (2018b). Radiographie des néobanques [Radiography of neobanks]. *Revue Banque*, *820*, 65-68.

Romānova, I., & Kudinska, M. (2017). Banking and fintech: A challenge or opportunity? *Contemporary Issues in Finance: Current Challenges from Across Europe Contemporary Studies in Economic and Financial Analysis*, *98*, 21–35. doi:10.1108/S1569-375920160000098002

Rooney, K. (2018). *After the crisis, a new generation puts its trust in tech over traditional banks*. https://www.cnbc.com/2018/09/14/a-new-generation-puts-its-trust-in-tech-over-traditional-banks.html

Ryu, H. S. (2017). What makes users willing or hesitant to use Fintech?: The moderating effect of user type. *Industrial Management & Data Systems*. Advance online publication. doi:10.1108/IMDS-07-2017-0325

S&P Global Platts. (2018). *Blockchain for Commodities: Trading Opportunities in a Digital Age*. Author.

Sahay, R., Allmen, U., Lahreche, A., Khera, P., Ogawa, S., Bazarbash, M., & Beaton, K. (2020). *The Promise of FinTech: Financial Inclusion in the Post COVID-19 Era New*. Journal Issue.

Saksonova, S., & Kuzmina-Merlino, I. (2017). Fintech as Financial Innovation – The Possibilities and Problems of Implementation. *European Research Studies Journal, 10*(3A).

Sandelowski, M. (2010). What's in a name? Qualitative description revisited. *Research in Nursing & Health*, *33*(1), 77–84. doi:10.1002/nur.20362 PMID:20014004

Sarmah, S. S. (2018). Understanding blockchain technology. *Computing in Science & Engineering*, *8*(2), 23–29.

Saunders, M. N. K., Lewis, P., & Thornhill, A. (2012). *Research methods for business students* (6th ed.). Pearson Education Ltd.

Saunders, M. N. K., & Rojon, C. (2014). There's no madness in my method: Explaining how your research findings are built on firm foundations' coaching. *An International Journal of Theory. Research and Practice*, *7*(1), 74–83.

Say, J. B. (2018). *A Treatise on Political Economy*. HardPress. (Original work published 1803)

Schaeffer, C., Haque, A., Booton, L., Halleck, J., & Coustasse, A. (2016). Big data management in United States hospitals: benefits and barriers. *Proceedings of the Business and Health Administration Association Annual Conference.*

Schmidt, J., Drews, P., & Schirmer, I. (2018). *Charting the emerging financial services ecosystem of fintech and banks: Six types of data-driven business models in the fintech sector.* Academic Press.

Schueffel, P. (2016). Taming the beast: A scientific definition of FinTech. *Journal of Innovation Management, 4*(4), 32–54. doi:10.24840/2183-0606_004.004_0004

Schueffel, P., & Vadana, I. (2016). Open Innovation in the Financial Services Sector – A global literature review. *Journal of Innovation Management, 3*(1), 25–48. doi:10.24840/2183-0606_003.001_0005

Seebacher, S., & Schüritz, R. (2017). *Blockchain technology as an enabler of service systems: A structured literature review.* Paper presented at the International Conference on Exploring Services Science. 10.1007/978-3-319-56925-3_2

Sgourev, S. (2013). How Paris Gave Rise to Cubism (and Picasso): Ambiguity and Fragmentation in Radical Innovation. *Organization Science, 24*(6), 1–17. doi:10.1287/orsc.1120.0819

Shamim, S., Zeng, J., Shariq, S. M., & Khan, Z. (2019). Role of big data management in enhancing big data decision-making capability and quality among Chinese firms: A dynamic capabilities view. *Information & Management, 56*(6), 103135. doi:10.1016/j.im.2018.12.003

Shim, Y., & Shin, D. H. (2016). Analyzing China's fintech industry from the perspective of actor–network theory. *Telecommunications Policy, 40*(2–3), 168–181. doi:10.1016/j.telpol.2015.11.005

Shmeljov, O. (2017). Banking in the Digital Age-Impact of Fintech on Banks' Business Models. *The Journal for Money and Banking, 66*(11), 22–28.

Sia, S. K., Soh, C., & Weill, P. (2016). How DBS Bank Pursued a Digital Business Strategy. *MIS Quarterly Executive, 15*(2).

Silva, P. M., & Dias, G. A. (2007). Theories About Technology Accepentace: Why The Users Accept Or Reject The Information Technology? *Brazilian Journal of Information Science: Research Trends, 1*(2), 69–91. doi:10.36311/1981-1640.2007.v1n2.05.p69

Sinha, S. (2017). A Glimpse into the World of FinTech Accelerators? The Open Vault at OCBC. *IEEE Potentials, 36*(6), 20–23. doi:10.1109/MPOT.2017.2737238

Sironi, P. (2016). *FinTech Innovation: From Robo-Advisors to Goal Based Investing and Gamification.* Wiley. doi:10.1002/9781119227205

Skan, J., Dickerson, J., & Masood, S. (2015). *Future of fintech and banking – Accenture.* Retrieved May 14, 2020, from https://www.accenture.com/us-en/insight-future-fintechbanking

Smaoui Hachicha, Z., & Mezghani, K. (2018). Understanding Intentions to Switch Toward Cloud Computing at Firms' Level: A Multiple Case Study in Tunisia. *Journal of Global Information Management*, *26*(1), 136–165. doi:10.4018/JGIM.2018010108

Sood, A., James, G. M., Tellis, G. J., & Zhu, J. (2012). Predicting the path of technological innovation: SAW vs. Moore, Bass, Gompertz, and Kryder. *Marketing Science*, *31*(6), 964–979. doi:10.1287/mksc.1120.0739

Staff Discussion Note, I. M. F. (2017, June). Fintech and Financial Services. *Initial Considerations, SDN*, *17*(05), 2–49.

Stewart, L. A. (2010). The impact of regulation on innovation in the United States: A cross-industry literature review. *Information Technology & Innovation Foundation, 6.*

Sung, A., & Leong, K. (2018). FinTech (Financial Technology): What is it and how to use technologies to create business value in Fintech way? *International Journal of Innovation, Management and Technology*, *9*(2), 74–78.

Sutton, R. I. (1987). The Process of Organizational Death: Disbanding and Reconnecting. *Administrative Science Quarterly*, *32*(4), 542–569. doi:10.2307/2392883

SvD. (2014). *Swedbank lägger ned betallösningen Bart* [Swedbank closes down the payment solution Bart]. Retrieved June 20, 2020, from www.svd.se/naringsliv/swedbank-lagger-ned-betallosningen-bart_8913772

Svensson, C., Udesen, J., & Webb, J. (2019). Alliances in Financial Ecosystems: A Source of Organizational Legitimacy for FinTech Startups and Incumbents. *Technology Innovation Management Review, 9*(1).

Swacha-Lech, M. (2017). The main challenges facing the retail banking industry in the era of digitalization. *Journal of Insurance. Financial Markets and Consumer Protection*, *26*(4), 94–116.

Swan, M. (2015). *Blockchain: Blueprint for a new economy*. O'Reilly Media, Inc.

Swartz, N. D. (2014). Bursting the Bitcoin bubble: The case to regulate digital currency as a security or commodity. *Tul. J. Tech. & Intell. Prop.*, *17*, 319.

Swift White Paper. (2018). Retrieved August 20, 2020, from https://www.swift.com/sites/default/files/documents/swift_whitepaper_transformation_european_payments_landscape.pdf

Sy, A. N. R., Maino, R., Massara, A., Perez-Saiz, H., & Sharma, P. (2019). *FinTech in Sub-Saharan African countries: A game changer?* IMF, Departmental Papers. No. 19/04. Retrieved May 16, 2020, from https://www.imf.org/en/Publications/Departmental-Papers-Policy-Papers/Issues/2019/02/13/FinTech-in-Sub-Saharan-African-Countries-A-Game-Changer-46376

Tanda, A., & Schena, C. M. (2019). *FinTech, BigTech and Banks: Digitalisation and Its Impact on Banking Business Models*. Springer. doi:10.1007/978-3-030-22426-4

Tardieu, H., Daly, D., Esteban-Lauzán, J., Hall, J., & Miller, G. (2020). *Deliberately Digital. Rewriting Enterprise DNA for Enduring Success*. Springer. doi:10.1007/978-3-030-37955-1

Tassev, L. (2020). *China Adopts Security Standards for Blockchain Applications in the Financial Sector.* Retrieved from https://news.bitcoin.com/china-adopts-security-standards-blockchain/

Taylor, P. J., Dargahi, T., Dehghantanha, A., Parizi, R. M., & Choo, K. K. R. (2019). *A Systematic Literature Review of Blockchain Cyber Security*. Digital Communications and Networks. doi:10.1016/j.dcan.2019.01.005

Teece, D. J. (2010). Business models, business strategy, and innovation. *Long Range Planning*, *43*(2-3), 172–194. doi:10.1016/j.lrp.2009.07.003

Terazono, E. (2018). Commodities Trader Louis Dreyfus Turns to Blockchain. *Financial Times*. https://www.ft.com/content/22b2ac1e-fd1a-11e7-a492-2c9be7f3120a

Thakor, A. V. (2019). Fintech and banking: What do we know? *Journal of Financial Intermediation*.

The History of Electronic Payments. (n.d.). http://blog.e-money.com/the-history-of-electronic-payments-part-1/

Thiruchelvam, V., Mughisha, A. S., Shahpasand, M., & Bamiah, M. (2018). Blockchain-based technology in the coffee supply chain trade: Case of burundi coffee. *Journal of Telecommunication, Electronic and Computer Engineering, 10*(3-2), 121-125.

Thompson, K. (2017). Wealth management advice in the digital age. *Journal of Securities Operations and Custody*, *10*(1), 6–11.

Timmers, P. (1998). Business models for electronic markets. *Electronic Markets*, *8*(2), 3–8. doi:10.1080/10196789800000016

Tnani, F. (2019). *Pourquoi la Tunisie est-elle en retard en matière de fintech? L'économiste Maghrébin.* Available at: https://www.leconomistemaghrebin.com/2019/02/27/la-tunisie-en-retard-en-matiere-de-fintech/

Trujillo, Fromhart, & Srinivas. (2017). *Evolution of blockchain technology*. Retrieved from https://medium.com/@crowdmachine/evolution-of-blockchain-technology-9ee208c000e2

Tsang, C. Y. (2018). A Tentative Analytical Framework and Developing Roadmap for SupTech. *Management Review*, *37*, 105–120.

Underwood, S. (2016). *Blockchain beyond bitcoin*. Academic Press.

Union, O. J. (2015). *Directives*. Retrieved June 13, 2020, from https://eur-lex.europa.eu/legal-content/EN/TXT/PDF/?uri=CELEX:32015L2366&from=EN

Utoyo, I., Fontana, A., & Satrya, A. (2019). The role of entrepreneurial leadership and configuring core innovation capabilities to enhance innovation performance in a disruptive environment. *International Journal of Innovation Management*, *24*(06), 2050060. doi:10.1142/S1363919620500607

Valarie, A., Zeithaml, A., Parsu, P., & Arvind, M. (2002). Service Quality Delivery Through Web Sites: A Critical Review of Extant. *Journal of the Academy of Marketing Science, 30*(4), 362–375. doi:10.1177/009207002236911

van Winden, W. (2017). Boosting The Entrepreneurial Local Scene. *Maximizing The Ecosystem Approach. Thematic Workshop*, Torino, Italy.

Vanderlinden, S. L., Millie, S. M., Anderson, N., & Chishti, S. (2018). *The INSURTECH Book: The Insurance Technology Handbook for Investors, Entrepreneurs and FinTech Visionaries*. John Wiley & Sons.

Vardi, M. (2017). Cyber insecurity and cyber libertarianism. *Communications of the ACM, 60*(5), 5. doi:10.1145/3073731

Varga, D. (2017). Fintech, the new era of financial services. *Vezetéstudomịny-Budapest Management Review, 48*(11), 22–32. doi:10.14267/VEZTUD.2017.11.03

Vasiljeva, T., & Lukanova, K. (2016). Commercial banks and fintech companies in the digital transformation: Challenges for the future. *Journal of Business and Management, 11*, 25–33.

Vasiljeva, T., & Lukanova, K. (2016). Commercial banks and FINTECH companies in the digital transformation: Challenges for the future. *Journal of Business and Management*, 11.

Vassakis, K., Petrakis, E., & Kopanakis, I. (2018). Big data analytics: applications, prospects and challenges. In *Mobile Big Data* (pp. 3–20). Springer. doi:10.1007/978-3-319-67925-9_1

Vauplane, H. de. (2015). Les FinTech et la réglementation bancaire et financière [FinTech and banking and financial regulations]. *Banque & Stratégie, 339*, 32-36.

Veeramotoo, M., Nunkoo, R., & Dwivedi, A. (2018). What determine sucess of an e- government service validation of an aintegartive mode of E filing continuance usage. *Government Information Quarterly, 35*(2), 161–174. doi:10.1016/j.giq.2018.03.004

Ventura, A., Koenitzer, M., Stein, P., Tufano, P., & Drummer, D. (2015, October). *The Future of FinTech: A paradigm shift in small business finance.* World Economic Forum, Global Agenda Council on the Future of Financing and Capital. https://www.weforum.org/reports/future-FinTech-paradigm-shift-small-business-finance

Verina, N., & Titko, J. (2019, May). Digital transformation: conceptual framework. In *International Scientific Conference Contemporary Issues in Business, Management and Economics Engineering*.

Verma, M. (2019). Data-oriented and Machine Learning Technologies in Fintech. *Fintechs and an Evolving Ecosystem*, 1.

Visnjic, I., Neely, A., & Jovanovic, M. (2018). The path to outcome delivery: Interplay of service market strategy and open business models. *Technovation, 72*, 46–59. doi:10.1016/j.technovation.2018.02.003

W.UP. (2019). *Tech Giants in Banking: Will Amazon Launch a Bank?* https://wup.digital/blog/tech-giants-banking-amazon-in-banking/

Walker, A. (2014). Banking without banks: Exploring the disruptive effects of converging technologies that will shape the future of banking. *Journal of Securities Operations & Custody, 7*(1), 69–80.

Waller, S., & Masse, C. (1999). *L'analyse documentaire: une approche méthodologique* [Thedocumentary analysis: a methodological approach]. ADBS Edition.

Wamba, S. F., Akter, S., Edwards, A., Chopin, G., & Gnanzou, D. (2015). How 'big data'can make big impact: Findings from a systematic review and a longitudinal case study. *International Journal of Production Economics, 165*, 234–246. doi:10.1016/j.ijpe.2014.12.031

Wang, J., Wu, P., Wang, X., & Shou, W. (2017). The outlook of blockchain technology for construction engineering management. *Frontiers of Engineering Management*, 67-75.

Wang, L. (2020). Post–COVID-19: China's Machinery Production and Automation Equipment Market Cannot be Immune to the Global Pandemic. *Omdia Technology*. https://technology.informa.com/624995/postcovid-19-chinas-machinery-production-and-automation-equipment-market-cannot-be-immune-to-the-global-pandemic

Wang, Y., Singgih, M., Wang, J., & Rit, M. (2019). Making sense of blockchain technology: How will it transform supply chains? *International Journal of Production Economics, 211*, 221–236. doi:10.1016/j.ijpe.2019.02.002

Wass, S. (2019). komgo Unwrapped: Financing Commodity Trade on Blockchain. *GTR Global Trade Review, 17*(1). https://www.gtreview.com/magazine/volume-17-issue-1/komgo-unwrapped-financing-commodity-trade-blockchain/

Weatherston, J., Brooks, I., & Wilkinson, G. (2010). *The international business environment: challenges and changes*. Prentice Hall.

Weichert, M. (2017). The future of payments: How FinTech players are accelerating customer-driven innovation in financial services. *Journal of Payments Strategy & Systems*, 23-33.

Wewege, L., & Thomsett, M. C. (2019). *The Digital Banking Revolution: How FinTech Companies are Transforming the Retail Banking Industry Through Disruptive Financial Innovation*. Walter de Gruyter GmbH & Co KG. doi:10.1515/9781547401598

Williamson, O. E. (1981). The Economics of Organization: The Transaction Cost Approach. *American Journal of Sociology, 87*(3), 548–577. doi:10.1086/227496

Wirtz, B. W., Pistoia, A., Ullrich, S., & Göttel, V. (2016). Business models: Origin, development, and future research perspectives. *Long Range Planning, 49*(1), 36–54. doi:10.1016/j.lrp.2015.04.001

Wong, M. C., Yee, K. C., & Nohr, C. (2018). Socio-technical consideration for blockchain technology in healthcare. *Studies in Health Technology and Informatics, 247*, 636–640. PMID:29678038

World Economic Forum. (2017). *Beyond FinTech: A pragmatic assessment of disruptive potential in financial services.* http://www3.weforum.org/docs/Beyond_FinTech_-_A_Pragmatic_Assessment_of_Disruptive_Potential_in_Financial_Services.pdf

World FinTech Report. (2018). https://www.capgemini.com/news/capgeminis-world-FinTech-report-2018-highlights-symbiotic-collaboration-as-key-to-future-financial-services-success/

Wragg, E. (2019). Tech Company Unveils 'Network of Networks' to Solve Blockchain's Interoperability Issue for Trade. *GTR Global Trade Review*. https://www.gtreview.com/news/fintech/tech-company-unveils-blockchain-network-of-networks-to-solve-interoperability-issue/

Wright, A., & De Filippi, P. (2015). *Decentralized blockchain technology and the rise of lex cryptographia.* Available at SSRN 2580664

Yan, T. C., Schulte, P., & Chuen, D. L. K. (2018). InsurTech and FinTech: banking and insurance enablement. In Handbook of Blockchain, Digital Finance, and Inclusion, Volume 1 (pp. 249-281). Academic Press. doi:10.1016/B978-0-12-810441-5.00011-7

Yan, J., Yu, W., & Zhao, J. L. (2015). How signaling and search costs affect information asymmetry in P2P lending: The economics of big data. *Financial Innovation*, *1*(1), 19. doi:10.118640854-015-0018-1

Yap, B. (2017). India's new payment banks need a regulatory boost. *International Financial Law Review*.

Yazici, S. (2019). The analysis of fintech ecosystem in Turkey. *Journal of Business. Economics and Finance*, *8*(4), 188–197. doi:10.17261/Pressacademia.2019.1162

Yeoh, P. (2017). Regulatory issues in blockchain technology. *Journal of Financial Regulation and Compliance*.

Young, J. (2017). *Bitcoin and Ethereum Price Recover From Korea ICO Ban as Japan Licenses Exchanges.* Retrieved from https://www.ccn.com/bitcoin-ethereum-price-recover-korea-ico-ban-japan-licenses-exchanges/

Zaheer, S. (1995). Overcoming the liability of foreignness. *Academy of Management Journal*, *38*(2), 341–363.

Zaheer, S., & Mosakovski, E. (1997). The dynamics of the liability of foreignness: A global study of survival in financial services. *Strategic Management Journal*, *18*(6), 439–464. doi:10.1002/(SICI)1097-0266(199706)18:6<439::AID-SMJ884>3.0.CO;2-Y

Zalan, T., & Toufaily, E. (2017). The promise of FinTech in emerging markets: Not as disruptive. *Contemporary Economics*, *11*(4), 415–431.

Zambrano, E. (2017). The 'troubling tradeoffs' paradox and a resolution. *Review of Income and Wealth*, *63*(3), 520–541. doi:10.1111/roiw.12235

Zavolokina, L., Dolata, M., & Schwabe, G. (2016). Fintech–What's in a Name? *Thirty Seventh International Conference on Information Systems.*

Zavolokina, L., Dolata, M., & Schwabe, G. (2016). The FinTech phenomenon: Antecedents of financial innovation perceived by the popular press. *Financial Innovation*, *2*(16), 16. Advance online publication. doi:10.118640854-016-0036-7

Zetzsche, D. A., Buckley, R. P., Arner, D. W., & Barberis, J. N. (2017). From FinTech to TechFin: The regulatory challenges of data-driven finance. *NYUJL & Bus.*, *14*, 393. doi:10.2139srn.2959925

Zhao, J. L., Fan, S., & Yan, J. (2016). *Overview of business innovations and research opportunities in blockchain and introduction to the special issue*. Academic Press.

Zhao, O., Tsai, P., & Wang, J. (2019). Improving financial service innovation strategies for enhancing China's banking industry competitive advantage during the Fintech revolution: A hybrid MCDM model. *Sustainability*, *11*, 1–29. doi:10.3390u12010001

Zhou, T. (2013). An empirical examination of continuance intention of mobile payment services. *Decision Support Systems*, *54*(2), 1085–1091. doi:10.1016/j.dss.2012.10.034

Zott, C., Amit, R., & Massa, L. (2011). The business model: Recent developments and future research. *Journal of Management*, *37*(4), 1019–1042. doi:10.1177/0149206311406265

Zveryakov, M., Kovalenko, V., Sheludko, S., & Sharah, E. (2019). FinTech sector and banking business: Competition or symbiosis? *Economic Annals-XXI*, *175*(1-2), 53–57. doi:10.21003/ea.V175-09

Zwinoira, T. (2020). *CBZ clinches digital currency deal.* Retrieved May 15, 2020, from https://www.thestandard.co.zw/2020/03/22/cbz-clinches-digital-currency-deal/

# About the Contributors

**Amira Sghari** is an Assistant Professor in Management studies at the Faculty of Economics and Management of Sfax, Tunisia. She received her Ph.D. degree in management science, in 2013, from the Aix-Marseille University, France and University of Sfax, Tunisia. She received her HDR, in 2018, from the University of Sfax, Tunisia. Dr. Sghari is member of a Laboratory PRISME and is a regular contributor to scientific conferences and Journals in both French and English languages. Her research interests include strategy and organizational structure, organizational change and change management, especially in the banking sector.

**Karim Mezghani** is an associate professor of Business Administration at Imam Mohammad Ibn Saud Islamic University, Saudi Arabia (College of Economics & Administrative Sciences). He received his M.Sc. degree and his Ph.D. degree from Sfax University, Tunisia (specialty: Management Information Systems). In addition to his experience as an associate professor in Tunisia and Saudi Arabia, Dr. Mezghani is a regular contributor to scientific conferences and indexed Journals including "Journal of Global Information Management", "International Journal of Enterprise Information Systems", "International Journal of Technology and Human Interaction" and "Electronic Journal of Information Systems Evaluation". His researches focus on Enterprise Resource Planning (ERP) implementation, cloud computing adoption, big data analytics and consultant-client relationship.

* * *

**Bilal A. A. Al-Khateeb** is an Assistant Professor in the Department of Business Administration, Faculty of Economics and Administrative Sciences, Imam Mohammad Ibn Saud Islamic University, Riyadh 11564, Saud Arabia. He received his B.A degree in Business Administration specialization (MIS) from Sindh University in 2007, his M.B.A degree in Business Administration specialization (MIS) from Sindh University in 2007, and his PhD degree in Management Information System from

Universiti Utara Malaysia, Kedah, Malaysia in 2015. His research interest includes information sources and information channels, personal and situational characteristics, information choice strategies, information sharing, Blockchain.

**Wassim J. Aloulou** is an associate professor at the Department of Business Administration of the College of Economics and Administrative Sciences in Imam Mohammad Ibn Saud Islamic University (Saudi Arabia) and of the ISAAS in Sfax University (Tunisia). He received his B.Sc. degree in Higher Commercial Studies from IHEC Carthage (1995), his M.Sc. degree in HR management from ISG Tunis (1998), and his Ph.D. degree in Management Sciences (Specialty: Entrepreneurship) from Pierre Mendès FranceUniversity (UPMF) of Grenoble 2, in France (2008). Currently, he is a member of the French Academy of Entrepreneurship and Innovation, of the Tunisian Association for Entrepreneurship and Spin-off and the Saudi Association of Entrepreneurship. He is a Certified Entrepreneurship Trainer of the ILFEN (International License For ENtrepreneurship) in Saudi Arabia. His research interests include (social) entrepreneurship and SMEs, knowledge-based startups, (social) entrepreneurial intentions, and orientations of individuals and organizations. He is an article editor of Sage Open and has published in journals including EJIM, IJGE, JSBED, JEC, JEEE, JIBED, and MEJM among others.

**Sonia Arsi** is an assistant professor in finance at Carthage Business School, the University Tunis Carthage, Tunisia. She holds a Ph.D. from the Institute of Higher Business Studies of Carthage (IHEC Carthage). She has been teaching topics of corporate finance, international finance, treasury management, derivative securities, and asset pricing. Her current research interests include commodities markets, derivatives, and behavioral finance.

**Fatma Bouaziz** is assistant professor in Management at the Faculty of Economics and Management of Sfax - Tunisia. She got her Ph.D. in management in 2011 from the same faculty. Her doctoral thesis deals with the risk management of e-government projects in the case of the Tunisian government. Her research interests include the use of ICTs by government, their organizational impacts and abilities to improve public services delivery, human resource management and organizational resilience in the context of transition.

**Mufaro Dzingirai** is a PhD candidate in Business Management at Midlands State University and a lecturer in the Department of Business Management, Midlands State University. He received his Master of Commerce in Strategic Management and Corporate Governance degree from Midlands State University in 2016. He was hired as a teacher by the Ministry of Education from 2014 to 2016. In 2013, he received the MSU Book Prize. His research interests include Higher Education, Strategy, Management, Finance, and Entrepreneurship.

**Yasmin Mahgoub** is a Ph.D. candidate in Department of Industrial Economics and Management, KTH Royal Institute of Technology. Her research focuses on innovation and disruption in payments industry via researching: Developing of digital platforms, payments providers strategies for payments, regulation views on field of payments, and Transformation in Payments.

# Index

## T



## Z

www.ingramcontent.com/pod-product-compliance
Lightning Source LLC
LaVergne TN
LVHW061538290926
849162LV00004B/837